River of Hope

River of Hope

Black Politics and the Memphis Freedom Movement, 1865–1954

ELIZABETH GRITTER

UNIVERSITY PRESS OF KENTUCKY

Scholarly publisher for the Commonwealth,
serving Bellarmine University, Berea College, Centre College of Kentucky, Eastern
Kentucky University, The Filson Historical Society, Georgetown College, Kentucky
Historical Society, Kentucky State University, Morehead State University, Murray
State University, Northern Kentucky University, Transylvania University,
University of Kentucky, University of Louisville, and Western Kentucky University.
All rights reserved.

Editorial and Sales Offices: The University Press of Kentucky
663 South Limestone Street, Lexington, Kentucky 40508-4008
www.kentuckypress.com

Library of Congress Cataloging-in-Publication Data

Gritter, Elizabeth.
 River of hope : Black politics and the Memphis freedom movement, 1865-1954 /
Elizabeth Gritter.
    pages cm. — (Civil rights and the struggle for Black equality in the twentieth
century)
 Includes bibliographical references and index.
 ISBN 978-0-8131-4450-4 (hardcover : alk. paper) —
 ISBN 978-0-8131-4475-7 (pdf : alk. paper) —
 ISBN 978-0-8131-4474-0 (epub : alk. paper)
 1. African Americans—Tennessee—Memphis—Politics and government—20th
century. 2. African Americans—Civil rights—Tennessee—Memphis—History—
20th century. 3. Civil rights movements—Tennessee—Memphis—History—20th
century. 4. Memphis (Tenn.)—Race relations—History—20th century. I. Title.
II. Title: Black politics and the Memphis freedom movement, 1865-1954.
 F444.M59N486 2014
 323.1196'0730768190904—dc23   2013048838

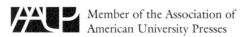

Contents

Photographs follow page 136

Introduction

Memphis, Tennessee, was on the cutting edge of black political mobilization in the Jim Crow South. An unusually large number of black Memphians could vote compared with their counterparts in the rest of the South, and many African Americans, both in the South and elsewhere, saw Memphis as a model for political mobilization. The story of Memphis illuminates the small but significant number of black southerners who retained the right to vote and engaged in formal political efforts from the disenfranchisement campaigns of the late nineteenth century through the *Brown v. Board of Education* decision of 1954, which overturned the "separate but equal" doctrine of *Plessy v. Ferguson* (1896). In the face of the disenfranchisement, violence, segregation, and poverty in the region, black southerners fought these injustices through electoral action. Their political activities constituted a major prong of the "long civil rights movement," and they often engaged in legal, direct action and labor efforts for civil rights as well. Ultimately, they contributed to the demise of legal segregation and the democratization of southern politics in the 1960s. They laid the groundwork for the Voting Rights Act of 1965, which resulted in a dramatic increase in the number of black voters and public officials in the region and, eventually, the election of the nation's first black president.

This study asks: How and why did black southerners engage in formal political efforts in the Jim Crow era? What was the impact of their efforts? It uses Memphis as a case study to more broadly explore the formal black political mobilization taking place in the Jim Crow South, an aspect of the long black freedom struggle and southern politics that scholars have largely overlooked. By connecting the post-Reconstruction era with the mass civil rights mobilizations of the 1950s and 1960s, this book shows the long duration and depth of the black freedom struggle. It focuses on electoral politics, specifically on African American voter registration and education activities, voting

1

behavior and patterns, candidacies for public office, activities in political campaigns, interactions with public officials, and participation in political clubs and party organizations.[1]

This emphasis on electoral politics is not meant to suggest that politics took solely this form. One important development in scholarship over the last few decades is a recognition that politics encompasses not only the electoral process and government institutions but also broader power relations and struggles. Although such encompassing definitions of politics are useful and important, they can lead historians to lose sight of the crucial importance of the government. This book, by contrast, remains sharply focused on direct efforts to influence it through the electoral process. It brings into the spotlight the power structure that wields influence over all and, at the same time, examines the influence of black leaders and ordinary people on it. The government's capacity to formulate policy, mobilize resources, and change and shape the course of American life cannot be overestimated. At the same time, the structure of the government ultimately is created by people, put in place by people, and sustained by them.

Consequently, this book does not provide an exploration of the political culture of Memphis or claim to be a comprehensive community or political history of it. It centers on the electoral process in order to show how and why African Americans engaged in formal political mobilization in the Jim Crow era in Memphis and other urban areas in the South. To be sure, black electoral action was a complex process that was enmeshed with the institutions and culture of the black community. Although not focused on the intersection of black political activity with churches or schools or other sociocultural institutions, this study is not saying that these aspects of black electoral mobilization are not important or significant. Already, fine studies exist of the political culture and history of Memphis on which this book has relied, such as works by Laurie B. Green, Michael K. Honey, and G. Wayne Dowdy. To expand the focus of this study would dilute its purpose. Rather, it is hoped that this book will raise questions for future scholars to explore.

Memphis both serves and does not serve as a representative southern city for looking at African American political participation. On the one hand, it was distinctive in being the cotton capital of the world and the business center of the Mid-South area. One of the largest southern cities, it reportedly had more registered black voters than any other community in the South. It is also unusual because of Edward H. Crump. A white Democrat, he was the most powerful political figure in Memphis from the time that he became mayor in 1910 until his death in 1954; he built the longest-running political machine in US history to date. On the other hand, Memphis effectively functions as a case study because of its location and the nature of the black political mobilization that took place there. Perched on the Mississippi River just north of Mississippi, the city, located in Shelby County of West Tennessee, straddles the Deep South and Mid-South, thus containing features of both regions. Most importantly, the abundance of black electoral action in it offers a window into the range of political activity that occurred in other areas as well.

Even after disenfranchisement swept the South, many black Memphians engaged in electoral mobilization. They maneuvered for political access and negotiated with white elites in complex and sometimes conflicting ways. Crump relied on black votes to maintain his power, and a two-way relationship developed that gave black Memphians a degree of leverage. They formed political clubs, ran for office, engaged in voter registration and education activities, held the balance of power in elections, participated in party politics, used the political arena as a forum for advocating civil rights, and petitioned public officials for better public services and employment opportunities.

African Americans continued to vote in at least twenty other cities as well, including Nashville, Richmond, Raleigh, Durham, Atlanta, Birmingham, Jacksonville, and Houston. Although thousands of African Americans voted in Memphis, no more than a few hundred usually voted elsewhere until the 1930s. By the end of that decade, thousands registered to vote, mainly in large urban areas of the Peripheral South.[2] More became eligible to vote after the Supreme Court ruled the white primary unconstitutional in *Smith v. Allwright* (1944).[3] By being restricted to whites, the Democratic primary had served as the most powerful of all disenfranchisement measures. Because southern white Democrats held such dominance in the region, whoever won the primary was virtually guaranteed election. Democratic party rules had established the white primary in all southern states except Texas, which mandated it by state law, and Tennessee and North Carolina, both of which never had a statewide white primary. The number of black voters in the South rose after the *Smith* decision from less than 5 percent of those eligible to nearly 25 percent by the time of the 1954

Brown v. Board decision.[4] The number of African Americans in elective
or appointive office remained small, however: at least one held elective
or appointive office in less than 5 percent of southern cities from 1945
to 1960. Not until the Voting Rights Act of 1965 did a large increase
in the number of black public officials occur, from only one hundred
in 1964 to some fourteen hundred by 1970.[5]

Black electoral activity took place mainly in cities rather than in
rural areas, where African Americans were disenfranchised to a greater
extent until the civil rights activism and federal interventions of the
1960s. Despite the vigor of their activism, rural African Americans
suffered from less economic independence and faced greater isolation
and more violence and intimidation than their urban counterparts,
all of which served as a barrier to their formal political mobilization.
Exceptions occurred in places such as Tuskegee, Alabama, and Fayette
and Haywood Counties of West Tennessee, where African Americans
waged voting rights campaigns before 1960, but they, too, largely did
not gain the right to vote until after that time. In cities, an independent professional class developed that formed the leadership for electoral efforts and made up a disproportionate number of black voters.
The proximity of black institutions and neighborhoods to each other
allowed for concerted activities and sometimes provided for safety
in numbers. And the higher education and income levels of African
Americans in urban areas correlated with higher voter participation.
Black voter registration numbers also correlated with population figures: African Americans were more likely to become registered voters
if they made up a smaller share of the population than whites, which
occurred more often in urban than in rural areas.[6]

This study also challenges persisting notions of a "Solid South"
of white Democratic control by arguing that black Republicans had
more political influence than has been assumed. Scholars have largely
dismissed or not deemed significant black participation in the Republican Party in the early decades of the twentieth century before
the New Deal of the 1930s, even though the vast majority of African
Americans were Republicans. As a result, historians have underestimated the importance of the party's conduct toward African Americans, the significance and influence of black Republicans, and the
meaning the party held for African Americans.[7] For black southerners
who wanted a place in the two-party system, the Grand Old Party was
the only real alternative. Although it was very limited in its approach

to African Americans and certainly not a bastion of racial tolerance, it differed from the Democratic Party in allowing black southerners a venue for participation and leadership, offering some support for civil rights, and affording blacks the dignity of political participation. Black Republicans could participate in party organizations and serve as delegates to the Republican national conventions. They pushed the party to embrace racial advancement and include them in party circles.[8] White southerners dominated the Democratic Party regionally and nationally, and the party largely excluded African Americans from its operations, failed to support civil rights, and did not take steps on blacks' behalf until the 1930s.

This book focuses particularly on Robert R. Church Jr., a black Memphian who tirelessly fought for civil rights his entire life and emerged as the country's most prominent black Republican in the 1920s. He remained a Republican until his death in 1952. Church, widely known as Bob Church, first and foremost saw politics as the key way to secure civil rights and otherwise push for racial advancement. He urged African Americans to mobilize politically. Secondarily, he urged them to be Republican. He believed that they needed to participate in the political party system in order to exercise political influence. He saw the Republican Party as their best hope because of its historic support for the Reconstruction amendments and its acceptance of some black political participation in the party. In addition, unlike the Democratic Party, it advocated civil rights to a limited degree. In 1916, Church formed the mass-based Lincoln League in Memphis to politically mobilize African Americans and support the Republican Party. Its success led him to found the Lincoln League of America in 1919, a move that furthered his rise to national political power. Because Church engaged in local, state, and national political activism across most of the time period of this study, his life illuminates the political activities of black southerners and the impact of their efforts. Church was a highly respected leader, and many African Americans saw him as reflecting their political aspirations. This book especially focuses on his local and national activities. Even though Church remained a Republican during the 1930s, when most African Americans shifted to the Democratic Party, an exploration of his rivalry with Dr. Joseph E. Walker, who became the most prominent black Democrat in Memphis, not only helps reveal the process of partisan change but also gives a complex portrayal of the partisan history of African Americans by putting a spotlight on African Americans who remained Republican.

The other main character is Edward H. Crump, the white machine politician who dominated Memphis politics from 1910 until his death in 1954. Crump was unique compared to other white southern politicians in allowing African Americans the ability to vote, negotiating with them politically, and providing them with better public services compared to many of their southern counterparts. Still, he was no racial liberal. Like other white southern politicians, he believed in segregation and second-class citizenship for African Americans. Because he included black Memphians as part of his political coalition and they took advantage of this access, the interactions between him and local African Americans further provide a window into black electoral activities. The story of Memphis forces us to acknowledge the important role that white political actors played in black politics. Because black southerners were essentially barred from holding office during the Jim Crow era, they often had to negotiate with whites in order to exercise political influence. Black leaders, like Church, faced the challenge of striking a balance between keeping the trust of their followers and wheeling and dealing with white politicians who had the power to affect African American lives. Black southerners could not elect one of their own to office, but they sometimes could determine which white candidate was elected. Many scholars have examined Crump and the role of African Americans in his machine, but this book is the first to focus primarily on this relationship.

This study is not a biography of Robert R. Church Jr. or Edward H. Crump; rather, it uses their lives to illuminate black political efforts. The decision to focus on these two figures is also pragmatic. Because relatively few copies of local black newspapers from the time frame of this book have survived, the Robert R. Church Family Papers represent the best source of archival materials on black political mobilization in Memphis. Where they exist, the papers of other key black electoral figures and related groups do not contain as much information on black politics for the time period covered by this study. Similarly, the Edward Crump Papers and those of two mayors installed by him, Walter Chandler and Watkins Overton, include extensive information on black politics for the first half of the twentieth century because these officials interacted with black leaders and ordinary black Memphians and also monitored developments occurring in the black community. In addition, this book draws on oral histories, newspaper articles, pamphlets, and government reports in order to reveal the electoral efforts of both well-known and ordinary black political activists and the meaning that political participation held for them.

Most historians have neglected the black southerners who retained the right to vote and engaged in formal political activities during the Jim Crow era. Rather, scholars see this period as "the nadir," a time when African Americans were politically powerless because the vast majority were disenfranchised and, consequently, exercised little influence on electoral and party politics. Yet we know that African Americans commonly secured better public services, such as improved parks and school facilities, in the places where they could vote in the South. This book contends that the benefits that African Americans received from politics went far beyond even these significant gains. They ensured that the Republican Party supported black involvement in party operations and took stands for civil rights, and they helped transform the Democratic Party into a vehicle for civil rights and black political participation. Realizing that an inherent dignity existed in staking out a place in the political process, African Americans used political activity to get their voices heard and to upset ideas that they were inferior and apathetic. And they achieved some success in working to make a reality their vision of the political process as a means by which to better the lives of the disadvantaged, eradicate racism and discrimination, and achieve the American promises of freedom and equality for all.

By exploring the involvement of black southerners in both political parties, this book reveals a more complex political landscape than historians have acknowledged. Scholars have recognized the significance of the northern black vote to a much greater extent than they have the southern black vote.[9] While the vast majority of African Americans continued to live in the South during this study's time period, the mass migration of black southerners to the North, particularly during and after World War II, led to a powerful black vote in key urban areas of the North. African Americans increasingly held the balance of power in elections, and Republicans and Democrats were forced to pay attention to them. This study argues that the impact of black southerners on national politics cannot be ignored. Church and other black politicians exerted significant, albeit limited, national political influence that led to gains and held meaning for African Americans. While most African Americans remained registered Republicans during the 1930s, they voted for Democratic candidates in unprecedented numbers at that time mainly because they benefited from Franklin D. Roosevelt's New Deal programs. Roosevelt's presidency led to one of the most major partisan shifts in US history as African Americans increasingly turned to the Democratic Party. Along with trade unionists, liberals, nonsouthern African Americans, and whites from all regions of the country, many black southerners became part of a New Deal coalition that helped weaken the long-standing power of conservative southern white Democrats and influenced Democrats to embrace civil rights policies and black participation in party operations.[10] While scholars have focused on the black shift to the Democratic Party in 1936, many African Americans remained committed to the Republican Party because of a strain of racial liberalism that persisted in the party, the party's historical association with them, and the Democratic Party's history of supporting the Jim Crow system.[11]

A spotlight on southern black electoral mobilization thus adds to the growing body of scholarship on the complexity and nuances of African American life in the nadir period.[12] This book is similar to Steven Hahn's Pulitzer Prize–winning *A Nation under Our Feet* because Hahn too examines black political struggles in a time and place in which scholars traditionally have assumed that little political activity took place and shows the importance of such struggles to broader developments in the South and the nation overall.[13] To be sure, it is crucial to realize that black political mobilization was limited in the South because of widespread disenfranchisement measures and violence. Yet it is equally important to give adequate attention to black agency. Doing so gives not only a fuller, more accurate picture of the black experience but also a better understanding of the human condition more broadly. Human beings often have displayed amazing resilience in the face of oppression and worked to better their conditions. Although they have not always seen changes in their lifetimes, their efforts have led to a better tomorrow. These stories, then, provide us with an essential reason for studying history: its capacity to inspire hope, especially in the face of current injustices.

Chapter 1 uses the lives of Robert R. Church Sr. and Robert R. Church Jr. as a window into political developments in Memphis and the South from 1865 until 1916. During Reconstruction, African American men were enfranchised and held public office. However, before and after federal troops withdrew from the South in 1877, white supremacist campaigns led to the ascendancy of conservative white Democrats to office in southern states. Especially from the late 1880s until the early years of the twentieth century, southern states passed laws that disenfranchised and segregated African Americans, and lynching reached its peak. Black Memphians saw a sharp decline in their political and social status, but they retained the right to vote and remained politically mobilized. Church Sr. ran for office and helped register African Americans to vote. The first African American millionaire in the South, he mainly focused on business and black institution building as a means for racial advancement. His daughter, Mary Church Terrell, emerged as a nationally recognized women's rights and civil rights leader. In the 1910s, Church Sr.'s son, Robert R. Church Jr., also a businessman, got his political start. Edward H. Crump began building a political machine and became mayor in 1910. Local black political efforts culminated in 1916 when Church Jr. formed the Lincoln League. Although a league-sponsored ticket of black Republicans for local, state, and national offices lost at the polls, they beat its white Republican challengers, leading to the establishment of Church's Republican faction as the "regular Republicans" in the area and greater political influence as a result.

Chapter 2 explores the period from 1917 to 1927, which led to a new era in the political mobilization of black Memphians. The success of the local Lincoln League attracted regional and national attention, inspiring Church Jr. to form the Lincoln League of America in 1919. As a result of his political successes, he emerged as the most prominent African American Republican in the country, held local, state, and national positions within the party, and wielded great influence through dispensing patronage. Black Memphians also expanded their civil rights activism into new venues. Following a local lynching, Church Jr. and his political associates formed the Memphis branch of the NAACP. They faced a challenge to their leadership from black clergy who were part of the city's Commission on Interracial Cooperation (CIC) chapter. The CIC group became an influential organization that advocated for improvements within the existing Jim Crow system. Despite their differences, both groups were dedicated to racial advancement. While Church Jr. shifted his attention to national politics and disbanded the local Lincoln League in 1920, he and his associates continued to involve themselves in local elections. Their efforts, and those of other African Americans, were key to defeating most of a Ku Klux Klan ticket of office seekers in 1923. Four years later, black Memphians united to make their biggest mass political mobilization of the decade: Church and his political lieutenants founded the West Tennessee Civic and Political League. They formed an alliance with Crump and mobilized black Memphians to successfully vote the incumbent mayor out of office and elect the mayoral candidate who offered the most promise for meeting their demands.

Chapter 3 examines political transformations occurring from 1928 through 1939. While the Republican Party had always been limited in its support for civil rights and acceptance of black participation in the party, President Herbert Hoover took fewer steps toward racial advancement than his Republican predecessors and alienated many African Americans from the party. Church and his fellow black Republicans made sure that the party did not completely disregard them. In 1932, Franklin D. Roosevelt was elected president. Although most African Americans continued to identify themselves as Republican during the 1930s, a majority first voted for the Democratic Party in the 1934 midterm election, and more backed Roosevelt in 1936, becoming part of a new coalition that weakened the long-standing power of conservative southern white Democrats. In Memphis, Church Jr.'s power declined with the rise of Roosevelt to the White House, while Crump's power increased. Crump's machine encompassed both city and county politics, and he became the most powerful figure in state politics. Crump cracked down on whites and blacks who threatened his control, including Church. At the same time, like African Americans elsewhere in the region and the country, black Memphians increased their political activity. Local black Democratic organizations formed, and the businessman J. E. Walker emerged as a Democratic rival to Church. Spurred by New Deal legislation, a powerful biracial labor movement emerged in Memphis and the South that resulted in better working conditions for African Americans and put cracks in the Jim Crow system.

Chapter 4 assesses African American political activity in Memphis and in the South during the period 1940–45, a time of increased activism among African Americans as they pressed the United States for the democracy at home that soldiers were fighting for abroad. However, Crump became more antidemocratic than ever before. He cracked down on African Americans campaigning for the Republican presidential candidate in 1940, leading to the exile of Church and two other black Republicans from Memphis. In a well-publicized incident, he banned the black labor leader A. Philip Randolph from speaking in the city. Randolph used the ordeal to press for a more democratic Memphis and South. With the departure of Church and his political lieutenant J. B. Martin from Memphis, black political leadership fell into the hands of local African Americans who took a less assertive political approach and largely did not challenge the Crump machine. But other African Americans joined the local NAACP branch, engaged in individual protests against the Jim Crow system, and involved themselves in the labor movement. While many black Memphians praised the city for its release of a booklet detailing its provisions for African Americans, a black lieutenant and his soldiers criticized the local government for its limits. They signified a new generation of black southerners and Memphians who would more aggressively pursue civil rights in the postwar era and take advantage of the *Smith* decision to further engage in political activities.

Chapter 5 examines the watershed years from 1946 to 1954. Black and white Memphians became increasingly disenchanted with Crump. White reformers, black and white unionists, and black political activists came together in 1948 to support the first non-Crump-supported candidates to win public office in more than a decade. That year, President Harry S. Truman supported civil rights measures in a way that no president had done since Reconstruction. The Democratic Party fissured as many white southerners, including Crump, supported the Dixiecrat Strom Thurmond, who opposed Truman's civil rights stance, for the presidency. After the 1948 elections, a more democratic political environment developed in Memphis, and Crump's power declined. While the labor movement suffered from the wave of anticommunism sweeping the country, black and white Memphians engaged in increased levels of political activity. An independent white leadership group rivaled Crump and his associates, and a white Republican group emerged that challenged the local party organization dominated by African Americans. In 1951, black Memphians mobilized behind J. E. Walker when he made the first African American bid for local office in decades in a race for the school board. In 1952, Church Jr. made an effort to come back to Memphis to regain control of the local Republican Party's leadership, but he died before he could come closer to making these plans a reality. His daughter, Roberta Church, carried on his mission by becoming involved in Republican Party politics. In 1954, Crump died, leaving no successor to take his place, and an era of Memphis politics came to an end. That same year, the Supreme Court handed down the *Brown* decision, shaking the South to its core.

This book ends with a brief examination of the period from 1955 to 2013. In 1960, the sit-in movement swept Memphis and the South. Political activists in Memphis embraced direct action as a new part of their struggle, while the younger generation supported the Democratic Party, which spearheaded the Civil Rights Act of 1964 and the Voting Rights Act of 1965. As a result of civil rights activism and legislation, de jure segregation saw its demise in the region, and black Memphians and southerners saw better employment opportunities and won public office on a larger scale. Martin Luther King Jr. was murdered in Memphis in 1968 after coming to the city to support striking sanitation workers, and the gains of black Memphians and other black southerners were stunted by the persistence of poverty and racial polarization. Nevertheless, this study concludes that the political activities of black southerners in the Jim Crow era not only led to racial advancement at the time but also forwarded the civil rights movement of the 1950s and 1960s, which forever changed the United States for the better.

1 "To Regain the Lost Rights of a Growing Race"

Black Political Mobilization, 1865–1916

W. Herbert Brewster grew up in a community "with very little opportunity" in rural West Tennessee near the small village of New Castle.[1] Until a life-changing night in 1916, he had never been in an auditorium before and did not even know what one was. When he and his fellow black students pressed their way into Memphis's crowded Church's Auditorium that evening, they looked up and saw a beautiful place. After the singing of "The Battle Hymn of the Republic," Brewster remembered, "there strode out to . . . the platform a young man of great personal carriage and personality. We had never seen a man who charmed us like he did." The man was Robert Reed Church Jr. Church introduced Roscoe Conkling Simmons, the nephew of Booker T. Washington and a prominent journalist and civil rights leader in his own right. Simmons gave a rousing address. "When I heard that speech and saw [Church Jr.], [I] resolved that night to be somebody someday," Brewster said. "That determination . . . was inspired by Bob Church and that crowd of people in that black auditorium. I never knew before that I had a chance."[2] Brewster went on to work with Church in political efforts and, eventually, became a prominent minister in local and national Baptist circles, the head of a ministerial school, and one of the most influential gospel songwriters of the twentieth century.[3]

Brewster's meeting with Church Jr. occurred at a rally of the Lincoln League on the night before election day. Church had formed this mass-based Republican organization in order to mobilize African Americans politically, press for civil rights, and support the Grand Old

Party. During Reconstruction, the Republican-controlled federal government had granted African Americans citizenship rights and black men voting rights. White Republicans took charge of southern state governments, and black men registered to vote and occupied public office in Memphis and elsewhere in the region. But the alliance between white Republicans and African Americans was tenuous; most white Republicans were not committed to ensuring black equality. Former white Confederates resumed control of southern state governments, and Reconstruction ended in 1877. A surge of white activism, compounded by white extralegal violence, led to the removal of black officeholders, the widespread disenfranchisement of African Americans, and the enactment of legal segregation across the South by the early twentieth century. Although black Tennesseans retained the right to vote more than most other black southerners, the number of black officeholders in the state and in Memphis declined to zero. The number of Republicans in the South also decreased; a sizable proportion of the remaining whites joined "lily-white" factions that largely excluded African Americans. African Americans mainly stayed involved in the Republican Party in "black-and-tan" factions that included a few whites and often competed with the lily whites for control of local party organizations, while white Democrats monopolized southern politics and excluded African Americans from their party organizations.

In 1916, the lily-white faction was the most prominent Republican group in Memphis. Church wanted his black-and-tan faction to displace it as the dominant party organization. For the November election, he organized a Lincoln League ticket of black candidates to run against the white Republican slate for state and national positions. If the black office seekers polled more votes, the black and tans would become the "regular Republicans" and, consequently, exert more political influence, bettering their chances for racial advancement. With the backing of many of the city's black leaders, the Lincoln League mobilized ordinary black Memphians in support of the candidates. League leaders portrayed the Republican Party as the vehicle that had delivered African Americans from slavery and as their best hope for wielding political influence in the two-party system.[4] While historians have emphasized the ideology and programs of individual African Americans during the post-Reconstruction years and the community building that African Americans engaged in to protect themselves from the prevailing environment, the story of Memphis reveals how black southerners mobilized politically.

Elsewhere in the South, a small but significant number of African Americans continued to participate in the political process after the end of Reconstruction, particularly in urban areas. Hundreds voted in some cities, including Atlanta and Richmond, while a few cast ballots despite facing the white primary. Some voted in nonpartisan municipal elections, bond and tax rate referenda, and occasional special elections; in some cases, they secured the passage of measures beneficial to the black community. While cities served as the headquarters of black-and-tan Republican committees, black women petitioned municipal governments for better public services. In addition, the number of African American urban civic organizations and nonpartisan political leagues increased: these groups conducted discussions of public matters affecting African Americans and coached them on how to overcome registration requirements. By challenging disenfranchisement in the courts and raising funds for such litigation, these organizations joined the black southerners engaged in legal battles against disenfranchisement. The NAACP, founded in 1909 in part to secure black voting rights, began a legal battle to overturn disenfranchisement measures and achieved success when in 1915 the Supreme Court ruled the grandfather clause unconstitutional.[5]

In Memphis, Brewster called Church Jr.'s father, Robert Reed Church Sr., the "forerunner" of the 1916 political developments because his rise to prominence from humble beginnings had left a "legacy of inspiration."[6] Church Sr. was the most influential African American in Memphis from the Civil War until his death in 1912. His life testifies to the frustrations and travails that all black southerners experienced during these years; the wealth that he amassed underscores the opportunities of which only a very small number were able to take advantage. Born in Holly Springs, Mississippi, in 1837, Church Sr. was the grandson of Lucy, a daughter of a royal family of the Malay Islands who was taken prisoner during a time of civil strife. It is unclear who captured her or why, but she arrived in Norfolk, Virginia, between 1805 and 1810 and was sold into slavery. Church Sr. was the son of her daughter Emmeline and Captain Charles Beckwith Church, a white steamship owner. Contradictory evidence exists as to whether Church Sr. was a slave. He claimed that he was, but his daughter and granddaughter later unearthed firsthand accounts saying that he and his mother were not slaves; rather, Emmeline worked as a seamstress for the Lynchburg, Virginia, planter family that purchased her and then later moved to Holly Springs.[7]

In the 1850s, Church Sr. served as a steward on his father's steamboats, which ran up and down the Mississippi River from Memphis to New Orleans. During the Battle of Memphis on 6 June 1862, a Federal fleet captured the steamboat *Victoria*, but Church escaped. The Confederates lost Memphis to the Union in a naval battle that day, resulting in Union troops occupying the city for the rest of the war. Church stayed in Memphis and saved money while working as a helper at a livery stable. After the war, he became one of the city's first black saloonkeepers when he opened a saloon at the corner of Beale and Gayoso.[8]

The unsettled social, political, and economic conditions that followed the Civil War led to racial friction, and Church was a target. Whites of all classes confronted growing competition from black workers. For a brief period after the war, whites were forced to accept the authority of black soldiers stationed just south of Memphis. In 1866, these simmering tensions exploded into the first large-scale urban race riot in the South. Following a verbal confrontation between members of the Irish-dominated police force and black troops on a Memphis street corner, white rioters targeted black property and businessmen, but Church refused to close his saloon. Members of a white mob shot Church in the back of the head at his business, leaving him to die. The injury left a hole in his head where one could insert the tip of a little finger; he subsequently suffered from headaches so severe that he sometimes threatened to commit suicide. By the time order was restored, at least seventy-five people had been wounded, some one hundred blacks robbed, at least five black women raped, and forty-six blacks and two whites killed. After the riot, no whites experienced punishment, and no African Americans received compensation despite Church's testimony before a congressional committee investigating the riot. African Americans rebuilt their churches and schools and increasingly sought solace and protection in their own neighborhoods and through their own institutions.[9]

More than any other person, Church transformed the Beale Street area into a center of commercial activity and community life for black Memphians. Church invested his business profits in rental properties and came to own more property than any other black Memphian. His first wife, Louisa Ayres, a former slave, ran a successful hair salon, the first one for black women in Memphis, in the downtown area. With her profits, they bought their first carriage and house, which was located in an interracial suburb. Church accrued a fortune mainly through real estate, and he served as an architect and civil engineer for his buildings: he designed them and supervised their construction. Called the "Boss of Beale Street," he dominated the street's business affairs by 1883. He operated several saloons in the area and owned a hotel, a restaurant, and other properties on the street, including in the vice district. He also owned valuable business property on South Second Street, more than 350 residences in Memphis, and several hundred acres of land on the city's edge. His real estate empire eventually encompassed properties in other large municipalities. Recognized across the region and the nation for his success, Church became the first black millionaire in the South and, reputedly, in the United States.[10]

Reflecting and symbolizing Church's financial success was his palatial house, which he built in 1884. He and Louisa had divorced around 1867.[11] He lived there with his second wife, Anna Wright Church, in a silk-stocking neighborhood that included prominent whites and blacks. The three-story, fourteen-room Queen Anne–style home at 384 S. Lauderdale ranked with the white mansions of the city and included frescoes and elaborate lace curtains on bay windows. As was common during that time, the showplace of the house was the parlor, which was hand-painted by French artists and featured velvet Brussels carpets and two crystal chandeliers. The *Commercial Appeal,* a local white daily, noted that the family had earned the respect of their white neighbors, but Church's success stoked jealousies among whites as well.[12]

Although Church was first and foremost a businessman, he participated in political movements aimed at advancing the collective interests of African Americans. In the late 1860s, the Republican-dominated state legislature passed laws providing for the suffrage of black men, removing restrictions on black officeholding, and protecting black voters from economic intimidation. Taking advantage of these new laws, black Memphians formed political clubs, held elected and appointive office, and built coalitions with whites in the 1870s and 1880s. Black fraternal organizations encouraged black political participation and officeholding, while black churches hosted political meetings. Whites of both parties competed for the black vote. Nearly every branch of government included black officials or employees, and African Americans served on the grand jury and as police officers and firefighters. African Americans usually were elected to office from predominately black districts. Like most African Americans of his era, Church was a lifelong Republican. He helped African Americans register to vote and campaigned for James Garfield, who won the 1880 presidential election. In 1882, Church made a bid for a city council seat but lost.[13]

The political scene in Memphis reflected the revolution in politics and society occurring across the South. During Reconstruction, some two thousand African Americans held elective and appointive office at the local, state, and national levels, with the majority at the local level. Most black officeholders were former slaves, attesting to the radical social transformation by which enslaved African Americans not only became free but also occupied political positions over their former masters. Black churches especially provided the space for political organizing, and African Americans used the political process to press for racial advancement. Although not granted suffrage, black women participated in politics through such means as petitioning local officials to hire black police officers. Black political activists and officeholders were full of hope, but the road was not smooth anywhere. They faced violence, intimidation, and economic repercussions. While whites mainly occupied the most important political positions, African Americans were represented in public office in numbers disproportionate to their population size. Southern white Republicans generally could be counted on to support black political rights, but most did not see racial equality as a priority.[14]

Church Sr. knew many of the most prominent African American political figures of the day and interacted socially with them. Family friends included Pinckney S. B. Pinchback, Frederick Douglass, Blanche Bruce, and John Lynch. Pinchback was the only black governor during Reconstruction, as governor of Louisiana. Most well known as an abolitionist and orator, Douglass was the first African American to have his name entered into nomination for president at a major party convention, the Republican national convention in 1888. Bruce, of Mississippi, was one of two black US senators during the Reconstruction era, and Lynch served as speaker of the Mississippi House of Representatives, a US congressman, a justice of the peace, and the temporary chair of the Republican national convention in 1884.[15]

While Church participated in economic and political efforts on behalf of black Memphians, he helped white residents as well. Memphis was severely affected with yellow fever epidemics in 1873, 1878, and 1879; its population fell from more than 40,000 in 1876 to 18,500 in late 1879 because of death and emigration. The city, which had become a business center in the Mid-South, lost its charter and became a taxing district run by the state. Having faith in the city's recovery and potential, Church stepped up his investments in local real estate and bought the first bond for $1,000 to restore the city's charter, spurring white capitalists to purchase bonds. Memphis regained its financial standing and status as a city, and its population rose to 64,495 in 1890.[16] Recalling Church Sr.'s role in buying the first bond, the *Memphis Evening Scimitar* in 1891 called him "a firm believer in Memphis," adding that "war and plagues have never shaken his faith in her."[17]

In spite of his contributions to Memphis, Church, along with other assertive and economically successful African Americans, remained the target of white violence and hatred. Fearful of the new freedoms afforded to African Americans, white southerners embraced Jim Crow measures and racist demagoguery in order to elevate their relative status, control black workers, and limit black advancement. Extralegal violence emerged as a crucial weapon in this new campaign to affirm white privilege and dominance. Lynching and mob violence reached a height during the 1890s and threatened black progress into the 1930s. A group of white hoodlums, wanting to gain economic control of Beale Street, threatened to shoot Church, but he was not hurt. Other African Americans were not so fortunate: at least fifteen lynchings occurred in Shelby County between 1892 and 1914.[18]

While Church emerged safe from lynching, he and his generation could not stop disenfranchisement from occurring across the South from 1888 to 1908. Conservative white Democrats regained control of all southern state legislatures, and federal troops left the region in 1877, effectively ending Reconstruction. Southern state legislatures soon began enacting disenfranchisement measures that dramatically diminished the political power of African Americans and that of some marginalized whites, including impoverished farmers and laborers, who had occasionally sought alliances with African Americans. Eleven black men still were elected to Congress from the South, with the last one ending his service in 1901, after the end of Reconstruction. Black men served as state legislators in Mississippi into the 1880s. But the number of registered black voters plummeted to less than 5 percent of those eligible, the number of black elected officials dropped to zero by the early years of the twentieth century, and the number of white registered voters fell as well. In Louisiana, for example, the number of African Americans registered to vote decreased from 130,000 to 5,000.[19]

Tennessee was no exception to this wave of disenfranchisement. Black officeholding had peaked in the 1870s in Memphis but then declined. Restructuring of the local government after the yellow fever epidemics led to a reduction in electoral positions, and the state legislature passed laws that enacted stricter registration requirements, the secret ballot, and the poll tax in 1889 and 1890. In the general election, voter turnout statewide dropped from 78 percent in 1888 to 50 percent in 1890. Race-baiting, fraud, intimidation, and hostile press coverage undermined black political power and elevated growing numbers of conservative white Democrats to positions of power at the local and state levels. White Republicans and Democrats no longer sought the black vote or gave jobs to black supporters to the extent that they had previously. In Memphis, black public officials were no more, and African Americans occupied only the most menial government jobs by 1910. The question became not whether African Americans would hold office but whether they would be successful in uncovering new means of asserting political influence.[20]

It was no coincidence that disenfranchisement occurred alongside the imposition of legal segregation. After the Civil War, new laws chipped away at the newfound freedom of African Americans. After conservative white Democrats resumed control of the Tennessee state government in 1869, they repealed measures that the Radical Republicans had enacted, including laws curbing the Ku Klux Klan and preventing the segregation of railroad travel. They spearheaded a new constitution in 1870 that prohibited school integration and strengthened the existing statute against intermarriage. In 1875, Tennessee legalized the segregation of public accommodations by allowing those places to refuse service to African Americans. Six years later, the state legislature passed the first law in the South to mandate segregation; it required separate coaches with equal accommodations for first-class black passengers on trains.[21] Throughout the region, the Volunteer State's lead was followed: laws mandating segregation came to fruition in the 1890s and reached into nearly every area of southern life by the early years of the twentieth century. The US Supreme Court legitimated these actions by ruling in *Plessy v. Ferguson* (1896) that separate facilities for African Americans were constitutional as long as they were equal to those of whites.

Even with the double blow of disenfranchisement and segregation, black Tennesseans, especially those residing in large cities, enjoyed greater success in exerting political power than their counterparts in other southern states. The state legislature left it up to counties to decide whether to adopt a white primary rather than establishing one statewide. Tennessee did not enact common measures of disenfranchisement such as a literacy test or a grandfather clause.[22] Furthermore, the state had more of a two-party system than the rest of the South; white Republicans dominated the political scene in East Tennessee, while white Democrats controlled the state government and local governments elsewhere. Intense party rivalries fostered continued black political participation.

Black Memphians proved particularly successful at taking advantage of the unique opportunities for political participation in Tennessee. Shelby County did not have a white primary. The local Democratic Party experienced significant factionalism, with different wings running against each other, so at least one candidate in close local elections sometimes sought black support, especially given that African Americans made up between 40 and 49 percent of the population from 1890 and 1910. Politicians often coached illiterate African Americans and paid their poll taxes to try to secure their votes. Black women participated in women's suffrage meetings, and Julia Hooks, a community leader and the grandmother of the future civil rights leader Benjamin L. Hooks, urged black men to pay the poll tax and called for greater state funding for schools.[23] According to the local black observer Green P. Hamilton in 1908, African Americans could vote as easily in Memphis as in the North. "Political passion is not . . . intensely aroused against [black voting]," he said. "No political hocus pocus has been resorted to to deprive [the black voter] of his political rights. . . . All must meet the simple requirements of the law."[24] "When the Negroes turn out in strength at the polls, it requires only a very few additional votes to elect anyone they support," the *Com-*

mercial Appeal reported in 1898. "This is, after all, their privilege and we cannot blame them for exercising it."[25]

Black Memphians joined forces to use politics as a tool to better their condition following the enactment of legal disenfranchisement in 1889, but the scarcity of sources makes it difficult to determine how extensively.[26] According to G. P. Hamilton, who was Columbia University educated and the principal of Kortrecht High School, the first black public high school in Memphis, African Americans did "not blindly adhere to any political party," although they supported Republicans in presidential elections. In municipal and state elections, they were "largely independent and disposed to vote for the man that they consider[ed] least hostile to their interests . . . [and] least likely to deny [them] opportunity or punish [them] because of [their] color." Some black political leaders criticized African Americans for voting solidly as a bloc because they thought that their united force would "always force the white voters to be united under another political banner," Hamilton observed, noting that "this division of the races into two opposite and hostile political camps has been the cause of serious misunderstanding and friction between them."[27]

African Americans also used the written word to speak out against disenfranchisement, stereotypes, and racial violence. In 1903, on behalf of a group of local black pastors and professionals, the Reverend John H. Grant of Avery Chapel African Methodist Episcopal Church wrote an opinion piece, published in the *Commercial Appeal,* in response to that newspaper's editorial degrading African Americans. The columns were later included in a short pamphlet titled *Defense of the Negro; or, A Review of the "Commercial Appeal's" Attack on the Negro.* The *Commercial Appeal* had argued that black suffrage was a failure because African Americans were biologically and mentally inferior to whites. To evidence its argument, the paper called black people a "monumental failure among the nations of the world," saying that they never had had "any form of civilization, any code of morality, any conception of abstract justice, any religion, any literature, any art, or any science." Evoking social Darwinism, the paper said: "He is an incomplete and arrested race, and if there is anything in the survival of the fittest he, as the unfittest, will perish from the earth." The only hope for betterment for African Americans, according to the paper, was through contacts with whites, although, even then, they would remain inferior.[28]

The editorial "caused no little stir" among black Memphians: they discussed it on street corners, in their offices, and in their homes. They decided that a committee should discuss the editorial with the editor and call for space in the *Commercial Appeal* for an opinion piece in response. Grant and the Reverend T. J. Searcy, a former slave, met with the editor, who received them with courtesy and agreed to publish their views. In his opinion piece, Grant deconstructed and discredited the editorial point by point, calling the *Commercial Appeal*'s claims of biological inferiority of African Americans "ethnological humbuggery, a stretch of the imagination, a hiss in the teeth of knowledge, and an insult to God." He dismissed claims that black people were savages by detailing their historic and modern achievements, including W. E. B. Du Bois's success at Harvard; he pointed out that Du Bois had flourished in this top-notch educational institution dominated by whites. At a time when African Americans could face severe repercussions for protesting lynching, he denounced racial violence by quoting a white Chicago pastor's words that white men lynch African Americans "again and again for crimes that white men have not outgrown and do frequently commit." Grant concluded: "It is God's will that we should be friends and not enemies; that we should love, not hate each other; that . . . one cannot degrade the other without degrading himself." In a parting word in the pamphlet, he called on African Americans to "promote the cause of justice, humanity and social reform, and by our lives [dis]prove the false charges of our enemies."[29]

Further disproving ideas of their inferiority and unworthiness for political participation, black southerners took advantage of the access that the Republican Party allowed them to the party system, given that Democrats denied them participation in their official circles. Local Republican organizations often consisted of African Americans with some white allies; black men headed some local and state organizations. Although white Democrats largely dominated southern politics, local Republicans could distribute thousands of patronage jobs when their party occupied the White House. Southern mores dictated that whites gained the most important positions, but African Americans received and could distribute some patronage. Patronage positions carried prestige and a good salary and ranged from postal jobs, including postmasterships, to judicial posts.[30] Black Republicans also wielded influence by serving as delegates to Republican national conventions, where they could help determine which presidential candidate was nominated. Especially because Republicans largely occupied the White House from the Civil War through the first decades of the twentieth century, black Republicans were not without hope that they could make a difference.

In order to do so, black-and-tan factions battled with lily-white groups over participation in the Republican Party. By the 1880s, a lily-white movement had arisen in the South. Lily whites, who desired to attract more white southerners to the Republican Party, wanted to purge party organizations of black leadership and control; they wanted only whites to distribute and receive patronage. Black-and-tan and lily-white factions desired recognition as the regular Republican organization. Regular Republicans held more influence in local, state, and national circles: they received and distributed patronage and were more likely to serve as delegates to state and national conventions and to participate in official local, state, and national committees and organizations. Yet a complex, complicated political scene could result in which, say, one faction could be recognized as the regular Republican organization while members of the other faction could occupy the most seats on official party committees. In some cases, black-and-tan and lily-white factions held separate conventions in order to nominate delegates to the Republican national convention; the credentials committee there would decide which faction to seat. In Memphis and Shelby County, African Americans participated in official Republican Party politics at the same time that they vied with the local lily-white faction. They served on the local Republican Executive Committee and as delegates to the Republican national convention. Church, for instance, traveled as a delegate to the Republican national convention in Philadelphia in 1900, which nominated William McKinley for president. He had enough national political weight to obtain appointments in the Department of State's Foreign Service for two black Memphians.[31]

Republican presidents in the early twentieth century varied in their support of black political participation. During his first term, Theodore Roosevelt sought a middle ground between appealing to black and tans and lily whites. He infuriated many white southerners, including ones in Memphis, by dining with Booker T. Washington at the White House. He consulted with Washington about patronage matters and southern policies, made a number of black political appointments, and expressed strong disapproval of an exclusively lily-white party in the South. But his backing among African Americans dwindled in his second term; he no longer made dramatic gestures supporting them. He dishonorably discharged all 167 members of a black regiment in Brownsville, Texas, in 1906 for inciting violence locally, even though they claimed and evidence suggested their innocence. As a result of the Brownsville affair, some African Americans turned away from the Republican Party. William Howard Taft, who won the presidency two years later, showed even less concern for African Americans. He supported the lily-white movement in the South and did not make any black political appointments, although he retained some of Roosevelt's appointees.[32]

W. E. B. Du Bois, who became a vocal African American critic of the Republican Party, emerged as a civil rights leader in the early twentieth century. Du Bois began publication of the *Moon Illustrated Weekly,* a black magazine, in 1905 in a Beale Street building. Although the magazine lasted only a year, he used it to promote the principles of the Niagara Movement, an organization that he formed in 1905 outside Buffalo, New York, that called for civil rights, black enfranchisement, and equal education opportunities. The group was assimilated into the NAACP when Du Bois, other black leaders, and white liberals formed that organization four years later. The NAACP advocated political rights, and the *Moon* was a precursor to the NAACP's *Crisis* magazine.[33]

Du Bois coined the term "Talented Tenth," referring to the responsibility of successful African Americans to use their wealth and resources to spearhead civil rights and uplift efforts in order to help the masses. Although the number of well-off African Americans actually made up less than a tenth of the population and not all engaged in these endeavors, Church, like other members of the black elite in the South, often took the lead in movements to establish black institutions, such as schools, as a way of pressing for racial advancement.[34] Church was closer philosophically to Du Bois than to Booker T. Washington. Church and Washington were friends, and Church became one of the first members of Washington's National Negro Business League. The two men shared a common belief that black economic progress was crucial to improving black conditions, but Church disagreed with Washington's accommodationist stance. According to his daughter Annette Church, he did not believe that African Americans should forsake political participation or higher education in order to focus on uplifting themselves through industrial work and training.[35]

Church's support of civil rights activists included the antilynching crusader Ida B. Wells and his daughter Mary Church Terrell, both of whom were founding members of the NAACP. Wells used her Beale Street–based newspaper, the *Free Speech and Headlight*, to speak out against lynching and other racial injustices. In 1892, she was forced to leave Memphis after she protested the lynching with impunity of three black men of the local Peoples' Grocery Store by a white mob. Black Memphians turned out for the largest funeral procession in the city's history to mourn the victims, while a black town meeting adopted resolutions condemning the lynchings and calling for emigration. Many black Memphians fled to the West to start a new life. A number of the most politically active ministers left the city, leaving behind pastors who appear to have largely eschewed protest and, rather, preached accommodation. Wells moved to Chicago and became nationally and internationally known for her antilynching activism; she also fought for black and women's suffrage. Church assisted her financially when she lived in Memphis and after her exile. Born in 1863, Terrell was the daughter of Church and his first wife, Louisa. She became one of the country's best-known activists for black and women's rights, including voting rights, and was a pioneer of the women's club movement. Church Sr. supported Terrell financially as well.[36]

One of Memphis's most philanthropic citizens, Church apparently contributed to all local charities and met all requests for funding. He donated to orphanages and churches of all denominations, bought a fire and patrol wagon for the city, and saved Beale Street Avenue Church from financial disaster.[37] "Mr. Church has never been appealed to in vain," the *Memphis Evening Scimitar* said in 1891. "Whether it was to contribute to a fair, a trades display, the reception of a president, republican or democrat, to a church an orphan asylum or to a private charity, he has always responded promptly and liberally, regardless of whether the beneficiaries were of his own color or political faith."[38]

Church ran into controversy when he made a $1,000 donation to the entertainment fund of the United Confederate Veterans Reunion in Memphis in 1901. Attended by representatives of the country's Confederate associations, the reunion required local citizens to cover its costs. The only prominent African American who gave to the Confederate fund, Church was among its most generous contributors; many African Americans condemned him for his gift.[39] The *Commer-*

cial Appeal, in contrast, praised him as "acquiring credit for himself and his race by such acts of liberality."[40] "I have been a citizen of Memphis all my life, and believe this is a great opportunity [through] which I am sure the people of Memphis will improve," Church wrote the chairman of the finance committee of the Confederate Veterans Reunion.[41] He told the *Commercial Appeal:* "It is a pleasure for me to make this donation, because the men of the South have been my friends, and I feel it my duty to aid in entertaining those men who fought bravely for the Lost Cause." He further explained:

> I have tried to be liberal at all times and to help along this city when-
> ever I could. . . . I want to see the veterans enjoy themselves and I
> want to see Memphis do herself credit in the matter of the entertain-
> ment. What ever I have I made here in Memphis and I made it here
> with these people. My experience has shown that nowhere on earth
> will the colored man be treated better or be given better opportunity
> to make something of himself than here in Memphis, in the center of
> the South. There is nowhere that more is done in a substantial way
> to elevate the negro than right here. Nowhere is more money spent
> by the white people for the education of the colored youth than
> here. No persons on earth are more disposed to their former slaves
> than are the veterans of the Confederacy; those old men who yet re-
> member the negro in slavery. That is how I find the conditions here;
> those are the sentiments I feel; and that is why I, for myself, and on
> behalf of my race, desire to be allowed to make this contribution to
> the cause in which all the people of Memphis are now interested.[42]

Fred L. Hutchins, a black Memphian and an astute observer and historian of the city's life from 1892 on, later wrote that Church was well liked by all and attributed his donation to the belief that the "war was over and there should be no more fuss about it, and all should work together to promote one common feeling of unity for our great nation."[43]

Although Church intended to benefit Memphis and to contribute to harmonious race relations, his donation and statements, in effect, perpetuated the "Lost Cause" myth that had been taking hold across the South since the end of the Civil War and that helped fuel the development of the Jim Crow system. Memoirs, novels, folklore, and historical works painted slavery as an "antebellum Eden." Monuments, markers, and memorials that glorified the Confederacy and erased any memory of slavery as an evil institution pervaded the landscape. Black officeholding during Reconstruction came to be seen as corrupt and immoral, while the system of segregation and disenfranchisement cast African Americans as not worthy of participation in public life or the fruits of citizenship.[44]

The reunion donation appears to have been an exception to Church's overall support of civil rights and black institution building. One of his most significant contributions was Church's Park and Auditorium, developed in 1899 along Beale Street. Church had hundreds of trees planted in the park and provided an extensive playground for children. The six-acre, privately patrolled park featured peacocks and rare plants alongside beautiful walkways. The auditorium, which seated two thousand, was reputedly the world's largest black-owned theater. Costing $50,000 to construct, it included fireproof features and a drop-curtain mural. This "vast pleasure ground" was the country's only enterprise of its kind owned and operated by African Americans. Black Memphians had no parks at the time because of their exclusion from municipal ones. Throughout the South, separate parks for African Americans and whites or segregation within existing ones had become the norm by the 1890s.[45]

Church's Park and Auditorium fulfilled recreational, cultural, political, educational, and religious needs for both white and black citizens. With no large theater until this time, the city had been limited in its cultural offerings. Local and out-of-town groups of both races used the grounds for church bazaars, carnivals, picnics, and band concerts. The auditorium accommodated vaudeville troupes, theatrical performances, concerts, public school graduation exercises, social and civic club meetings, and political rallies and meetings. In addition, the establishment housed the private music school of Julia Hooks, the community leader. Frederick Douglass, Blanche Bruce, and Booker T. Washington were among the public figures who spoke and W. C. Handy, Duke Ellington, and the Fisk Jubilee Singers among the national and international artists who performed at the establishment. Washington spoke there in 1909 and 1913. For his last appearance, the auditorium was packed, with nearly as many people milling outside. He spoke three hours straight at the urging of the crowd.[46] Born in 1873 in Florence, Alabama, the blues musician W. C. Handy got his start as a band and orchestra leader at Church's Park and Auditorium;

he later credited Church for inspiring him "to do worth while things and be somebody in this life."[47]

Church's Park and Auditorium hosted President Theodore Roosevelt and Luke Wright in 1902. The gathering, attended by ten thousand, marked Wright's return to his hometown after his tenure as Vice Governor of the Philippines. Roosevelt and his party drove into the park in twenty-five horse-drawn carriages. A number of distinguished whites, including the Democratic governors of Tennessee and Mississippi, the mayor of Memphis, and the editor of the *New York Sun*, sat on the platform. The prominent black ministers T. O. Fuller and T. J. Searcy gave the invocation and benediction, respectively. Before leaving the grounds, the procession paraded around the park three times so that those unable to enter the auditorium had a good view of the president.[48]

Church Sr. was devoted to his community as well as his family, but his private life did not escape public criticism. He was self-educated, while his second wife, Anna Wright Church, was highly educated. She was born in Memphis in 1856 to Lucy Jane Wright and Colonel James Coleman, who owned a plantation and general store near the city and a wharf boat on the Mississippi River. After service in the Civil War, Coleman operated a telegraph office in Memphis where Thomas Edison worked; Anna later had vivid memories of Edison. Anna's mother, Jane, was a free African American who was part Native American; she lived with James as his confidante and secretary. Interested in civic affairs, she held political salons in their parlor. Frederick Douglass stayed in their home when in Memphis. She and Colonel Coleman ensured that Anna received an education that was exceptional for the time: they employed white schoolteachers from the North to instruct her and her twin sister, Eliza, and Anna received piano lessons from German professors in Memphis praised for their skill. In 1876, Anna was a member of the first graduating class of the LeMoyne Normal Institute, the predecessor of LeMoyne College, the first black college in Memphis. Afterward, she studied at the Music Institute of Antioch College in Yellow Springs, Ohio, and later (from 1900 to 1901) at the Oberlin Conservatory of Music. An acclaimed piano player who was recognized as one of the best in Tennessee, she was the principal of Winchester School, a black public school in Memphis, until her marriage.[49] Anna and Robert Sr. were both second-generation members of the Episcopal Church. Robert Jr. was born to them in 1885, and

Annette was born in 1887. The children received private and paro-
chial educations. When they attended Oberlin Academy, Anna moved
to Ohio with them. She rented a house because the children were too
young to stay in a dormitory.[50] The Church family saw the school system up North as "more adequate" than the one in Memphis, according to Church Sr.'s granddaughter, Roberta Church.[51] According to
Walter P. Adkins, the author of a 1935 master's thesis on Beale Street
politics, however, it was "a popular rumor that 'Bob' Church, Sr.,
sought to minimize his identity with the Negro race. The fact that he
sent his children to Oberlin College to get their college training was
interpreted by the general run of the colored population of Memphis
as a move to repudiate his racial identity."[52]

Church Jr. grew up in an environment that shaped his perspectives
and growth as a civil rights leader; he could remember what life had
been like before the decline of black officeholders and the harden-
ing of segregation. He knew black politicians and civil rights leaders
through his family's associations, and black and white public officials
lived in his neighborhood.[53] He recalled: "As I grew up the City of
Memphis had Colored Policeman, Squires, Magistrates, a Wharfmaster and at one time there were Colored members of the school board.
As time passed and the city grew these Colored men were replaced
by White employees." He also witnessed the enactment of Jim Crow
laws. The 1905 statewide law requiring segregation on streetcars particularly affected him. Seating had been integrated, but now signs appeared saying "This end for colored" at the back and "This end for
whites" at the front. In Memphis, Nashville, and other cities, black
Tennesseans had protested the new law and raised funds at Church's
Park for a legal challenge—but to no avail. Church recalled: "Prior to
the passage of this law, one of my pleasures was that of standing by the
motorman as he guided the car, and being permitted to guide it myself as it turned at the end of the line where I boarded it going to and
returning from school. This pleasure was ended." The Church family
members refused to cooperate with legal segregation and used their
wealth to protect themselves from Jim Crow's indignities. When on
trips, they took nonsegregated Pullman cars. No family member ever
rode on the segregated streetcars; instead, Church Sr. arranged for
personal transportation. By having meals at home, the family avoided
restaurant segregation. "We would eat and drink before we left home
and go hungry or thirsty until we returned if necessary," Church Jr.

recalled. They did not attend any theater, concert, movie, or meeting where separate entrances or segregated seating arrangements existed.[54] Although the Church family was exceptional because of its wealth, other black southerners, too, turned inward and concentrated on developing black institutions and strong communities to shield themselves from the prevailing environment.

Through his travels, education, and work outside the South, Church Jr. expanded his horizons and realized the peculiarity of the region's segregation and disenfranchisement. "As a child I travelled frequently with my parents [through] the northern and eastern United States, and we also made a trip to Europe," he remembered. "I noticed . . . that it was possible to stop at hotels in the north and east [and] . . . for all children to attend the same schools. . . . [T]his was not possible in the south."[55] After receiving his schooling in Memphis and Ohio, Church graduated from Morgan Park Military Academy in Morgan Park, Illinois (near Chicago), and took classes at Packard School of Business in New York City, where he circulated among elite African Americans, including the famed entertainers Bill "Bojangles" Robinson and Bert Williams. He spent nearly five years on Wall Street gaining banking experience.[56]

When he returned to Memphis, Church Jr. became the cashier of Solvent Savings Bank and Trust Company, the first bank in the city owned and managed by black people and the third largest in the country by 1912. Church Sr. helped found it in 1906 and was its first president. One of its organizers was R. W. Ware, a cashier of the Bank of Mound Bayou in Mississippi. (Mound Bayou was an all-black town founded by two black men in 1887 where African Americans could vote and black enterprises flourished.) Part of the increase in black business institutions across the South during this time, the bank was located across the street from Church's Park and Auditorium, where father and son maintained offices as well. Heralded outside Memphis as a successful black business, it inspired confidence in the business ability of African Americans, encouraged thrift among the masses, and gave black businesses the credit that often was unavailable to them from white institutions. The bank survived and fared better than most local banks during hard financial times in 1907.[57]

Church Jr. held one of Solvent Savings Bank's most difficult and responsible positions as its cashier. In 1909, at age twenty-four, he took over the bank's presidency from his father. In addition to his business duties, he experienced social and personal success. G. P. Hamilton, the local black observer and writer, noted that he was "popular with all classes and a general favorite with young and old." In 1908, black and white citizens endorsed him for the position of surveyor of customs for the Port of Memphis in a petition to President Theodore Roosevelt, although he ended up not receiving the appointment. In Washington, DC, in 1911, the tall and handsome young man married Sara Paroda Johnson, a member of the black elite there who had been a friend during their childhood and youth. W. E. B. Du Bois and his wife sent their congratulations. Three years later, Sara gave birth to their only child, Sara Roberta, who became known by her middle name. Throughout his life, Church Jr. was a very active and loyal member of the Elks, to which he donated money, as well as the church and the college fraternity Omega Psi Phi. Like his parents, he was Episcopalian. He enjoyed reading and hunting and going to the theater, baseball games, prizefights, and horse races, where he rarely bet. Personable, optimistic, direct, and well mannered, he was moderate in temperament except for incessant cigarette smoking and an occasional cigar.[58]

In 1912, a year after Church Jr.'s marriage, Church Sr. died at age seventy-four after an illness of some eighteen months. Booker T. Washington was one of the last persons to see him alive, and Solvent Savings Bank officers passed a resolution in his honor. At the funeral, the Church family's white neighbor Mrs. Mudge sang. Black newspapers nationwide reported his passing, while both white dailies in Memphis ran lengthy and praiseworthy obituaries, although these papers rarely devoted that much positive coverage to African Americans. A year later, the *Commercial Appeal* commented: "The triumph of Memphis as a great city could not be written without an account of the marvelous career of the late R. R. Church." Church Jr. and his sister, Annette, inherited the vast fortune left by their father, estimated at between $1 and $2 million, with more than $50,000 coming in per month from rental properties, including hundreds of houses. Bob resigned the Solvent Savings Bank presidency in order to become executor and manager of the more than three hundred properties of his father's estate. As she had done for his father, his mother assisted him in business matters.[59]

By this time, another major personality in Memphis life was making his mark. The rise to power of the white politician Edward

Hull Crump irrevocably changed Memphis. Although Memphis and Shelby County elections were nonpartisan, he was a lifelong Democrat. He became the longest-serving political boss in US history to date. Born in Holly Springs, Mississippi, in 1874, Crump was raised by his mother after his father, a cotton planter and Confederate officer, died in the 1878 yellow fever epidemic. She struggled to keep the family out of poverty. The young man came to Memphis in early 1894 and went from initially struggling to find permanent employment to becoming an executive of the Woods-Chickasaw Manufacturing Company, which specialized in carriages and saddles. Well liked, courteous, considerate, and with a streak of fun and adventure, he socialized with young and ambitious businessmen and professionals. In January 1902, he married Bessie McLean, one of the most beautiful and, as the only daughter of a rich businessman and his wife, most sought-after young women in Memphis. Two children soon followed, Edward Hull Jr., born in 1903, and Robert McLean, born in 1905. After the Woods-Chickasaw Manufacturing Company went bankrupt in December 1902, Crump, aided by security put up by his wife's parents, borrowed $50,000 from the Memphis National Bank and bought the company, which he ran with a partner. Not one who liked sharing authority, he purchased the partner's share of the business in 1906 and renamed it the E. H. Crump Buggy Company.[60]

Although Crump himself later admitted that he was unsure when he got his start in politics, he worked as a poll watcher in Memphis and in 1902 was elected from the Fourth Ward to the local Democratic legislative convention. Two years later, he was elected director of the Memphis Business Man's Club, the forerunner of the Memphis Chamber of Commerce. This position made him a well-known figure across the city and gave him important political connections.[61] In 1905, he won a seat on the public works board, one of two bodies of the city council. He was elected to the other body as fire and police commissioner two years later.

In 1909, Crump ran for mayor against J. J. Williams. A campaign official recruited the up-and-coming blues musician W. C. Handy to compose a song for Crump's bid. At that time, campaigns employed music to draw a large number of people to one place and to help people remember the candidate's name. Handy and his band opened Crump's race by playing "Mr. Crump Don't 'Low No Easy Riders Here." The song caught fire, and Handy rewrote the piece as "Memphis Blues" three years later. One of the first blues songs published, it led Handy to worldwide fame. Crump did not win the backing of most African Americans, however. He used race-baiting as a campaign tactic and punched an African American, Robert Houston, for violating an election law. When voters went to the polling place, they were handed a blank paper ballot. Houston arrived with a marked paper ballot, leading to an argument between him and Crump. When Houston tried to bypass Crump, Crump hit him. Crump was charged with assault, and Houston was charged with illegal election activity, but both dropped charges. Beale Street was one of the few sources of black support for Crump. A center of saloons, dance halls, gambling joints, and brothels, it was one of the vice wards that Crump swept. He captured wards controlled by criminals as well. Crump won over Williams by only seventy-nine votes, with Williams receiving more black support.[62]

Crump sold his buggy company in 1910 on becoming mayor. His and his wife's third son, John, was born later that year. A devoted father and strict disciplinarian, he regaled his sons with Civil War stories, occasionally took them fishing and hunting, and enjoyed taking them to the circus. He and his wife sent them to Memphis University School, a private school favored by well-off families.[63]

As a city councilman, Crump had led the movement to switch the structure of the Memphis government to the commission form. Now, he headed this new system as the leader of the third largest city in the South; more than 130,000 lived in Memphis. A Progressive-era reform, commission governance was adopted in more than three hundred cities during this time; it emphasized a managerial style by "experts" in order to centralize authority and increase efficiency. In Memphis, Crump and a handful of commissioners controlled the city's budget, enacted its policies, and served as department heads. Shelby County followed suit and adopted the commission form in 1911. The commission form, which lacked official checks and balances, lent itself well to dictatorship.[64] An inherently elitist system of government, it could limit democracy by placing control in the hands of a small group.

Crump "was a combination of showman, dictator, humanitarian, progressive, and hard-as-nails, ruthless administrator," as one historian said.[65] Over six feet tall, and with red hair, he earned the nickname the "Red Snapper." After becoming mayor in 1910, he feverishly worked to ensure numerous city reforms and improvements. "Plan your work, and work your plan" was one of his favorite sayings. He often got to work before most Memphians had awakened and ended his day after most had gone home from their jobs. He attended to both the large picture and the small details of his job, jotting down items in a small memo book, and following up to make sure the necessary work was accomplished. He personally inspected city services periodically and ensured that lower municipal taxes were enacted. Like other Progressive politicians, he improved public services.[66] To maintain and increase his power, Crump built a campaign organization with city and county employees as ward workers. A strong voter turnout was fundamental to his local control and statewide influence; many ballots from Memphis provided him with leverage over other white politicians seeking state office. By 1914, he exercised statewide power.

A two-way relationship ensued between Crump and African Americans in which African Americans had a degree of leverage. Making up between 38 and 49 percent of the city's population during the first two decades of the twentieth century, African Americans represented a potentially powerful base of votes; Crump needed their support to secure his influence. Black Memphians took advantage of their opportunity to vote and participate in politics. They formed political clubs and used professional, community, and neighborhood organizations for electoral activities. Political and civic groups sometimes overlapped in leadership and membership, providing their activism with unity and cohesion. At times letting Crump know that they supported him at the polls, African Americans asked him for better public services, improved employment opportunities, and other favors. Black saloonkeepers and underworld figures secured votes for him in order to receive protection for their illicit activities, while some African Americans asked him for the suppression of prostitution and gambling. Yet others called for better care for prisoners, an end to lynching, and the appointment of black police officers. Crump sometimes granted African American appeals. In 1914, for instance, he supported the Colored Men's Civic League's request to ban Thomas Dixon's play *The Leopard's Spots* from showing in the city because of its negative portrayal of African Americans. He referred the matter to the board of censors, which promptly forbade the play from being performed.[67]

To a degree, Crump believed in being civil toward African Americans, treating them fairly, and recognizing their citizenship rights. His conduct fit within his paternalistic philosophy of providing for citizens as the "city father" and helping the disadvantaged. After a black man complained about rude behavior from a city employee, Crump replied: "It has always been the policy of this . . . administration to treat everyone with uniform courtesy, regardless of their station or mission and you were entitled to like treatment."[68] His correspondence with African Americans appears the same as his letters to whites: he addressed them with courtesy titles and wrote in a respectful manner.[69] The boss met with black leaders as well, including Church Jr., who thanked him for the "cordial and generous courtesies extended" during the visit.[70] He also met with W. C. Handy in 1910 and agreed to his request to change the title of the campaign song that he wrote for Crump to "Mr. Crump's Blues."[71]

Although Crump incorporated African Americans into the body politic more than most southern politicians, his actions masked his derogatory views and activities. Some African Americans campaigned for him of their own free will, but he also manipulated the support of some African Americans by "herding" them to the polls: he arranged his supporters to pick them up by the carload, pay their poll taxes, and reward them with barbeque and liquor. Like white politicians across the South, he embraced segregation. He perpetuated black inequality by providing public service improvements within the context of the Jim Crow system. African Americans were excluded from participation in the local Democratic Party and occupied the lowest rung of government employment. They had virtually no chance of winning seats on the city commission because these positions were few and at-large and most whites would not vote for them. As a result, they ceased running for city positions. Because of their inability to hold office, they had no direct say in local government, unlike in the late nineteenth century, when they occupied municipal positions.[72]

Robert Church Jr. began his journey as a political leader during the Crump era. He followed in his father's path as a businessman but differed in taking up politics as his primary avocation. Church Jr. engaged in electoral efforts mainly as a means to secure racial advancement. His faith in the democratic process convinced him that this goal could be best achieved through politically mobilizing African Americans.[73] He later acknowledged his "firm conviction" that African Americans "should and wished to enjoy rights as . . . stated in the Bill of Rights, Constitution and elsewhere" as the primary factor behind his rise to political leadership.[74] During the 1910s, he and his fellow Solvent Savings Bank officials were the most important local black political actors. Perhaps inspired by Church Sr.'s legacy, these independent black professionals, who were among the richest black Memphians, used their wealth to finance their political efforts. They included Bert Roddy, the operator of Iroquois Café across from Church's Park; T. H. Hayes Sr., an undertaker and close friend of W. C. Handy and Booker T. Washington; J. W. Sanford, one of the city's leading contractors and largest property owners; and Harry Pace, who graduated from Atlanta University at age nineteen, came to Memphis at the request of W. E. B. Du Bois to help him launch *The Moon,* and later formed a blues publishing company with W. C. Handy. These men spanned a generation, from Hayes and Sanford, who were born in the early 1860s, to Church Jr., Pace, and Roddy, who were born in the mid-1880s.[75] Although they were Republican, they supported Democratic candidates in the nonpartisan local elections if they promised to be the best hope for African Americans.

For the 1911 election, Church, Pace, and Roddy formed the Colored Citizens Association (CCA), and Church organized a mass voter registration drive.[76] In a rematch of their race two years earlier, mayoral candidates J. J. Williams and Ed Crump vied for the black vote. Black voter registration numbers increased to levels unseen since the 1870s. The *Commercial Appeal* reported that African Americans were registering by the thousands, although because of police pressure in many cases. Black Memphians were divided as to whether to press for improvements within a segregated society or fight against segregation altogether. They were particularly concerned with parks. No law forbade African Americans from using city parks, but they were not welcome. To be sure, Church's Park was a space for both blacks and whites, but it was privately owned and operated. Harry Pace, the CCA president, wrote Crump on behalf of the Solvent Savings Bank directors. Acknowledging a movement among African Americans for their own municipal park, Pace said that the CCA believed that black Memphians should have access to public parks enjoyed by whites because of their constitutional rights and their status as taxpayers. The CCA wanted street paving and sprinkling service in black neighborhoods as well. At the time, most city streets were made up of dirt, and they became nearly impassable after heavy rainfalls. After interviewing Crump and Williams, CCA officials endorsed Crump.[77] "[Williams] promises everything and I fear he'll do nothing," Pace said. "But this redheaded fellow frankly declines to promise us some of the things we want, but convinced me he will fulfill promises he did make."[78]

While the CCA saw Crump as the better of two less-than-ideal choices, other black voters saw him as "a patriotic citizen working for the best interest of the people," and yet others opposed him.[79] The *Bluff City News* blasted him for the city's rampant crime and the police protection of illicit activities. Deeming him incapable and unfit, it ran a cartoon portraying him securing the black vote with a clenched fist. Crump ended up receiving most of the black vote and was reelected. The city did not admit African Americans to parks frequented by whites but opened its first park for African Americans the next year despite white opposition.[80]

The CCA appears to have discontinued operations after the election, but these same Solvent Savings Bank officials made a more ambitious political effort in 1912. They supported the candidacy of H. C. Purnell, a prosperous merchant and popular black Memphian who ran for the county commission in an attempt to achieve black representation on that body. His wife, Fannie, was a well-known caterer in the city. For the 1911 election, Purnell had headed the Eleventh Ward Improvement Club, which had endorsed Crump.[81] Church, Hayes, Roddy, and Pace served on his campaign committee. In a letter to Crump responding to his "queries and advice," the committee wrote that Purnell was not antagonistic to but rather supportive of local authorities. Quoting the political boss in calling the county office "insignificant," the committee members said they believed that one African American on the county commission would not jeopardize the "dominant race" but rather would help white officials by attending to complaints of the black community. Acknowledging that Crump could ensure Purnell's defeat, they asked him not to endorse their candidate but rather to allow him a fair chance.[82] The committee's words further revealed the changed political climate caused by the political ascension of Crump, the advent of commission government, and the decline of black officeholding. African Americans had gone from serving as elected officials in the late nineteenth century to arguing for the right to make a fair bid for public office. By saying that a black representative would not jeopardize the "dominant race," the committee members tempered their challenge to the status quo. Nevertheless, Purnell lost the race.

Mayor Crump's quest for power rose to new heights during the 1914 election, when he decided to run for county sheriff. Holding this position would increase his control over government affairs in Memphis and Shelby County. After learning that the city charter forbade any city official from holding two offices simultaneously, Crump withdrew from the race and entered J. A. Reichman instead. A technicality kept Reichman off the ballot, however, so Crump ran a write-in campaign for him and had the police set up blackboards on Beale to teach illiterate African Americans how to write his name. Reichman won by nearly ten thousand votes despite significant white opposition, including that of the two white newspapers. On election day, the *Commercial Appeal* reported its discovery of nearly five thousand registration receipts and thousands of poll tax receipts illegally secured by the Crump machine to distribute to African Americans at the polls. The paper found city and county employees soliciting votes, painting campaign signs, and instructing African Americans how to vote; all these actions violated the city charter.[83]

After the election, Crump came under further attack. A campaign manager for Malcolm R. Patterson, the gubernatorial candidate in 1915, assailed him as the "most baneful influence in politics this state has ever known" and charged him with using "the votes of dead men, fraudulent negro votes and every conceivable and rotten method of ballot box manipulations."[84] The editor of the *Commercial Appeal*, C. P. J. Mooney, criticized the machine through editorials, articles, and cartoons. One cartoon depicted Crump reading a book titled "How to Use 12,000 Registration Certificates." In early 1916, the newspaper presented the first solid evidence of the illegal use of black voters by publishing photographs of fraudulent registration certificates and poll tax receipts. It reported that one police officer had handled thirty thousand voter registration certificates during his six years on the force. These public criticisms were not the only troubles that Crump was facing. Two county commissioners resigned after Mooney charged them with graft, and two judges were impeached for corruption. In late 1915, Crump pled guilty to violating state prohibition laws and was convicted for failing to enforce prohibition.[85] He was ousted from office in February 1916 but elected six months later to the powerful office of county trustee (treasurer). In light of these troubles, why would local citizens vote Crump back into office? He had, after all, provided them with improved public services and lower city taxes. The positive aspects of his machine must have outweighed the negative ones for many voters.

In the meantime, Robert R. Church Jr. was becoming increasingly involved on the national political scene. Church was determined to keep African Americans active in the Republican Party as leaders and members even though the lily-white movement had gained strength across the South during the first two decades of the twentieth century. He was active in the local black-and-tan Republican faction by 1912. That year, he served as a delegate to the Republican national convention for the first time. He supported President William Howard Taft in his bid for reelection, but Taft lost. Still, Church's growing influence made him in demand among national Republican leaders, who asked him in 1915 to send them the names of black political leaders in five southern states. That year, Church wrote his national political associate Roscoe Conkling Simmons that he wanted to be in Washington, DC, when the Republican National Committee met to consider reducing southern representation to the Republican national convention; he urged Simmons to write a forceful letter opposing this move. Even though southern states rarely went to Republican office seekers, southern delegates made up a substantial portion of those needed to nominate the presidential candidate. As a result, black political activists continually combated moves to reduce southern representation because their service as delegates provided them with political influence and leverage.[86]

Despite its limitations, the Republican Party remained a better alternative for African Americans than the Democratic Party. Because of the small number of white Republicans in the South, the national party often depended on African Americans to maintain a Republican presence in the region, distribute patronage, and campaign for candidates where they could vote. Unlike the Democratic Party, the GOP allowed integration in its southern operations; African Americans could serve as members and leaders of party organizations. They could use their party involvement as a forum for speaking out against racial injustice publicly. In their roles as delegates to the Republican national convention, members of local and state Republican Party committees, and campaign officials for the Republican National Committee, African Americans could influence party and government policies. The party's platforms commonly included antilynching planks and calls for protecting the constitutional rights of all US citizens;

some Republican officials publicly endorsed these measures. From 1892 forward, Democratic Party platforms did not contain these or similar statements. Moreover, the Democrats had never seated an African American delegate at their national conventions.[87]

The Democratic administration of Woodrow Wilson, a Virginia native who was elected in 1912, further exposed the differences between the two parties. Some African Americans, including W. E. B. Du Bois, had supported Wilson in 1912 because they thought that he represented a better choice than Taft. They were quickly disappointed, however, because Wilson did not hire any black civil servants and dismissed, segregated, and reduced in rank black government employees. He dismissed all black political appointees except for one and made only two black political appointments. Although Republicans had not made a large number of black political appointments, they had a better record than did the Democrats.[88]

Yet the Republican Party also exhibited apathy, neglect, and even hostility toward African Americans. The vast majority of African Americans resided in the South, where they were overwhelmingly disenfranchised; they made up only a small percentage of the voting population in the North.[89] As a result of these factors, the party had relatively few votes to gain from embracing positions appealing to African Americans. The lily-white wing was a vital component of the party and an attempt to build up Republican influence in the region. Like most white Americans, white Republican leaders generally paid little attention to African American concerns. Although the party and its officials made statements promoting civil rights and denouncing lynching, Republicans largely failed to sponsor and enact legislation to end disenfranchisement, segregation, and other racial injustices.

Reflecting its contradictory attitudes toward African Americans, the Republican Party had a mixed approach toward them. It tried to appeal to southern segregationists and northern racists while cultivating black southerners, but this strategy proved difficult. The success of the lily whites and black and tans for control of local and state party committees and seats to the Republican national convention varied by state in the South, and the national Republican Party had a mixed record when giving official recognition to party organizations at its conventions. Tours of the South conducted by presidents and presidential candidates reached out to white southerners at the same time that rhetorical appeals, often invoking the name of Lincoln, were made to African Americans.[90] In the 1916 campaign, for example, the party released public statements endorsing the presidential candidate Charles Hughes's promise: "I stand for the maintenance of the rights of all citizens, regardless of Race or Color."[91] Hughes, however, had no history of working on racial issues and exhibited little knowledge of such matters.[92]

Church Jr. and his associates took their political activity to a new level in early 1916 in an attempt to make the Republican Party more responsive to African Americans. Church Jr. founded the Lincoln Republican League of Tennessee for the goals of "regain[ing] the lost rights of a growing race" and achieving "political and economic emancipation" for African Americans.[93] As he later said: "It has been my firm conviction that if Colored people were instructed in and learned how to actively use the Ballot . . . their united strength would result in the election on local and national scenes [of] candidates for various offices who would be compelled to adhere to the demands of the voters who elected them." He continued: "With this in mind I founded and organized the Lincoln League . . . the purpose of which was to get colored citizens to register en masse, pay their poll taxes, get instructions on how to use the ballot, and go to the polls and vote."[94] Church believed that local partisan organizations provided the foundation for political parties and that wielding influence in the two-party system necessitated aligning with a political party. Observing that nonpartisan or independent voters usually voted for Republican or Democratic candidates, he believed that active, vote-producing members of a partisan organization would be most likely to influence the party's policies and legislative stances.[95]

Through his Lincoln League endeavor, Church wanted to bolster Republican Party strength in West Tennessee, help elect Republican candidates in the November election, and gain official recognition for his black-and-tan group in party circles. Locally, lily-white Republicans, who made up the official Shelby County Republican organization, would not allow black Republicans to join or align with them. They supported local Democrats by campaigning for their candidates in elections; they often did not run Republican office seekers. They denied African Americans patronage and had contested Church's seating as a delegate to the national convention in 1912.[96] Church thought that many white Republicans were, in reality, "disgruntled Democrats" who were unable to rise in the party and, thus, wanted "power, patronage and status as . . . Republican[s]."[97] In Memphis and elsewhere in Tennessee, lily whites who controlled Republican organizations excluded African Americans from their local conventions, in which they decided who would be delegates to state and national conventions. If African Americans developed a strong enough organization, they bettered their chances of challenging these white Republicans for seats as delegates. In addition, Tennessee was considering amending its constitution to impose a literacy test to disenfranchise black voters. The Lincoln League hoped to mobilize African Americans across the state so they could take a stand against the proposal as delegates to the constitutional convention.[98]

Church gathered together a group of black male professionals to form the league. They adopted a constitution and elected the organization's officers, including Church, at age thirty-one, as president. Businessmen and professionals dominated the league's offices and executive committee, including the Solvent Savings Bank officials T. H. Hayes Sr. and Bert Roddy.[99] The black newspaper *Beacon Light* observed that the officers ranged in age and that each had a "wide circle of friends and a large measure of influence in the community." It predicted that the league's power would be "tremendous" with "this influence combined."[100] Among the league's eighty-seven directors were ministers and Lymus Wallace, the last African American on the city council. His very presence provided a reminder of the black officeholding that had once been.[101]

The official founding of the Lincoln League took place in Church's Auditorium on 1 February 1916. Church asked for "real men and real Republicans" to be present.[102] On this bitter cold night, some one thousand black men and women attended the public meeting, including Church's grandmother, mother, wife, and sister, Annette. Aiming to gain public approval for the league and its officials, Church told the audience that any league officers would be removed if objections were voiced. Prominent black citizens, including Lymus Wallace and the Reverends Sutton Griggs, J. A. Grant, and T. J. Searcy, made enthusiastic speeches endorsing the organization and its officers. "We have at last a political leader in the south," proclaimed Griggs about Church to the cheering crowd. "Let us sink self and lift him; lift him where he can stand among giants and say 'I am a voice of millions.'" The attendees, some of whom stood in the aisles because the auditorium was so packed, unanimously approved the league, its officials, and its constitution.[103]

"Mr. Church has a most pleasing personality," reported the *Beacon Light* in a profile that shed light on why many black Memphians followed Church in his Lincoln League endeavor. "His bearing is cordial, modest, manly and dignified under all circumstances. He is patient, never grows excited, and is always, even when under fire, as cool as the proverbial cucumber." Noting that Church accepted political advice from others, it characterized him as "thoroughly interested in the welfare of his people" and observed that his wealth placed him "beyond the range of temptation to do anything merely for the sake of money." Black Memphians respected Church and watched him "with unusual interest" because of the "remarkable brain power" that was "known to run in his family," the paper said, pointing out that his father was a "business genius" who had become the wealthiest African American in the United States and that Mary Church Terrell was admired by many for her intellect. The paper concluded: "With such an evident strain of genius in the Church family, thoughtful persons will hesitate to fix a limit to the heights to which R. R. Church, Jr., may climb in his efforts to enable his race to make an effective use of the ballot."[104]

Observing that "the storms of division" had "kept the Negro down," league leaders hoped to unify black Memphians politically in order to advance their collective interests.[105] The only requirements for league membership were supporting the Republican Party, paying the poll tax, and registering to vote.[106] A year earlier, when Booker T. Washington had died, Church had observed the "magnificent tribute" paid by local black Memphians: schools were closed in Washington's honor, and between four and five thousand people came together at Church's Park and Auditorium to pay their respect. "It was really a wonderful gathering and remarkable in more ways than one, because the brother in Memphis does not get together on any one thing or subject," he had written Roscoe Conkling Simmons.[107] Now, the *Beacon Light* reported the goals that he later said motivated him to start the league: "In a republican form of government, where men gain office by the favor of the people, the one means of commanding the attention of those in power is an effective ballot; and the Lincoln Republican Club is organized for the purpose of teaching the Negro race the power of the ballot, and for the purpose of having the race to make a wise use of this power in defending itself and advancing the interests of all the people."[108] Like many other black middle- and upper-class activists at the time, the league's leaders felt a responsibility to uplift the black masses: they wanted to lead the league members not only in political activities and the "calm assertion" of their constitutional rights but also in "ways of character and intelligence."[109] A league profile further declared: "When Afro-Americans who reside in the South are as safe in life and as secure in their rights as in the North, then the goal of this organization will have been attained."[110]

To forward these objectives, Church put out a ticket in late August of twelve black candidates to challenge the lily-white slate in the November election; he acted as its campaign manager. Roddy, Hayes, and other black professionals and businessmen sought state and national positions in Tennessee's Tenth Congressional District, which encompassed Shelby, Tipton, Hardeman, and Fayette Counties. They knew that a win over the lily-white ticket would lead to the establishment of the black and tans as the area's regular Republicans. To support the candidates, the Lincoln League formed clubs in every black ward, while Church financed and set up voter education schools. More than one thousand African Americans attended the schools held almost nightly in churches. The teachers, mainly female and apparently well paid, educated them about the importance of the Republican Party and taught them how to vote. Only those who paid their poll taxes and registered to vote could attend.[111]

Church also ensured that rallies occurred weekly from August until November in Church's Auditorium. He brought in outside speakers, including Roscoe Conkling Simmons, at gatherings such as the one W. Herbert Brewster remembered so vividly. As with the schools, only African Americans with poll tax receipts and registration certificates were admitted. News of these meetings spread, and African Americans paid their poll taxes in order to come even though most were poor and had little time to spare. At these rallies, ministers and league officials condemned Jim Crow laws and lynching. Church said that African Americans would free themselves from these injustices through their political participation.[112]

The two white dailies took note of these developments: while the *Press-Scimitar* pointed out that "heavy black registration" was occurring, the *Commercial Appeal* planted white and black spies in the voter education schools and reported that African Americans were "coming back" in politics and showing an "unequalled interest" in it. Fearing that the white vote would split between the lily-white ticket and the

Democratic ticket and result in the election of the black candidates, the *Commercial Appeal* called on whites to cast their ballots for the Democrats in order to "write the brand of shame across the hideous plot" of the Lincoln League.[113]

At the same time that Church was using it to strengthen the Republican Party locally, the Lincoln League furthered his rise in the party nationally. In May 1916, he became the first African American since 1892 to serve as an at-large delegate from Tennessee to the party's national convention. The national Republican Party appointed him to its black advisory committee, which was devoted to securing the black vote. That August, Church met with Theodore Roosevelt at his home in Oyster Bay, New York. Roosevelt believed in the biological inferiority of African Americans as a group, but he enjoyed friendships with some black individuals. The two men had a pleasant meeting, and the former president gave Church a signed photograph. After the meeting, Church subsequently courted Roosevelt with praise, telling him that the picture held a prominent place on his wall and that he was the greatest man that he had ever met. The men went on to maintain a professional and personal relationship.[114]

Church's national ties and recognition did not lead him to lose sight of his goal of politically empowering ordinary black Memphians. At the Lincoln League's first public meeting, he said: "This club is not going to be an organ of any fraternal or religious body, any business firm, any bank, [or] of any other particular or special corporation. It is distinctly founded for the good of the masses and not classes of men."[115] By clarifying the nature of the organization, he fought off any suspicions that he and his fellow bank officials were focused on their own self-interest. He demonstrated through this statement— along with his use of mass rallies, voting schools, and voter registration efforts—his interest in advancing ordinary African Americans. He knew that their support and grassroots mobilization were crucial to the league's success.

At a September mass meeting, Lincoln League members unanimously adopted a platform that unequivocally embraced civil rights. The league denounced all Jim Crow laws as "a wicked abuse of power" and as "barbarous relics of [the] unenlightened days" of slavery. In response to President Woodrow Wilson's success in segregating the government workforce, the organization advocated an end to racial discrimination in the civil service. World War I had begun, and the platform pressed for more African Americans in the armed services. In addition, it called for the integration of labor unions, the establishment of integrated federal trade schools, federal aid to supplement inadequate southern state educational budgets, and improvements to and higher appropriations for black and white schools within the existing state system. Condemning lynching as "a barbaric attack upon order and a rape attempted upon the law" and something that "makes a great country the shame of all nations," the league advocated for federal antilynching legislation and said that its nominee for Congress would introduce such a measure if elected.[116]

Calling suffrage an "inherent" right, the league supported the "immediate extension of the vote to women."[117] Although initially opposed to women's suffrage, Church had changed his mind, perhaps because of the influence of his half-sister, Mary Church Terrell. In 1910, she had written to him:

> Now, my dear boy, you say you do not believe in woman suffrage. You just mean to say you have never thought previously on this subject. I have always been impressed with your sense of justice. . . . Whatever *white* men may think about woman suffrage, no *colored* man who believes in suffrage for colored men can consistently oppose it. Unless you believe that all men who are born colored should because of that accident of race be deprived of the right of citizenship you [cannot] insist that all human beings who are born girls should because of that accident of birth be denied rights which others enjoy simply because they happen to be born boys instead of girls.[118]

Although the league involved women and supported their suffrage, its statements stipulating that voter registration was necessary for joining the league and attending its rallies and voter education schools indicate that women faced limits to their political participation.

Despite the league's stress on improving the status of African Americans, Church reached out to white citizens as well. In response to false allegations spread during the campaign, the black office seekers took out a full-page advertisement in both white dailies the day before the election, and Church signed it.[119] Faced with a prevailing environment of negative racial constructions, the candidates fashioned a counternarrative about black identity and expressed reasons for their endeavor. They identified themselves as the regular Republican candidates and the Lincoln League as "composed of the backbone of labor and industrial supremacy of Memphis." Assuring white readers that the league members loved their neighbors, city, state, and the South, they tied their cause to Memphis's economic advancement, saying that the city's prosperity depended on mutual cooperation. The candidates emphasized that they had conducted the campaign free of bitterness, prejudice, and hate and that they desired an atmosphere of peace and goodwill.[120]

Instead of attacking whites as enemies who supported the Jim Crow system, the Lincoln League ad linked the organization's cause with American principles of freedom, fairness, and democracy—values that had special resonance during World War I. Like so many black activists before and after them, the candidates exposed contradictions inherent in the American creed and pressed the country to live up to its ideals. The ad stated: "We are citizens. We are taxpayers. We believe in law and order. . . . [W]e have sought to conduct ourselves as men worthy of American citizenship. We ask not only for the suffrage of all good citizens, but particularly for a fair chance at the polls—the freeman's battlefield—and for an honest count in the reckoning. More than this we could not ask, less than this no honorable man would ask to accept. . . . The present contest will decide the power of the universal claim we live beneath a flag of law and love." By stressing political rights and not directly confronting segregation or lynching, the ad avoided these contentious matters and, instead, appealed to values shared by blacks and whites.[121]

When election day arrived, the Lincoln League had reached five thousand members and was credited with registering nearly ten thousand black voters, bringing the black electorate up to nearly one-third of the total electorate in Shelby County. The league ticket won a resounding victory of a four-to-one margin over the lily-white slate. The league helped the Republican presidential nominee, Charles Hughes, carry Shelby County by sixty-seven hundred votes, although he did not win the state or the election, and the Republican gubernatorial and senatorial candidates lost as well. Nonetheless, the Lincoln League's strong showing at the polls established Church's faction as the regular Republican organization in West Tennessee, and the state did not enact a literacy test as the league had feared it would.[122]

The Lincoln League's victory generated favorable coverage from black publications across the country.[123] *Champion Magazine* said:

"The Lincoln League is in politics not for the elevation of any individual politician, [or] for the establishment of Negro supremacy, but to regain the lost rights of a growing race. It is not revolutionary, it is not a color line organization, it is not a political Ku Klux Klan, but [it is] the outgrowth of that type of idealism that produced . . . the Sons of Liberty during the days prior to the American Revolution."[124] The *New York News* commended Church and the Lincoln League for running a slate of candidates in the South. "It requires [in Tennessee] not only political wisdom but [also] physical bravery for Colored men to secure civic recognition," the paper said. "The action of the Colored citizens . . . in naming a Colored ticket is one of the most courageous things that Colored citizens have ever done in this country." It urged black men in New York and New Jersey to pay "special attention" to this "splendid example."[125]

After the election, some white newspapers called on the Lincoln League to dissolve or face dire consequences. An editorial in the state capital's *Nashville Banner* accused the league of inflaming prejudice through manipulating black voters, promoting bloc voting, and perpetuating the color line in politics. Declaring that whites would not "tolerate [Negro voters'] attempt to gain political supremacy," the paper said that the main aim of black leaders "should be to make their people capable through character and intelligence for the duties of citizenship and to exercise individual judgment in voting." The *New York Age* attacked back, saying: "The spectacle of a southern daily preaching against race solidarity in politics is a bit unusual not to say incongruous." It pointed out that the league's efforts were in response to racial discrimination and that the league would not exist if not for solid white opposition.[126]

Years later, Church remembered: "The ticket was successful beyond our expectations."[127] To prove his point, he quoted from the *Western World Reporter,* a local black newspaper, which said at the time: "If the league did nothing more than teach colored men the dignity of the ballot and white men that all colored men cannot be purchased and a great number misled, that is enough for the first time." The newspaper reported that the leaders and candidates had announced their "determination to go ahead with the fight year after year until the political chains are broken, and colored men are treated as citizens."[128]

Indeed, the Lincoln League served as a milestone for black political activists in Memphis. At a time when most black southerners were deprived of the right to vote and engaged in institution building within their own communities to shield themselves from the indignities of the Jim Crow system, black Memphians used the vote to press for a better tomorrow. They spoke out against Jim Crow laws and lynching and advocated for civil rights, political power, and economic advancement. They were not willing to accept the loss of the rights that they had won during Reconstruction or forsake the life that they remembered before the imposition of segregation ordinances and the removal of African Americans from public office. By engaging in voter education and registration efforts and using the Lincoln League as a forum for independent black political action, black Memphians protested and broke free of the manipulation of the black vote, demonstrating that they were not mere pawns in the hands of Crump's machine.

Church and the Lincoln League operated from the premise that civil rights flowed from political rights. He and league members had faith in the democratic process and pragmatically sought change through formal political channels. Faced with a Democratic Party that excluded black southerners, they turned to the Republican Party and urged it to live up to its historical principles of freedom and equality and to reject its lily-white component of prejudice and exclusion. Although the Lincoln League candidates had no chance of winning against the Democrats, their victory over the lily-white slate provided black Memphians with newfound access and leverage. Church could serve as a voice for African Americans through his national political activities and connections, and the establishment of his organization as the regular Republicans in West Tennessee allowed for a greater degree of influence in party operations and control of patronage when Republican administrations were in power.

Church received the most credit and praise for the Lincoln League effort from the black press; he certainly was the organizational genius and chief strategist. Yet the league's success equally reflected the efforts of the masses of black Memphians. These ordinary black men and women propelled Church to prominence by sacrificing their time and money to participate in the campaign and ensuring that votes were cast for the Lincoln League ticket. Like W. Herbert Brewster, they were willing to open themselves to the possibility of politics as a way to improve their lives and were motivated to participate in electoral battles to come.

2 "The Fight . . . to Make America Safe for Americans"

Memphis as a Political Model for the Region and the Country, 1917–1927

The Lincoln League's 1916 victory at the polls inaugurated a new era of formal political mobilization for black Memphians. They also expanded their activism into new avenues such as NAACP and Commission on Interracial Cooperation (CIC) chapters. They pressed for economic opportunities, civil rights, improved public services, political influence, and an end to lynching. Robert R. Church Jr. became increasingly involved on the national political scene and emerged as the country's most prominent black Republican. He transformed the local Lincoln League into the Lincoln League of America, an influential black political organization that was part of the upsurge of black activism during the World War I era. The political efforts of black Memphians culminated in 1927 when they mobilized to vote the incumbent mayor out of office and elect a candidate who incorporated their demands into his platform. In all these ways, Church and black Memphians upset social constructions of African Americans as politically apathetic, carved out a political space for themselves, and influenced the political process to meet their goals.

World War I and its aftermath exacerbated racial tensions nationwide. Many whites resented the authority of black servicemen and the dramatic spike in civil rights agitation. The NAACP and other activist organizations grew in size, black periodicals advocating racial advancement enjoyed wide circulation, and union drives and black migration north increased.[1] African Americans pressed white Americans to face the contradiction of the United States fighting for democracy and freedom abroad but not granting them its constitutional protec-

51

tions at home. Instead of seeing their hopes fulfilled, however, African Americans faced new and continued obstacles. They saw riots break out in urban areas, with the violence peaking in the Red Summer of 1919: 120 whites and blacks died, and 15 African Americans were lynched in more than a dozen communities nationwide.[2]

Although no wartime or postwar riots occurred in Memphis, racial tensions were heightened.[3] Just six months after the Lincoln League's success in 1916, black Memphians experienced a blow when Ell Persons, a black woodchopper, was burned to death in May 1917. Even though evidence strongly pointed to a white killer, Persons had been charged with murdering a white teenage girl on the outskirts of the city. Law enforcement officials forced him to confess after beating him. A posse of local citizens formed, and government officials and the police failed to protect him. After the local press published his whereabouts, the posse captured him. The press publicized the upcoming lynching to take place five miles outside Memphis. Fifteen thousand local residents, some of whom took their children out of school, came. While the mother of the dead girl voiced her approval of the lynching, vendors sold sandwiches to the crowd. The mob tied Persons to a log, and two men cut off his ears before flames engulfed him. Afterward, many whites mutilated his body. Some onlookers, including women with children in their arms, scrambled to get bits of his body and clothing for souvenirs. The mob tied an American flag to the log, and whites proceeded to throw Persons's bodily remains onto Beale Street.

The lynchers were never prosecuted. Only after the tragedy did local white clergymen accept responsibility for failing to warn against mob violence. The white *Memphis Press* called all white citizens complicit and asked them to determine whether they wanted a society of law and order. Engaged in an antilynching campaign at this time, the national office of the NAACP investigated the tragedy. Robert R. Church Jr. drove the field secretary, James Weldon Johnson, a long-standing friend of his, to the lynching site. Johnson interviewed the sheriff, journalists, many African Americans, and some local whites. He wrote a special report, and the organization's magazine, the *Crisis,* used the incident to highlight the regionwide phenomenon of lynching, reporting that 2,867 black men had been lynched from 1885 to 1916.[4] That July in New York City, the NAACP spotlighted the Persons tragedy in its Silent Parade against lynching, segregation, disenfranchisement, and discrimination. As a result of the Persons lynching, many black Memphians migrated north, joining the 1.2 million black southerners who from 1915 to 1929 left the violence, segregation, disenfranchisement, economic exploitation, and daily indignities that they faced. Better economic opportunities in the North generated by the rise of wartime industries also spurred their movement.[5]

Church and his political associates responded to the lynching by forming the first NAACP branch in Tennessee and using their national connections to battle racial violence. A month after the tragedy, an organizational meeting occurred at Church's Park and Auditorium. Fifty-three people, mainly middle- and upper-class black professionals, became charter members, with Annette Church, Anna Wright Church, and Sara Paroda Church the only women among them. Although many African Americans initially feared joining, branch membership rose to 1,024 by 1919; Annette recruited many members, while some ministers and churches financially contributed to the chapter. A forceful presence in the region, the branch acted as a clearinghouse for the reporting of racial violence. Church and the NAACP national office developed a secret code for telegramming reports of lynching and mob violence. For example, the name "Fred" meant the Ku Klux Klan. National NAACP officials made Memphis a base on their investigative tours of the region, while Church sought greater national condemnation of racial violence. After at least thirty-nine African Americans died at the hands of a white mob in the East St. Louis riots of 1917, he took advantage of his close ties with Theodore Roosevelt to praise him for denouncing the violence and to urge him to speak out further.[6]

African Americans across the South followed Memphis's lead by joining the NAACP; the national organization targeted the region in its membership drive. The number of branches in the region rose from six in 1916 to fifty-eight by 1918, when Church accepted James Weldon Johnson's invitation to serve on the NAACP national board as its first southern representative. By becoming a board member, he hoped to influence others to join the organization. He represented fourteen states with nearly ten thousand members; by 1919, most NAACP members were southern and working class.[7] In introducing Church to the association's membership, NAACP publications mentioned his Lincoln League and Republican Party activities, saying that he had "done much to prove that the disenfranchisement of Negroes in the South can be broken up." The national organization also detailed his business activities, calling Solvent Savings Bank a strong black institution. It praised his late father as "an active and aggressive leader" in Tennessee and his half-sister Mary Church Terrell "as one of the ablest speakers among all American women."[8]

Two-and-a-half weeks after the Memphis NAACP chapter was organized, the Lincoln League held its first gathering since the Persons lynching, marking the first time that a local black leader or group publicly condemned or spoke openly about the incident. More than three thousand African Americans, including one thousand women, packed Church's Auditorium. Hundreds were turned away. When Church got up to speak, the crowd's "pent-up feeling . . . found expression in a burst of cheers," according to the *Nashville Globe,* the state capital's black newspaper. Church said: "I would be untrue to you and to myself as your elected leader if I should remain silent against shame and crime of lawlessness of any character, and I could not if I would hold my peace against either the lynching or burning of a human being." Acknowledging the migration north, he urged the audience to not give up hope and to throw their support behind the NAACP, announcing that the Lincoln League endorsed it.[9]

When the meeting was held, the Lincoln League was a rallying point and a source of hope for African Americans in Memphis and West Tennessee. The Reverend W. Herbert Brewster later called the organization a "bridge over troubled waters for black people" and "the greatest thing that happened among black people." "[For] black people, next to God and the church, was the Republican Party. It was the party of Lincoln," he recalled. "They were by the Republican Party like Moses was by the burning bush. They thought of it as . . . their trip into the land of freedom." He remembered that the naming of the league after Abraham Lincoln drew black Memphians to it, owing to his emancipation of African Americans from slavery. According to Brewster, next to the name of Jesus, African Americans were most familiar with that of Lincoln, and many could relate to his poor roots.[10]

Church and his lieutenants saw politics primarily as a tool to improve racial conditions; secondarily, they hoped to convert African Americans to the Republican Party. As a consequence, while the Lincoln League backed Republican candidates at the state and national levels, it endorsed Democrats locally. Because Republicans had no chance of winning local office, the league supported Democratic candidates who seemed most likely to treat African Americans fairly. Elsewhere in the South, African Americans who could vote saw politics as a means for racial advancement as well. In Atlanta, for instance, black community leaders marshaled their forces in local bond elections in 1919 and 1921 and, as a result, secured new black schools.[11]

The year 1918 saw a number of political successes for the Lincoln League. The organization supported nineteen of the twenty winners in the August election in Memphis, including Frank Monteverde as mayor, Crump as county trustee, and two non-Crump-supported candidates. Black Memphians held the balance of power in some cases. Calling the outcome "one of the greatest victories we have ever won," Church asked Roscoe Conkling Simmons for favorable publicity in the *Chicago Defender,* for which he was a columnist. "Get this dope in the paper this week and the next time I see you I will buy you a package of peanuts," Church said.[12] The year 1918 also saw Church's election to the state Republican Executive Committee and appointment to the Republican State Primary Board; a black Tennessean had not held either of these positions in twelve years. By January 1919, he served on the Shelby County Republican Executive Committee.[13]

The Lincoln League grew to at least six thousand members by 1919 and expanded its membership to include women after they became eligible to vote that year. The state legislature granted women voting rights in municipal and presidential elections, so more than one thousand black women, including Annette Church, registered to vote in Memphis that election season.[14] The federal government's guarantee of women's suffrage would come a year later. In urban areas elsewhere in the South, black women registered to vote and formed and joined black political clubs, including Republican ones. Black men often supported their efforts because they hoped that increased black political power would further their chances for civil rights. Yet many black women faced the widespread disenfranchisement measures. In Columbia, South Carolina, for instance, black women registered to vote on the first day of a voter registration campaign but then were stymied by literacy tests and harassment. The local NAACP chapter filed a lawsuit against the Board of Registrars but was unsuccessful.[15]

The Lincoln League faced obstacles to its political efforts as well. In 1919, it supported the mayoral candidate Frank Monteverde and his entire ticket. Church, a friend of Monteverde's, made a deal with him to appoint six African Americans to the police department in exchange for the organization's backing. No blacks had served as police officers since 1895. After Monteverde was elected, he put three black men on the detective force. Their service collectively lasted only a few months, however. A violent scuffle, apparently provoked by whites, resulted in the death of one and the subsequent dismissal of the other two.[16]

While Church and his black-and-tan faction, which included whites, made up the area's regular Republicans, the local lily-white faction challenged it for local power, representation at the Republican national convention, and seats on official Republican committees. Church funded all the legal expenses associated with his black-and-tan faction's battles with the lily whites over who should achieve delegate seats at the national conventions.[17] The fights between the factions were noticed by African Americans both locally and nationally. Among those who supported Church and his group were his mother, Anna Wright Church, postal employees, railroad union men, fraternal members, and Beale Streeters in general.[18] The *Chicago Defender* and other black publications reported on these battles.[19]

John W. Farley, a local white Republican lawyer, wrote a short book titled *Statistics and Politics* (1920) that apparently reflected the philosophy of his fellow lily whites. Adhering to the widespread belief that black voting threatened to disrupt social harmony, he characterized most African Americans as politically apathetic and preferring white government control. Calling attention to Church's light skin, Farley attributed his political participation to his "white blood." He argued that white Republicans should eliminate African Americans from their party organization because the Lincoln League had spurred some whites to vote Democratic in order to maintain white supremacy.[20]

Church himself faced obstacles to his political and civil rights activism. His political enemies tried to have him drafted into the army during World War I because they wanted to regain control of local Republican Party politics. Church refused to request exemption but never received a call to military service. In 1918, a sniper tried to murder him by using a high-powered rifle to shoot into a bedroom window of his home. Church was in his business office, and the gunman narrowly missed his niece, who had been sitting on the bed sewing. Church's daughter, Roberta, was near her.[21] The combination of his elite class status, political power, and interracial support did not shield Church from this fierce opposition, but that opposition did not deter him from his goals. When he received a noosed rope sent anonymously through the mail in 1921, he said that it was not the first time he had received "such presents" and that the incident had not "disturbed [him] in the least," that "it ha[d] just about as much effect as 'pouring water on a duck's back.'"[22]

Despite difficulties, Church and the Lincoln League operated in a time of rising hope: it increasingly appeared that the Republican Party could make a difference in the lives of African Americans. The black migration north resulted in an increasingly powerful black vote in urban centers, a point that black Republicans made in urging the party to support civil rights. Republicans regained Congress in 1918 and hoped to capture the White House in 1920. Some white Republicans recognized that many African Americans had become alienated from the party because of its lily whitism. All these factors influenced the party to take more concrete steps to advance civil rights. Between 1918 and 1920, a few Republican members of Congress, including Leonidas Dyer of Missouri, introduced bills against lynching and calling for an investigation of the country's racial problems. A congressman from a predominantly black Chicago district submitted a bill to ensure equal accommodations and prohibit racial discrimination in interstate transportation. All these bills died in committee, but they nevertheless provided an important recognition of civil rights.[23]

On the state level, Church was encouraged by and benefited from his alliance with the East Tennessee congressman J. Will Taylor, a lawyer who was born in 1880 in Union County, Tennessee, near Knoxville. After moving to La Follette, Taylor became its postmaster and then its mayor from 1910 to 1913 and 1918 to 1919 before resigning to become a member of Congress in 1919. He served as chair of the state Republican Executive Committee in 1917 and 1918, the same time period in which Church began his service on that body. Church made a $100 contribution to Taylor's campaign for Congress in 1918.[24] Tennessee remained unique among southern states for its strong Republican presence, although Democrats usually won local, state, and national elections. East Tennessee, a pro-Union region during the war, was heavily Republican. Most African Americans were Republican, and a sizable number voted in Tennessee. All these factors, along with Democratic Party factionalism, made the chance of Republican victories in Tennessee at the state and national levels a real possibility and inspired white Republicans to work with black Republicans.

Church later credited J. Will Taylor with doing more than any other person to further his rise in political circles. He recalled that Taylor "always firmly and sincerely believed that all men were equal," that he was "an exceptional White man from the south."[25] Taylor spoke out against the immorality and illegality of lynching in a speech in the House of Representatives in 1922, and his correspondence with Church reveals a friendly and cordial relationship built on trust. The two worked closely together and headed the statewide black-and-tan faction, which dominated Tennessee's Republican Party politics throughout the 1920s and early 1930s despite fierce competition from the lily-white faction. Whereas lily whites contested Church's authority, Taylor and other whites at the state and national levels worked with him; some voted to seat his black-and-tan faction at conventions instead of the lily-white one. These supportive whites recognized Church's ability to mobilize votes for the party and submerged any prejudices that they had in order to align with him. By accepting black authority and participation in the party, they countered persisting beliefs that African Americans were not worthy of political involvement or capable of exerting political leadership. They stood with these African Americans even though they could face attacks for doing so.[26] Church, for instance, wrote Taylor in 1928 about a rumor a rival Tennessee Republican was spreading that Church and Taylor had shared quarters together during the Republican national convention. Writing Taylor and stating that this rumor was untrue, Church said that Taylor could publish his letter if he wished.[27]

Most white southerners, however, saw the Republican Party as a threat; they blamed it for contributing to their defeat during the Civil War and then compelling them to accept black officeholders during Reconstruction.[28] The *Commercial Appeal* expressed these views in its editorial "The South Republican? Never!" Declaring that the "Republican Party always may be relied upon to drive the Southern Democrats back into their party shell," it said: "The people of the South may be oppressed by taxes; they may be misgoverned; the affairs of the nation may be mismanaged; they may believe that a Republican administration will be best for the country and for themselves from an economic standpoint, but they will not support a candidate, a ticket or a platform, no matter what it may promise, if to do so means that they must acknowledge the leadership of a negro. This is not an argument, it is just a plain statement of fact."[29] This newspaper piece revealed what the white author Lillian Smith called the "schizophrenic" mind-set of the South—a society so psychologically wedded to white su-premacy that its members were willing to forgo a better nation instead of accepting black political leaders. Elsewhere in the South, whites also viewed the Republican Party negatively because they saw its ac-ceptance of black leaders as undermining white political and social control. As a result, lily whites were limited in number because whites were reluctant to join the party.[30]

As local black and tans and lily whites vied for influence, Crump worked to regain control of local politics following his ouster from the mayoral office in 1916. He used his new position as county trustee to dominate the county political machine and the executive committee of the local Democratic Party from behind the scenes. Despite his sup-port of women's suffrage, newly enfranchised white women in 1919 joined the anti-Crump Citizens' Non-Partisan League; their efforts resembled those of southern suffragists elsewhere who denounced and campaigned against political machines. But they, like other Mem-phians, could do little to stymie Crump. He endorsed the successful mayoral candidates from 1917 through 1923. When they did not ad-here to his demands, he exercised influence through other city officials and ran tickets to place his subordinates in elected positions. Cover-ing the gamut of organizational life in Memphis, Crump's campaign organization consisted of black and white workers, both male and fe-male. Sometimes under pressure, teachers and other city employees campaigned for his candidates. He kept lists, such as of local black ministers and barbershops (even to the point of how many chairs there were), in order to maximize the number of voters reached. He contin-ued to secure black support at the polls by ensuring that his political workers paid their poll taxes, providing them with poll tax receipts, and plying them with barbeques and other enticements. Operators of illicit saloons, brothels, and gambling establishments provided him with a slush fund for registering and mobilizing working-class black voters. His supporters allegedly brought to town by the carload Af-rican Americans who worked on nearby plantations in order to have them vote for the Crump machine. They also transported local black Memphians to the polls, as evidenced by photographs published pe-rennially in the *Commercial Appeal*.[31]

While Crump took advantage of illiterate and poor African Ameri-cans during election time, the Lincoln League remained a vital presence locally and attracted widespread attention beyond Memphis for mobilizing black voters. African American leaders—including party officials, ministers, union officials, teachers, and doctors—from across the region and the nation visited Church in Memphis or corresponded with him in hopes of learning the secrets of his success. Black leaders in several southern, midwestern, and western states contacted him about organizing their own groups. As a result of all this interest, Church and his fellow black Republicans Roscoe Conkling Simmons and Walter L. Cohen, the secretary of the Louisiana Republican State Committee, called for a meeting to see about forming a national organization.[32]

A cross section of black leadership traveled to the two-day meeting in the summer of 1919 at the famed Iroquois Club on Canal Street in New Orleans. Only men participated. The *Chicago Defender* reported: "Albert Workman, head of the Longshoremen, took a leading part, while Tom Woodland, head of the Screwmen, was the most effective debater on the floor." It noted that these labor leaders sat side by side with black professionals, including doctors, lawyers, and businessmen.[33] The attendees officially founded the Lincoln League of America and nominated Church as its president. He declined in favor of serving as its director and chairing its executive committee. As president, he would have had a very public role; he preferred politically maneuvering behind the scenes. Roscoe Conkling Simmons became president instead. The participants passed several resolutions, including calls for federal aid for black education and an end to black disenfranchisement. Responding to the violence of the Red Summer, they demanded federal intervention to stop lynching and declared that the black soldier deserved the citizenship rights for which he had fought. Elsewhere in the country, black activists also pointed to black veterans to argue that African Americans should have a greater place in the country's democratic system, that black veterans demonstrated their civic worth and national loyalty. The meeting participants made plans for a national convention and invited black men and women to attend.[34] After the gathering, the Lincoln League of America's headquarters, located in Church's business office at 391 Beale Street, was swamped with more than one hundred applications for local charters from as many cities. "Letters Endorsing the Lincoln League have simply poured in on us," Church said. "Everywhere branch leagues are being formed. Old organizations are changing their names to Lincoln League."[35]

When the Lincoln League of America's first convention occurred in Chicago on 11 and 12 February 1920, thousands attended this public event, including four hundred delegates from across the country who represented all classes; some were members of local Lincoln Leagues, including Bert Roddy and Wayman Wilkerson of Memphis. Although the convention was a nonpartisan meeting, with the idea that delegates would decide which party to endorse, most delegates were prominent black Republicans from thirty-three states, including most southern states.[36] Calling the topic of "Political parties and Colored Americans" the most significant one on the meeting's agenda, the *Afro-American* said: "Undoubtedly this is a great step in advance. Too long have Negroes voted the Republican ticket blindly and unanimously."[37] Church encouraged women to attend, and many did, including Ida B. Wells-Barnett.[38] Men held the league's top offices, while women served as delegates and planned and hosted social affairs. The *Chicago Defender* reported: "No part of the convention proceedings was more interesting than the manner in which the women present pointedly discussed issues as presented."[39]

Prominent black and white speakers regaled the attendees at the South Park M.E. Church auditorium, which was draped with American flags and housed a large oil portrait of Lincoln that looked down at the audience. Each session began and ended with prayer and song. Preferring, as noted, to take a behind-the-scenes organizational role, Church did not have an official part in the program, but the crowd recognized him with a standing ovation. James Weldon Johnson, field secretary of the NAACP, reported on lynching. Simmons inspired the audience with his oratory and paid tribute to Governor P. S. B. Pinchback, who was honorary president of the league but too ill to attend.[40] Three former black officeholders spoke; their very presence symbolized the league's desire to reclaim black political rights. Invoking Woodrow Wilson's words about making the world safe for democracy, these leaders said that "the fight was to make America safe for Americans—safe against disfranchisement, against prejudicial labor organizations, against Jim Crow cars, against mob violence and lynching."[41]

Prestigious white Republicans who made remarks included the mayor of Chicago, William Hale Thompson, and the governor of Illinois, Frank O. Lowden. Calling black soldiers among the bravest of the war, Leonard A. Wood, a retired US Army major general, asked each one in the audience to stand, and he saluted them in turn. To thunderous applause, he said that all citizens deserved the privileges of and protections guaranteed by the Constitution.[42] Republican National Committee chairman Will Hays, responsible for the party's fall campaign, utilized Church's talking points in making a forceful address for civil rights and against racial violence that led to a standing ovation from the delegates and favorable comments from the black press. Across the country, white newspapers carried his remarks against lynching.[43] Yet the *Afro-American* commented that, while "old conservative, dyed-in-the-wool Republicans" saw Chairman Hays's presence at the convention as a sign of recognition from the national Republican Party, African American supporters of the "more progressive Socialist and Labor Parties regard the move as a probable attempt to prevent the League from taking any radical step."[44] It noted elsewhere that Governor Lowden spoke only on Lincoln and "dodged the color question."[45]

At the closing-night session, attended by some three thousand, the delegates unanimously passed resolutions calling for the Republican Party to condemn mob violence and to take federal action against lynching. They endorsed the League of Nations and suffrage for women and all black southerners. They urged black workers to join nondiscriminatory labor unions. And they said that no black delegate to the Republican national convention should vote for the nomination of any presidential candidate unless he endorsed antilynching legislation and voting rights for black southerners; they urged black voters not to support any US presidential or congressional candidate who did not support these measures and their enforcement.[46] The delegates' endorsement of the Republican Party as the "channel through which the League activities [were] to be carried out" led the *Chicago Defender* to report: "The league, as interpreted by its orators, thinks the Race will get a better hearing fighting in its own backyard rather than by threatening to leave home because everything isn't pretty." The *Afro-American* remarked that the league's official support for the party could mean "a few plums" for the organization's officers.[47] Afterward, the league established its headquarters at the Idlewild Hotel in Chicago.[48]

The league's founding increased Church's prominence in national political circles. He attended the meeting of the Republican National Committee in 1919, at which women sat as members for the first time. National committee chair Will Hays appointed him and four other Lincoln League of America officials to the Advisory Committee on Policies and Platform for the 1920 Republican national convention. Citing his advisory committee credentials in a magazine article, Church called disenfranchisement a crime that hurt both blacks and whites. Now that the war was over, he said, the battle must be fought inside the country for equal rights, and Republicans must not build up their party in the South at the expense of African Americans. For the 1920 election, Hays named Church and two league officials as directors of campaign activities for black voters. For the Republican national convention, Church was also assigned to a subcommittee dealing with international trade, an indication that Hays requested his opinions on matters other than race relations.[49]

Despite the involvement of African Americans in the campaign, Republican presidential candidates paid little attention to racial matters, and the Republican national convention largely sided with lily-white factions in 1920. Only three of the seventeen presidential primary candidates returned an NAACP questionnaire about their positions on racial issues. One was Warren Harding, but he, like the other responders, was vague in his responses. At the Republican national convention, no black delegates were seated from five southern states.[50] The platform included only a noncommittal statement against lynching, as opposed to the lengthier planks dealing with civil rights that the party had endorsed in years past. The *Chicago Defender* reported that the party's leaders, including Hays, were "as still as shadows in a deserted graveyard—and as silent—against the plot and plan to rob the Race [of] the South of its place in the Republican household."[51]

At the national convention, Memphis lily whites manipulated white anxieties about interactions between white women and black men to contest Church's attempt to be seated as a delegate. In the South, charges of the rape of white women by African American men—most often untrue—were used to justify lynching. This hysteria, most prevalent in the region, occurred nationwide. For instance, the popular 1915 film *Birth of a Nation,* which President Woodrow Wilson screened at the White House, perpetuated these stereotypes. At the 1920 convention, Mrs. Eddie McCall Priest, on behalf of the lily whites and as the sister of John McCall, an avowed lily-white enemy of Church, charged Church with running vice operations and characterized him as so disreputable that local white women would leave the party if he were seated as a delegate; delegations of white women sent telegrams backing her up. Knowing the potential volatility of challenging white women, Church refused to reply publicly to their charges, although behind the scenes he did, in his own words, "burn the two men up, who were hiding behind her skirts." The National Committee voted to seat Church as a delegate, but the party's credentials committee voted twenty-three to eighteen to unseat him.[52] When Church had the opportunity to contest the vote before the convention delegates, he said that he was entitled to a seat but planned to take his fight to Memphis instead of dealing with the matter there. The black Memphian Lieutenant George W. Lee characterized the speech as one "of a trained diplomat who was wise enough to sacrifice the glory of the moment for a commanding place in the future." According to Lee, Church's graciousness in defeat increased his standing among national party leaders, and he "extracted from them certain promises that made his future in the Republican Party secure."[53] Afterward, Church and his black-and-tan faction were always seated at national conventions.

The 1920 convention was not all bleak for black Republicans. Lincoln League of America president Roscoe Conkling Simmons aided African Americans fighting to be seated as delegates, while the league's executive secretary attended meetings of the Republican National Committee and monitored lily-white opposition. On behalf of the league, Church helped ensure the seating of the league official Henry Lincoln Johnson as a national committeeman representing Georgia. The league helped influence the recognition of the black-and-tan faction of New Orleans, headed by the league official Walter Cohen, rather than the city's lily-white delegation, as the regular party organization. All this work and success led Simmons to say that the organization's activities were not in vain. Another league official commented that the lily-white victories at the convention further revealed the necessity of the organization.[54]

After the convention, black leaders pushed Republicans for civil rights and antilynching legislation. In his NAACP leadership capacity, James Weldon Johnson, also a member of the executive committee of the Lincoln League of America, met with Harding to discuss racial issues. Although not willing to publicly commit to alleviating racial injustices, Harding privately denounced the Ku Klux Klan and said that the problem of black voting rights in the South would be resolved in time. Johnson's combination of behind-the-scenes diplomacy with tangible civil rights demands reflected strategies deployed by Church and other black political leaders. Moreover, Johnson's work in overlapping civil rights organizations mirrored the participation of Lincoln League members in other organizations for racial advancement as well. Both Church and Walter Cohen, for instance, served as officers of the National Negro Business League.[55]

For the 1920 election, Lincoln League of America members rallied for Republican victories. Church mobilized his local league for Republican candidates and led efforts to register black voters across Tennessee, including newly enfranchised women. On behalf of the Republican Party, he traveled to Maryland and Kentucky to campaign for candidates there. Wayman Wilkerson, a member of the Lincoln League and a political associate of Church, ran for Congress. For the first time since Reconstruction, Tennessee went for a Republican presidential candidate as some 170,000 African Americans voted the straight Republican ticket. Harding won 60 percent of the popular vote in his successful bid for the presidency, while Republicans retained their majorities in Congress. Further breaking the stranglehold of the largely Democratic South, Tennessee voters elected a Republican governor and five Republican members of Congress, although Wilkerson lost his bid. Church's work enhanced his stature in the eyes of national Republicans, and he attracted attention as far away as Delaware for helping ensure these victories. Making their headquarters at the Whitelaw Hotel, the luxury hotel for African Americans in segregated Washington, DC, Church and his fellow Lincoln League of America officials Ben Davis of Georgia and Perry Howard of Mississippi attended the inauguration.[56]

After the election of 1920, Church declared that his local Lincoln League had accomplished its purpose, and it was dissolved. Whether the league met to make this decision or he alone had the power to disband it is unknown. Yet its goals for "political and economic emancipation" and "regain[ing] the lost rights of a growing race" had not been fulfilled. Church probably decided that he could not concentrate on both local and national activities, although, if this was the case, it is unclear why he did not appoint one of his political lieutenants to lead the league. He later expressed his belief that national efforts provided him with a better opportunity for promoting the economic and political interests of African Americans than did local activities.[57] Similarly, he may have thought that the best way to improve conditions for African Americans locally was through national activities. According to the *Chicago Defender:* "His slogan always has been to help better the condition, first, of the Race in Memphis, then the members of the Race in the United States."[58] The decision to focus on national activities made sense in light of the political context and his success. Church was a rising star among Republicans. He had helped pull off a tremendous electoral sweep for Republicans in Tennessee in 1920 and had a close relationship with Will Hays, one of the party's most powerful officials. After the dark years of the Wilson administration, the White House had now returned to Republican hands. As executive director of the Lincoln League of America, Church had influence over prominent black Republicans and ordinary African Americans nationwide. It was a truly exciting time for Church as he had an increasing amount of influence and access to aid him in the pursuit of his ultimate goal of using politics as a tool for racial advancement.[59]

After the election, Harding's first message to Congress called for the elimination of lynching and noted a congressional proposal for an interracial commission to investigate racial problems, although he did not endorse it. In a letter to Congress, W. E. B. Du Bois called this message the strongest pronouncement on racial problems ever made by a president, both attesting to the significance of these presidential remarks and, given the obvious limits of those remarks, bespeaking the Republican Party's lack of commitment to African Americans. Harding made his most extensive comments on racial issues in a 1921 speech in Birmingham, Alabama, that generated a mixed reaction from African Americans and white southerners. On the one hand, the president said that African Americans should be able to vote and have equal educational and economic opportunities. On the other hand, he spoke out against social equality, saying that racial amalgamation should not exist, that recognition should exist of the differences between whites and African Americans. The Lincoln League of America officials Henry Lincoln Johnson and Perry Howard wrote Harding letters of congratulations, whereas other African Americans, including Du Bois, criticized his comments on racial differences. Several white southern newspapers responded favorably, but many southern congressmen denounced Harding for his remarks.[60]

By the end of his first year in office, Harding became increasingly unpopular among African Americans. In his messages to Congress, he was silent on race. Devoting little attention to racial issues, he made few black appointments and took no action against segregation, disenfranchisement, or racial violence. He advocated a lily-white strategy in the South in an attempt to bolster Republican strength in the region. As a result, some state Republican committees "reorganized," leading to a decline in black members.[61] Harding's administration also convicted Marcus Garvey, the leader of the largest mass movement of people of African descent of the time, of mail fraud in 1923 despite Garvey's protestations of innocence and later scholarly claims and congressional findings that he was set up in order to weaken his movement. Garvey headed the Universal Negro Improvement Association (UNIA) and had attracted millions of followers. After founding the organization in his native Jamaica in 1914, he based it in Harlem shortly after his move there in 1916.[62] Through its branches across the country and around the world, the UNIA advocated black pride, self-reliance, and nationalism. In the South, 423 branches existed by 1926, with nearly 500 elsewhere in the United States.[63]

After Harding died in 1923, Calvin Coolidge became president. Like Harding's, his approach to racial matters was mixed. On the one hand, he displayed little understanding of or concern about racial matters and resorted to platitudes instead of tangible action for civil rights. With Republicans in control of Congress, the Dyer antilynching bill had a chance of becoming law during the Harding and Coolidge administrations, but neither president endorsed it. Coolidge especially angered African Americans by remaining silent about a Ku Klux Klan march in front of the White House. On the other hand, Coolidge made a few well-received black appointments. Largely as a result of black protest, segregation was ended in some federal government bureaus during his administration. More African Americans were seated as delegates at the 1924 convention than in 1920, in part because Coolidge did not embrace lily whitism to the same extent as Harding did.[64]

Despite the restrictions of the Republican administrations, Church and other African Americans still could influence the party's operations; the GOP remained the most powerful political party in which they had a voice. Harding and Coolidge made more black appointments than Wilson, Republicans were more receptive to black participation in their party than were Democrats, and they were generally less hostile to African Americans. A vigorous black presence prevented the party from further turning toward lily whitism. The US House of Representatives passed the Dyer antilynching bill; if southern Democratic senators had not filibustered the bill, the Senate may have passed it. The NAACP conducted a campaign to pass the Dyer bill, and the Lincoln League of America supported it. While the bill was debated in Congress, the number of lynchings declined; the congressional action may have played a role.[65]

Church became the most prominent black Republican in the country during the Harding years and held that status for the rest of the 1920s. Black newspapers nationwide covered his activities. Deft at interpersonal relations, Church cultivated ties with high-ranking white leaders in order to secure political access and leverage. Cultured, well mannered, courteous, modest, quiet, frank, and recognized as a man of integrity, he was well liked by white Republicans and bold enough to speak forthrightly for civil rights. He further earned respect by financing his own political efforts in order to maintain political independence and avoid ties to special interests. Nicknamed the "roving dictator of the Lincoln Belt," an area that stretched north and south from Missouri and through Illinois, Kentucky, Tennessee, Indiana, and Ohio, he was regularly sent by the Republican National Committee into states with close races during presidential election time in order to garner black support for Republican candidates.[66] Republican officials consulted him about political strategy, and he acted as the party's codirector of activities for black voters for the 1924 campaign. Tennessee lily whites called the Republican National Committee chairman "every name out of the dictionary" for appointing Church to this position.[67]

Church's influence reached as high as the White House. During the Harding administration, Church would visit with the president, secretary of state, attorney general, and Will Hays there. A story went around Memphis that he could call at the White House any time he pleased and enter by the front door. He visited it during Coolidge's administration as well. He met with Coolidge, for instance, to urge him to appoint the African American attorney James A. Cobb to be judge of the Municipal Court of the District of Columbia to succeed Church's late brother-in-law, Robert H. Terrell; Coolidge subsequently made this appointment. Several top Republican officials believed that Church, as opposed to J. Will Taylor, mainly controlled the state's black-and-tan faction, the dominant state Republican organization. They thought that Church, on whom Taylor relied heavily, was probably his greatest source of strength in national politics. In Tennessee, Republican politicians believed that Taylor had to go through Church to go to the White House if he was in a hurry.[68]

Church's work on the national political scene was inextricably intertwined with his local and state activities. His local black-and-tan group was more powerful than and outnumbered the local lily-white group. As a member of the Shelby County and state Republican Executive Committees, a delegate to the Republican national convention, and the head of the regular Republican organization in the Tenth District throughout the 1920s, he had leverage and credibility in official party circles and pushed for African Americans to have a greater role in the party as members of committees and as delegates to conventions.[69]

One of the key ways in which Church exerted political influence was through patronage. During Republican administrations, he controlled patronage in West Tennessee. Congressman J. Will Taylor, who was in charge of federal patronage for Tennessee, often asked Church for recommendations for whites and African Americans and usually accepted those recommendations without question. Church assisted white Tennesseans who sought federal appointments and appointed at least two white federal judges for West Tennessee. In 1921, Republican National Committee chair Will H. Hays, pointing out that Church had principally formed the Lincoln League of America, recommended to President Harding that Church be the administration's point person for dispensing black patronage across the country. On assuming this position, Church made frequent trips to Washington, DC, to submit requests for black political appointments through Hays. Although frustrated that the Harding administration did not follow many of his recommendations, Church controlled thousands of jobs. His influence led to the appointments of black officials nationwide as well as whites whom he thought would treat African Americans fairly. He demanded that all whites that he recommended for federal appointment agree to use merit instead of race as a basis for hiring civil service workers in their agencies; as a result, more African Americans were employed. Although invited to serve on federal delegations to Haiti in 1922 and the Virgin Islands in 1924, Church did not accept and never sought any political appointments. He did not want to be under any obligation to the Republican Party that might compromise his civil rights efforts. Instead, he wanted the party to be in his debt.[70]

Church took pride in his ability to appoint postmasters general in Memphis. He selected whites for this role, adhering to the social convention of whites receiving the most important patronage positions. In one dramatic case, he overturned the appointment of his lily-white foe, Charles B. Quinn, as the postmaster. In 1921, Quinn influenced the acting national postmaster general to select him when Will Hays, who had become the national postmaster general, was sick. After Church telephoned Hays, Hays revoked the commission from his hospital bedside and appointed Church's choice. Quinn received the news via telegram when traveling by train from Washington, DC, to Memphis to assume the position. Church made successful recommendations for postmaster appointments in 1927, 1929, and 1932 as well, all of which led to more job opportunities for African Americans in the postal system. When a young man, Church had observed that black teachers and principals were paid less than whites for the same work. Federal employment was an exception to the widespread practice of unequal pay. Like his father, he encouraged young black men to consider a career with the US Postal Service, where white and black employees received the same salary. Church used his political influence to provide black Memphians with civil service positions at the post office, where they worked as mail clerks, mail carriers, and special delivery men, and in the federal court system, where they could work as bailiffs.[71]

Church used his national political influence to stand against segregation as well. The only African American chosen for membership in the exclusive Congressional Country Club of Washington, he declined the honor to protest the club's all-white membership, denying himself the opportunity to hobnob with such prominent members as the publishing giant William Randolph Hearst and the auto executive Walter Chrysler. In 1924, lily-white Republicans invited the Republican vice presidential candidate, Charles Dawes, to speak in the municipal auditorium in Memphis. With regional newspapers spreading the word about the visit, lily whites of Alabama, Arkansas, and Mississippi were expected to come. Local lily whites planned to let whites occupy the main floor and to seat African Americans in the balcony and have them use a separate entrance. Considering this arrangement an insult to loyal Republicans, Church telephoned Republican National Committee chair William Butler, a senator from Massachusetts, and explained the situation. Consequently, Dawes canceled the engagement.[72]

Church's success inspired black Memphians and influenced some to join the Republican Party.[73] In 1921, the *Memphis Times,* a local black newspaper, praised Church for "standing in the forefront of Negro leaders" and winning "a place among the powers of the Nation that but few can claim." By pressing for constitutional rights, justice, and equal opportunity, Church represented all African Americans in his political work, according to the *Times.*[74] Raymond Lymon, who became part of Church's political group, was born in 1913 to a family that had long supported the Church family. "I [was] a convert and a follower of the Church activities, successes and trials ever since I was a lad. . . . He was my hero," he remembered. "When we were children, we would ride down Lauderdale Street [and] the Church house . . . was always pointed out." Lymon saw the mansion as a symbol of what could happen to any African American who was successful and "dared to lead." "We looked at Mr. Church as our emancipator," he recalled. "Memphis was held in the grip of strict segregation and many instances oppression. We would read about Mr. Church's exploits and his visits to the White House and at that time it was almost unknown for Negroes to go to the White House. We each felt that if we were to be delivered, Mr. Church would be the one to do it."[75]

Church carried on with his work with the Lincoln League of America, which held the second of its quadrennial conventions in 1924 in Chicago at Bethel A.M.E. Church on Lincoln's birthday. That meeting resembled the one held four years earlier. Black leaders and journalists from forty-six states attended, among them many black Memphians.[76] Prominent black and white Republicans spoke, including Republican National Committee chair John T. Adams and Senator Medill McCormick of Illinois. McCormick received a particularly warm reception for saying that racial violence and disenfranchisement "endanger[ed] the rights of every citizen in America."[77] Not everyone was pleased with the proceedings, however. Women remained involved in organizational operations, but men continued to serve as the top officials.[78] Lethia C. Fleming, a member of the executive and credentials committees from Cincinnati, Ohio, protested that "women ought to have a place along with the men in the league."[79] The delegates also engaged in a heated debate about to what extent they should criticize the Republican Party. Ben Davis of Georgia presented strongly worded resolutions charging the Republican National Committee with lily whitism and criticizing it for its treatment of Henry

Lincoln Johnson of Georgia; he pointed out that the committee did not print a biographical sketch of his career as it did for its white members. The delegates passed the resolutions but in toned-down language.[80]

By the time of the 1924 convention, the Lincoln League of America had moved its headquarters to Pennsylvania Avenue in Washington, DC, and had taken significant steps for black political rights and against lily whitism. In 1923, Roscoe Conkling Simmons helped end party proposals that would have undermined the influence of black Republicans by reducing southern representation at the Republican national convention. The league secured black political appointments: Perry Howard of Mississippi became assistant attorney general of the United States, and Walter L. Cohen became comptroller of customs for the Federal District of New Orleans. In his Republican National Committee position, Johnson had advocated for Howard. Among the most prominent black Republicans of the time, Cohen, Johnson, and Howard were all patronage dispensers and Lincoln League of America officials. The league also urged African Americans to run for office and to register to vote. In 1921, John Mitchell, a Richmond newspaper editor and Lincoln League of America member, ran for governor in Virginia. On his ticket was Maggie Lena Walker, the first black woman to make a bid for statewide office in Virginia, as a candidate for the superintendent of public instruction post. Mitchell and Walker were among the few black southerners who ran for public office in the 1910s and 1920s.[81]

The 1924 meeting marked the last of the Lincoln League of America's conventions, however. The league appears to have hardly operated past 1925, although it is unclear why. In the *Chicago Defender*, which among the major black newspapers reported the most on its activities, the last mention of it occurred in March 1925. The paper reported that the league planned to hold an executive committee meeting, that its leaders and members had made a strong showing for Coolidge's inauguration, and that it planned to propose that Coolidge give African Americans more political recognition. A December 1927 article of the *Afro-American* only briefly referenced the league, mentioning that Simmons remained president. By 1930, the organization had ended its operations.[82]

The Lincoln League of America may have declined because of a lack of support from its members. During the mid-1920s, African

Americans became increasingly alienated from the Republican Party because of its lily whitism, its failure to live up to its campaign promises, and its inaction on civil rights. The *New York Amsterdam News* later criticized the league for disbanding after placing its officials in political positions.[83] Reporting on the league's 1924 convention, the *Pittsburgh Courier* had characterized it as "a meeting of men fighting for political prominence and a job."[84] Although, as noted, Church did not accept or seek political appointments for himself, he did use his influence to ensure that his political associates received these positions. He was widely seen as an unselfish man and one of integrity, but, in assisting his associates in this manner, he arguably contributed to charges that nationally prominent black Republicans were self-serving.[85]

Correspondence between Lincoln League of America president Roscoe Conkling Simmons and Wayman Wilkerson sheds light on the league, suggesting that a divide between the league's leaders and its members may have led to its demise. A local political and business associate of Church, Wilkerson had been involved with the league from its start.[86] He believed that the 1920 national convention was a "rousing success." But, after attending the league's 1923 executive committee in Chicago, he wrote Simmons that he and other Tennessee leaders saw the league as a "farce and a joke" that had yielded "neither beneficial results to the success of the Republican party in general nor the colored voters in particular." He said that he had tried to point out to Church the problems of the organization, that its "program of pretense" was "beneath him and dangerous to his position," but Church had not believed him. Wilkerson did not provide more specifics, saying only that Simmons, who wrote for the *Chicago Defender*, should not be so connected with the publication because other papers thought the organization favored the *Defender*.[87] An article in the *Pittsburgh Courier* echoed some of Wilkerson's remarks. Reporting that the league's executive committee planned to meet privately in 1923, it criticized the organization for its failure to hold more meetings and quoted an unnamed independent political leader in Chicago saying: "That has been the trouble with this group of fellows who are seeking to play the national game—they have always had too much 'closed door' stuff, and they are liable to wake up and find, when they open the door, that the people have all scampered into open fields."[88]

Simmons responded to Wilkerson with a vigorous defense of the organization. He said that the league did not and had not benefited him personally—he had spent time and money on its behalf and also undergone "mental hardships" in carrying out its work. Expressing that he was "astounded" that Wilkerson failed to see the possibility of the league, Simmons said that Church had risen above "folly" by not heeding Wilkerson's comments. He claimed that the league had secured every black appointment made by the Harding and Coolidge administrations, that it had made Church the political spokesman of the people, and that it had ensured black representation in Republican circles. He defended the league's ties to the *Defender* by saying that its publicity had popularized the league and that rival newspapers suffered from jealousy.[89] This defense did not stop criticism of the league. For instance, in 1924 Simmons said that the league was responsible for "recent political victories": "[It] had Harding's ear. It has the ear of Mr. Coolidge. It has the eye and ear of the people." William N. Jones, a columnist for the *Afro-American*, responded that, if these claims were true, the organization should ensure that more African Americans receive more government jobs, that the Fourteenth and Fifteenth Amendments be enforced, and that segregation be abolished.[90]

The league's decline did not keep Church from maintaining his national political influence. According to a May 1927 profile, politics was not his occupation, as some supposed; rather, he made a living in real estate and was a millionaire. Now age forty-two, he worked out of two offices, a modest brick building on Beale Street and an unmarked office in a rickety old building on Pennsylvania Avenue, one of many unidentified Republican headquarters throughout DC. "He seldom makes a trip to Washington without calling [at the White House]," the profile said. "He gets in to see the President and shakes the chief executive by the hand." In his DC office, the walls were covered with autographed photographs of practically every prominent Republican politician of the past fifteen years. Church never had to ask for them. "These men appreciate what I do for them," he said.[91]

For all his accomplishments, access, and influence, Church could rise only so high in the Republican Party. "Had I not been a Colored Republican, many, many opportunities and avenues would have been open to me in the Party," he later said.[92] He had to battle not only to prevail over the lily whites but also to get his message heard by and acted on by more progressive party members. For instance, he pressed Will Hays to urge Harding to make more black political appointments, but Hays apparently did not spread the word.[93] Still, Church's voice was heard and his presence felt in these circles of power. Although the Lincoln League of America operated in problematic ways and eventually disbanded, it had increased the stature of Church and other black Republicans in the eyes of party, led to the placement of African Americans in political leadership positions, served as a vital force against lily whitism, and empowered African Americans to engage in political activity in their own communities.

While Church had shifted his attention to national activities, his black-and-tan faction in Memphis had operated as the backbone of black political activity during election time. Church exerted influence over a large number of black voters, so he could swing elections for his white candidates of choice; he was so shrewd politically that he apparently never backed a losing candidate for local office. He acted as the master strategist and organizer for political campaigns while his lieutenants remained business leaders and independent professionals. Largely conducting his political and business operations out of the public eye, he entered and exited his office through the rear entrance and used the back room for meetings. He preferred political negotiations in conferences rather than protests; he rarely gave interviews or speeches.[94]

Lieutenant George Washington Lee became one of Church's right-hand men in Memphis in the 1920s. Born in 1894, Lee grew up poor in Indianola, Mississippi. He attended Alcorn College, the state college for African Americans, before World War I interrupted his schooling and spurred him to attend a selective training school for black officers in Des Moines, Iowa. He became a lieutenant and was called "Lieutenant Lee" for the rest of his life. When on leave, he walked around Vicksburg in his uniform. A false rumor spread that he had forced a white soldier to salute him, so local whites formed a posse to lynch him. Lee escaped unharmed. Other black soldiers and veterans of World War I were not so fortunate as they were lynched by whites feeling threatened by their authority and seeking to keep the status quo. After the near lynching, Lee was sent to France, where he commanded a black regiment, narrowly escaped death, and received a citation for bravery. The war exposed him to both combat experience and racial transformation. Observing that the French had stereotypes of African Americans, he saw Frenchmen change their views after he and others became their friends.[95]

Lee returned to the States and secured an appointment in 1919 with Church, who he knew was a man of "unusual power."[96] Aware that Church had national political connections, he sought his help in securing a lifetime military career.[97] Lee told Church about his army experience and near lynching, and Church was immediately taken with him. Encouraging Lee to use his fighting spirit not to serve the military but to improve racial conditions, Church said that he could help him tremendously. "You need to get on the firing line of racial activities and racial progress," Church said.[98] Lee moved to Memphis and became the manager of the Atlanta Life Insurance Company's branch there. Lee and Church worked on the same block on Beale Street and grew professionally and personally close. Lee would join Church and his family for Christmas.[99] Like Church, he became very active in the Elks, the black fraternal organization, throughout his life. Church opened up business connections for Lee, and Lee became Church's political protégé. Lee developed what would become a lifelong admiration for Church, whom he later characterized as the "great crusader, the great civil rights battler long before any civil rights laws had been passed, and a man of unusual courage."[100] Lee himself became one of the most important political leaders in Memphis for decades to come. Involved in the Lincoln League of America, he got his start in national campaigns by 1920 when he spoke on behalf of the Republican National Committee. In 1924, Church convinced the Republican Party to appoint Lee to secure the votes of African Americans in the Midwest. During the campaign, Lee also organized the Lincoln Legion, a group of black soldiers for Coolidge.[101]

Church was the driving force behind a group of African American businessmen and professionals—of which Lee was a key figure—that engaged in a nonpartisan voter registration movement for the 1923 city election in Memphis. Black Memphians stepped up their political efforts to protest the Ku Klux Klan, which took the unprecedented step of running a ticket for local offices. The 1920s was the height of the Klan's influence nationally. Composed largely of lower- to middle-class white native-born Protestants, the organization displayed anti-black prejudice and xenophobic views toward others not sharing its members' race, citizenship, or religious beliefs. According to one estimate, the city's Klan numbered ten thousand members in the early 1920s. Despite its large membership, many white citizens opposed the Klan, and so did the *Commercial Appeal*, which won a Pulitzer Prize for its three-year campaign against the Klan; it spotlighted its use of violence and the secrecy of its operations as opposed to its antiblack views.[102]

During the 1923 election, the influence of African American voters and the presence of black powerbrokers significantly affected the white politicians who came out against the Klan candidates. Mayor Rowlett Paine and his ticket officially denied Klan affiliation or sympathy. The other mayoral candidate, Judge Lewis T. Fitzhugh, filed a $50,000 lawsuit against the *News-Scimitar* for publishing the charge that the Klan had picked the candidates on his ticket. Both Mayor Paine and Judge Fitzhugh appealed for African American support by appointing black campaign managers; Lieutenant Lee worked in this capacity for Paine. Because Paine did not associate with the Klan and promised street improvements and a new black high school, the Church faction supported him. Crump, who saw the Klan as a threat to his control, endorsed him at the last minute. Paine was reelected. Cliff Davis, who ran for city judge, was the only victorious Klan candidate. The election marked the peak of the Klan's power locally; the organization soon found that its influence was negligible.[103] Plagued by internal scandals and public opposition, the Ku Klux Klan nearly collapsed nationally by the end of the decade.

Church and his associates were victorious in 1923, but their efforts were never easy. Many white Memphians resented Church's national political standing. His black-and-tan faction constantly battled with the lily whites for recognition as the local regular Republican organization. It apparently faced a more difficult situation than did black Republicans in other southern states where the Republican Party was not as viable and blacks consequently faced less white opposition.[104] "I have seen [Church] in action at political fracases when he clashed with white opponents in such turmoil that mob action was openly suggested," William N. Jones of the *Afro-American* later commented.[105] Moreover, Church was the object of negative newspaper coverage, editorials, and cartoons. His foes strung banners across Main Street appealing to voters to "Stop Church and his associates."[106]

Church had to overcome black opposition as well and faced criticism for his leadership methods. According to the Reverend W. Herbert Brewster, some members of his black-and-tan group deserted and betrayed him. Believing that he should make public appeals instead of conducting his political activities behind closed doors, some African

Americans saw his leadership style as undemocratic. Others disliked him for his wealth or shunned him for fear of what whites might think. "During the early days of his struggle," he was "dodged by members of his own race who feared that contact with him might throw them into disfavor with the majority group," Lieutenant Lee wrote in 1927.[107] Many black Memphians disliked Church for being so different from the masses. "Many were impressed; others were not. Just as soon as you start up, there will always be someone who will hate to see you go up whether they are white, black, blue or gray or got a stripe down your back," Brewster recalled. "So all black youngsters were not inspired. They wanted everybody to be the same."[108] Yet others thought that Church's advantages were due to his light skin.[109] Nat D. Williams, a local black political observer, recalled that black Memphians made distinctions based on whether an African American was light skinned, brown skinned, or black skinned. "We judged the development of Negroes in Memphis on the area of different shades of color. The blacker you were, the further down you went," he said. He remembered that Church was a friend of his even though he, Williams, was dark skinned.[110]

Church also faced a very personal challenge that interfered with his local political activities in the early 1920s: when his wife, Sara, who had taken a keen interest in his political activities, became ill, he abandoned business and politics. They traveled to Washington, DC, in January 1922, where she convalesced. He and their daughter, Roberta, stayed there until she died in July. Church never remarried. Instead, his sister, Annette, became his housekeeper and the caretaker for Roberta, to whom he was very devoted.[111]

Although Church and his adherents helped defeat most of the Ku Klux Klan slate in 1923, his focus on the national level came at the expense of local activism. In 1924, he and his lieutenants withdrew from leadership positions in the city's NAACP branch, which had seen its activities decline in the immediate postwar era. Across the South, NAACP branches became dead or dormant after their growth during the World War I era; their members experienced violence, harassment, and economic intimidation from white southerners determined to quell their activism. The Memphis branch reorganized, had an encouraging start, and supported the Dyer antilynching bill, but it declined the offer of Congressman Leonidas Dyer, the Missouri Republican who sponsored the measure, to lecture in Memphis for fear of an overly small turnout. By 1926, black Memphians apparently saw the branch as powerless.[112]

Even so, the City Federation of Women's Clubs achieved political success while Church was gaining influence on the national scene. Begun in 1905 in response to the state law mandating streetcar segregation, the organization helped secure state funding for a vocational school for delinquent black girls. These girls had by law not been permitted in institutions for delinquent white girls, so they had been taken to jail. J. Frankie Seay Pierce, a black women's suffrage leader based in Nashville and the organizer of the Tennessee Federation of Women's Clubs, spearheaded the campaign for the school, which the granting of women's suffrage energized. The Tennessee General Assembly passed a bill creating the school in 1921, and it opened its doors two years later.[113]

In addition, the Inter Racial League stepped into the activism void in Memphis and became an important force for racial advancement in the mid-1920s. The league was a branch of the Atlanta-based CIC, an interracial organization formed in 1919 to defuse postwar racial tensions, promote peaceful black-white relations, and engage in black uplift and protest efforts. Local committees and women's auxiliaries formed across the South, and the CIC became a major interracial reform movement by the mid-1920s. The group advocated against lynching and for better housing, equal education opportunities, a more equitable justice system, and black voting rights. Like other liberal organizations, the CIC did not directly attack segregation. It embraced a paternalistic stance in which its middle-class white members often determined the best ways to improve conditions for African Americans.[114]

The Memphis CIC branch was one of the first in the South; it became the largest and one of the most active branches in the region. The white chamber of commerce supported the chapter's formation, and prominent black men and women made up its staff and membership, which grew to twelve hundred by 1926. Middle- and upper-class African Americans composed its executive committee, and women headed and served on committees. Much of the black community backed the branch, including pastors of all denominations, teachers from county and city schools, the Federation of Women's Clubs, hotel and railroad employees, social workers, and business and fraternal organizations. Through its programs, it reached some twenty-five thousand local citizens and supplemented the efforts of the Rosenwald Fund, the philanthropic organization that built schools in partnership with state and local governments by using funds raised by local African Americans. African Americans often petitioned their government officials to build these schools, and Shelby County had the largest number of Rosenwald schools in Tennessee. Manassas High School, the largest Rosenwald school in the world and part of the county school system until 1930, had a library, laboratories, and home economics resources owing to the fund-raising of its principal, Cora Taylor. In addition, the CIC chapter protested lynching and pushed for public improvements. It educated the *Commercial Appeal* editor about derogatory press coverage of African Americans and spurred the city administration to make improvements to black playgrounds and to construct five new school buildings and a high school. Black and white businesses and individuals, including Crump, financially contributed to the league's campaign to erect a wading pool for black children in Church's Park.[115]

Individual supporters of Church served on the chapter's executive committee, including his longtime political associate T. H. Hayes Sr. Yet his lieutenants criticized the organization for not pushing harder for racial advancement. Church and his associates engaged in partisan politics and spoke out against the Jim Crow system, but the Inter Racial League avoided partisan politics and pressed for improvements within segregated conditions. While the league received funding from whites intent on maintaining the Jim Crow system, Church and his lieutenants financed their own political efforts. His group especially clashed with two black ministers, T. O. Fuller and Sutton Griggs, who had helped organize the chapter and were the two most significant politically active ministers in Memphis. They had been two of the eighty-seven directors of the Lincoln League's campaign in 1916, and Fuller had been a charter member of the NAACP branch, but they had parted from Church and his group.[116]

The most prominent black minister in Memphis, T. O. Fuller acted as the Inter Racial League's president. Born in Franklinton, North Carolina, to former slaves in 1867, Fuller worked his way through Shaw University and joined the North Carolina State Senate in 1898 when conservative white Democrats gained control of the state government and staged a successful coup to overtake the municipal government of Wilmington, the state's largest city. In the riot that ensued, innocent African Americans were murdered and injured, a black newspaper office fell victim to arson, and many African Americans and whites were forced to leave the city, particularly successful black businessmen, black leaders openly opposed to white supremacy, and whites who received black voting support. As the only black member of the legislature, Fuller faced pressure from black leaders to advocate civil rights, but instead he pled for harmony and cooperation. He spoke out the next year against a proposed constitutional amendment to disenfranchise African Americans, but it was enacted in 1900, leading to his removal from office and to the end of black officeholding in the state. All these experiences undoubtedly shaped his worldview and help explain why as a leader he embraced an accommodationist stance rather than one of protest.[117]

In 1900, Fuller moved to Memphis to become the minister of the First Colored Baptist Church. One of the most highly educated black Memphians, he had received master of arts and doctorate of divinity degrees from Shaw, and Alabama's A&M College granted him an honorary doctorate of philosophy degree in 1906. A fervent advocate of black pride, he wrote books and articles on black history and life that praised black achievements, criticized slavery, and extolled black participation in Reconstruction. He was also the principal of the Howe Institute, which was established in 1888 as the Memphis Baptist and Normal Institute for West Tennessee Baptists. The institute offered an academic education as well as training and courses in music, industry, printing, domestic science, and clerical, ministerial, and missionary work. On the one hand, it fit within the industrial education movement that was promulgated by Booker T. Washington and other prominent African Americans across the turn-of-the-century South. On the other hand, it offered a broad, liberal arts education at a time when few schools in Memphis taught African Americans above the grammar school level and no local colleges existed for them. The Howe Institute was the most influential local educational organization for training black ministers. Fuller shrewdly emphasized its religious and vocational training and downplayed its academic side when publicizing the school.[118]

Fuller aimed to promote peaceful interracial relations throughout his career even if that meant acquiescing to segregated conditions. When the streetcar segregation law took effect in 1905, he pled for peace and cooperation instead of joining black Memphians protesting the measure; he believed that protests would result in strong white opposition.[119] In 1922, he gave a speech that echoed Booker T. Washington's Atlanta Exposition address, saying: "Let the races find a way to advance along separate and distinct parallel lines, each race reaching its highest possibilities and cooperating in matters that are mutually helpful."[120] Throughout his career, Fuller cultivated close relationships with Crump and Memphis mayors by campaigning for them and contacting them to secure benefits for African Americans such as improved job opportunities. In a letter to Crump, he said that he opposed Church's use of race-based bloc voting because political organization along racial lines inflamed white prejudice.[121]

The Reverend Sutton Griggs, a member of the executive committee of the Inter Racial League, started his career as a militant advocate of racial equality but came to embrace an accommodationist approach similar to Fuller's. Born in 1872 in Chatfield, Texas, to a former slave, Griggs graduated from Bishop College in Marshall, Texas, and Richmond Theological Seminary in Richmond, Virginia, before becoming the minister of Baptist churches in Berkeley, Virginia, and Nashville, Tennessee. One of the few southern pastors to join W. E. B. Du Bois's Niagara Movement, he wrote books promoting civil rights such as *The Hindered Hand* (1905),[122] which castigated lynching and white racism. By the time of his move to Memphis in 1913 to pastor the Tabernacle Baptist Church, he shifted to believing that appealing to whites and engaging in uplift efforts was the best strategy for racial advancement. He believed that African Americans needed to change behaviors that buttressed stereotypes detrimental to the race and that they could advance only with white support. Like many middle- and upper-class African Americans active in uplift efforts, he worked to equip African Americans with practical skills and instill them with virtues associated with the middle class. His church, for example, taught domestic science to help black women serve as better cooks for their white employers. His church also functioned as a community center, with a gym, an employment bureau, educational facilities, and a swimming pool to serve the social and educational needs of black Memphians.[123] Griggs believed that African Americans should not rely so heavily on the Republican Party or publicly criticize the white South. He saw the party's failure to do more for African Americans as a sign that it took their votes for granted; he believed that African Americans should make clear that they would not back the party if it did not support their interests. Although Griggs believed to some degree in black inferiority, his work to change the behaviors of African Americans represented an indirect attack on lynching by attempting to counteract stereotypes used to justify it. At a time when civil rights activists faced violent repudiation, this conservative strategy was less dangerous.[124]

In Memphis, Griggs put into practice his theory that cooperation with whites was essential to racial progress. Whites funded Griggs's publications and financially contributed to his church, and he campaigned for Crump during election time. In 1917, he organized the all-black Public Welfare League, an Urban League affiliate of which Fuller was a leader as well. Supported mainly by white philanthropists, the Urban League, formed six years earlier in New York City, focused on improving economic opportunities and living conditions for African Americans rather than on civil rights. Griggs reached thousands through his Public Welfare League pamphlets and books, which were distributed through churches, schools, and other black institutions. He used these publications to promote his theory that the black community must unite to engage in the moral development of its members before African Americans could advance as a race. In his book *Guide to Racial Greatness; or, The Science of Collective Efficiency* (1923), he enumerated thirty-three characteristics for African Americans to adopt to move forward, including courtesy, persistence, self-respect, and honesty. It is unclear to what degree black Memphians accepted his beliefs, but school principals did not adhere to his request to use his publications as textbooks, and Griggs admitted that whites backed his ministry more than African Americans. Some black Memphians viewed him as a traitor because of his flattery of whites.[125]

Church's group did not agree that blacks held responsibility for their own subordination and publicly spoke out against the Inter Racial League. After Memphis gained a reputation as the world's murder capital, the CIC chapter led a city-sanctioned campaign to decrease black crime.[126] Focusing on black behavior as the reason for crime, it called on blacks to stay away from "bad company," obey the law, avoid idleness, and abstain from alcohol and carrying dangerous weapons.[127] In response, Lieutenant Lee pointed out structural reasons for black violence, including that the city did not provide recreational facilities that might help deter black youths from crime. Church's associates also protested the league's successful campaign to get the city to change the name of Kortrecht High School to Booker T. Washington

High School. While white newspapers generally praised Griggs and Fuller and spotlighted their views, Lieutenant Lee and others succeeded in publicizing their own viewpoints. Bert Roddy, the long-standing Church associate, wrote a letter to the *News-Scimitar* that criticized Griggs, Fuller, and others who espoused their views. He accused them of duplicity, saying that they pandered to whites in the hope of receiving funds for their pet projects while they condemned white discrimination, prejudice, and violence to black audiences.[128]

More than any other group in Memphis, Church, Lee, and their associates represented the "New Negro" of the 1920s. Rejecting Booker T. Washington's philosophy of accommodation, the New Negro spoke out against racial violence and discrimination, assertively pressed for civil rights and better economic opportunities, and embraced the Harlem Renaissance, the outpouring of black culture in New York City that emphasized black history and pride. Church was recognized as a New Negro by other African Americans, including the labor leader and socialist A. Philip Randolph, who eventually became one of his closest friends and political associates. Randolph specifically pointed to Church's "matchless courage and inflexible determination" in opposing lily whites and dominating Republican politics in Memphis.[129] Lieutenant Lee called Church a "fearless champion of human rights" and a "new leader for a new day, whose ideas are in keeping with a new order."[130] While Fuller and Griggs embodied aspects of the New Negro, they also resembled the "Old Negro," who stressed the negative characteristics of African Americans and portrayed them as needing uplift.[131]

For all their differences, however, Church's group and the Inter Racial League shared much in common. In addition to calling for better public services and an end to lynching, they sought improved race relations, advocated racial pride and advancement, and worked with the city administration. Fuller used his publications to counteract ideas of black inferiority, and Lieutenant Lee thought that racial pride would lead African Americans to secure equal rights.[132]

In 1927, Church's group, Inter Racial League members, and thousands of black Memphians came together to make the most ambitious African American electoral effort in more than a decade. They were spurred to political activity after the city built an incinerator only two hundred yards away from the new Booker T. Washington High School building. Considering the action a grave insult, African Americans feared the facility's potentially negative effect on students. Black business leaders had unsuccessfully filed a lawsuit to stop the incinerator's construction. After Church called a mass meeting at Beale Avenue Baptist Church, leaders of nineteen ward organizations formed the West Tennessee Civic and Political League. Church was the league's central figure, Lieutenant Lee was its president, and its major figures included black professionals, ministers, and women's club leaders. Some members had been involved with the Lincoln League's effort in 1916.[133]

The West Tennessee Civic and Political League leaders and members had a number of goals, many of which forwarded the agenda of the Inter Racial League. They wanted African Americans to participate in municipal affairs and resist voter manipulation. Seeing Mayor Paine's administration as indifferent and hostile, they thought that the municipal government should devote more funds to improving public services; of the $3 million spent to improve the city, less than $500,000 had gone to black neighborhoods. The league called for street lighting and paving services, better pay for black schoolteachers, more playgrounds and parks, black admission to white parks, better hospital care for African Americans, and black police officers and firefighters. Except for the brief appointment of three black police officers in 1919 previously mentioned, none had served since 1895. No black firefighters had served since 1874.[134]

League members waged an intensive campaign to mobilize black Memphians. They held mass fund-raising meetings, and black leaders underwrote league expenses. While the *Memphis Triangle* urged registration, Roscoe Conkling Simmons returned to Memphis to speak at black political rallies, where Church and his associates gave speeches as well and "register, register, register" was the cry.[135] Black men and women from all walks of life joined the effort. "ALL Memphis entered the campaign, pew and pulpit, the learned and unlettered—the PEOPLE without distinction," the *Memphis Triangle* reported. "[They] joined the fight to re-enter THEIR government, write their names in the books of CITIZENSHIP, and help Memphis, the state of Tennessee, and COUNTRY to a better, a fairer day for all, whether Aryan or Ethiopian."[136]

That election season, Crump ran a ticket for public office. He enlisted Watkins Overton, a Memphis lawyer and state legislator, to oppose Mayor Paine in his reelection bid. Although Crump had supported Paine in 1923, Paine had not always followed his directives.

Crump had remained in the county trustee position through 1924 but then decided to focus on his insurance business, exercising political influence without occupying public office himself. In 1920, he had formed an insurance and brokerage firm, the E. H. Crump Company, which had become increasingly successful. He had also further turned his attention to state politics. Although his gubernatorial candidates of choice lost in the 1920s, he became one of the most influential politicians statewide, and he rallied Shelby County voters for office seekers on the state level.[137]

Crump developed a working relationship with Church's group for the 1927 election. Lee, the campaign manager for Overton's Beale Street office, would meet with Frank Rice, Crump's right-hand man. Feeling very secure about black support, Crump publicly boasted that the Overton ticket would receive 99.1 percent of the black vote.[138] His interactions with black supporters like Annie Brown surely bolstered his confidence. President of the City Federation of Colored Women's Clubs and a member of the Inter Racial League and the NAACP branch, Brown was a leader of the West Tennessee Civic and Political League and the chair of the black women's division of the Eleventh Ward. Informing Crump that she "heartily endorse[d] the Overton ticket," she wrote: "I know you are a friend to my race, and to me personally." In response, Crump thanked her for endorsing the Overton ticket, saying: "I know you are in a position to do a great deal of good."[139]

Overton courted the black vote in a number of ways. He implicitly included African Americans in his ticket's motto: "For All the People." Most significantly, he wrote the league's demands into his campaign platform. In a specific plank for African Americans, he called for adequate school facilities, better-paid teachers, more parks, playgrounds, and swimming pools, and improved health facilities and public services. The platform painted Paine as a double-crosser for not fulfilling his 1923 campaign promises to improve public services for African Americans, and it castigated him for building the incinerator. Overton secretly promised to appoint black firemen and policemen and grant African Americans admission to municipal parks. After a league member leaked the deal to the press, Crump called Lee to the courthouse basement for their first-ever political meeting.[140] Criticizing Lee for the disclosure, Crump said that he would have to deny the deal and that black police officers would have to wait. "All I can promise now is a chance to destroy your worst enemy," he said.[141] Overton then publicly denied the deal.

Overton's inclusion of the league's demands in his platform further revealed how African Americans exercised political leverage to shape government according to their needs. Black Memphians maneuvered to persuade Crump to give them better public provisions, taking advantage of his paternalistic governing style and desire for their ballots. Instead of yielding to his voter manipulation tactics, league leaders and members mobilized black Memphians into a powerful electoral force. At the same time that Crump and Overton responded to their concerns, they underscored the distinct limits of black political action in denouncing the deal for black police officers and firefighters and black admission to white parks. The inability of black activists to effectively protest Crump's public denials of the private promises further demonstrated barriers that they experienced in their political efforts.

The black political activists faced a racially hostile atmosphere in Memphis more broadly as well. The *Pittsburgh Courier* published a scathing article on the city during the election season. Observing that "Memphis [was] the gateway to the cotton belt, the center of many railroads, [and] the headquarters of many important business concerns," the paper said that "for all of its modernity . . . [it was] culturally barbarous" and "reflect[ed] all of the colorphobia of its next door neighbors . . . barbarous Arkansas and unspeakable Mississippi."[142] Like Crump, many white Memphians had Mississippi roots and hardened and paternalistic racial attitudes. Local police officers mainly hailed from the state and were known for their brutality, surely a reason why black Memphians pushed for black police officers.[143]

Unwilling to relent to this environment, black Memphians mobilized to the point that they made up some 40 percent of registered voters, causing Mayor Paine to become increasingly alarmed by their effort. He tried to interest Church in organizing a Republican ticket for the election. Local elections were nonpartisan, but Overton and Paine clearly were Democratic candidates. Paine thought that a Church-sponsored ticket would take votes of African Americans away from Overton. After this unsuccessful attempt, Paine resorted to more drastic tactics and appealed to white prejudice. His campaign published full-page newspaper ads opposing the black political movement and spotlighting Church as a "boss" who would rule local politics, pointing to his national influence and his ability to name the local postmaster and district attorney. Similarly, local newspapers warned that the league's campaign was part of a nationwide conspiracy for black equality.[144] At the Paine campaign headquarters, a large portrait of Church hung, underneath which were the words: "Will Southern white men and women allow this Negro man to name the Mayor of the great city of Memphis?"[145] African American leaders experienced threats of personal violence, and Paine supporters allegedly bombed a school where the Overton campaign was instructing black Memphians how to vote as well as Prospect Baptist Church on Beale Street when Church was speaking at a mass meeting there. No one was killed or, apparently, injured, but the blast damaged the church considerably and scared the crowd.[146]

Paine also issued a statement castigating Crump and Overton's overtures to African Americans and rejecting the West Tennessee Civic and Political League. He criticized politicians for manipulating black voting support for the 1926 state election, saying that they "paved the way for the situation now confronting the people of Memphis and constituting the greatest menace to white supremacy in this city since the reconstruction days." Declaring that there was "nothing to fear from votes of [the] class [of] intelligent law-abiding negroes," he said that office seekers could appeal for "the support of a negro who votes his own convictions." He opposed the "the recent appeals for racial solidarity and political mass action" that would give African Americans "the balance of power in [municipal] political affairs." He disapproved of the league's demands for black firefighters and policemen and park admission. Claiming that he had provided African Americans with better public services, he said that he had tried to treat them fairly and justly and pledged to continue to do so.[147] League members responded that "they were determined to show the city officials with the citizens' ballots that their demands were not idle jests, but declarations for their rights."[148]

Paine's statement revealed the balancing act that Memphis's white politicians engaged in as they tried both to appeal for the black vote and to adhere to the Jim Crow system. Paine gave typical white southern reasons for opposing black political activity—it threatened white control and superiority. Yet the mayor knew that black voters were an entrenched part of Memphis politics; he felt compelled to accept their voting rights and to ask for their support. As a result of his concerns, Paine released a nuanced campaign statement that spelled out what he thought was and was not proper black political activity. He accepted certain individual African Americans supporting white candidates but not African Americans mobilizing for political change. Crump and Overton engaged in this balancing act as well by making promises to and aligning with African Americans but then going back on their secret deal to avoid alienating white voters.

The Paine campaign's opposition made black Memphians more determined in their electoral effort. Surpassing the 1916 Lincoln League effort in the number of African Americans mobilized, the West Tennessee Civic and Political League reached a membership of some six thousand African Americans; more than twelve thousand African Americans registered to vote and paid their poll tax. Shortly before the election, the league accepted Church's recommendation to endorse Overton, although it initially did not plan to endorse either candidate. The official explanation was that Paine had attacked the league's platform, whereas Overton had agreed to most of its requests. Church also backed Overton because their families shared a longtime friendship.[149] Not all African Americans supported the league's endorsement or effort. Reverend Boyd, one of the league leaders, warned that endorsing any office seeker would be the equivalent of giving him "a whip by which to hit us back."[150] Griggs, a Paine supporter, accused the league of "laying the foundation of a race riot."[151]

The day before election day, the Paine campaign made a final appeal to white prejudice. Full-page ads appeared in the white press characterizing Church as "intoxicated with his success in matters of Federal patronage and aiming to become [the] real dictator in local politics." Paine further declared that victory for Overton would mean "that in the future candidates for office in this city, like applicants for Federal appointment, must see 'Bob' Church."[152]

On election day, some one hundred black women worked at the polls from 8:00 A.M. until 7:00 P.M. in an atmosphere that Lieutenant Lee called "tensely exciting."[153] With 80 percent of African Americans voting for his ticket, Overton won the election by thirteen thousand votes. Many black Memphians celebrated his election as a personal victory even though they had not technically held the balance of power.[154] Declaring that the city "underwent the greatest civic and political campaign in its history," the *Memphis Triangle* said: "The response of the people to the West Tennessee Civic and Political League took us back forty years, back to the days when freedmen cherished freedom. Sons and daughters of freedmen . . . heard, many for the first time, of lost power, and of the ballot, the only bloodless weapon of liberty." It reported that thousands saw Church as the "gallant and bravest figure of the New Day."[155] After the election, black leaders declared that they and black citizens would "seek more ardently in the future to secure their full citizenship rights, and especially assert themselves at the polls."[156]

With almost every major black newspaper carrying the election results, the league's success won the praise of African Americans from afar.[157] The *New York Amsterdam News* called the victory significant for "knock[ing] to pieces the argument made by southern advocates of disfranchisement that the Southern Negroes do not really want to vote."[158] In a roundup of the recent elections throughout the country, the *Pittsburgh Courier* called the campaign in Memphis the "greatest victory" achieved by African Americans.[159] Noting that a "voteless man is voiceless in a democratic republic," the *Houston Informer* expressed hope that "the example set by 'Bob' Church and the Negroes of Memphis, Tennessee, who organized their forces, put up their own money and waged their own campaign for the successful mayoral candidate . . . will have a salutary effect upon Negro leaders and followers in . . . the South." Declaring that the election signified a "new day" in the South, it said that "the race's political salvation could be worked out right in the heart of the South" if more men like Church existed. The paper commended the city's white citizens by pointing out that Paine's appeals to white prejudice had not led to his victory and by praising Overton for openly seeking black votes.[160]

Despite its victory at the polls, the West Tennessee Civic and Political League immediately faced problems. After the election, the organization was forced to disband because of a lack of funds and patronage. As was the case elsewhere in the South, most African Americans were poor and could not fund ongoing political efforts. The collapse of the one remaining black bank further contributed to the league's decline. Beset by financial troubles, the Solvent Savings Bank and the Fraternal Savings Bank, the two black banks in Memphis, had merged to survive in 1927; the new bank was called Fraternal and Solvent Savings Bank. Church had given up his presidency of and professional association with Solvent Savings Bank earlier in the decade and was not connected with these financial problems. He tried to assist the new bank by depositing and raising money, but his efforts were not enough: by the end of 1927, state bank examiners took over the institution. Black businessmen, who had led and funded political efforts, could no longer do so to the same extent as a result of this blow to their livelihoods.[161]

The league saw limits to its political approach as well. Although black Memphians helped kick Paine out of office, they bolstered Crump's control. Crump's overtures to African Americans did not erase his record of illegal activity and voter manipulation. Memphis had reportedly provided better public services to African Americans than cities elsewhere in the South, but Crump and the city officials who granted these provisions exhibited a "plantation mentality" that constructed African Americans as dependent and inferior and perpetuated the construction of whites as superior. By supporting Overton's ticket, African Americans helped elect Cliff Davis, the only successful candidate on the Klan slate in 1923, as vice mayor.

Nonetheless, the 1927 effort served as a fitting culmination of the victories experienced by Church and black Memphians over the past ten years. In his leadership roles in the NAACP and the Lincoln League, Church mobilized thousands of black Memphians for political action and civil rights. In Republican Party circles, he served as a voice for racial advancement. His political successes inspired young black Memphians at a time when society deemed them inferior. African Americans outside Memphis saw the Lincoln League as a model for political activity and led Church to form the Lincoln League of America. Black Memphians joined him in participating in the national organization, which opened more doors for black political involvement. As with the local Lincoln League, African Americans used the national Lincoln League to publicly denounce the Jim Crow system and lynching; these activists represented an important and courageous voice of protest. Church used his national leverage to secure more black political appointments, appoint fair-minded whites to political posts, and provide local African Americans with civil service positions. A vital force against lily whitism, he and his associates helped keep alive a racially progressive strain in the Republican Party.

Locally, black Memphians differed in their political philosophies, but they shared a dedication to racial advancement and worked through the Inter Racial League and political and community organizations for this purpose. They played a key role in the decline of the Ku Klux Klan by mobilizing to defeat most of its slate in 1923. Through their work

in the Inter Racial League, they successfully pressed the local government for public service improvements and engaged in uplift efforts.
The 1927 campaign demonstrated the commonality and interlock-
ing nature of the various strategies and goals of black Memphians by
bringing together members of Church's faction and the Inter Racial
League. They succeeded in their most massive political mobilization
ever by helping elect the candidate who wrote their demands into his
platform and by helping depose the candidate who had disappointed
them.

In the end, Church, black Memphians, and those black southerners who politically mobilized elsewhere knew that disenfranchisement,
segregation, and other racial injustices weakened the United States.
They desired to better the lives of African Americans and the country
as a whole. Influenced by World War I, they wanted to make their own
country safe for democracy.

3 "Come . . . and See What a Negro Democrat Looks Like"

The Diversity of Black Political Activity, 1928–1939

The years from 1928 to 1939 brought new political challenges for black Memphians. The Republican Party became less attuned to African American concerns with Herbert Hoover's election to the presidency in 1928. Edward H. Crump, who became more powerful locally as a result of the 1927 election, saw Franklin D. Roosevelt's election to the presidency in 1932 solidify his control. He held greater national influence than he had when Republicans occupied the White House and cracked down on Memphians who challenged his power. In addition, Memphians faced the blow of the Great Depression. Despite all these difficulties, black Memphians engaged in a variety of electoral activities. While some found it beneficial to work with the Crump machine, others protested it. Church's black-and-tan faction remained the most powerful local Republican group, and Church continued to be an influential Republican figure nationally. Rivaling Church in power, the businessman J. E. Walker emerged as the city's most prominent black Democrat. The local NAACP chapter pushed for racial justice, and a powerful, biracial labor movement emerged in Memphis and the region. In all these ways, black Memphians worked to make democracy real in their city, the South, and the country.

The 1927 election had led to the consolidation of the Crump machine. That machine now encompassed both the county and the city, and no political rivals challenged Crump's power. Crump ran Memphis from behind the scenes, installing his followers as mayors, approving all officeholders, and even handpicking the heads of white civic organizations. Crump apparently worked with Church to support city, county, and state candidates, although Church's daughter, Roberta Church, and two historians later contended that they just happened to back the same people. Political observers of the time, however, pointed out or charged that Crump and Church had an alliance. The *Memphis Triangle,* for example, reported that Church lined up twelve thousand African Americans in the Shelby County primary election for Crump's gubernatorial endorsee in 1928. Moreover, Lieutenant George W. Lee later supported the contention that an alliance existed. After collaborating with Crump's lieutenant Frank Rice during the 1927 campaign, Lee continued to see Rice as Church's political liaison to the Crump organization. According to Lee, Church ensured that a congressional committee investigating fraudulent elections did not take steps to prosecute the Crump machine, and in return the city did not charge Church property taxes.[1]

Church's partnership with Crump came at a time when the collapse of the black bank hurt black political efforts. Some twenty-eight thousand depositors saw more than 90 percent of their savings wiped out, and more than fifty black-owned businesses suffered major losses. The bank's troubles had resulted from bad loans, a shortage of funds, and criminal activity. Six black officials received jail sentences, including Church's political associate T. H. Hayes Sr. Wayman Wilkerson, the political lieutenant of Church and a business leader affected by these developments, committed suicide. Some white Memphians, to no avail, tried to connect Church to the scandal. Although the bank personnel were guilty, an anonymous pamphlet released by a Beale Street publishing company accused white businessmen of encouraging black businessmen in unwise activities and white bank examiners of negligence in carrying out their duties.[2] After the bank closed, Mrs. Wayman Wilkerson, the local NAACP president, wrote the national office: "Everything possible is being done to intimidate the colored people. For that reason we are being as quiet as possible." With the business and professional class no longer able to financially support the NAACP, the branch lost funds and ceased activity for two years.[3]

Black Memphians benefited from aligning with Crump in a number of ways. Although it is unclear how many viewed him positively, the local black journalist Nat D. Williams later contended: "Mr. Crump had the admiration and respect of most Negroes . . . because he did things for Negroes nobody had done before."[4] Those who backed him considered him a "benevolent dictator"; Lieutenant Lee shared this view.[5] Writing about the Watkins Overton administration, Lee said: "I have seen parks and playgrounds spring up in densely populated Colored sections where Negro children lived in two room shanties without . . . places to jump the rope. . . . I have seen muddy . . . streets that marked the section in which my people lived, beautified, paved and made passable."[6] These public service improvements revealed that Overton had fulfilled some of his 1927 campaign promises to African Americans. After the election, African American leaders detected a "favorable change in the attitude of white administrators towards the Negro population," according to Walter P. Adkins in his 1935 master's thesis on Beale Street politics. "[They] discern[ed] an attitude of cautious solicitation . . . despite their refusal to commit themselves to those larger demands of the colored constituency."[7]

The Crump machine appeared racially progressive in other ways as well. The police protected black Republicans in their battles with lily whites. Church, for example, could call the police if lily whites locked them out of official Republican meetings. Crump refrained from race baiting, which was prevalent among southern politicians. Furthermore, black Memphians could contact city administrators or Crump directly to ask for and secure benefits such as city jobs.[8] Other black Memphians went through Church and his lieutenants when they sought assistance from the machine. Whereas local government officials elsewhere in the South might have been repelled by these communications or concerned about the effect on their image, this was not the case in Memphis and Shelby County.[9]

While Church benefited from his ties to Crump, Crump benefited from an alliance with Church: Church could deliver votes for his candidates and provide him with important national connections. As long as Republicans occupied the White House, Crump saw limits to his power. In 1930, he was elected to the House of Representatives. But, as a Democrat, he remained a member of the minority party. By working with Church, the most powerful Republican in West Tennessee, he bolstered his influence in national politics. According to Lieutenant Lee, Crump and black Republicans collaborated because "he needed us on the national scene; we needed him on the local scene."[10] African Americans distributed the patronage that Crump wanted for his white supporters; he did not want local political appointees to interfere with his organization. Elsewhere in the South, black Republican leaders occasionally could trade political appointments for a degree of influence with white Democratic politicians who wanted their officials or allies in these positions.[11]

Even those black Memphians involved with Crump's voter manipulation schemes could sometimes work the system to their own benefit. "People were only making fourteen to seventeen cents an hour, until [Roosevelt] brought in the minimum wage of thirty-five cents an hour," recalled George Holloway, a black union activist who grew up in the city during this time. "A lot of blacks were paid to get [poll tax] receipts, and since they didn't have jobs, they'd marked the ballot the way they were told, to earn some money."[12] To maximize the monetary rewards, some African Americans cast votes at least four times on election day, showing up at different polling places and disguising themselves in different clothes. Crump used underworld figures to manipulate African American support, and African Americans used him to serve their ends. By maintaining a partnership with the machine, black bootleggers and gambling and brothel proprietors could continue their operations.[13]

Some black ministers used their authority to persuade their parishioners to support Crump or otherwise work for the machine during election time. Memphis had a vibrant church culture, with the black church playing a major role in the black community. Most black churchgoers belonged to Baptist churches and then the Methodist and Church of God in Christ denominations. By 1924, 107 black churches existed in Memphis. The Church of God in Christ was headquartered in Memphis and became an international presence by the 1930s. Whereas this denomination and shouting Baptist churches attracted the poor and uneducated masses, Methodist congregations consisted of the poor and the middle class. Other Baptist churches varied in class status according to congregation.[14] George Holloway recalled: "A lot of black preachers went along with Crump. They would persuade people to do what Crump asked. The church was the big philosopher who told people what to do."[15] The Reverend A. D. Bell, the pastor of Mount Moriah Baptist Church, for instance, assisted the machine by distributing watermelons to black Memphians as an incentive to vote the Crump ticket.[16]

Through mobilizing votes for Crump, black ministers could receive benefits from the machine, including securing teaching contracts for their parishioners and the release of African Americans from jail. They could borrow money for church improvements or receive charitable donations from Crump himself. Many black pastors held outside jobs, where they were dependent on white employers, because the ministry did not pay them enough.[17] Others had wives who worked in the school system and, thus, opposing Crump or not publicly supporting him could mean that their wives might lose their jobs. "Therefore, it was not too difficult [to] . . . put pressure on these people to come out and praise Mr. Crump and be advocates of the local Democratic point of view," Roberta Church later said. "I understand that they were forced to write letters to newspapers here in Memphis and praise him and do other things that were done under pressure. I think that was just a situation in which they found themselves helpless on the account of the economics involved."[18]

Although some black ministers played a subservient role in the Crump machine, most stayed out of politics. Like most black ministers in the South, black pastors in Memphis, most of whom lacked formal training or higher education, generally focused on otherworldly concerns and not political or social activism. In the 1970s, Randolph Meade Walker conducted interviews with black ministers across the sociopolitical spectrum for his study of the role of the black clergy during the Crump era. According to him, the Church of God in Christ was particularly otherworldly minded and never a major force in local politics.[19] "They said in those days, stay in your place," the Reverend Calvin Mims, a Baptist minister, told Walker. "If you could stay in your place as a Negro Preacher here, why you could have it very fine, very good. That is, don't bother with no politics, don't bother with the status quo, just preach and shout the folks and you'd get a good congregation." The Reverend A. E. Campbell, a Baptist minister who backed Crump, added that it was best to stay out of politics if you did not support Crump.[20] Ralph Bunche, in his 1930s study of the political status of African Americans, wrote: "Negro preachers of Memphis as a whole have avoided social questions. They have preached thunder and lightning, fire and brimstone, . . . but about the economic and political exploitation of the Negro in Memphis they have remained silent."[21] "Accepting the political tactic of accommodation and compromise did not mean that a pastor had repudiated this world and become altogether otherworldly," however, as the historian David M. Tucker points out.[22] Similarly, Walker noted: "Complacency among the clergy . . . did not mean that most of the clergy actively supported Crump, but simply that most of them allowed the 'machine' to have its way."[23]

Yet ministers had more of a political role during the Crump era than scholars have suggested. Not all ministers and churches shied away from politics as a tool to better social conditions, as in the cases of the Reverends T. O. Fuller and W. Herbert Brewster. Some opened their churches to voter education schools during the 1916 Lincoln League effort and made speeches endorsing it. The meeting to organize the West Tennessee Civic and Political League in 1927 was held at the Beale Avenue Baptist Church. During the 1927 campaign, the Prospect Baptist Church was bombed when Bob Church was speaking at a mass meeting there.[24] The black church and black ministers continued to play an important role in politics in the 1930s.

It appears that most African Americans engaged or did not engage in political activities of their own free will, although some fell victim to Crump's manipulation.[25] Some shrewdly backed the machine, while others signaled their opposition to it by voting only in the Republican primary. Yet others, including black ministers, steered clear of manipulative tactics by silently abstaining from voting.[26] According to the Memphis NAACP official Florence McCleave, many African Americans registered "to keep their vote from being stolen, but [did] not vote."[27] Dr. R. Q. Venson, a black community leader, dentist, and World War I veteran, said: "The majority of self-respecting Negroes in Memphis . . . pay their poll tax and vote their own convictions."[28] The scholar Paul Lewinson observed that black voting in Memphis occurred more as a result of state political conditions and skilled black leadership than manipulation.[29] Tennessee never did enact a statewide white primary or disenfranchisement measures that could not be surmounted. A degree of political competition existed statewide that was conducive to black voting, and the Republican Party in Tennessee depended on African Americans to maintain its strength. To be sure, not just black leaders but also ordinary African Americans who registered and cast ballots accounted for black voting.

Marie Fort, a black Memphian born in the city in 1904, resisted Crump's voter manipulation schemes. She recalled: "[Crump's operatives] would come around with cars and pick up a lot of people and take them to different polls. They would vote at every poll." She continued: "Then they would take them to a house right back here . . . and would make spaghetti in big tubs and they would serve spaghetti and whisky." When they came by one day and asked her whether she was going to vote, she said: "No." They asked why not. She said:

"You won't ever vote me. I am going to be my own woman." When her husband's employer, working on behalf of the machine, tried to put whisky in their barn, she told him: "The day you put whisky in my barn is the day that I am going to put a pistol in your mouth. I am not going to disrespect my race, my neighbors, my children with your whisky." As a result, he threatened to fire her husband. Fort replied: "Go on and fire him. He'll get another job." And, when her husband was fired, she secured her husband a job at the railroad through her connections.[30]

Crump needed the black vote to increase and maintain his influence in local and state politics. Luke Lea of Nashville acted as the undisputed boss of state politics until 1930, when he was jailed for corruption. Crump then emerged as the boss of Tennessee politics, a position that he would hold for the next eighteen years. It became impossible to win the governor's race without his support. Memphis's position as the state's chief commercial center increased its power on the state political scene as well. Tennessee historically had a strong Republican presence in East Tennessee, but Republicans typically ran only nominal candidates for the governorship in light of the Democrats' monopoly of this office. Because Crump faced Democratic Party factionalism, he benefited from securing African American voting support. The Memphis returns came in last in state elections, so he and his cronies knew how many votes their candidates needed to win. Crump fraudulently held some black votes in suspension and used these ballots to tip the balance if necessary.[31]

The Crump organization had two main areas of voting strength: the Democratic counties of West Tennessee and the Republican counties of East Tennessee. Although Crump wielded substantial influence in Middle Tennessee, a rivalry existed between Middle Tennessee and West Tennessee. Nashville politicians resented Crump's influence, including his ability to determine the governorship. In contrast, a power-sharing situation occurred between West Tennessee and East Tennessee. The Crump Democrats respected the Republicans' control of local offices in East Tennessee, while the East Tennessee Republicans respected the Democrats' domination of statewide offices. It was widely believed that the Crump Democrats, the East Tennessee Republicans, and the East Tennessee Democrats all worked together: East Tennessee Democrats supported Republican candidates locally, and East Tennessee Republicans voted for Crump's candidates for statewide office in the Democratic primaries. Rumors spread that Crump ensured that East Tennessee Republicans received patronage during Democratic administrations; this gossip made Middle Tennessee politicians more resentful of Crump.[32]

Because Church headed the state Republican organization along with the East Tennessee Republican congressman J. Will Taylor, the alliance between Crump and Republicans on the state level further indicates that Church worked with Crump. A July 1930 political cartoon in a Chattanooga newspaper pictured Taylor, Church, Luke Lea, Crump, and Henry Horton, the Democratic governor running for reelection, in bed together, calling them "strange bedfellows." Lea and Crump had politically collaborated before Lea's imprisonment.[33] By bolstering Crump's control through their votes, however, Church and other black Memphians arguably did more for Crump and his endorsees than they did for African Americans. Facing the Jim Crow system, the black bank's collapse, and the Great Depression, black Memphians were faced with a dilemma: should they support Crump even with the negative aspects of his machine and see benefits firsthand in their lives, or should they fight his machine and most likely lose those benefits? They chose the former course of action, albeit at an unforeseen cost.

One of the few public voices against Crump was R. E. Johnson, a white Democrat, Mississippi native, and Memphis citizen since 1910. An engineer and construction contractor by trade, he held local and state positions at various times. To protest Crump, whom he called "the Red Headed Monster," he founded the Loyal Tennesseans League and contacted national and state politicians, journalists, and the political boss himself. Johnson, who was not financially well off, experienced physical attacks and economic repercussions from the machine for his whistle-blowing. Shortly before the August 1932 election, he published *Edward H. Crump: Public Enemy No. 1.* A takeoff on the popular 1931 gangster movie *Public Enemy,* the witty, well-researched, and astute booklet described Crump and his cronies as gangsters in an attempt to convince white Tennesseans to elect state officials not beholden to Crump. Johnson castigated Crump for manipulating the black vote, attacking white opponents, and partnering with vice.[34]

Johnson called Crump egotistical, a characteristic that he used to illuminate the boss's political operations. Johnson quoted a profile of Crump in the *Albany (NY) Evening News* that the boss "proudly showed to his friends" and had reprinted in the *Memphis Press-Scimitar*. In the article, a white Memphian said, "Why, we have a mayor now—his name is Watkins Overton. Well, he's a good man. Smart, honest, capable. But nobody is fooled about him. . . . [E]verybody knows Crump is really mayor." The white Memphian observed that Crump was "an organizing fool." "He's the greatest organizer you ever heard of," he said. "He's not so handsome and he's never made a speech in his life, but just let him stay in the House of Representatives two or three years and you will find those Democrats taking orders from him!" Reporting that a portrait of Napoleon hung in Crump's business office in Memphis, Johnson wrote: "In Crump the Napoleonic complex burns with lambent flame."[35]

Arguing that an honest election had never occurred in either the city or the county in his twenty years as a legal voter in the area, Johnson accused the Crump machine of burning ballots in the courthouse basement in order to cover up evidence of election fraud. He wrote: "Ribald observers of Memphis politics watch the smoke from the chimney of the court house; when smoke rises Crump has won another 'victory'—and destroyed the evidence!" The courthouse custodian, Joe Boyle, admitted to burning ballots, claiming he did so to make more room in the basement.[36] "Stories of ballot-box stuffing, boxes stolen from the court-house cellar, herding, and bribery, fill the air," reported Walter Adkins a few years later. "No determined or effective effort is ever made to fight these charges in court, or before the Democratic state executive committee."[37]

Johnson further called on white citizens to mobilize against Crump because of his use of the black vote; he quoted prominent white Memphians concerned about its potential impact. "It is only a matter of time until the negroes, now comprising almost half of the total registration of the county, demand representation in the legislature and county [commission]," he wrote. "Already they are talking [about] such representation at Orange Mound, a Crump controlled suburb."[38] Rembert Moon, an anti-Crump member of the Shelby County Election Commission, called black voter manipulation a "menace to the white social system in the South."[39] Despite Johnson's battle against the machine, Crump's candidates won in 1932. It appears that Johnson's opposition had little impact.

While Johnson campaigned against the machine, Church was fighting a new battle to secure his place in the Republican Party. In

1928, local lily whites attempted to have him indicted on trumped-up charges of graft relating to post office appointments.[40] In response to the allegations, the Reverend S. A. Owen, the head of the elite Metropolitan Baptist Church and one of the most prominent and scholarly black ministers in Memphis, wrote Church: "Truly we are proud of you and of the heroic accomplishments to your credit. We believe in you now and the unsullied integrity you have sustained through all of the intricate and delicate experiences of the past." He continued: "Many of the citizens of Memphis are willing to be directed by your wise counsel and stand ready to champion your cause when unfortunately the fight centers on you. We remember that your defeat means the ultimate annihilation of the rights and privileges of a great host of people."[41] The first black female high school principal in Memphis, Cora P. Taylor, the head of Manassas High School and a well-respected community leader, wrote Church that she and the entire faculty were holding him "up as a spokesman and martyr" to hundreds of students and their families. "Should the time ever come when you have a message to send or when you should need to rally this Section, for any purposes, I can assure you of a hearty response," she said.[42] Further backing Church was Congressman J. Will Taylor, who said that "not one word of truth" existed in the charges.[43] Church was exonerated of the graft charges the next year.

Lily whites kept up their attack on Church during the election season, as did the white newspapers and Clarence Saunders, the founder of the grocery store Piggly Wiggly and one of the few local political opponents of Crump. For the primary, two male and two female lily whites formed a ticket to oppose Church and three whites who ran as a slate for the state Republican Executive Committee. Calling Church a "menace" and a Democrat, the lily whites distributed campaign literature saying that he "must be eliminated from domination of the Republican Party in Shelby County" and that the "pernicious influence of the negro" had an "injurious effect on the *whole* community."[44] The *Memphis Evening Appeal* accused Church of having a machine, while white newspapers across the state proclaimed that white supremacy was threatened by the possibility of African Americans holding the balance of power in the Democratic primary. Saunders took out full-page advertisements in the *Commercial Appeal* attacking the Church-Crump alliance.[45] Calling Crump "a traitor to the race," he said that the "stench" of the Crump-Church partnership was "enough to stop every decent man's nose in Tennessee from taking a single breath."[46] Nevertheless, Church's ticket won by a ten-to-one margin, with Church receiving twenty-eight hundred votes as opposed to his opponent's two hundred.[47]

The *Commercial Appeal* took a different approach to battling black political mobilization that election season: it launched a crusade to exclude African Americans from the Democratic primary. At the same time, it decried the attempt of local whites to challenge Church's power.[48] "It is one of the traditions of the South that the Democratic party is the white man's party and the Republican party is the Negro party," the paper editorialized. "To exclude the negro from the Republican party . . . would deprive him of his natural party affiliation and of the right of franchise." Calling Church an undisputed leader of the Republican Party, the paper said: "His work is done in his Beale Street office in Memphis and in the White House in Washington." It continued: "No federal appointment is made in Memphis or Shelby County under a Republican administration without his endorsement. Federal office-holders and applicants for federal favor not only admit his authority, but seek his favor. . . . His influence in the Republican party is more extensive in the south than any other man white or black."[49]

On the one hand, the editorial provided an important recognition of Church's leadership. The newspaper's acceptance of his leadership, even over whites, revealed that Church and other black Republicans could counteract prevailing stereotypes of black inferiority through occupying positions of power within the party. On the other hand, the *Chicago Defender* warned: "Don't take the Memphis Commercial Appeal too seriously. . . . [It] cares nothing for Bob Church, for Mr. Church is not of the race to which the [paper] caters." It continued: "Whom is this paper kidding when it starts out to champion you and your rights to vote?"[50] The *Pittsburgh Courier* called the editorial "vicious," saying: "To exclude the Negro from participation in the Democratic primary in Tennessee or anywhere else in the South is to exclude him from participation in the government of which he forms a part."[51] Indeed, the *Commercial Appeal* promoted a segregated party system, with African Americans occupying the less powerful party. Black Republicans controlled patronage, secured some political rewards, and held some party leadership positions, but white Democrats remained in charge locally and regionally.

National developments occurring in the Republican Party energized the local lily-white opposition to Church. During his presidential campaign, Herbert Hoover was determined to make inroads among white southerners in order to build up the party in the region. He supported a reform program that would ensure that southern party organizations consisted of elite, honest leadership. While Hoover generally has been portrayed as a bigot determined to strip the black and tans of their power and, instead, make the party lily white, his plans were more complicated in reality. Southern party organizations had a reputation for corrupt leadership. Officials abused patronage privileges by selling federal jobs, and there were perennial charges, apparently true, that Republican presidential hopefuls from McKinley forward bought the support of southern delegates in order to ensure their nomination as the party's candidate. Hoover hoped to attract elite white leaders to take over corrupt party organizations. Like other Republican politicians, he knew that the party's acceptance of black leaders and members drove many whites away. Although he thought that honest black leaders and members should remain in the party, he did not publicize these intentions. As a result, his reform program took on the cast of lily whitism, compounded by the fact that his southern campaign officials erroneously declared that he promoted a whites-only party in the region.[52]

At the Republican national convention in June, Church and his fellow black delegates pushed the party for planks in its platform supporting the enforcement of the Fourteenth and Fifteenth Amendments, the enactment of antilynching legislation, the prohibition of discriminatory civil service hiring, and the disavowal of lily whitism, but the platform called only for antilynching legislation. Further raising suspicions among African Americans about Hoover's intentions toward them, the convention's credentials committee seated only delegations that supported Hoover, resulting in the seating of Church's faction and black-and-tan groups from Mississippi and Georgia but not black-and-tan factions from other southern states. Hoover's campaign officials appointed black professionals who had little political experience to head the advisory committee devoted to securing black votes for the party. College-educated and businessmen or university administrators, they had no political power base of their own and did not run for office or get out the vote, although they were committed to securing equal rights and working through the party for this goal. Of an older generation, they embraced Booker T. Washington's approach of advocating racial advancement through educational and economic means.[53]

Church was a member of the other major faction of black Republicans, the professional politicians. This group was diverse, unorganized, and actively participated in politics, although some of the leaders faced criticism from other African Americans for not attacking disenfranchisement in or politically mobilizing their communities but instead focusing on rounding up southern delegates for presidential nominees and dispensing patronage. Church was the most widely respected leader of this group. African Americans nationwide praised him as a bold, skilled, and militant leader who was committed to racial advancement and had successfully mobilized African Americans in Memphis.[54]

Because Church disagreed with the Hoover campaign's selection of the black professionals for the advisory committee, he refused to accept his appointment to the body. In a public protest to the campaign, he said that the black professionals could not effectively represent African Americans or their issues because they lacked political experience and political standing in their communities. He asked Hoover to restructure the committee's leadership, but the candidate refused. Church's protest led to criticism from black politicians who accused him of not joining the committee not because of his expressed reasons but because he was not chosen to head the group. Some thought that he was upset that the men on the committee had ideas that were counter to his way of thinking.[55] "Mr. Church says he is trying to help Mr. Hoover's cause and that of the Republican Party," Emmett Scott, a member of the committee, remarked. "His actions, however, suggest that he is laboring under hallucinations of super perpetual grandeur and self-exaltation in his all-too-apparent attempt to destroy party harmony."[56]

Church considered the 1928 campaign the bitterest one in his memory. Not only did black Republicans fight among themselves, but also the Hoover campaign and that of the Democratic candidate, Al Smith, engaged in race baiting in an effort to attract white support. Church initially did not endorse Hoover and hardly campaigned for him. Although Hoover desired to remain distant from African Americans during the campaign, he could not afford to ignore Church's influence or to lose his support. He called Church to Washington, DC, for a personal meeting and heard his grievances against lily whites. He assured Church that his administration would respect black leadership and concerns and that white and black Republican leaders would work together in the South. He said that his southern campaign manager, Horace Mann, had misled southerners in thinking that Hoover promoted lily whitism.[57]

As a result of Hoover's courting, Church supported the candidate fervently in the last days of the campaign. According to *Time* magazine, all but six of the leading twenty-five black newspapers supported Al Smith, but "most of the rebellious journals, at Church's command, changed front and Hooverized vociferously" during the last week of the campaign.[58] Three days before the election, the *Chicago Defender* published an open letter by Church backing Hoover, which by no means was a wholehearted endorsement. Church acknowledged that countless African Americans had asked him, "Why, if things are as they seem to be, do you support Hoover for president?" He said that they had "every right to halt and question" him and that he had "neither fault to find [with] nor criticism to bestow" on those leaving the Republican Party. Admitting his confusion about the "undeserved indifference of the party of our love and hope," he made clear that he did not "wish the ascendancy of the Republican party as we have it now." Expressing his belief that Republican black leadership would not be destroyed, Church framed the election as a choice between two bad options: "The Republican party offers us little. The Democratic party offers us nothing." He said that he chose the Republican Party "because its history is a better assurance of justice to us, while the history of the Democratic party is a guaranty of injustice to all of us." "If I err, I err in thoughts of you," he said about his decision. "Long have I waged war in your name and for our children. . . . I have known deadly and unrelenting fire. I have fled from no battle. . . . My contests have been waged with a support from people among whom I was born and as loyal as man ever knew in any cause."[59]

When election day arrived, Hoover swept Tennessee and four other southern states in his successful bid. Oscar DePriest of Chicago, a former member of the Lincoln League of America, was elected as the first black congressman since the turn of the century; he became a leading spokesperson for civil rights in the House of Representatives.[60] In Shelby County, Hoover captured the black vote, while Smith received the white vote. Although Hoover had tried distancing himself from black voters, he had needed to cultivate their support; this strategy alienated whites, as he had feared. Many local whites feared any kind of alliance between African Americans and national political figures. They thought that it would lead to "negro bossism" in West Tennessee, resulting in the everlasting "humiliation of the white man," and that a Republican administration would place African Americans in positions of political power, primarily postmasterships, over whites. They assumed that Church would be rewarded for his campaign work by becoming the local postmaster.[61]

One day after the election, Church sent Hoover a telegram. Pointing out that most African Americans had voted for him, he called on the president-elect to promote peace, freedom, and justice "for a people . . . who are still in bondage."[62] Shortly after meeting with Church in March, Hoover fired Horace Mann, who had promoted lily whitism in the South, as a party official. Black newspapers credited Church with his dismissal, and it appears that he had an impact.[63] Observing that Church exerted enough influence over black voters in eight states that he could hold the balance of power in a presidential election, the *New York Amsterdam News* said that Hoover granted his request because "the complete espousal of the 'lily white' policy by the Republican party might easily alienate this vote without gaining enough Southern white votes to offset its loss."[64]

But Hoover remained committed to bolstering southern white leadership in hopes of a stronger Republican Party in the region. He sanctioned the removal of blacks from leadership positions nearly everywhere in the South in the name of reform.[65] The president worked to replace allegedly corrupt white leadership as well, but Kelly Miller, a nationally syndicated political columnist, African American intellectual, and Howard University professor, observed: "[His southern policy is] ostensibly based on corruption and political scandal, which in the last analysis is laid at the door of the Negro race and is calculated to damn the Negro to everlasting infamy. Practically every white leader in the South has or does lie under allegation. The Negro is made to bear the chief brunt of the stigma."[66] Miller also noted that the "simple fact that Mr. Hoover does not pose for photographers with Negro delegations, as Mr. Coolidge was wont to do, may be suggestive and significant."[67]

Church protested Hoover's reform program. In April, he sent members of Congress a series of editorials rebuking Hoover for his perceived policy to create an all-white Republican leadership in the South.[68] In an eloquent four-page letter to Hoover exactly one year after his election, Church reported the "grievous disappointment" of African Americans, reminding the president that they had helped elect him. He expressed dismay that, unlike his Republican and Democratic predecessors, Hoover had made no black political appointments. "When a Republican president disregards both our citizenship and our party regularity and joins the cry of 'Down with the Negro,' we have a spectacle that calls for tears," he wrote. The continuation of the present policy would "leave the Republican party a wreck upon the shores of the political ocean, but a memory to those who once loved it." He concluded that he was willing to talk to Hoover any time.[69] Church's impassioned plea apparently had little overall impact on Hoover, although, working behind the scenes, the president ensured that Church was not stripped of his party leadership positions in Tennessee. An honest politician, Church represented the type of leader that Hoover was trying to cultivate, and the president personally liked and respected him. Church, who did not know of Hoover's work on his behalf, remained disillusioned.[70]

In Tennessee, Church supported the Democratic candidate in the 1930 gubernatorial race over C. Arthur Bruce, a prominent lily white in Memphis who ran as the Republican. Members of the defunct Ku Klux Klan campaigned for Bruce, he never appeared before black voters, and he unsuccessfully attempted to persuade Church to secure him campaign money from the Republican National Committee. He turned down an invitation to speak before the Baptist Pastors Association, composed of some two hundred pastors of black churches in West Tennessee. Receiving some 100,000 fewer votes than Hoover had in 1928, Bruce was defeated by nearly 70,000 votes. High-ranking Democrats attributed his loss to his failure to follow Church's advice to campaign for black support; other leaders of the state's regular party organization had urged him to do so as well.[71]

Locally, Church saw Memphis provide its black citizens with an important cultural recognition by naming a new municipal park on Beale Street after W. C. Handy. Following the Ell Persons lynching in 1917, Handy had fled Memphis to escape racial violence and relocated his publishing company to New York City. He had been among those to find the remains of Persons thrown on Beale Street; now his park was on the same block. Not forgetting his roots, Handy had returned almost annually to Memphis to visit, and the city had inspired his compositions. In 1931, Lieutenant Lee suggested to Crump that the city name a park for him. After Crump agreed to do so, the city organized the park's dedication ceremony before an election. Twenty thousand from the city and surrounding states attended the ceremony, including city and county officials, federal judges, Handy, Crump, and Church. Among the speakers were Lieutenant Lee and Judge Harry Anderson, whom Church had appointed and who had returned African Americans to federal jury service in the area.[72]

While Church experienced some success on the local and state political scenes, Hoover appeared indifferent and even hostile toward African Americans. He met with nearly universal black protest when he nominated John Parker to the Supreme Court. Parker, a member of North Carolina's lily-white Republican faction, had publicly supported disenfranchisement. Mainly because of the NAACP's pressure, the nomination was defeated. Church, an NAACP board member, worked against it. Like his Republican predecessors, Hoover took no action against segregation, disenfranchisement, or lynching. His administration mandated that black and white Gold Star mothers take separate ships when they went overseas to visit their sons' graves. He made vague statements that African Americans interpreted as a desire to carry out a lily-white policy in the South and also appointed a lily-white proponent as the chairman of the Republican National Committee. Black leaders were further alienated by Hoover's unwillingness to solicit their views and exchange ideas with them.[73]

After 1930, Hoover largely abandoned his deeply flawed and ineffective southern reform policy, which had alienated blacks and whites and weakened the party. In South Carolina, Georgia, and Mississippi, black Republicans had maintained their influence despite his administration's attempts to weaken their power. Lily-white Republicans had hoped that the president would go further in stripping African Americans of leadership positions and were alienated by his protection of Church and Walter Cohen, whom he allowed to remain collector of customs of New Orleans. Because they wanted to maintain their dominance, some southern white Democrats had opposed Hoover's attempts to strengthen the Republican Party in the region. Still, the damage of Hoover's southern policy had been done. The percentage of black delegates at the 1932 Republican national convention was smaller than at previous conventions, and even fewer would have been seated but for the pressure of Church, who was a delegate and the sole African American member of the credentials committee. He told Hoover's personal secretary that he would stop giving the $1,000 campaign contribution that he made to Republican presidential candidates every four years if black-and-tan delegations were not seated; instead, he would use his funds to campaign against the administration.[74]

The 1932 presidential race between Herbert Hoover and Franklin D. Roosevelt demonstrated the growing political independence of African Americans. The number willing to speak on behalf of Hoover was fewer than normal, while a substantial number defected from the party. The majority of black newspapers and journals endorsed the Republican Party, but a significant number actively supported Roosevelt, attacked Hoover, or did not endorse either candidate.[75] Criticisms of the Republican Party that the *Chicago Defender* raised during the 1928 campaign rang just as true in 1932: "Today, with segregation, disfranchisement, lynchings . . . and all other forms of humiliations facing us, the Republicans are in control of government. With . . . the government flaunting segregation signs in our faces under the dome of the nation's capitol, the Republicans are in control."[76]

Roosevelt seemed worse to many African Americans than Hoover, however. Nothing in Roosevelt's background suggested any sympathy toward African Americans or any understanding of their problems. He chose a southern senator, John Nance Garner, as his running mate. His campaign sought black votes in the North to a limited extent, and Hoover's campaign continued the Republican tradition of having a black voters division, but neither candidate answered the NAACP questionnaire on racial concerns. During the campaign, Hoover took more steps on behalf of African Americans than did Roosevelt: he sent a message to the NAACP convention and delivered the commencement address at Howard University. The Republican National Committee invited two hundred African Americans to meet with Hoover on the White House lawn. In response to their call for him to take a firm stand on racial issues, the president assured them that the party would not abandon its traditional duty to African Americans. He cited the Republican platform, which pledged to "maintain equal opportunity and rights for our negro citizens," and declared: "We do not propose to depart from that tradition." In contrast, the Democrats had no such language in their platform. Hoover's remarks assured some African Americans.[77] A few weeks later, Church opened an office on Beale Street to support Hoover, although his campaign efforts were halfhearted and he had not attended the White House gathering because of his disgust with the president.[78]

Roosevelt won the election by a large margin. He provided more hope than Hoover for alleviating the Depression. Most of the voters in predominantly black wards in Memphis went for Hoover, as did most African Americans nationally.[79] Yet, according to the Associated Negro Press, commentators believed that the extent of black support for the Democratic Party as well as the Communist and Socialist Parties meant "the beginning of the end of party solidarity insofar as the Negro vote is concerned." It continued: "Negroes surged over into the Democratic camp as much because of resentment at the failure of Republican promises and performances as they did because of well founded hope of Democratic favor."[80]

During Roosevelt's first one hundred days in office, the Democratic-controlled Congress passed a flurry of legislation to alleviate the Depression. Like most southern members of Congress, Crump supported the New Deal initially. He voted for every piece of New Deal legislation in the first one hundred days, and he ensured that the city administration in Memphis successfully applied for New Deal funding. During the early years of the Depression, few businesses failed in the city, and unemployment rates for blacks and whites were low. But the number of unemployed people rose to about 14 percent of the workforce by mid-1932, and many businesses went bankrupt. The number of families helped by community relief organizations increased, with black Memphians experiencing greater economic distress than whites; they experienced a scarcity of jobs and disproportionately applied for and received government assistance compared to whites.[81] The Reverend Sutton Griggs was one of many black Memphians severely affected by the Depression. He saw his church, Tabernacle Baptist, foreclosed on because of the inability of both his church members to make the necessary mortgage payments and his white friends to financially support him. He moved to Denison, Texas, in 1930, to become pastor of Hopewell Baptist Church and died three years later.[82]

Although the Mayor's Commission on Employment and Relief, created in December 1930, helped hundreds secure temporary jobs and handed out clothing and food, Memphis, like most southern cities, kept taxes low, limiting funds available for relief. As a result, black Memphians relied on New Deal programs. Between 1928 and 1937, the city devoted more than $6 million to provide them with jobs, improved health services, better schools, a library, public housing, and street and park improvements; at least $3.5 million of the total came from New Deal programs. The construction of housing projects for African Americans improved housing conditions for more than two thousand families and provided much-needed jobs. African Americans across the South and the country saw increased job opportunities and better public services owing to the New Deal as well. In a move that benefited all Memphians, the Crump machine also ensured that Congress passed legislation authorizing $9 million for a Memphis flood-control project following the great Mississippi River flood of 1937, the worst natural disaster of the decade. Memphians had escaped inundation by the floodwaters in part because of the work of Crump to round up Works Progress Administration workers and African Americans on Beale Street to erect makeshift levees.[83]

However, the Crump machine administered the New Deal programs in racist ways. Relief programs buttressed the existing socioeconomic hierarchy, in which African Americans occupied low-level positions and received less pay than whites did for the same work. Local Works Progress Administration officials, for instance, trained African American women in domestic service. The black library branch's resources were inferior to those of white library branches, and black recreational facilities were in poor shape. By placing black housing projects in black neighborhoods, local authorities perpetuated housing segregation. Despite the protests of the Reverend T. O. Fuller and the black community, the city administration demolished Fuller's First Colored Baptist Church, the Howe Institution, and black businesses, institutions, and residences in the late 1930s in order to erect the Foote Homes public housing project. The machine's actions evidenced that no African American was spared its mistreatment as Fuller was a staunch supporter of Crump. He was forced to find another location for his church.[84]

Discrimination plagued New Deal programs across the South. By charging local government agencies with carrying out these programs, the Roosevelt administration provided the opportunity for southern officials to act in racially discriminatory ways. The president knew that white Democrats from the South, who held powerful positions in Congress, might not vote for his legislation if he mandated that federal officials control local programs, given the region's emphasis on states' rights. Because he feared alienating these southern politicians, he was not a forceful advocate for civil rights or antilynching legislation either.[85]

Yet many African Americans believed that they had a friend in the White House. New Deal programs included and economically uplifted African Americans, leading many to view Roosevelt as a hero. He made more black political appointments than any previous president and involved an unprecedented number of African Americans in policymaking circles—steps that Church and black Republicans had long advocated. While the expansion of the civil service led to the tripling of the number of black federal employees, his administration began to desegregate federal cafeterias, secretarial pools, and restrooms.[86]

The "Black Cabinet" and racially progressive whites played influential roles during Roosevelt's presidency. A group of his racial advisers for New Deal programs, the Black Cabinet met informally and conferred with civil rights leaders. It made government officials more attuned to African Americans' concerns, raised the black public's awareness of the New Deal, and helped African Americans become federal employees. Moreover, First Lady Eleanor Roosevelt was a forceful and genuine advocate for civil rights. She had close ties to civil rights organizations and friendships with African Americans, including Mary McLeod Bethune. As a member of the Black Cabinet and the most powerful black official in the administration, Bethune influenced the government to sponsor conferences and reports examining problems affecting the black community, criticizing the New Deal for its shortcomings, and calling for civil rights.[87]

Filled with hope because of the Roosevelt presidency, African Americans shifted to the Democratic Party, and black political action grew throughout the South and the country. The number of African Americans who registered and voted increased nationwide. The Agricultural Adjustment Act allowed black farmers to cast ballots in cotton-making quota referenda, resulting in many rural black southerners voting for the first time. Even though none won, black southerners ran for local, state, and national offices. More than 400,000 African Americans migrated North, where they increasingly held the balance of power in elections, forcing politicians of both parties to pay attention to them. African Americans were elected to political offices in state legislatures in the North and elsewhere, many as Democrats. In 1934, Arthur Mitchell beat Oscar DePriest in Chicago to become the first black Democrat ever elected to Congress. That year, the mid-term elections signified the first time that Democrats captured the majority of black votes.[88]

Black voter organizations rose in number in the 1930s and appeared in cities in every southern state, paving the way for later civil rights mobilizations. Amelia Boynton Robinson, for instance, registered to vote in Selma, Alabama, and founded a black political organization there, laying the groundwork for her and others' participation in the voting rights movement in the 1960s. In Georgia, black Democratic clubs were organized in most urban areas, although these groups were discouraged from affiliating with the regular party organizations. The Reverend Martin Luther King Sr. led a voting rights march in Atlanta, and he later joined the black Atlanta Voters League formed in the 1940s. In Greenville, South Carolina, the local NAACP branch organized a voter registration campaign and voter's club in 1939. Although its efforts were met with harassment, arrests, and a violent crackdown led by the Ku Klux Klan, the foundation for the formation of the statewide organization of NAACP branches in South Carolina was laid; the right to vote became the organization's chief goal in the 1940s.[89]

Civil rights activists engaged not only in more political action but also in more labor activism. The Wagner Act of 1935 spurred unionization by legitimizing the rights of employees to unionize and have union representatives negotiate with management. The Congress of Industrial Organizations (CIO) formed that year and welcomed African Americans, unlike the American Federation of Labor (AFL), which generally maintained discriminatory policies. Throughout the South, CIO members conducted interracial strikes. Many of these labor activists were part of a broad, sprawling movement of civil rights activists, black voter organization members, progressive New Dealers, communists, and others promoting labor and civil rights for all that had developed in the region by 1938. A biracial coalition of labor and civil rights activists, for instance, undertook anti–poll tax and voter registration campaigns as part of the Southern Conference for Human Welfare, formed in 1938 in Birmingham, Alabama.[90]

There was a rise in union membership and activism among black Memphians, as there was among black southerners generally. Black men and women participated in interracial CIO strikes and joined non-CIO unions. Founded in Arkansas in 1934 and headquartered in Memphis, the interracial Southern Tenant Farmers Union attracted members of different political persuasions, including socialists, New Dealers, and NAACP members. Although black strikers in the Memphis area generally received minor wage increases and did not have all their demands met, riverboat workers carried out successful interracial strikes in 1937 and 1939 that led to better working conditions.[91]

Black Memphians experienced a greater degree of politicization during the 1930s as well. In contrast to the 1916 and 1927 mobilizations, they relied less on figures such as Bob Church for political guidance and were more likely to form their own outlooks. They developed more political groups and engaged in more political debates than in the 1920s. Some became Democrats, whereas others turned to the Socialist and Communist Parties, which gained strength nationwide during the 1930s. Civic clubs formed and engaged in political action. Black Memphians kept up with political developments elsewhere, such as the NAACP's legal battle against the white primary in Texas. Rising black literacy and education levels, along with the growth of black periodicals and the spread of radio, furthered the increased political consciousness in Memphis and elsewhere. Although the momentum of the 1927 effort had not been sustained, black Memphians saw it as an important example of their political potential.[92]

Roosevelt's election further affected black Memphians by increasing Crump's power. Because the federal administration was now Democratic, Crump no longer had to rely on local Republicans for national influence. His two-term service in the House of Representatives from 1930 to 1934 increased his influence in Washington. After he stepped down in order to focus on his business interests and local politics, he controlled his former seat as well as every important office in Memphis and Shelby County, the seats of the two US senators, and the governorship. From 1931 to 1943, his candidates received almost 99 percent of the votes in the four mayoral elections; no politician in any major US city has matched that record to date.[93]

Crump began a personal campaign against Church after Roosevelt took office. Although Crump had aligned with him, Church was a powerful black leader and well-known civil rights advocate who potentially threatened Crump's control. Crump no longer needed Church on the national scene, and it became less necessary for him to secure black votes as his power grew. He harassed Church by finding building-code violations in his properties. As Church's daughter, Roberta

Church, later explained: "It took the form of things like this: if you put in a fire escape after the fire inspectors had been to your property, then they'd find some trouble with the electrical wiring; after you got the electrical wiring repaired, there'd be some troubles with the exits. . . . It was one constant thing after another, so that you always had to be spending money for repairs. The city wouldn't approve inspection unless you did this, that, or the other."[94] By 1937, the machine reneged on its apparent promise to exempt Church from local property taxes and ordered him to pay city, county, and state back taxes. Hurt economically by the Depression and the costs associated with paying the building code violations, Church could not pay all this money. His funds were limited partly because he allowed some people who occupied his rental properties to stay for free until they could pay their rent as a way of alleviating their economic distress. In a move that generated attention from the national black press, city officials took legal action against him: they collected rent from his tenants and filed a lawsuit to seize and sell twelve pieces of the Beale Street property of Church and his sister, Annette, in order to satisfy more than $80,000 in back taxes from 1915 to 1937.[95]

Crump took steps against white political adversaries as well. After Silliman Evans bought the *Nashville Tennessean* in 1938, he attacked Crump through its pages for ruling the state with an iron fist. It became the state's only newspaper to make a sustained fight against Crump, although Ed Meeman, the editor of the *Memphis Press-Scimitar* since 1931, made some headway there.[96] Because he opposed Crump, politicians ostracized Evans, leading him to feel like a "leper." Crump destroyed "scores of men financially, [drove] men out of the state, destroyed their homes [and] . . . businesses, and no Hitler was ever more dictatorial than Crump when we started the fight against him," Evans later said.[97]

City officials had previously tolerated and worked with selected labor organizations. With the rise of labor activism in the 1930s, Crump worked with the conservative AFL, but he and local business leaders opposed the CIO, the Southern Tenant Farmers Union, and other progressive unions. Local government officials consistently publicized the low wages offered in the city to attract more business to the area, but labor activism threatened to force higher wages. Like other southern politicians, Crump became disenchanted with the more liberal components of the New Deal, such as the establishment of the minimum wage and the protections offered to unions. Militant unions, with their legal strikes, illegal sit-down strikes, and other direct-action protests, threatened to interfere with his desire to present Memphis as a peaceful and orderly city. Moreover, unionists potentially could join forces and oppose him at the polls. At the hands of the machine, black and white unionists suffered beatings, harassment, and death. The brutality attracted publicity and attention from national civil rights organizations.[98] Ironically, it was the Crump machine that undertook activities that threatened the social harmony of Memphis by violating the civil liberties of its opponents and violently attacking them.

As Crump and his cronies grew increasingly repressive in the 1930s, they favored relationships with black leaders who did not challenge them politically. Lieutenant Lee shifted from being a leader focused on protest to one who accommodated to the machine. He developed a working relationship with the city administration in political and social relief efforts. Like other African Americans, he acted as an informant for Crump. In turn, Lee could recommend African Americans for city employment, receive a special police permit to carry a gun, and succeed in pressing the city to build a football stadium and two swimming pools for the black community. In order to forward his political agenda, Lee developed an acute and perceptive understanding of Crump's personality, observing that he was forceful and had a temper but could be manipulated.[99] "Beyond all that crust and thunder, beyond it was a kindly heart," Lee later said. "You had to dig for it, but if you didn't rile him, if you could find a way to neutralize him, you could get almost anything out of him."[100] Lee did not end his advocacy of racial pride. With the assistance of Bob Church and James Weldon Johnson, he published *Beale Street: Where the Blues Began* (1934), a social, political, and cultural history of the thoroughfare that discussed the Church family's achievements. The book received national acclaim, including Lee's selection as the first black author to have a book advertised by the Book-of-the-Month Club.[101]

Dr. Joseph Edison Walker, more commonly known as J. E. Walker, emerged as Memphis's most prominent black Democrat in the 1930s. He grew up poor in Indianola, Mississippi, and self-financed his undergraduate education at Alcorn College in Mississippi, graduating with a B.S. in 1903. He received his M.D. from Meharry Medical College in Nashville in 1906. After moving to Memphis, Walker in 1923 founded the Universal Life Insurance Company, which became one of the country's largest black life insurance companies. He organized the Negro Chamber of Commerce in 1926.[102] He was a leader of the West Tennessee Civic and Political League in 1927, but tension between him and Church grew out of unpleasant business relations and their similar ambitions. After Church denied his request to be a delegate to the Republican national convention in 1932, Walker became a political rival and turned to the Democratic Party.[103] The tension between Church and Walker suggests that Church was undemocratic when it came to power sharing.

Walker personally experienced the benefits of federal action against poverty. Hit hard by the black bank's failure in 1927, Universal Life suffered further losses during the Depression.[104] In 1933, Walker borrowed money from the Reconstruction Finance Corporation, set up by the Hoover administration in 1932, to save his business from financial disaster. Three years later, he observed: "Better conditions were reflected soon after the beginning of the Roosevelt administration, and conditions have continued to improve without a hitch. In 1934, in fact, our business was better than in any year of the existence of our company."[105]

During the 1930s, Walker worked to increase the economic security of African Americans and to mobilize them politically. In 1932 he formed the nonpartisan Independent Business and Civic Association, which encouraged civic responsibility and participation, advocated for black economic advancement, and worked with the Crump machine. It called on Memphians to take a stand against segregation, unfavorable publicity in the press, and other racial injustices. With its membership representing a fairly representative cross section of ages, the association held regular monthly meetings. In contrast to Walker, Church no longer had any extensive or permanent organization beyond his black-and-tan faction. Representative Walker's group made appearances at most public gatherings of African Americans. Its officers included J. B. Martin, Matthew Thornton, M. S. Stuart, and T. H. Hayes Jr., some of whom were political adherents of Church.[106] In the spring of 1932, the organization paid college students to conduct a survey of who was registered to vote in the black community and to present "intelligent reasons" to black Memphians to register and become politically active; these efforts helped lead to an unprecedented registration of black voters in the summer.[107] That same year, Walker served as president of the Community Welfare League, a social welfare organization affiliated with the local government and created to provide relief for African Americans. Its tasks included distributing flour to needy families. At a time in which the activities of the Inter Racial League and black welfare organizations had waned, this group served an important function. In 1939, enhancing his national prominence, Walker assumed the presidency of the National Negro Business League, the organization founded by Booker T. Washington.[108]

Walker and his lieutenants became leaders of the local NAACP branch as well, a move that intensified the Church-Walker rivalry because Church and his associates had once controlled the chapter. The branch protested racial discrimination in New Deal programs and distributed information to African Americans on how to take advantage of relief initiatives. It supported the lawsuit of William B. Redmond II of Nashville to integrate the University of Tennessee School of Pharmacy. The NAACP national office, which was working on similar legal challenges elsewhere, supported Redmond, with the assistance of Church.[109]

Church resigned from the national board of the NAACP in 1931. He privately indicated that the organization had become too partisan. By this time, the NAACP was becoming identified with the Democratic Party. Church's longtime associate and friend James Weldon Johnson's action of stepping down as the organization's executive secretary further influenced his decision. Publicly, Church indicated that his business and political activities had kept him from participating in board meetings and that the organization was now so well established that it no longer needed him on the board. Nevertheless, he did not stop aiding the NAACP. In 1932, two national officials, Roy Wilkins and George Schuyler, bypassed the Memphis branch's leader, M. S. Stuart, an executive of Universal Life and a political lieutenant of Walker, to work with Church in their tour investigating discrimination and peonage faced by African Americans working on a flood control project in response to the Mississippi River's 1927 flood and living in levee camps in Arkansas, Mississippi, and Louisiana. Church let them use his home as a contact point, briefed them on the area, and helped them acquire clothes for their undercover mission. National officers of the NAACP found Stuart unsympathetic to their investigation and thought that he might discredit any charges they might ultimately make if white contractors invited him to visit the camps.[110] According to Walter Adkins, many black Memphians found Stuart, who headed the local branch until 1935, "more concerned with the exploitation of the Negroes in favor of his insurance company than with the welfare of the group."[111]

In 1934, the first black Democratic club in Memphis formed, calling itself the Roosevelt New Deal Negro Democratic Organization. It is unclear whether Walker and his associates were involved. The group's leaders pledged cooperation with the machine. Because they supported the New Deal, they backed Roosevelt and wanted to line up with the regular Democratic organizations on the local, state, and national levels. The club had four hundred members, including a number of male college students. Independent black professionals led the organization, while working-class blacks primarily served as members. The younger generation's embrace of the Democratic Party was symptomatic of similar dynamics taking place across the South and the country. Unlike their parents' and grandparents' generations, which could have vivid memories of the Democratic Party's history of racial repression and the Republican Party's steps for racial justice, young voters saw the Democratic Party as a more viable political alternative. Many viewed the older generation of black Republicans that Church and his counterparts represented as self-serving politicians more interested in patronage and bolstering whites in the party than in serving the broader interests of African Americans.[112]

As of 1935, Church and his group held more influence over and enjoyed more support from black Memphians than did the black Democrats. Although Church and his associates had collaborated with Crump, they had retained their independence from the machine, whereas the black Democrats had tied themselves to it. While Church could serve as a delegate to Republican national conventions and control patronage during Republican administrations, Walker could not do either during Democratic administrations because the local, state, and national organizations did not include black southerners. Until the New Deal, the Democratic Party had never seated an African American delegate at a national convention; African Americans had been accepted as alternates in 1924 and 1928 but had been segregated from white delegates and other alternates in 1928.[113]

While Bob Church was steadfastly loyal to the Republican Party in the 1930s, he had reached the height of his power in the 1920s and would never be so influential again. Still, in 1932, African Americans in Memphis and Shelby County engaged in their greatest political mobilization in years to reelect him to the state Republican Executive Committee; it was understood by both African Americans and lily whites that the winner of the election would determine whether Church's black-and-tan faction or the local lily-white faction would serve as the regular Republican organization. Largely owing to the work of Walker's Independent Business and Civic Association, black Memphians registered to vote in unprecedented numbers, with thirty-three thousand ending up on the rolls. Lieutenant Lee, Church's campaign manager, headed an organization on his behalf with members from forty-three wards and two hundred precincts. Church's campaign committee included longtime black political activists such as the Reverend W. H. Brewster, Mrs. T. S. Brown, Laura Jackson, J. B. Martin, and Matthew Thornton. At a rally at Church's Auditorium, Lee, Thornton, and other leaders trained the record 346 African Americans who acted as officials, including as registrars, at twenty-four wards and fourteen precincts on election day.[114] Joseph Marks, a white member of Church's ticket who was active in Republican politics in Tennessee for fifty years, told the attendees: "You have not a better friend and leader than Mr. Church."[115]

Church won a spot on the state committee, as did the three other members of his ticket. The lily whites had withdrawn their ticket a few weeks before the election; they said that they did not feel that "they would get a square deal," but the black press commented that they did not want to risk sound defeat at the hands of the massive black vote.[116] With the support of black Memphians and the Crump machine, Hill McAllister was elected in the gubernatorial race of the Democratic primary and later in the November election despite the efforts of his opponent, Malcolm Patterson, and white daily papers to paint the black vote as fraudulent and to intimidate African Americans by printing confusing voting instructions. More than thirty-one thousand black voters, whom the *Afro-American* termed "Republi-Crats," registered as Democrats in order to participate in the primary. McAllister, whom Church backed, did not run an antiblack campaign like his opponents did; rather, he stayed silent on the issue of black voters. The black vote held the balance of power that allowed for his election in the primary. In the November election, he received most of his support from Shelby and Davidson Counties, where African Americans solidly backed him. He defeated the Republican candidate for governor, John McCall, the fierce lily-white opponent of Church, who played the race card throughout the campaign. On the eve of the election, McCall attacked Church while addressing a small, cheering crowd in Memphis.[117]

When the white press and particularly those whites opposed to black voting in the Democratic primary had charged that black voters were being "herded" to the polls that election season, African American leaders responded that "the increased registration had grown out of educational campaigns and the determination of colored people in general to take a more positive part in governmental affairs."[118] "The facts are that not by any means is this heavy registration of people of color made up of illiterate Negroes," J. E. Walker had said. "There are thousands of very intelligent and discriminating Negroes here in Memphis who have registered and are preparing to assert themselves in no indifferent manner in an effort to change the ridiculous civic disadvantages under which they labor."[119]

Church also faced dissension within his own ranks that election season. "That the real power of Church is based upon voter strength, even his political enemies admit. People believe and follow him," the *Afro-American* reported. "That does not mean, however, that he has no colored opposition. There are people in Memphis even, who criticise the Tennessee leader for the manner in which he has handled the mandate given him by the voters." Although the article did not provide more specific details, it noted: "There has developed bitter opposition to his leadership in the middle and eastern parts of the state. A group led by J. W. McClelland of the Nashville Independent have accused him of jeopardizing the whole party because of personal greed. . . . A desperate effort to drive a wedge into his leadership was made during the primary fight and some few, including several ministers, did go over to the other side."[120]

After 1932, Church spent a great deal of time in the East working with party leaders, including the industrialist Joseph Pew of Pennsylvania, to strengthen the GOP so that Republicans would regain the presidency in 1936. Pew largely opposed the New Deal, and the eastern wing of the party promoted business interests. While Church supported Republican candidates seeking election in the East, he called on the GOP to support measures for voting rights, including the end to poll taxes and closer federal supervision of elections, in order to stem the exodus of African Americans from the party. Despite his work and that of others, however, the Republican Party floundered, experiencing factionalism and no strong leader. It offered little to counter Roosevelt's work to alleviate the Depression. A visible strain of racial progressivism persisted in that some white party leaders made statements in support of civil rights and African Americans remained involved in party operations, yet the damage of the Hoover years and the popularity of Roosevelt hurt efforts to attract African Americans.[121]

Church stayed active in Memphis and state politics and as a major figure on Beale Street. His black-and-tan faction remained the city's regular Republican organization and consisted mainly of men. In 1932 and 1936, Church's black-and-tan group was seated over the lily-white faction at the Republican national convention. Church held mass meetings that generated large crowds; these gatherings asserted the rights of African Americans to political participation and cultivated feelings of pride in taking part in politics. Highly regarded in the banking and business world, Church enjoyed friendships with members of official political circles in the city, the county, and the state regardless of their party affiliation.[122] While Church was "very democratic in his manner," it sometimes was not "the easiest thing in the world to gain an audience" with him, the *Pittsburgh Courier* reported.[123] "Among the masses of blacks there . . . was a great deal [of], not reverence, but . . . respect in that Mr. Church, you see, was associated with the top people of the city, and the average Negro didn't have occasion to know him too well but always more or less knew him at a distance." Nat D. Williams later commented: "They looked at him with a degree of awe because he had a commanding personality, and he had light skin, and he was a man who had intelligence. The result was . . . that . . . the average Negro liked Mr. Church and respected him."[124]

On the state level, Church received a temporary setback in 1934 when delegates at the state convention voted to seat the lily-white faction instead of his faction, thus bringing to power John McCall's group as the regular state organization after years of dominance by the Church-Taylor faction. McCall, one of Church's most outspoken enemies, attacked him for collaborating with Democrats and providing votes for Democratic candidates. White Republicans who spoke on behalf of Church were shouted down. According to the *Pittsburgh Courier*, Church's defeat was "the culmination of years of envy and jealousy on the part of peanut white politicians who have resented the ability of Bob Church to exercise leadership in the party councils and to dominate the Republican organization in Shelby County."[125] The dominance of the McCall faction, however, was short-lived. At the state executive committee meeting later in the year, members aligned with Church defeated the supporters of McCall by a three-to-one vote on nearly every issue. In 1936, Church's faction, which outnumbered the lily-white one, regained control as the state's regular Republican organization when delegates voted to seat it over the McCall group at the state convention.[126]

In a 1934 editorial commenting on the temporary lily-white victory over the black and tans, the *Commercial Appeal* pointed out Church's status as the most powerful black Republican nationally, as a welcomed visitor to the White House during the last three Republican administrations, and as someone Republicans eagerly sought assistance from in national campaigns. Calling Church "rich, cultured, quiet, and unassuming," the paper said: "He makes no speeches, has never been known to answer a criticism, and seldom appears on the scene of political action. He does not seek publicity and has never by act or word encouraged race prejudice." The *Pittsburgh Courier* excerpted the editorial's praise of Church in an article titled "Even His Enemies Pay Tribute."[127] In his characteristically colorful style, Nat D. Williams heralded the editorial in his column in the *Memphis World*, a black newspaper started in 1931. Noting that the *Commercial Appeal* typically carried negative coverage of African Americans, he wrote about the praise: "Caesar, himself, could have appreciated a back-pat like that, even if Brutus had said it."[128] The Reverend S. A. Owen wrote Church about the editorial: "To be able to come through the many upheavals, stresses, and storms of heated political campaigns . . . and then to have such commendable things said of you by . . . the opposite race group . . . in the heart of the country's prejudice, is indeed a noble triumph."[129] Such praise struck a blow against not only stereotypes of African Americans but also the internalization of these falsehoods by African Americans. After a young black woman asked Lieutenant Lee whether news stories of Church's political power and support from whites were true, Lee commented that the black southerner "had been trained to look for greatness only under white skin and to underrate worth and achievement when they were expressed to a member of his own group."[130]

During the late 1920s and the 1930s, Church mentored Lonnie Briscoe, a young black Memphian born in 1911 who graduated from Booker T. Washington High School in 1930. On his way to high school, Briscoe would pass by the palatial Church family home. He recalled: "I enjoyed just looking over there because it seemed like to me [Bob Church] was doing more than anybody I knew as far as influence and that sort of thing was concerned." One day, when he was seventeen, he and a friend of his, Bert Cumby, stopped by to see about meeting him. Greeted by two men who worked for Church, Briscoe told them: "I want to see him and shake hands with him and see if I can't get some of the gusto that he is passing along the way, see if I can't have some of that stick to me." They told him that Church was busy, but Church, in Briscoe's words, "eventually . . . came in . . . and was very, very generous in his greeting to us." Bert Cumby told him that he hoped to become a politician like him, which made Church laugh and say something to the effect that he would have to be better than him.[131]

As he did for other young black men, Church secured a job for Briscoe at the post office, one of the best places for African Americans to work at that time. Briscoe bought a new overcoat and school supplies with his earnings; he recalled that most of the young postal men were devoted to Church and attributed their success to him. According to Briscoe, Church had "implicit confidence in youth" and was happy to mentor young men like himself. Church told him: "Briscoe, every time there is a baby born in this world, when the doctor pats him on the back and brings him into life, we have new inspiration. Every time there is one born there is that possibility." Briscoe's contacts with Church inspired him to join the Republican Party and to secure a job as a traveling salesman for a company that manufactured commencement materials, class rings, and yearbooks. When Briscoe asked Church for advice about how to tackle unfamiliar sales territory in Texas and Louisiana, he said: "Friendliness is the best thing that anyone can do on any foreign job. Just be friendly—not over friendly—just friendly. Use common sense in everything you do. Don't let people push you around. . . . stand up and be a man." Briscoe would tell Church about his work, and Church enjoyed hearing about his interactions with others.[132]

Briscoe found Church to be an energetic, likable, modest, cultured, and dignified person who had a sense of humor and little time to socialize. "[Church] wanted to know about things. He wanted to know why things ticked. He wanted you to tell him what it was all about," Briscoe later said. At his Beale Street office, Church had a library with an extensive selection of newspapers. He usually was on his feet when he met with Briscoe. Church's energy "made me want to do something," Briscoe recalled. An immaculate dresser with beautiful gray hair, Church enjoyed kidding Briscoe and spoke in a "smiling like manner" to him. He once teased him about the fact that Briscoe was going out with a woman who he did not know was married. Briscoe would have liked to have socialized with him more but remembered that Church "kept mostly to himself" and "was always engaged in something that was always bigger than social[izing]. He would socialize for a short time, yes. He was right in and right out so to speak. Everybody was glad he could come."[133]

"Nobody ever thought of Bob Church as being an ordinary man. No, he was special in everything he did. He carried himself in such a way that you had to respect him," Briscoe said, echoing the observations of Nat D. Williams on black Memphians' views toward Church. "People kind of admired him to the extent that they stayed away from him. They felt . . . if they needed him, okay. He was there. If you didn't need him, you don't bother him. That's the way it was." Briscoe further recalled: "They always respected him for his principles and what he thought about things. If he didn't have anything to say, he didn't say anything. And when he said something, everybody was willing to listen." Briscoe and Cumby would recruit people to attend mass political meetings held by Church during election time. "We'd go out and beat the bushes, so to speak, and have everybody that was interested in civil rights, civil liberties and civic pride, personal pride . . . go there. We always had a big crowd," Briscoe remembered. He said that Church would call the meetings and then let other people handle the logistics. "He was just like a general in an army," Briscoe said. "He doesn't have to do anything, but give signals and seemingly things were happening on the basis of his signals."[134]

Church also attracted the attention of and inspired African Americans outside Memphis in the 1930s. In his work as a salesperson Briscoe met people in Texas and Louisiana who admired Church and gave him a greater reception as a result. The National League of Republican Colored Women asked Church to speak at its conference in 1935. That same year, John Wesley Dobbs of Atlanta, who had organized the Republican-affiliated Atlanta Civic and Political League, invited him to speak at a mass meeting.[135] Informing Church that he had long kept up with his local and national political activities, Dobbs said: "You have attracted the attention of many citizens and have set a concrete example to be patterned after by other men of like temperament, desiring to be of service to an under-privileged minority group of citizens." When in Memphis earlier, Dobbs had learned firsthand of Church's political activities, which had inspired him to register voters in order to "get rights and privileges right here in Atlanta that we do not now enjoy."[136] Later, at a February 1936 gathering of his league, Dobbs called for ten thousand African Americans to register to vote in order to develop enough political strength and leverage to better their hopes of receiving better parks and playgrounds, better hospital facilities and schools, and black policemen and firemen. "We've got to do like the Memphis Negroes," Dobbs told the crowd, pointing to Church's success in mobilizing voters there.[137]

In a rare interview in 1934 with Walter Adkins, Church explained his political philosophy and expressed skepticism about the New Deal. His paramount goal was not that African Americans become Republican and vote for the party's candidates but that most be politically active and use the ballot as a vehicle for racial advancement. Realizing that black political influence thus far had been small, Church justified his work to "[keep] an active Negro constituency in the Republican Party" as a way "to arouse the masses of colored Americans to a consciousness of the potency of the ballot, and to use it most effectively." He believed that African Americans were Republicans out of tradition and circumstances, as incipient capitalists, and because the party was one of "rugged individualism." "The Negro Democrat and colored adherents of other parties are not regarded seriously by the 'Boss of Beale Street.' . . . To him the colored Democrat, Socialist, and Communist are merely back-sliding Republicans beguiled by ephemeral promises, or moved by a childish recalcitrance," Adkins observed. "The electoral triumph and the social experimentation of the present Roosevelt administration find [Church] an interested and avowedly cynical spectator. He still expresses faith in the fundamental Republicanism of the country at large."[138] As someone who had a career in business, belonged to a family that had grown rich through real estate, and believed that black capitalism was a key to racial advancement, Church supported a party that did not advocate government intervention in the economy to the extent that the New Deal did.

Church was a member of the black professional class and the older generation of African Americans, two groups more likely to support

Republicans than were young and poor African Americans.[139] He and these black Republicans invoked history to urge African Americans to support the party. In 1936, John Lynch, the prominent Reconstruction-era politician, said: "The colored voters cannot help but feel that in voting the Democratic ticket in national elections they will be voting to give their Endorsement and their approval to every wrong of which they are victims, every right of which they are deprived and every injustice of which they suffer."[140] Yet these black Republicans held an increasingly outdated view of their party. Whereas Republicans dominated national politics after the Civil War, the Democrats now were gaining strength, and the power of conservative white southern Democrats was declining as a coalition of African Americans, labor activists, and working-class citizens across regions put hope in the party as a vehicle for social change.[141] The New Deal economically uplifted African Americans in tangible ways, in contrast to the platitudes the Republican Party offered when it came to civil rights.

For the 1936 election, the Democratic Party, along with the Republican Party, made an unprecedented effort to secure the votes of African Americans through such steps as full-page ads in black newspapers and an active black voters division. For the first time the Democrats accredited African Americans as delegates at their convention. For African Americans, the election, in essence, served as a referendum on the New Deal. Would they support the president despite the pervasive discrimination that plagued his New Deal programs? Or would African Americans turn to the Republican candidate, Alf Landon? He supported civil rights to a greater degree than the president did and spoke out against discrimination in New Deal programs, but he and his party did not fully support Roosevelt's relief measures.[142]

J. E. Walker and the local black attorney William H. Foote organized the Shelby County Colored Democratic Club for the election under the guidance of the Crump machine. Walker claimed that it was the first black Democratic club recognized by a regular white Democratic organization in the South. The club held its first public meeting at the Universal Life Insurance Company. J. Ashton Hayes, the principal of Manassas High School, called on black educators to "come to Universal and see what a Negro Democrat looks like." Sound trucks parked outside a football game at the Booker T. Washington High School stadium spread the word about the meeting. Speakers at the meeting included Hayes and Jeannete Shivers, another school principal. Walker returned for the gathering from Texas, where he spoke on behalf of John Nance Garner, the vice presidential candidate. The crowd at the meeting was small, but community interest soon grew. More than twenty-five hundred attended its last meeting before the election.[143]

While Walker recruited support for the Democratic Party, Church acted as codirector of the Midwest division of the black voters committee of the Republican Party. In Landon, the governor of Kansas, loyal black Republicans found a candidate who seemed to validate their belief that African Americans remained better off as Republicans than Democrats. "With Landon G.O.P. Begins Its Recovery," a *Chicago Defender* headline blared.[144] In contrast to Hoover, Landon openly embraced black members of the party. He met with black leaders, and his pictures with them were featured in black newspapers and Republican campaign material. Following a meeting with Church, Landon called for the passage of an antilynching bill. Roosevelt had condemned lynching but did not support antilynching legislation.[145] Kelly Miller, the astute black political commentator, was skeptical of Landon's antilynching stance given his lack of action against racial violence. Miller criticized Church for allowing "candidate Landon to pull the wool over his eyes . . . by such guileful campaign promises as Republican politicians have been using for the past fifty years."[146] Later in the campaign, Landon angered Church and other African Americans by choosing Colonel Arthur W. Little, who was white and the former commander of a black regiment in France, as the primary spokesperson in his outreach effort to African Americans, whereas the Democratic campaign was using Mary McLeod Bethune and other African American leaders for this purpose.[147]

During the election season, Church became the first African American in forty years to sit on the Republican National Committee's executive committee, which was charged with directing all aspects of the campaign and shaping future campaigns. Church had sat in on these meetings for years; he now held the proxy for the East Tennessee congressman and Republican national committeeman J. Will Taylor, his loyal ally on the state and national political scenes. The *Chicago Defender* noted: "[Church] entered into the deliberations of the committee with his accustomed modesty. He was given a most cordial reception. No members sought to flatter his presence. . . . His presence was noted as [a member] and not as a 'leader of the Race.'"[148] Reporting on his participation in the committee, the *Pittsburgh Courier* called him "probably the most powerful and most influential single figure in the high ranks of the Republican party to-day." At his urging, the committee set up an African American youth division for the campaign.[149]

In a Republican Party campaign booklet directed at African Americans, Church and more than seventy other prominent black Republicans, including Lieutenant Lee, Roscoe Conkling Simmons, and Oscar DePriest, signed a statement focusing on ways that the New Deal discriminated against African Americans. For instance, they pointed out that the Social Security Act excluded domestic and agricultural workers from its provisions. They also castigated the New Deal for not protecting black southerners against mob violence. The Democratic Party's platform did not explicitly deal with African Americans, so they spotlighted the plank of the platform adopted at the Republican national convention that stated: "We favor equal opportunity for our colored citizens. We pledge our protection of their economic status and personal safety. We will do our best to further their employment." And they quoted a telegram from Governor Landon to them reiterating his support for the platform, invoking the history of the party's treatment of African Americans, and saying that he employed "neither platitudes nor mottoes." They argued that a Republican administration would better provide African Americans with jobs than a Democratic one and that it would continue relief for all needy persons. "We cannot forgot nor should the youth of the colored race ever forget," the statement concluded, "that the Democratic Party . . . remains the Party of disfranchisement, of the Jim Crow car. . . . It remains the party of lynching and the stake."[150]

For most African Americans, however, the New Deal's benefits outweighed Roosevelt's inattention to civil rights, their traditional loyalty to the Republican Party, and the racial conservatism of southern congressmen. Republicans had not provided a viable alternative to the New Deal and had a history of making empty promises to African Americans. At the same time that the black Republicans who signed the campaign statement declared their support for the party, they showed their distance from other African Americans by not acknowledging how the New Deal positively affected the black community by providing economic relief and involving African Americans in the federal government. In 1936, a majority of African Americans voted for a Democratic presidential candidate for the first time, and Roosevelt swept the election. In contrast to 1932, when some 70 percent of African Americans voted for Hoover, now some 70 percent backed Roosevelt. Black Memphians voted for Democrats on a greater scale than they had previously.[151]

Most African Americans remained registered Republicans in the 1930s despite their support of Roosevelt in 1936. Church, to be sure, was motivated to stay a Republican for the reasons mentioned in the campaign booklet. In addition, he did not become a Democrat because he felt that he could make more of a difference within the Republican Party than outside it. He had standing in and a history with the party. If he left the party, he likely would not be as influential a political figure, and he would be forced to give up the personal prestige of his recognition within its councils. It was important that he remain a Republican in order to continue to serve as a voice in the party for civil rights and black political participation and to keep alive these strains of the party. After 1936, he urged the party to take more steps for racial advancement in order to win back African Americans, such as supporting federal government control of all elections for federal offices. Yet he had gotten increasingly out of step with most African Americans and was unsuccessful in his attempts to get them to return to the party. His stubborn advocacy for the party revealed a degree of rigidity and a lack of creativity in his political approach for which Robert Vann, the prestigious editor of the *Pittsburgh Courier*, criticized him.[152] Church continued to devote tremendous time and energy to a party that offered him so little in return with regard to meeting his goals for racial advancement.

It was no wonder that J. E. Walker came to enjoy a greater degree of mass political support locally than did Church. While Church was skeptical of the New Deal and spent a great deal of time out of town working to strengthen the Republican Party with elite leaders in the East, Walker supported the New Deal and embraced the turn of African Americans to the Democratic Party through his local, on-the-ground organizations. Black Memphians experienced firsthand the administration's attention to them in 1937 when Eleanor Roosevelt visited Douglass Junior High School, where students, supported by the National Youth Administration, carried out a garden and canning project for the benefit of their school lunches. Dr. and Mrs. J. E. Walker, African American principals, and other notables were on hand to meet the First Lady. In 1938, a high-ranking Democratic leader in Memphis observed that many black Memphians who formerly supported the Republican Party now were actively supporting the Democratic Party because the Democrats gave African Americans more recognition.[153]

While Church immersed himself in Republican activities, he stood against the police brutality that black Memphians faced, which intensified after 1933. In 1937, police officers murdered two black men, wounded African Americans in seven shooting incidents, and otherwise harmed African Americans at least six times. Church tried to rectify at least two cases of police brutality. He called for the dismissal of the guilty police officers. If the victim was not killed, he pressed the mayor to hear the victim's side and give him a fair trial if he faced prosecution. In early 1938, the police arrested William Glover, a member of the Brotherhood of Sleeping Car Porters, the large black union headed by A. Philip Randolph. After accusing Glover of flirting with a white woman, officers beat him to the point that they left a hole in his forehead. The police chief ordered Glover to resign his job with the Pullman Company and leave town. Glover did so, fleeing with his family to Cairo, Illinois, to stay with his brother. When he made an official statement there on the police brutality, J. T. Settle Jr., a lawyer and political associate of Church's, represented him. Ten days later, the Reverend S. A. Owen and Julian Bell, an employee of Booker T. Washington High School, praised Church for his handling of the case.[154] Proclaiming himself an "interested observer" of black leaders, Bell said: "I'm sure Memphis would be a much better place in which to live if our Religious, Political, and Social leadership were dotted with a few more men like yourself, and those with whom you are connected."[155]

As the decade came to a close, the year 1938 revealed the various political approaches of black Memphians. Inaugurated under the sponsorship of the *Memphis World,* the Mayor of Beale Street contest saw African Americans elect a mayor and city council in a symbolic campaign modeled after one in Harlem.[156] The contest was designed to promote civic participation among African Americans, educate them about the city government, and encourage cooperation with city officials "for the betterment of Memphis as a whole."[157] Matthew Thornton Sr., the black Memphian who was one of the three police officers who had served in 1919, was elected mayor because of his popularity. His inaugural ceremony occurred at Beale Street Baptist Church, and Mayor Overton issued a proclamation giving an official seal of approval to his election. A former member of the local Lincoln League and a charter member of the city's NAACP branch, Thornton operated a barbershop and worked for the US Postal Service. Active in political, social, fraternal, and civic circles, he was credited with spurring W. C. Handy's move to Memphis in 1873 by inviting him to lead the Knights of Pythias Band, the first black brass band in the city, which Thornton organized. Elsewhere in the South, African Americans elected "bronze mayors" as well.[158]

For the actual 1938 election, Taylor C. D. Hayes wrote his pastor, Dr. J. A. G. Grant, about the disappointment of young black Memphians with Grant's participation in an upcoming mass meeting to feature free watermelons, fireworks, and speeches promoting Crump's candidates by black leaders, including J. E. Walker, Lieutenant Lee, T. O. Fuller, Nat D. Williams, and Lucie Campbell, the famed songwriter. A traveling representative for the Elks, Hayes, who was around thirty years old, was the son of T. H. Hayes Sr., the oldest businessman in Memphis and a longtime political associate of Church.[159] "News has it that a Committee of colored men, *working with the city administration,* are to stage a Mass Meeting in Memphis for the purpose of pointing out to the colored people what the city administration has done (?), is doing (??) and will do (???) for them," he wrote. Having heard that Grant, along with Walker, Fuller, and Lee, were members of this committee, he suggested that Grant point out to these black leaders the problem of police brutality; the lack of black police officers, firefighters, and city health officials; the low pay for black teachers; and the inadequate recreational facilities and "many other inconvenience[s] . . . for a down-trodden people." Hayes wrote that he and other young Memphians would be watching the committee "to determine the type of leadership that we desire and the type that we can so well do without."[160] What Hayes might not have understood is that the machine could exert pressure on leaders to support it. As a public school teacher, Campbell, for instance, could have faced repercussions if she did not campaign for Crump, as the city administration had the authority to appoint and fire teachers.[161]

Grant admired the young men and sympathized with their views. Along with Lieutenant Lee, T. O. Fuller, J. E. Walker, and Blair Hunt, he had formed a committee by early 1938 to vigorously protest police brutality.[162] Although "not at all satisfied with the treatment that has been awarded to our people" by the city administration, he wrote Hayes that he felt that "if we have any hope at all it will be through them." He said: "I believe that if we stick to them at this crucial time it will mean that we will be in a position to get more for our people."[163] In response, Hayes called Grant "weak-minded" for believing that Crump and Lee would ever give black people a chance. "The administration of Memphis can never change; it is too deeply rooted in evil," he declared. "They condone murder, proven by the fact that no officer has ever been fired for the murdering of a Negro, since they were in office. Those that support them, support murder, which is against all the teachings of the Bible." He further condemned the machine for graft and for using money to buy votes. "It is with deep regret that I not only find my faith in the Church shaken, but my faith in you shattered," he wrote. "I'm sorry you have taken your stand."[164]

Crump faced further resistance and did not seek black support as vigorously as usual during the 1938 election. Governor Gordon Browning, elected with his backing in 1936, had turned against him. The state crime commission had conducted an investigation of his tactics for securing the black vote, so he faced the possibility of the Tennessee National Guard being sent out to monitor elections. In addition, he no longer worked with black operators of illegal establishments as much as he had previously to get votes. His administration had begun to clean up vice in the city partly because of unfavorable national publicity; Tennessee repealed prohibition the next year. Church advised black Memphians to protest police brutality by not supporting Crump's choice for governor. More black Memphians stayed away from the polls than usual, ignoring attempts to coerce them with watermelon and whisky. Although many black Memphians cast a protest vote for the anti-Crump office seeker, Crump's candidate won. Still, Crump did not completely ignore the black protests. He had a police officer who killed an African American fired, a step that he had never taken previously.[165]

Despite obstacles, the Crump machine remained well in control by the decade's end. Mayor Overton and Crump split over a policy disagreement and Overton's desire for more power, so Crump ran for mayor in 1939 to temporarily serve in place of Walter Chandler, a lawyer and World War I veteran who was his choice for the position. Chandler, serving in Congress, was needed to cast an important vote. Crump was elected and held office for just fifteen minutes, long enough to rescind the city's invitation to the CIO's American Newspaper Guild to hold its national convention there. Chandler then resigned from Congress to become mayor. That year, city authorities attempted to murder Thomas Watkins, the black leader of a successful interracial riverfront strike of the AFL's International Longshoremen's Union and the CIO's Inland Boatmen's Union. The local NAACP branch helped him flee to East St. Louis, Illinois. At the request of the Memphis police, law enforcement officials there arrested Watkins twice, but the charges did not stick. The Memphis NAACP chapter, now headed by Utillus R. Phillips, a railroad postal worker, protested the Watkins case to the US Justice Department and the national office of the NAACP.[166] Phillips wrote US Attorney General Frank P. Murphy: "This instance is another of numerous violations of basic civil rights and liberties of Memphis Citizens, aided and abetted by the city administration and the police force."[167]

Although African Americans suffered at the hands of Crump during the 1930s, they benefited from their political activities in a number of ways. They supported the New Deal, which bettered their standard of living by providing them with improved public services and more job opportunities. In response to black political leverage, the city provided African Americans with significant benefits, including naming a park for W. C. Handy. Church served as a voice for civil rights in the Republican Party, and his role as a political leader inspired young black Memphians and disrupted stereotypes of African Americans as inferior, as demonstrated by the *Commercial Appeal* editorials. Black Memphians became more politically independent and formed more political organizations. J. E. Walker emerged as a significant black Democratic leader, part of the tide of African Americans turning to the party in light of Roosevelt's presidency and the New Deal. Under the leadership of Walker and others, the local NAACP engaged in important activism. The labor movement saw some victories and became an important local challenger to the Crump organization by working against the interests of the machine.

Church, Walker, and other African Americans, however, paid a major price for supporting Crump given the chronic police brutality, persistent voter manipulation, and other antidemocratic ways of his machine that hurt both blacks and whites. Some, like Church, rebelled and took a stand against Crump's repression, but Church began to personally suffer the consequences of his past political work that had bolstered Crump's power. Other black political activists, like Lieutenant Lee, took an accommodationist approach and could achieve some benefits for African Americans, but their support for the machine contributed to its power to subjugate blacks and whites. As leader of the Colored Democratic Club, J. E. Walker sought to gain bargaining power in the machine, but his impact was minimal.[168]

By permitting black voting, the machine was, ironically, planting seeds that challenged the prevailing southern political system of limited power for African Americans. African Americans took advantage of their ability to vote to serve their own ends. Even those who collaborated with Crump were building political skills and knowledge and could sometimes secure benefits. Black political activists ultimately wanted racial advancement despite their different approaches. All their activism indicated that they might ultimately break the Jim Crow system even if that outcome was not foreseeable in the near future.

Robert R. Church Sr. and family. Courtesy Special Collections, University of Memphis Libraries.

Lymus Wallace. Courtesy Memphis–Shelby County Room, Memphis–Shelby County Public Library and Information Center.

Ida B. Wells. Courtesy Library of Congress.

Church's Park and Auditorium. Courtesy Special Collections, University of Memphis Libraries.

Robert R. Church Sr. in Atlantic City. Courtesy Special Collections, University of Memphis Libraries.

Trolleys on Main Street. Courtesy Memphis–Shelby County Room, Memphis–Shelby County Public Library and Information Center.

Robert R. Church Jr. as a young man. Courtesy Special Collections, University of Memphis Libraries.

Walter H. Loving, Sara Johnson Church, Robert R. Church Jr., and Annette E. Church. Courtesy Special Collections, University of Memphis Libraries.

Robert R. Church Jr. and Roberta Church. Courtesy Special Collections, University of Memphis Libraries.

(Above) Lincoln League meeting in 1916. Courtesy Special Collections, University of Memphis Libraries.

(Left) Robert Church Jr., W. C. Handy, and Lieutenant George W. Lee. Courtesy Special Collections, University of Memphis Libraries.

Robert R. Church Jr., Henry Lincoln Johnson, Roscoe Conkling Simmons, Walter L. Cohen, John T. Fisher, and Perry W. Howard. Courtesy Special Collections, University of Memphis Libraries.

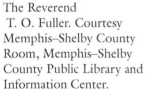

The Reverend T. O. Fuller. Courtesy Memphis–Shelby County Room, Memphis–Shelby County Public Library and Information Center.

Lieutenant George W. Lee. Courtesy Memphis–Shelby County Room, Memphis–Shelby County Public Library and Information Center.

Edward and Bessie McLean Crump. Courtesy Memphis–Shelby County Room, Memphis–Shelby County Public Library and Information Center.

Mayor Edmund Orgill and Lieutenant George W. Lee at Handy Park. Courtesy Memphis–Shelby County Room, Memphis–Shelby County Public Library and Information Center.

(Right) Dr. Joseph E. Walker and Mrs. Lelia Walker. Courtesy Memphis–Shelby County Room, Memphis–Shelby County Public Library and Information Center.

(Below) C. C. Spaulding, Dr. J. E. Walker, and B. G. Olive Jr. Courtesy Memphis–Shelby County Room, Memphis–Shelby County Public Library and Information Center.

Robert R. Church Jr. in his office. Courtesy Special Collections, University of Memphis Libraries.

Lonnie Briscoe. Courtesy
Special Collections, University
of Memphis Libraries.

Beale Street in 1944. Courtesy Memphis–Shelby County Room, Memphis–Shelby
County Public Library and Information Center.

(Above) W. C. Handy. Courtesy Special Collections, University of Memphis Librar-
ies. (Below) Dr. J. B. Martin, Robert R. Church Jr., Charles B. Washington, and
Senator Kenneth Wherry. Courtesy Special Collections, University of Memphis
Libraries.

(Above) George W. Lee (center), George Klepper (holding a gavel), and an unidentified man. Courtesy Memphis–Shelby County Room, Memphis–Shelby County Public Library and Information Center.

(Right) Benjamin L. Hooks. Courtesy Special Collections, University of Memphis Libraries.

Roberta Church at the White House. Courtesy Special Collections, University of Memphis Libraries.

Roberta Church modeling Anna Wright Church's sealskin coat. Courtesy Special Collections, University of Memphis Libraries.

(Above) A. W. Willis Jr.,
Benjamin L. Hooks, and Russell
B. Sugarmon Jr. Courtesy
Special Collections, University of
Memphis Libraries.

(Right) Maxine Atkins Smith.
Courtesy Memphis–Shelby
County Room, Memphis–Shelby
County Public Library and
Information Center.

4 "As Un-American as Any Dictator-Ridden Country in Europe"

Seeking Democracy during the War Years, 1940–1945

At a time of increased political opportunities for African Americans across the country during World War II, black Memphians confronted Edward H. Crump, who attempted to further restrict their political power. At the same time, he supported their voting rights to a limited degree and provided them with public services that were unequal to those of whites but better than those afforded to African Americans in other southern cities. Crump forced Robert R. Church Jr. and two other black Republicans to leave the city, and he also cracked down on whites who threatened his control. Within this environment, black political activists became more accommodating to the machine. Nonetheless, the labor movement challenged Crump, while Church worked from afar to oppose him. Seeking the democracy at home that black soldiers were fighting for abroad, black Memphians engaged in civil rights protests. Crump represented many of the larger problems facing black southerners, and African American soldiers and national leaders spoke out against him with the larger purpose of making the region more democratic. Their protests were intertwined with the efforts of black Memphians against Crump and for racial justice.

The Crump machine completely dominated the local political scene in the early to mid-1940s. Harry Woodbury, who worked as a reporter for the *Commercial Appeal*, recalled that elections from 1940 to 1947 "were just an exercise in muscle building." In 1944, Crump's ticket was unopposed except for one candidate for sheriff.[1] Wearing horn-rimmed glasses, and with thumb-thick eyebrows and a mop of

137

white hair, Crump directed the operations of his political machine from his business office downtown and named his candidates usually following get-togethers with his lieutenants. About his control, Crump told one reporter: "Work . . . hard work—that's what does it. I'm always working—a little buttermilk, a little orange juice keeps me going."[2] A vegetarian, Crump abstained from liquor, tobacco, and coffee.[3]

Despite the behind-the-scenes approach, it was well-known that the city's mayors held office nominally and that Crump really ran things. He publicly claimed that he placed "honest, competent, high class men in office." His organization reached into nearly every area of Memphis life. As a journalist observed: "Many of the politicians are active churchmen, many belong to the best clubs, and many are of prominent families long identified with . . . the town. Some are active in civic organizations while wives of city officials and friends of the administration are active club women."[4] Whites had little room to move politically because of Crump's dictatorial ways, and his machine continued to enlist the support of black leaders and citizens and to manipulate some black voters through its long-standing tactics of paying their poll tax, instructing them how to vote, and providing them with enticements.

Crump remained the most powerful political figure in Tennessee as well. Although his faction faced challengers during every state election, he outsmarted any opposition. He exercised his statewide power in a number of ways. He continued his political partnership with East Tennessee Republicans. His organization could expedite or delay local bills, which required passage by the state legislature, through the legislative process or the governor's veto. As a result, it simultaneously wielded influence over local officials and influenced state policies. Moreover, the machine ensured that leaders of poor, rural counties received campaign funds of at least $1,000 from the state headquarters for key races. This funding helped lead to Crump's candidates carrying their respective counties.[5]

An estimated fifteen thousand city, county, and federal officials were at Crump's command locally to marshal votes for his candidates during election season. Each needed to enlist the support of only three voters to bring in the sixty thousand ballots that would ensure victory in state elections; these votes signified the key to his control statewide. Organized like an industrial enterprise, the machine maintained a card index of voters and potential voters.[6] For instance, at a meeting of campaign workers in the Sixteenth Ward, the school board chairman, the city library director, the tax assessor, two probate judges, and fifty other local government employees gathered. "Each had his election day duties laid out before him," a *Chicago Sun* reporter observed. "The workers were busy, as in all other 51 wards. As voters came to the polls they ticked off their names. Those who didn't come were called. Those who still didn't come were sent for." He said that the campaign workers did these tasks joyfully and that each would "talk for hours about what a great man Crump is."[7]

Although Crump's machine could appear benign, it was ruthless when bucked.[8] A candidate for public office was playing gin rummy when Crump organized a softball game and commanded him to come. A woman begged him to stay with the game, but he declined, making the seemingly innocuous remark: "When the Old Man says you gotta go, you gotta go." The statement enraged Crump, and the man's name was removed from the ballot. Because of a lack of business, the candidate, who was a lawyer, eventually left town.[9] Anyone who defied Crump was subject to physical brutality or other repercussions from his machine. Labor leaders were beaten up, journalists suffered at his hands, and political opponents faced his wrath. During election time, Crump took out full-page newspaper ads to attack his rivals.

In a response to the famed journalist Lowell Mellett's charge that he maintained a "totalitarian political regime," Crump said:

There is nothing of a totalitarian nature in my make-up nor is there anything suggestive of totalitarianism in the manner in which . . . Memphis is governed. . . . [I]t [is] one of the cleanest cities, morally and physically in the entire United States. There is less graft and more efficiency in the governments of both Memphis and Shelby County than may be found in any other city or county in the United States. . . . We have none of the organized vice to be found in the average American city. . . . Indeed, a person would have a hard time making a bet on a horse race here. . . . Memphis is a clean city, a quiet city—the quietest in America—a city of beautiful parks, fine churches, excellent schools, splendid hospitals, with broad, well-paved streets. Ours is one of the few cities in America which owns its light, gas and water utilities. Our city and county tax rates are among the lowest in the United States.[10]

Indeed, the city received national recognition for its cleanliness. One Chicago-based reporter observed: "The cleanness of the city strikes the eyes of the visitor at once. It gleams in the sun."[11] Mellett responded to Crump's defense by writing: "Memphis is a clean city and a quiet city. . . . That was true also of Berlin and Tokyo before the war. They were two of the cleanest cities on this earth. You didn't dare drop a match on the sidewalk in either of them."[12]

In public statements, Crump steered clear of the key reason why whites allowed his control. A Chicago reporter termed it "something people did not talk about"—the fear that a different political system would allow African Americans, who made up some 40 percent of the city's population, to gain too much power.[13] Crump permitted black Memphians to cast ballots, but white citizens trusted Crump to keep them in check and settled for a political atmosphere of "fear and futility" in order to ensure white social and political control.[14] To be sure, white politicians across the South were trusted to keep African Americans in a subordinate position.

The 1940 elections demonstrated Crump's ability to rein in independent African American political mobilization and his increasing opposition to it. Bob Church was committed to electing the Republican presidential candidate, Wendell Willkie. Unlike in his previous campaigns for Republican office seekers, however, he faced resistance from Crump. Willkie not only had a chance of winning but also made vociferous statements against the Memphis machine, classing Crump with corrupt political bosses such as Frank Hague of New Jersey and Tom Pendergast of Kansas City. The Tennessee state Republican convention followed suit, saying that "a real Hitler and Mussolini" ruled in Shelby County.[15] Crump knew that a Willkie victory would hurt his organization and diminish his national influence.

Like past Republican presidential candidates, Willkie made statements supporting civil rights. These words were not merely a ploy for black votes, however; he seemed to genuinely believe in the civil rights cause. He called for antilynching legislation and the end of segregation in Washington, DC, and discrimination in the armed forces. In an attempt to win back black voters, the Republican Party had the strongest civil rights plank in its party platform in history. The platform called for the passage of antilynching legislation, the protection of black voting rights, and the ceasing of discrimination in the civil service and the armed forces. The Democratic Party signaled its support for racial advancement as well. For the first time, the party specifically mentioned African Americans in its platform: it did not have a civil rights plank but described how the New Deal benefited them. Pressured by the Black Cabinet and other black Democratic leaders to counter Republican statements in favor of civil rights, the Roosevelt administration announced nondiscriminatory policies for certain military programs and expanded opportunities for African Americans in the armed forces. The National Defense Advisory Committee, for instance, announced a new policy prohibiting discrimination in industries engaged in defense production, and the administration publicly gave information about a new AirCorps unit for African Americans based at the Tuskegee Institute in Alabama.[16]

Because Church had plans to organize black voters in the North and East, he asked J. B. Martin to head the local Republican campaign organization. Martin, a wealthy businessman and physician, had been a leader of the Lincoln League in 1916 and the West Tennessee Civic and Political League in 1927. He had attended every Republican national convention except for one since 1912. He coowned the Memphis Red Sox, the Negro leagues team in the city, and headed the American Negro Baseball Association, a national organization that supervised professional black baseball. Since 1910, he had run the South Memphis Drug Store, a popular business that included a sub–post office.[17] Church had helped establish the post office, the only one operated by African Americans in Tennessee. "Whenever visitors or prominent people come to Memphis, [black] Memphians take them to the South Memphis Drug Store to show them the branch post office," Church said. "I, myself, have taken hundreds of visitors there."[18]

Martin and his fellow black Republicans planned interracial rallies for October and November—as was usual for presidential campaigns—to promote Willkie and the other Republican candidates. At the first two rallies, held in October at two black churches, black and white speakers attacked the city administration for, among other things, condoning police brutality. The white and black press as well as Crump informants covered the meetings.[19] A local city official, Aubrey B. Clapp, reported to Crump that about four hundred African Americans, including some twenty-five women, attended one of the meetings. Three white Republicans spoke, and the black pastors George Albert Long and Harry B. Gibson gave "extremely severe and vitrolistic [*sic*]" talks, Clapp said. "In my opinion the speeches they made under certain circumstances and conditions might cause trouble. They both preached race equality without any reservations." They urged African Americans to organize and demand their percentage of state jobs and jobs in the fire department and police force in the city, county, and state in proportion to the amount of taxes that they paid. They called for the abolition of the poll tax and criticized J. E. Walker for working with the Crump organization.[20]

Infuriated by these rallies, Crump sent George W. Lee to tell Martin that his drug store would be "policed" unless he resigned as chair of the Republican campaign committee, closed his Republican headquarters, and called off the final political meeting. Martin voluntarily talked with a high-ranking city official, who also told him that his business would be "policed" if he did not call off the rally. The city made Martin take down a banner displayed in front of the Republican headquarters saying "Our Own Joe Louis is for Willkie," ostensibly because only candidates could have their names on campaign signs. Refusing to succumb to Crump's threats, Martin kept up his campaign work and held the rally. In response, Crump stationed two police officers in front of Martin's South Memphis Drug Store during all its operating hours under the pretense that Martin was running an illegal drug operation. No charges were filed against him, however, and no warrants were issued; Police Commissioner Joe Boyle claimed that the actions against Martin were based on "missing files." Police officers searched all African Americans and whites entering and leaving the store, including kindergarteners who went there to buy ice cream. In protest, black Memphians flooded the store, as did many whites, but the surveillance and searching continued. Police officers also frisked people entering and exiting the successful Beale Street saloon of Elmer Atkinson, another black Republican who had taken part in the rallies. Whereas Martin had no drug record, Atkinson had faced a drug charge some ten years previously. Martin suspected that city officials targeted Atkinson to legitimize their actions.[21]

The Crump machine turned against Church in an unprecedented way as well. Crump knew that a Willkie election would increase Church's power locally.[22] Church made a bid to serve as a Republican national convention delegate. Mingo Scott, who later wrote a history of black politics in Tennessee, led the effort to secure his victory. Crump lieutenants told Scott that Memphis had "had enough of Church's type of leadership" and to "go easy" in his campaign.

After Scott ignored them, thugs beat him with iron pipes and left him bleeding on Beale Street.[23] Thugs attacked Lieutenant Lee for supporting Church's bid as well, leaving him with a broken hand and a cut across his face requiring fifteen stitches.[24]

Church was selected as a delegate, but, in February, while he was engaging in political activity in the East, city officials auctioned off the twelve pieces of property that they had seized from him and his sister, Annette, in 1939 for overly high back taxes despite the local government's previous exemption of him from taxes. The city and the county bought eleven of the twelve pieces of property, including Church's home and office, for $83,000. In April, the state and Shelby County sued Church for nearly $3,000 in back taxes for the years 1931–1938 for 104 acres of land in the city's outskirts. Altogether, the city seized and sold through tax auctions at least twenty pieces of the Church family's property in rural and urban areas. These actions left Church in a state of financial disaster given that his real estate was his main source of income.[25]

Because of all these actions taken against his political power and economic livelihood, Church, who was fifty-five, and his sister, Annette, decided to leave Memphis until he could figure out a way to better deal with his difficulties there. They moved to Chicago in November, where he had established a home in 1938, although it had mainly served as a political headquarters. He continued to spend a great deal of time in Washington, DC. Later in November, the city dealt another blow by changing the name of Church's Park to Beale Avenue Park and Auditorium. Mayor of Beale Street Matthew Thornton and a committee of African American citizens petitioned the city's park commission for years afterward to reinstate the name but did not meet with success until 1956. The city sold the Church family home, replete with crystal chandeliers and mahogany mantels, in 1941 to private bidders who planned to use it as a boarding house, while Lieutenant Lee successfully negotiated with the city to buy Church's former office for use by the branch of the Atlanta Life Insurance Company for which he worked.[26]

In an oral history in the mid-1960s, Lieutenant Lee commented that Church's troubles were partially self-inflicted. He called him a "poor businessman" who spent so much money on his political activities that he was cash poor. Lee said that his company could easily have lent Church $30,000 to pay his back taxes but that Church had "a lot of pride and ego": "[He] was too prideful to let me or any of his friends help so the city gobbled up all that property."[27] In addition, Church evidently did not believe that the city would take these actions. A *Pittsburgh Courier* article reported that every few years a "for sale" sign had been attached to Church's property but that "through some mysterious manipulations Church has retained it, although he has never paid the taxes." The article continued: "Authoritative sources here state that Church has always been able to dodge the issue and escape losing his property through political influence." When the newspaper reached him for an interview, "Church appeared to be in the best of spirit and was not worried about losing his property." Lieutenant Lee told the newspaper that the sale would not be held and the property would be saved. But they both misjudged the situation. Roberta Church later commented that she thought that the death of Church's prominent white lawyer around that time also led the city to renege on any oral agreement that had existed between Church and the city concerning taxes.[28]

After leaving Memphis, Bob and Annette Church tried to buy back some of the lost property, but local officials were willing to allow them to repurchase only the family home. Bob did not do so because he preferred repurchasing the more valuable property downtown at Second and Gayoso or Beale Street. Roberta Church later said that she thought city officials refused to let him buy back most of his property because they feared his reestablishing himself in Memphis. Not until 1951 did a prominent and influential local white lawyer try to legally reobtain the property for them in appreciation for a favor that Bob had done for him many years previously. He thought that some of the tax sales could be set aside for irregularities. Although he was treated with hostility when undertaking this work at the courthouse, he secured some money for the Church family in 1952 before his death shortly thereafter.[29]

As the machine opposed black Republicans in 1940, it worked with black Democrats to bolster its power. It provided the Colored Democratic Club, the black wing of the local Democratic campaign organization, with a headquarters and funding and appointed its officials. Men mainly occupied its top leadership positions, with J. E. Walker heading the club. Businessmen, ministers, and other professionals served as its officers, including the Universal Life Insurance Company executive M. S. Stuart and the prominent ministers T. O.

Fuller and Blair Hunt. Female officers included J. E. Walker's wife, Lelia Walker, and Mary Murphy, who led the City Federation of Colored Women's Clubs. The black Democrats actively supported the Crump-backed ticket of Roosevelt for president, Prentice Cooper for governor, Kenneth McKellar for senator, and Clifford Davis for Congress. At the behest of the Democratic National Committee, Walker spoke to enthusiastic meetings of blacks and whites in Illinois. In addition to holding local rallies, the Colored Democratic Club distributed flyers extolling the benefits provided by the Roosevelt administration, including national black political appointees, National Youth Administration jobs, school improvements, and better public services. Walker also used his position to call for racial justice. Pointing out his support for his candidacy, he urged Prentice Cooper, who was the incumbent, to punish law officers in Brownsville, Tennessee, in rural Haywood County, who violently retaliated against African Americans trying to register to vote.[30]

Ordinary black Memphians worked with the Democratic club or campaigned for Democrats on their own. "I am with the administration and Pressident [*sic*] Roosevelt one hundred per cent," the Reverend J. H. Johnson wrote Walter Chandler, the new mayor installed by Crump. "I have canvassed from here to Knoxville. I have given out buttons and stickers for cars. . . . I have stickers on my car front and rear."[31] Letting Chandler know of his willingness to speak on behalf of Roosevelt anytime, the Reverend J. A. G. Grant wrote: "I feel that Mr. Roosevelt has done more for our Country than any president since Lincoln."[32] H. B. King, a teacher and funeral home director, aligned with the Colored Democratic Club by mobilizing his civic club members on behalf of the Democratic ticket.[33] King informed Chandler that he and his followers planned to vote for his reelection and that he and his associates had "reminded [their] listeners about the various advantages and conveniences that have been made available to the colored citizens by our city government, including good streets, adequate lighting facilities, wholesome recreation, excellent schools, and better housing conditions."[34]

Despite such support, the machine knew that many black Memphians disapproved of the harassment of J. B. Martin. Thinking that a "friendly word" would be "reassuring" at this time, Mayor Chandler sent a letter to black ministers the Sunday before election day.[35] Chandler pointed out the benefits that African Americans had received from the city government and Roosevelt administration. Calling for interracial peace and harmony, he accused a few black leaders of being "only interested in their personal gain and political welfare to the detriment of the masses of the colored people."[36] Many ministers responded that they and their congregations supported the mayor and the Democratic ticket. The Reverend Blair T. Hunt, a particularly loyal supporter of the machine, replied that Crump was "almost a human idol" to African Americans, although he thought that the policing of the two businesses was "inopportune."[37]

The Reverend G. A. Long was apparently the only black minister to respond negatively to Chandler in a letter. Originally from Arkansas, Long had served as the pastor of churches in Indiana and Illinois before arriving in Memphis in 1937.[38] He wrote the mayor that good city services were no substitute for constitutional rights. As for the comment about selfish black leaders, he indicated: "To whom this has reference I do not know. . . . I am the humble pastor of Beale Ave. Bapt. Church. I do not hold any political job. . . . I have not at any time sought to misguide my people." Noting that he had white Republican and Democratic friends and that his desire was for Christian love and not racial hate, Long said: "I want to meet you some time and have you see me and know me. I am sure you will like me. I just want to be a man and enjoy my rights as an American citizen."[39]

When election day arrived, most Memphis voters cast ballots for the Democratic ticket. Statistics do not exist on how black Memphians voted, but it appears that they continued to shift to the Democratic Party even though more voted for Republicans than in the 1936 and 1938 elections.[40] The black vote nationally remained largely in Roosevelt's corner. While Republicans had continually failed to fulfill their campaign promises to African Americans, the Democratic Party seemed most promising given its economic and civil rights efforts.

Victory at the polls for Crump did not end his crackdown. The machine's actions against Martin, Atkinson, and Church were part of a larger campaign that lasted through at least December; national civil rights and civil liberties organizations called it the "reign of terror." Martin's harassment attracted the most media attention, but the machine also attacked working-class blacks, black saloon patrons, and black labor activists. In addition to fearing Republican opposition, the machine felt threatened by the growth in local CIO organizing since the 1930s and its threat to the racial and class order. In mid-November,

Police Commissioner Joe Boyle announced a desire to rid the city of "undesirables." Police officers carried out raids on Beale and in black neighborhoods and arrested sixty-five black men one evening, calling them "suspicious persons." Accusing them of being idle, insolent, and vagrant, Boyle did not acknowledge that they helped make up the shortage of laborers needed for the cotton harvest. According to Collins George, the adviser to the NAACP Youth Council at LeMoyne College, any black man or woman on the street or at cafés or poolrooms was liable to arrest, bodily search, verbal abuse, and physical injury.[41]

After the election, blacks and whites increasingly spoke out against the reign of terror. Local white newspapers and Tennessee's black newspapers condemned the police surveillance of Martin's store. The Memphis Commission on Interracial Cooperation, made up equally of black and white clergy across faiths, petitioned the mayor to withdraw the police from the store. It said that a "state of tension and fear unprecedented in the recent history of our city" existed in the black community.[42] While the adult members of the NAACP branch were afraid to protest, the Memphis NAACP Youth Council condemned Martin's harassment in a letter to Chandler. National organizations that protested the reign of terror included the Southern Conference for Human Welfare, the Southern Negro Youth Congress, the national office of the NAACP, and the American Civil Liberties Union, all of which called on federal authorities to intervene.[43]

The reign of terror further exposed the racial views of the machine. Refusing to meet with the interracial committee, Police Commissioner Joe Boyle rebuked it for criticizing the police. Charging that Martin and his wife, who were light skinned, sat in seats reserved for whites at the circus, he accused Martin of gloating over "social equality." Attacking the black newspapers that protested Martin's treatment, he said: "They are not going to carry on and conduct themselves in Memphis as if they lived in Chicago, Pittsburgh, and Philadelphia. We have never had it before and we will never have it. For after all this is white man's country."[44] Crump made similar remarks when J. E. Walker, Blair Hunt, and T. O. Fuller, representing the black Democrats, asked him to end the police harassment of Martin. "He would not let them talk," reported the *Nashville Globe,* the state capital's black newspaper. "Tall, gaunt, and shaggy, he . . . fumed at the mouth. . . . He declared that Bob Church had been spending most of his time . . . up North, that he had been staying in white hotels there and had come back to Memphis 'spreading ideas of social equality' and that Martin had abetted him in it." Crump told them that African Americans should "learn their places."[45] According to the *Globe*, black Democrats were as indignant as the black Republicans over the treatment of Martin. The black businessman M. S. Stuart urged the machine to stop the harassment of Martin as well.[46]

The local and national outcry led to the removal of the police officers from the store on 5 December after six weeks of surveillance. The police had found no evidence of illegal activity, and Boyle had not prosecuted Martin or anyone connected with the establishment. Still, on 6 December, Boyle publicly commented that the store would be policed but in a different way. Police officers subsequently made short stops there daily. In mid-December, he declared that the Crump organization had its eyes on five black pastors, four black doctors, five black newspaper writers, one black drugstore operator, two black postmen, and one black undertaker who had been "fanning race hatred." Four were members of the interracial committee. Crump, Mayor Chandler, and the city commission publicly backed Boyle.[47]

Finally, in January, the US Department of Justice sent an investigator, Colonel Amos Woodcock, to examine the police harassment of Martin following the calls of national organizations, Church, and Martin for intervention. Woodcock talked only to Boyle and city officials, and black Memphians found out about his visit after he left. He did not contact Martin. Woodcock concluded that the police posting had been legitimate and that the case could not be tried in federal courts. Despite the calls of some African Americans for another investigation, the Justice Department backed his assessment.[48]

By this time, Martin had left Memphis for Chicago. The machine had begun building a criminal case against him for his work as an unlicensed bondsman even though it had previously tolerated this activity. Lieutenant Lee had found out and told Martin. "They're trying to put me in the workhouse, and I couldn't stand that," said Martin, who had suffered mental and financial distress during the ordeal. He moved away the day after Lee told him that Crump wanted him to leave town. He did not return to live in Memphis, and his brother took over management of the drug store.[49] In Chicago, Martin won the respect of whites and blacks alike; the *Chicago Tribune* said that the city "was gifted with a sterling citizen" as a result of the Memphis troubles.[50] Martin bought the Chicago American Giants, a black base-ball club that was nearly bankrupt, and led its financial recovery. He was elected a county commissioner in Chicago in 1942. Four years later, he became the first African American elected to the powerful position of trustee of the Sanitary District of Cook County. Approximately twenty-five Memphians, including Mayor of Beale Street Matthew Thornton, traveled to Chicago for his inaugural ceremony, while Church wired his congratulations from Washington, DC.[51]

Both Church and Martin sought justice against the Crump machine for the 1940 developments. Church persuaded Martin to join him in Washington, DC, to confer with Republican and Democratic officials, and he was present when Martin gave a deposition at the Department of Justice on 12 March 1941. The two men prepared an extensive memorandum, substantiated by quotes from black and white Memphians, attesting to Martin's impeccable reputation, and recounting his troubles with the machine. So respected was Martin that many white police officers had reported in sick when assigned to his store, and others had told him privately that they hated the assignment but had to carry it out because of their orders. Church and Martin presented the memo to officials of both parties and the Department of Justice, and Church monitored and publicized the case. Although Congress was investigating the matter as late as 1948, no action was taken against the machine.[52]

The Crump machine kept up its intimidation of Martin after his move from Memphis. Eight days after his deposition, Martin told Church that Lieutenant Lee had visited him in Chicago and informed him that Will Gerber, the Shelby County attorney general, wanted him back in Memphis. "I was careful what I said to him. I think they sent him here. He did not get a thing out of me," Martin said.[53] Lee called Martin four days later to pass on Gerber's message that he did not have anything against him and did not understand why Martin did not return. The next day, three men rode by Martin's house four times. They parked across the street and talked. "I said nothing to no one but it look [sic] bad to me," Martin wrote Church. "I don't go any place at night and a very few in the day [sic]. I think I may need some protection."[54]

Martin's suspicions of ill intent by the machine were confirmed when he came back to the city in 1943. He attended a party for Matthew Thornton in May. Thornton, who worked for the post office, was fired the next day. In October, Martin returned to watch a Negro leagues game as president of the American Negro Baseball Association. Three detectives arrested him, and the police chief told him that neither he nor anyone like him was wanted in Memphis. Martin left the next morning. At the next game, police officers came by to make sure he was not there.[55]

The atmosphere of fear and tension pervaded Memphis for years after the Martin incident. In some ways, the reign of terror continued and worsened as no Martin or Church-like political figure rose to challenge Crump's regime. Church wrote his uncle, James R. Wright, in 1943: "You asked me how people . . . feel towards the City Administration, they are scared to death, but there is nothing they can do about it."[56] According to Blair Hunt, African Americans could not express themselves "without being martyrs"; the black community's consensus was that "it was better to be a living soldier than a dead martyr."[57] Raymond Lymon, the long-standing black Republican, acted as vice president of the local NAACP chapter in the early 1940s; he later said that some members feared admitting involvement, that it took courage to be a member.[58] William Weathers, a black Republican who worked with Lee, recalled that the NAACP was "very, very, very weak in Memphis" at this time.[59] As Lymon later observed, however, these NAACP activists planted the seeds of future work. After Church and Martin left, Lymon also took charge of the local Republican ward and precinct work.[60] Black Republicans responsible for working at the polls on election day used storefronts for primaries. Lymon said: "You had many Negroes, I am sorry to say at that time [who] were afraid to have a ballot box out in the front yard of their business. Absolutely afraid!"[61]

The machine's exile of Church and Martin from Memphis led to changes in both African American views of Crump and black political leadership in Memphis. The Reverend Blair Hunt later said that Crump "was regarded very highly by all African Americans until the split came between him and Dr J. B. Martin." He elaborated: "Then a large group of blacks turned against him. . . . The blacks helped to build the Crump Machine. There is no doubt about that. What I have said concerning J. B. Martin and E. H. Crump is gathered from the opinion of many blacks."[62] With the most aggressive leaders gone, Lee, T. O. Fuller, J. E. Walker, and Hunt, who all worked closely with the machine, remained. In addition to acting as a messenger for Crump during the 1940 election season, Lee had avoided the Republican campaign headquarters and all of Martin's political meetings. His actions owed partly to his desire to remain in Memphis.[63]

Nevertheless, after the 1940 election, Crump accused Lee of not letting all he had done for him "seep down to the masses." In response, Lee organized a parade of black city employees to showcase the city's support of African Americans. It occurred at the Blues Bowl, a football game of the top two black high school teams in the Mid-South. Conceived by Lee, the bowl had segregated seating and was a fund-raiser for poor African Americans. He invited Crump and Chandler as the honored guest and keynote speaker, respectively.[64] Above all else, Lee wanted to survive during this time, according to his biographer. He did, but his actions damaged what was left of his reputation as a protest leader, and his relationship with the machine became increasingly unpopular among black Memphians.[65] Lonnie Briscoe, the young black Memphian whom Church mentored, saw Lee as a different leader than Church, one who "was trying to and clamoring for everything he could get for himself. . . . You could see that Mr. Church had prepared the way and he wanted to take over." As a result, Briscoe would have little to do with Lee.[66]

Lee took the place of Church as the most prominent local black Republican in the 1940s. Accepted as "token opposition" to Crump, he was a delegate to the Republican national convention and the only African American member from Memphis and Shelby County on the state Republican Executive Committee. Black Republicans made up most of the small Republican primary vote in Memphis and were mainly responsible for keeping the local party alive. They worked with a few white Republicans, including the attorney George Klepper, who chaired the local Republican Executive Committee. The machine monitored the Republicans, as it did virtually any group representing a potential threat, but they were not much of one. With Church and Martin gone and its leadership in accommodating hands, the local party declined to the point that no Republican primary was held in Memphis or Shelby County in 1942. The black-and-tan faction functioned as a mere shell of what had once been a vital local party organization that pressed for civil rights, economic advancement, legal justice, and political power. At a 1944 meeting of local Republicans, only twenty-seven whites and forty blacks attended, and they sat segregated from one another, an arrangement that Church never would have allowed.[67]

Despite Crump's ruthlessness, black Memphians campaigned and held rallies during election time, participated in political and civic clubs, and pressed public officials for demands such as city jobs. Ministers, businessmen, civic and women's club members, and ordinary citizens were among those who politically mobilized. As Mayor of Beale Street, Matthew Thornton sold thousands of dollars in war bonds, became an honorary navy recruiter, and convinced Kroger grocery stores in black neighborhoods to hire black butchers, clerks, and managers.[68] The Negro Chamber of Commerce and its female counterpart, the Housewives League, protested the White Rose Laundry's sign picturing a black female laundry worker washing a pair of underpants. In a letter to the storeowners with a copy sent to Mayor Chandler, these groups demanded the sign's removal, noting that hundreds of black Memphians objected to "its subtle although effective ridicule of the race." The letter continued: "Most colored people have to work hard for a living. . . . [W]e do not believe the many servile tasks that they have to perform should be held up in ridicule and be made a public laughing stock . . . [through the] immoral exhibition of underwear."[69] Chandler suggested to the storeowners that their sign did more harm than good, and they removed it.[70]

Like Church and his group, local black businessmen saw economics as a channel for black advancement. In May 1944, J. E. Walker resigned as chairman of the Colored Democratic Club.[71] The head of the National Negro Business League, he needed to focus on his new role as chairman of the War Bond Savings Club Plan, a project of the US Treasury Department whereby he visited cities nationwide to, as he put it, teach "thrift and preparation for life in the post-war world to colored people all over the country."[72] Two years later, Lieutenant Lee helped convince Walker to found the Tri-State Bank, one of thirteen black banks in the country and the first one in Memphis since the failure of the black bank in 1927.[73] "[The black man] can't always be in front of the counter and not behind the counter. He can't always be buying and never selling," Lee said. "He can't always be begging charity with no charity to bestow."[74]

While Crump accepted a limited degree of black protest, the Reverend T. O. Fuller represented the type of black leader that he most tolerated and encouraged, one who supported city officials and largely did not challenge them. Fuller cultivated ties to the machine as a way to improve black conditions within segregated Memphis, such as by seeking city jobs for African Americans, but his words and actions in support of the machine also served to legitimate it and undermine those who protested against it.[75] Despite ongoing police brutality, he brought business to the city by ensuring that the National Baptist Convention, of which he was the assistant secretary, met there, even though—as he wrote Crump—an "effort was made to give us the 'black-eye' on the account of some things that have happened here."[76] In addition, in 1942 he backed Will Gerber in his bid for reelection as attorney general of Shelby County. Even though Gerber had been active in the reign of terror, Fuller wrote Crump that he was "held in high esteem by all who are brought in touch with him."[77] Shortly before his death that year, Fuller criticized Church in a letter to Crump, accusing him of "never ma[king] any effort to organize an intelligent following." He said that Church "held the spotlight and prestige for what it meant to him in other quarters."[78] After Fuller died, Crump told the *Commercial Appeal:* "He thoroughly understood his own race as well as the white people and his work was always helpful and constructive. . . . He was held in high esteem by all white people who knew him. . . . [His] whole life [was] spent not only for the good of his own race, but for this entire community as well."[79]

The Reverend Blair Hunt began his service to the church as an assistant minister to Fuller and carried on Fuller's torch as one of Crump's closest black political associates in the 1940s. Born in Memphis in 1888 to former slaves, Hunt came from an elite black family with a history of political involvement. A relative, Fred Hunt, acted as recorder of deeds in Memphis in the 1880s. Hunt earned a bachelor of arts degree at Morehouse College and an associate of arts degree at Harvard followed by a master's degree from Tennessee State A&I College. After serving as a chaplain during World War I and receiving a bachelor's degree in theology from Roger Williams College in Nashville, he was ordained as a Baptist minister. In 1922, he began his fifty-one years as pastor of the Mississippi Boulevard Christian Church, the first African American congregation of the Disciples of Christ denomination in Memphis; J. E. Walker and other prominent black Memphians were members. Hunt's sermons were published weekly in the *Memphis World,* the local black newspaper. Hunt also moved up the ranks of the school system and became the principal of Booker T. Washington High School in 1932, a position that he held for twenty-seven years. He helped initiate the teaching of black history locally.[80]

Hunt's political approach was to campaign for and make friends with white politicians in order to secure benefits for his high school and otherwise improve the socioeconomic conditions of blacks. He could secure school supplies for his students when other black schools could not.[81] He sent holiday greetings and gifts to Crump and elected officials as well as congratulatory notes to those who won office; they often thanked him for these gestures.[82] Calling himself "a little brown nut" in the Crump machine, Hunt campaigned for Crump-backed candidates and supplied the organization with names of campaign workers.[83] In 1944, he worked with the Colored Democratic Club, as he had four years previously, and compiled a fact sheet on why African Americans should vote for Roosevelt.[84] Going so far as to suggest that Senator Kenneth McKellar of Tennessee nominate Crump to be vice president, he wrote: "Thousands of Memphis Negroes will be happy." Aware that the Crump machine manipulated black voters, Hunt contended that black participation in machine politics laid the foundation for future black political development. "I'm a desegregationist, but with it a gradualist. I'm not a revolutionist but an evolutionist," he explained in 1959.[85]

To be sure, at the same time that the Crump machine manipulated white and black voters and cracked down on activists, it held benefits for African Americans, a reason that Hunt, Fuller, and others supported it and used it to try to get their demands met. In 1943, Mayor Chandler summarized key aspects of the machine's approach to African Americans. "More than forty percent of the residents of Memphis are colored, and we try to maintain friendly relationships with the colored groups by giving them excellent schools, sufficient parks, playgrounds, housing and hospital facilities," he wrote. "We endeavor to take care of streets on which they live, and to encourage the proper understanding of their responsibilities as citizens."[86] Chandler made speeches at black institutions and participated in black-oriented events.[87] Like past mayors, he provided municipal assistance to the Tri-State Fair, the black counterpart to the white Mid-South Fair. He ensured that the city provided an office to Mayor of Beale Street Matthew Thornton after his reelection to this ceremonial position in 1940, and he addressed Thornton as "mayor" in his correspondence with him.[88] Adhering to long-standing machine policy, Chandler responded to letters from African Americans in a civil and cordial manner.[89]

The NAACP's *Crisis* magazine observed that Memphis ranked as one of the best places in the South for its material provisions to African Americans. Yet it reported: "In the congested colored sections . . . complaints persist of unlighted and unpaved streets, of underpaid Negro school teachers, of [the] lack of playgrounds and parks and of vast numbers of Negroes whose housing and hospitalization needs continue to be neglected."[90] Most certainly, public services were inadequate. And, in general, black Memphians were discontented: in a 1942 poll, 75 percent said that their treatment would improve if Japan defeated the United States.[91]

Not all whites agreed with the steps taken by the city administration on behalf of African Americans, particularly as racial tensions heightened during wartime. White Cotton Exchange workers, who considered themselves "friends" of Chandler, questioned the mayor's decision to allow a black Baptist convention in the city auditorium. "We all agree that it is certainly the wrong time to encourage a bunch of Northern Negroes to come down here, where there is certainly a most distinct feeling of animosity growing daily between the whites and the negroes," one wrote him.[92] With fewer white men around because of the war, numerous white women wrote the draft board about the increasingly visible presence of black men. These women feared that the black men carried venereal disease; they worried about miscegenation and the social and political dominance of African Americans over whites. The women said that the black men should be drafted.[93]

The war years saw increased racial friction as well as the explosive growth of the labor movement in Memphis and across the country. The demand for labor increased, providing a favorable environment for hundreds of successful strikes for union recognition and higher wages. Union membership jumped to more than 8 million by 1941, from a low point of 3 million in 1933. African Americans joined unions in large numbers in Memphis and elsewhere. In 1941, Roosevelt issued an executive order banning employment discrimination based on race, national origin, color, or creed in the defense industries and creating the Fair Employment Practices Commission (FEPC) for enforcement. A. Philip Randolph, the head of the Brotherhood of Sleeping Car Porters, had pressured Roosevelt to take this action by threatening to hold a mass-based march; he created the March on Washington Movement organization to monitor the FEPC.[94]

During the war, the number of factory workers doubled in Mem-

phis because of the economic growth generated by private invest-
ment, new industrial plants, and military facilities constructed by the
federal government. The CIO grew at a rapid pace, becoming the
most prominent union association in Memphis and reaching thirty-
two thousand members by the end of the war. Black workers were
the heart of its support; biracial organization became the key to its
success. The CIO gained bargaining rights in more than sixty workplaces—most with mainly black laborers—in Memphis and nearby areas as soon as September 1941. Black Memphians joined the AFL as
well and participated in strikes in that capacity. They also sought to
better their employment situation and combat job discrimination by
making appeals to the FEPC and asking for help from black community leaders.[95]

While the labor movement grew and experienced success, many
white Memphians, including Crump, saw the CIO as a "communist,
nigger-loving union" federation. CIO organizers experienced violence and intimidation from the police and antiunion employees, with
local authorities largely complicit. In a speech given in Nashville, Congressman Martin Dies, the head of the House Special Committee on
Un-American Activities, accused CIO organizers of fomenting racial
tensions, inspiring Memphis city officials and the *Commercial Appeal*
to justify the reign of terror as an effort to promote the security of citizens against communism and race warfare.[96] Joe Boyle accused "foreign born Communist agitators" of stirring up "the young element of
negroes."[97]

Although the reign of terror drove away many probable CIO supporters, the machine became more receptive to the CIO as it grew.
The Roosevelt administration sent down a Justice Department investigator after the beating of a union organizer, perhaps putting pressure on the machine to change its ways. City officials knew that totally
opposing the CIO was counterproductive because of its size and influence. Wartime workers were needed, and Memphis was experiencing unprecedented prosperity. Still, Crump disliked the organization,
police harassed union organizers, businesses resisted union demands,
and racial divisions hampered union activities. Like elsewhere in the
South, most white workers were not fully committed to interracial-
ism. They wanted to hold better jobs than African Americans and to
maintain segregation in the workforce and society.[98]

Despite these obstacles, black labor activists were the most vital force against the Jim Crow system in the absence of any strong civil rights or black political organization in Memphis. Black workers first fought for the right to unionize, sometimes risking their lives in the process. Then they used unions to battle workplace discrimination. By aligning with whites, they challenged the social code of racial separatism. Ultimately, they wanted the Jim Crow system to end.[99] Most, apparently, did not engage in formal political mobilization, but they helped create an environment that led to challenging Crump at the polls in the future.

Black Memphians, including unionists, became more overt in challenging the Jim Crow system during the war years than they had been in previous decades. Like African Americans across the country, they tried to make wartime rhetoric about democracy a reality in their own lives. Individual protests increased, especially on buses, where African Americans risked arrest for not complying with segregationist policies. Working-class ministers increasingly hosted union and civil rights meetings at their churches. As occurred elsewhere in the South and the country, local NAACP branch membership grew at a dramatic pace, rising ten times in size to a high of some four thousand members. In 1944, branch members helped organize the Tennessee State Conference of Branches in order to better coordinate NAACP activities. Black Memphians were further spurred to activism after hearing about the poor treatment of black soldiers stationed in the South, who experienced violent attacks from whites and saw prisoners of war receiving better treatment than they were. The black unionist Clarence Coe protested by signing up hundreds of NAACP members at his plant.[100]

Crump could not stop the rising tide of protest activity, but he did manipulate the fear of race riots to clamp down on efforts to promote black equality. During the war, at least 240 racial incidents occurred in forty-seven cities, most extensively in Detroit in 1943, where thirty-three people died. Rumors spread of race riots in Memphis, and city officials remained vigilant, but none broke out.[101] Still, race riots were not far from Crump's mind, and his political use of this potential disorder was epitomized in the A. Philip Randolph controversy.

The local branch of the Brotherhood of Sleeping Car Porters invited Randolph to speak in Memphis on 7 November 1943 at Mount Nebo Baptist Church. The day before the speech, the sheriff called a group of black leaders to meet with him at his office, including J. E.

Walker, Matthew Thornton, Blair Hunt, Lieutenant Lee, and H. L. Patton, the president of the local chapter of the brotherhood. The sheriff took them to the Shelby County jail. Serving as the spokesman of the Crump lieutenants gathered there, Attorney General Will Gerber reminded the assembled group of the city's actions on behalf of African Americans and said that the upcoming meeting must be stopped; each would be held accountable if Randolph spoke and a race riot occurred.[102]

Patton and a delegation of porters met Randolph at the train station and urged him to leave, but the labor leader came anyway and spoke at the national convention of the Southern Tenant Farmers Union taking place in Memphis. Comparing Crump to Hitler, Randolph denounced him for refusing to permit freedom of speech. He said that the city officials' actions challenged Memphians and the labor movement to invite him back to speak at a public meeting. Randolph's union was part of the AFL, and its president, William Green, organized a mass meeting to take place in Memphis in March even though the local Central Trades and Labor Council condemned the gathering.[103]

Crump's treatment of Randolph attracted national attention. The *New Republic,* the *Nation,* and the *Chicago Defender* covered the controversy, while the national office of the NAACP protested to federal authorities about Crump's behavior. Long a close friend of Randolph's, Bob Church monitored and publicized the incident from afar, calling it "the hottest thing in the South today."[104] He persuaded a Republican senator to place a *Chicago Sun* editorial against Crump in the *Congressional Record.*[105] Not all black Memphians appreciated the publicity, however. Lieutenant Lee wrote Church that he wanted to be left out of the *Chicago Defender's* coverage, which supported Randolph and opposed African Americans who tried to stay in the good graces of Crump. "There is a job here I am trying to do and its [*sic*] hard enough," Lee said. "To be envolved [*sic*] in something else will be an exceeding handicap in carrying out a political program where the opposition would try to stop me on the slightest pretense."[106]

In New York City at his Brotherhood of Sleeping Car Porters headquarters, Randolph thanked Church for publicizing the controversy and reported that he was "busy building fires under Boss Crump and his reprehensible gestapo."[107] To the Department of Justice, Randolph protested Crump's denial of his right to free speech. His March on Washington Movement organization came to his aid. Representing one thousand members, the New York City branch wrote Mayor Chandler to protest the situation.[108] Using letterhead featuring the organization's slogan, "Winning Democracy for the Negro Is Winning the War for Democracy," Layle Lane, a North Atlantic division official of the organization and black socialist who was a leader of the American Federation of Teachers, wrote: "If such things can happen in America of what avail is all the terrible slaughter in this war supposedly fought to preserve the rights of free men." Urging Chandler to invite Randolph to Memphis to assure him of his constitutional rights, she said: "Only in this way will Memphis redeem itself from the justifiable charge it has already become a part of Hitler's empire."[109]

Randolph returned to Memphis to speak at the AFL meeting on 31 March 1944, despite two black Memphians, the businessman G. L. Young and the drugstore operator T. J. Johnson, having traveled to Washington, DC, to try to convince AFL president Green to forbid Randolph from speaking in the city in March or at any time; the Crump machine had likely funded the trip. G. A. Long was the only minister who allowed Randolph to use his church, the Beale Avenue Baptist Church, for the March gathering. Doctors, schoolteachers, principals, and ministers largely stayed away. Physicians and businessmen claimed that they were either "too busy" to attend or "home with a cold." When a *Chicago Defender* reporter asked the wife of one black principal why she did not attend, she replied: "Now you know right well, honey, that we couldn't dare to go. It would jeopardize my husband's job." Long opened the meeting with prayer, and then Randolph spoke to a crowd of two thousand, made up primarily of black and white unionists, both male and female. They came despite rumors that before and during the day of the meeting the city planned to place machine guns on Beale Street in an attempt to scare people away.[110]

Declaring that Crump "out-Hitlered Hitler," Randolph engaged in a battle of words and ideas with Crump in his speech. He pulled apart a recent defense from Crump, published in the *Commercial Appeal*, of his actions against Randolph. "Free speech does not mean that anyone has the right to holler fire in a packed theatre," Crump had written. "Nor does it mean that anyone, white or black, has the right to incite race trouble." Randolph called his comparison of a public meeting to a disruption in a packed theater "an insult to the intelligence of decent citizens, black and white." The labor leader pointed out that no race riots had broken out in any place, including cities in the South, where he had spoken. If the city had friendly race relations, as Crump had stated, there "ought not be any fear that one speech by one man could upset or disturb" them. Randolph castigated the machine for "waves of police brutality and terrorism," trampling on the rights of J. B. Martin, manipulating the black vote, and providing few city jobs for African Americans. He pointed out that no African Americans sat on the city commission in Memphis despite their large percentage of the population.[111] In an attempt to discourage black activism, Crump had written: "About 99 percent of the negroes in Memphis appreciate what has been done for them—housing . . . medical centers, schools, playgrounds, parks . . . and innumerable other helpful things."[112] Randolph replied that these public services were "no proper justification or compensation for denying . . . freedom of speech"; moreover, he blasted the quality of these public services. He denounced the black schools for being typical Jim Crow schools—inadequate, poorly equipped, and with teachers who were both underpaid and unequally paid compared to whites. Instead of "crowing" about these schools, Randolph said, Crump should remedy the educational discrimination.[113]

Randolph criticized the black leaders who followed Crump's orders to prevent him from speaking, saying that they had failed the black people of the country and unborn generations of black children. "They failed when they refused to stand up and support the right of free speech," he said. "They went back on the noble and valiant traditions of Harriet Tubman, Sojourner Truth . . . Frederick Douglass . . . and a great galaxy of heroic Negro crusaders for freedom and justice in the dark days of slavery, reconstruction, and our own time." He reasoned that some of these African Americans sought to defend their stake in the Jim Crow system and others wanted the favor of whites. "But this is not typical of the Negro today," he declared. "Negroes want no part of the me-too-boss, hat-in-hand, Uncle Tom Negro leader."[114]

Randolph tied the situation in Memphis to larger problems across the South. Quoting Booker T. Washington's words that "a white man cannot keep a Negro in the ditch without remaining in the ditch with him," he observed that the region did not flourish economically, socially, or culturally because it was held down by segregation, disenfranchisement, violence, economic exploitation, and civil liberties violations. He called on black and white workers to unite to "save the South from destruction by jim-crowism, fascism, and Crumpism," noting that the "same forces that attack the Negro's struggles for their rights, attack the struggles of labor for its rights." Pointing out that Crump was both a lucrative insurance executive and a machine government boss, he said that businessmen and politicians aligned to racially divide black and white workers as a way of economically exploiting both. Randolph predicted that the day would "come when the black and white workers . . . stop this misrule and unholy alliance" for they would recognize that their shared interests trump racial divisiveness. "Like other powerful political dictators, [Crump] will . . . disappear in a blaze of political disgrace," he said.[115]

Randolph was correct in making the connection between Memphis and the South; both the city and the region hurt blacks and whites through undemocratic practices. With African Americans held down by legal, political, social, and cultural restrictions, their potential was limited, as was that of whites affected negatively by the Jim Crow system. The poll tax disenfranchised African Americans and poor whites and women; the Crump machine consistently opposed its repeal because it was part of its arsenal for maintaining social and political control. Most Tennesseans did not vote, which made it easier for Crump to exert influence statewide. In fact, voter turnout was low in states across the region, sometimes not reaching above 15 percent of the eligible population. The South also was the poorest region in the country, as spotlighted in the federal government's 1938 "Report on Economic Conditions of the South," which Randolph referred to in his speech. Segregation served as a powerful barrier to poor blacks and whites joining together to uplift their economic status, and a southern oligarchy controlled politics with influence particularly wielded by Black Belt planters. It was no coincidence that the white business community supported and made campaign contributions to the Crump machine.[116]

Part of the powerful social movement struggling for racial and economic justice in the region, Randolph considered the March meeting "epoch making" and wrote Church that the "crusade that is being waged to make Memphis civilized and also make the South democratic is bound to have far reaching consequences for the good of democracy in America and the Negro in particular."[117] Already, in 1941,

Charles G. Gomillion, a black professor in Tuskegee, Alabama, had founded the Tuskegee Civic Association, which engaged in voter registration and legal efforts against disenfranchisement into the 1960s. The Southern Conference for Human Welfare advocated for federal legislation abolishing the poll tax and saw the passage of the Soldier Vote Bill in 1942, which exempted soldiers serving in the armed forces and ensured that they received absentee ballots for primary elections. A 1944 *New York Times* ad targeting the Republican and Democratic conventions spoke of the rising activism as well. Sponsored by leading black organizations of the day and representing 6.5 million African Americans, the message called for the abolition of disenfranchisement measures, the continuation of the FEPC, the enactment of antilynching legislation, an end to discrimination in the armed services, and a stop to colonial exploitation and imperialism.[118]

After the speech, Crump railed against Randolph in the *Commercial Appeal*. Several black ministers had publicly affirmed their support for Crump and had said that Randolph did not represent the attitude of African Americans. Pointing again to public services, Crump said that he "hate[d] to think that [Randolph] voices the sentiment of the colored citizens of this community in his belittling the many things that have been done for them."[119] Randolph responded with an open letter to Crump published in the *Chicago Defender* and other black newspapers; he used all Church's suggestions for crafting the statement.[120] Challenging Crump to a public debate, Randolph said that black Memphians were "not satisfied with your jim crow charity and that they resent your tyrannical and Hitler-like policies." Referring to the black leaders who had ingratiated themselves to Crump, he said that these "'little black nuts in the . . . machine' have taken you for a ride and [have been] feeding you with a lot of baloney in order to get your good will and a little jim crow hand out from time to time." African Americans had not challenged Crump because they feared that he would use his "gestapo ruthlessly to beat them up and run them out of town." Again predicting the demise of Crump's regime, he declared: "Because of your political feudalism, Memphis is backward and benighted but the people will wake up."[121] Crump did not accept Randolph's invitation to a debate.

Randolph apparently suffered no repercussions from Crump beyond verbal attacks, but other black Memphians faced a violent crackdown in the months following the speech. The machine reasserted its power in the wake of the rebellion of the thousands of Memphians who attended Randolph's talk. While local government officials pressured families of Brotherhood of Sleeping Car Porters members to move out of the Foote Homes, a public housing project, the city banned the planned birthday celebration for Randolph by the ladies auxiliary of the brotherhood there, ostensibly because outside groups were not allowed to use the facility.[122] A number of black Memphians experienced physical attacks, including Lieutenant Lee and the labor organizer Benjamin Bell. Two black assailants, who the *Press-Scimitar* reported were "known to have done work at times for the police," beat them with an iron pipe. Others received threats of violence, even the steadfast Crump supporter Blair Hunt. Anonymous callers warned the journalist Nat D. Williams not to publicize the violence.[123] Appealing to the Justice Department for an investigation, the Workers Defense League, a national socialist organization committed to protecting the legal rights of poor workers and trade unionists, charged that the police, abetted by the Crump machine, were violating the civil rights of black leaders.[124]

For allowing Randolph to speak in his church, Reverend Long faced the most serious repercussions. Saying that Memphis was "better off" without him, Crump publicly accused Long of "spreading race hatred."[125] In a public letter titled "Christ, not Crump, is my Boss," Long replied that he was not beholden to Crump as to whether he could live in Memphis. Mayor Chandler sent Long a threatening letter, Boyle verbally abused him in comments publicized by the local white press, and two black assailants attacked him at night at his garage door. Police harassed his congregation on Sundays. The city condemned his church, forcing him to pay for more than $5,000 worth of improvements. Long only made $25 per week, and his parishioners were working-class and few in number. To meet the city's fees, Randolph ensured that his union paid Long $1,000, and a group of black sailors at the nearby naval air base at Millington contributed $136.50. Church monitored the repression against Long, while the pastor's congregation supported him through these trials. But Long finally left the city, moving north to Detroit by 1947, and harassment of his congregation stopped.[126]

Church and Randolph communicated about the labor leader's ordeal in Memphis for years, and Church remained interested in conditions in the city. A year after Church left Memphis, James C. Dickerson, a *Chicago Defender* reporter and the editor-publisher of the *Memphis Spot-Lite,* a black weekly based on Beale Street, had written him: "We miss you very much here, especially those of us who remember your true worth to the Memphis Negroes."[127] Church played an indirect role in guiding the local black-and-tan Republican organization from afar; he urged its members not to be intimidated by city officials, who he feared were taking over the rival lily-white faction. Yet his influence was not enough to prevent the black-and-tan faction's decline.[128] When Lieutenant Lee visited Church in Chicago during the Randolph controversy, Lee said that he "did not see how in three short years Memphis could be changed around like it is today." Church had said that Lee was "partly to blame for it, that Memphis had not changed, that it was the leadership of which he was part."[129]

Although Church seldom returned to Memphis, he tried to regain a couple of his political positions in Tennessee. His ownership of a small piece of property in Memphis made him eligible for political activity. In 1942, he sought to run for the state Republican Executive Committee in Tennessee in order to retain his prestige with national leaders. But Crump ordered the county court not to pay the bills for the Republican primary unless he withdrew from consideration. He did so, but no Republican primary was held anyway. Two years later, Church tried to become a delegate to the Republican national convention, but apparently Senator McKellar, one of Crump's associates, conferred with the East Tennessee Republican congressman B. Carroll Reece to help block this move.[130] J. Will Taylor, Church's loyal ally in state politics, had died in 1939. Reece was now one of the state's most powerful politicians.

Church met with more success in national politics after leaving his hometown. He wanted to push the Republican Party to meet the postwar concerns of African Americans, especially war veterans. He believed that unifying African Americans, as he had done with the Lincoln League of America, would help achieve this goal. As a result, he formed the Republican American Committee and was elected its first chairman at its organizational meeting held in Chicago over Lincoln's birthday in February 1944. The group consisted of black Republicans, both male and female, from more than thirty states; some were former members of the Lincoln League of America or their descendants. J. B. Martin, Lieutenant Lee, and Perry Howard, the prominent Mississippi Republican and former league official, joined.[131]

At its founding meeting, the Republican American Committee adopted resolutions outlining demands that it would push for in the coming years. It called for the end to racial discrimination in the armed forces, safeguards to protect the right of collective bargaining, the appointment of African Americans to policymaking positions, government aid for employment and housing, and the enactment of an antilynching law. It further called for legislation to equalize education opportunities regardless of race, to abolish the white primary system in the South, to end racial discrimination on the part of unions and employers, to extend Social Security legislation and include agricultural and domestic workers in its provisions, to prohibit discrimination and segregation in interstate travel, and to allow the president and vice president to be elected by popular vote. The committee held more meetings after 1944, and its members presented their resolutions and discussed them with the Republican National Committee and Republicans in Congress and state and local offices.[132]

The Republican American Committee achieved one of its greatest successes in 1944 when the GOP included the strongest civil rights language in its platform in its history. Church and an organizational delegation met with the Republican national convention's platform committee and helped persuade its members to include statements calling for a constitutional amendment to abolish the poll tax, legislation against lynching, the establishment of a permanent FEPC, and a congressional investigation into discrimination and segregation in the armed forces. They argued that the black vote held the balance of power in seventeen states and that Republicans could win this bloc by embracing a strong civil rights position. The Republican platform ended up containing stronger civil rights statements than that of the Democrats despite the turn of African Americans to that party.[133]

When it came to civil rights in the 1944 election, however, little difference existed between the two parties beyond the platforms. Civil rights was a minor concern, and both presidential candidates expressed their support for it in mere generalities. As a concession to the South, Roosevelt replaced as his vice presidential candidate the racially liberal Henry Wallace with Harry S. Truman, for whom African Americans had little hope when it came to civil rights. Nonetheless, most African Americans voted for Roosevelt, who won the election. The Republican Party had not provided an alternative to his economic programs or taken a civil rights position strong enough to distinguish itself from the Democratic Party. Its platform was part of the party's pattern of spouting platitudes about civil rights that were backed up by no real action.[134] In a letter to the Republican National Committee in early 1945, Church claimed that the efforts made by the Republican presidential campaign to reach out to black voters were "the least intensive of any Campaign ever conducted by the Party, and as a consequence of the stupidity of the present leadership, we lost thousands and thousands of votes."[135] Pointing out that the GOP had not won a presidential election since black voters left the party, Church and his Republican American Committee pushed Republicans to fulfill their platform promises.[136]

The Republican American Committee was one of Church's two main political projects after he left Memphis. The second was his work to make the FEPC permanent.[137] Calling the issue of fair employment "a human one which involves economic, social and moral justice for more than twenty million members of minority groups," he joined the board of directors of the National Council for a Permanent Fair Employment Practices Commission, an organization formed by A. Philip Randolph in 1943.[138] As its chief lobbyist on Capitol Hill, Church visited members of Congress of both parties to educate them about the issue and inform them of its importance; he also arranged conferences with them that included Randolph. His lobbying work commenced by 1946, and he advocated for fair employment into the early 1950s; he attended the Democratic national convention in 1948 in this capacity. He sometimes would wait in congressional offices for four to five hours in order to get a word with politicians.[139]

"I knew there was no other person of color in the country who could reach as many outstanding Republican spokesmen of power . . . [or] whose political wisdom was more highly cherished and sought after, by both black and white Republican leaders, than his," Randolph later said when discussing why he appointed Church as the chief lobbyist of his organization. "The basic reason for this was that he not only possessed a mind for careful evaluation of political personalities and forces but he [also] was impeccably honest and could not be influenced by money or political power." Randolph gave insight into their professional collaboration and personal friendship: "Although he knew that I was a Socialist and was critical of both the Democratic and Republican parties, he trusted my judgment even with respect to the expression of opinions about Republican leaders. He was immensely pleased over the fact that I was politically independent." Recalling that he and Church spent hours in Washington and New York in Church's hotel room discussing racial problems and strategies for solutions, he said that Church was happy to be his representative on Capitol Hill "not only because he was conscious of the impoverishment of black workers and believed in the principle of fair employment practice, but [also because] he enjoyed sitting down with me and various political leaders to argue over the feasibility of my program."[140]

Church involved himself in other national political activities as well. Virginia Durr, an official of the National Committee to Abolish the Poll Tax, enlisted him to persuade Republicans to support an anti–poll tax bill. He joined prominent black and white figures, including A. Philip Randolph and Eleanor Roosevelt, in working with this committee. He was a member of the Southern Advisory Board of the National Urban League. And he was willing to share his political skills: he taught Clarence Mitchell, the longtime lobbyist for the NAACP, how to lobby.[141]

As Church battled for political influence, civil rights, and fair employment, the Crump machine sought to portray race relations in Memphis as harmonious. In 1944, the city released a forty-page booklet titled *Benefits and Opportunities for Colored Citizens of Memphis: Civic Progress 1940–44,* which spotlighted health, educational, recreational, housing, and other municipal services for African Americans. It featured city jobs for African Americans, including as doctors, nurses, and public housing managers. Attractive photographs, portraying African Americans in a dignified light, showcased the city's offerings.[142] The city publicized the booklet to citizens, government agencies, and local and national organizations. Often in response to requests, city officials, along with the local chamber of commerce, distributed more than fifteen hundred copies free of charge from late 1944 through 1946 to a variety of recipients, including university and public libraries, chambers of commerce, municipal and federal officials, and ordinary citizens.[143] Mayor Walter Chandler ensured that all African American schoolchildren received copies for their families and that copies were available for distribution at Memphis's black library.[144]

The booklet served many purposes for the city beyond Chandler's assertion that it was "presented to challenge and arouse the colored people of Memphis to the exceptional opportunities offered to them for the promotion of their health, education, and general welfare, and to impress upon them their duty to take the fullest advantage of those opportunities, benefits and privileges."[145] The machine wanted to court black support in the midst of the civil rights and labor activism in which black Memphians were engaged. With the 1944 election approaching, Crump wanted black votes for his candidates. Because Memphis experienced a labor shortage owing to World War II, the machine wanted to discourage black migration away from the city. By giving the impression of good race relations, city officials wanted to attract business to Memphis.[146] Following the Martin and Randolph incidents, they also wanted to rehabilitate the image of Memphis nationally, and their effort resulted in some success. The Reverend A. J. Garvy of Chicago wrote the mayor: "It was a remarkably telling booklet. As you well know, Memphis has not always been presented in this light. It deserves fairer recognition than it has often obtained."[147]

Many local African Americans praised *Benefits and Opportunities* and requested copies. E. L. Washburn, president of both the Memphis Youth Service Council and the Twenty-Sixth Ward Civic Club, wrote Chandler that members of both organizations were asking for copies because they found the publication useful for informing them about city services. Washburn remarked that he had visited black schools in more than eleven southern cities, including Raleigh, Atlanta, and New Orleans. "None that I have visited [surpassed] the buildings and set up we have in Memphis," he said. "I am with you and your administration 100%."[148] Those black Memphians who had long supported the machine also commended the booklet. Businessman M. S. Stuart reported that he and other Memphis Negro Chamber of Commerce officials planned to send copies to southerners in other cities as an "expression of pride . . . for what has been done and is being done for us."[149] Blair Hunt and J. E. Walker added their voices to the chorus of praise for the publication.[150] Although the local government's benefits were significant, the words of all these black Memphians represented the "baloney" that A. Philip Randolph had spotlighted when he had said that some African Americans painted a picture of good race relations in order to win Crump's favor. At the same time, their comments signaled to Crump that the city had better continue to provide benefits for African Americans in order to keep their votes. The extent of the provisions revealed the degree to which black voters had successfully ensured that the government served their needs.

The businessman M. S. Stuart commended *Benefits and Opportunities* to Mayor Chandler for revealing that Memphis authorities "have a keen interest in, and fine attitude toward, the welfare of Negro citizens . . . in contrast to several large cities in the South where authorities almost entirely ignore the existence of Negro people except in regard to criminality." He gave him a column by the famed journalist George Schuyler of the *Pittsburgh Courier*.[151] Noting that no other southern cities had printed such booklets, Schuyler wrote that it "signified a new departure in race relations." He said: "It is not unusual for cities to boast of their assets and opportunities. . . . But it is certainly unusual for a Southern city to boast in print of what it is doing for its colored citizens." The journalist admitted that "many gaps [exist] in this flowery account" but said that the "City Fathers of Memphis deserve a hand" for the booklet.[152] Mayor William Hartsfield of Atlanta requested copies because of his desire to do more for African Americans, who made up 36 percent of his city's population. "While I retain certain views handed down from time immemorial in the South, still I am one of those that think the [economic] opportunities and privileges of blacks should be enlarged," Hartsfield wrote. "However, we meet with a lot of opposition and indifference from some of our officials."[153] Osceola E. McKaine, an editor of South Carolina's *Lighthouse and Informer,* a black weekly published in the state's capital, distributed *Benefits and Opportunities* to the mayor and city council, newspaper editors, and the chair of the South Carolina Interracial Committee.[154] He called it a "splendid booklet" that "registers a high mark [for its] constructive approach to better race relations."[155]

While the booklet showcased Memphis in a positive light, it also spread negative ideas about African Americans. It used *negro* instead of *Negro*. Spinning segregation as legitimate and even beneficial, it boasted that African Americans had an exclusive day each week at the zoo instead of emphasizing that it was the only day that they were allowed to visit. It characterized the city's one black library branch as a privilege for African Americans while ignoring the fact that they could not utilize the city's other library branches. Although the city government employed African Americans, *Benefits and Opportunities* did not mention that they mainly occupied the lowliest jobs and that black doctors and nurses treated only black patients. It did not address the city's lack of black policemen, firefighters, and public officials either. By framing essential human services provided to African Americans as "opportunities, benefits, and privileges," it made these rights out as something for which to be indebted. By saying that the city government should be commended because the costs of its services to African Americans exceeded the amount of taxes that they paid, it ignored the fact that the prevailing legal, social, and economic discrimination was at the root of their low contribution to the city treasury.

Although most responses to *Benefits and Opportunities* were positive, Lieutenant Dunbar S. McLaurin and his group of black soldiers sharply criticized it. Stationed overseas, many were from the South, and several were from Memphis. "It was . . . with a great deal of pride that we read of the publication put out by your city," McLaurin wrote Chandler when requesting copies. "It represents to us fighting men, a recognition of the fact by white southerners that the Negro citizen is definitely an integral part of the southern economic, political, and, yes, even social structure. . . . This is an example of what we are fighting for."[156] But then they received the booklet and saw the noncapitalization of the word *Negro*. McLaurin wrote again: "Our hopes, our visions, our excitement were blasted. For there was embodied in one incident the still vigorous antebellum spirit of the South—the deliberate, studied, and intentional degradation of a race by the refusal to allow it the dignity of a proper noun." He then talked about how even the word *Nazi* was capitalized and how no other race or ethnicity was referred to in the lowercase. He asked why the lowercase *negro* was used. "We agreed that it is because the South is determined that the Negro shall not be recognized as a man," he wrote Chandler. They reasoned that this recognition would entail recognizing the human rights of African Americans. Echoing A. Philip Randolph's observations, he reported that he and his men thought that the southern ruling classes used race to divide working-class blacks and whites, to keep whites from recognizing that they too were held down by disenfranchisement and segregation, and to prevent blacks and whites from joining together to battle these injustices.[157]

Because the lowercase *n* "screamed at the men from each page so that all the text was drowned out," McLaurin said that they could read the booklet only after they had gone through it and capitalized *Negro*. "Mr. Mayor, I went to bat for you," he wrote. "I told the men that your mistake in making the error was unintentional." But, he continued, he changed his view after they examined the publication more closely. "The booklet seemed to smack of smug completeness," he said. "Omitted was police brutality, the lack of Negro civil servants, of Negro firemen, police and others." Calling the chairman of the City Board of Censors a "Memphis Goebbels," he criticized the city's policy of banning or censoring movies with any semblance of racial equality.[158] "Mr. Mayor, I'm quite sure you won't reply to this letter. That is unfortunate. For we would like to have the South's side, briefly," McLaurin concluded. "We would like to know why you deliberately lower-cased the 'n.' . . . We would like to know what your city's real attitude is toward Negro policemen, firemen, doctors etc. In short, we would like to know: *Is Memphis afraid of its Negro and white citizens getting to know each other?*"[159]

The positive and negative responses to *Benefits and Opportunities* revealed the mixed approach of the Crump machine toward African Americans. On the one hand, it reportedly provided better public services to African Americans than were available elsewhere in the South and stood out for promoting its provisions to them. The city appeared racially progressive because African Americans could vote. On the other hand, it earned a reputation for its repression against its black and white citizens. Black political rights could mean little because of Crump. For all his concern about maintaining peace and harmony, Crump, ironically, was building up resentment among Memphis citizens that threatened to damage his control. Again and again, the machine pointed to its benefits to African Americans as a way to divert attention from and provide a justification for not giving them civil rights or otherwise meeting their demands. Pointing to the World War II context, the NAACP's *Crisis* magazine observed: "Politically, Memphis is as un-American as any dictator-ridden country in Europe."[160]

McLaurin's correspondence with Chandler came during a time of substantial steps for racial advancement. In April 1944, the Supreme Court declared the white primary unconstitutional in its *Smith v. Allwright* decision. Although southern states continued to find ways to disenfranchise African Americans, these new methods were not as effective. Black southerners took advantage of the *Smith* decision to engage in voter registration drives, which led to a dramatic rise in the number of black voters. Determined to make democracy work within their own country, black veterans especially became politically active. Black South Carolinians formed the Progressive Democratic Party through state NAACP networks to challenge the state's all-white Democratic Party. In 1944, Osceola McKaine made a bid for the Senate on its ticket, and the party sought recognition for its delegates at the Democratic national convention. Although unsuccessful in these goals, the Progressive Democratic Party and its efforts represented an important step forward. In Memphis, J. E. Walker sent Mayor Chandler a copy of his speech at a local church in which he praised the *Smith* ruling, advocated the permanent establishment of the FEPC, and called for other civil rights and labor measures. He said that these steps were necessary for advancing the masses, not the classes, of African Americans. By sending his speech to Chandler, Walker worked to carve out more of a space for African Americans in the local Democratic Party. As president of the National Negro Business League, he joined with prominent national black leaders in calling for the passage of legislation to abolish the poll tax in federal elections.[161]

During the war years, black Memphians had worked through the political system to improve their conditions in the face of the Crump machine. Leaders such as Blair Hunt, Lee, and Walker could secure a limited degree of employment opportunities, public service improvements, and other benefits for black Memphians. Working within the constraints of the time, they campaigned for Crump's candidates and cultivated ties with him and his officials as a strategy for achieving their goals, even to the point of being obsequious and pandering. In an era when most black southerners were poor, a better job or neighborhood improvement could have a positive effect on their standard of living. Most white southerners constructed African Americans as subhuman and inferior, so the recognition of their citizenship by white local officials, even though limited, was significant. These black leaders decided that it was best to work with the machine rather than risk reprisal or even death by going against it.

At the same time that these leaders sought to improve conditions for African Americans by working with Crump, they also perpetuated the Jim Crow system and the local political machine. By effusively praising Crump for his public services on behalf of African Americans, not speaking out against injustices of the machine, and claiming to speak for all black Memphians, they bolstered Crump's ideas that those opposing him or the Jim Crow system were troublemakers. In assuming this strategy, they hurt their own aims despite their good intentions. Hunt, for example, perhaps would have better improved the lot of his students by joining forces with A. Philip Randolph and speaking out against Jim Crow schools instead of pushing for benefits for his school within the segregated system. After all, when black businessmen, women, and others came together to protest the derogatory laundry sign, Crump made sure the sign was removed. It would be unwise to think that black leaders could convince Crump to change his position on segregation. If more black Memphians had challenged him, however, he may have become less repressive, especially considering that African Americans had some leverage because he needed their votes.

These leaders who stayed in the good graces of the Crump machine paid a price, and those who opposed Crump did as well. After rebelling against Crump, Bob Church, J. B. Martin, G. A. Long, and others found themselves stripped of their financial and personal security. Yet these figures, along with McLaurin and Randolph, provided an important challenge to Crump and the larger southern system. Seeing Crump as indicative of larger problems across the South, McLaurin and Randolph pointed out that the Jim Crow benefits of the Crump machine were no substitute for civil rights and liberties. They recognized that Crump's control was tenuous; the extent to which the political boss felt that he had to manipulate black and white votes and crack down on those who threatened his control revealed his own insecurity. Whites and blacks at the grassroots level had been crucial to his rise to power, and he knew that both could bring him down. Randolph worked from afar and locally against Crump, Long courageously took a stand against Crump and for racial equality, and Church successfully publicized Crump's actions and otherwise aided Randolph in his battle. Locally, black unionists supported Randolph in his ordeal, and other African Americans increasingly made public their opposition to segregation. With all this activism occurring, it looked like Randolph's prediction that the Crump regime would fall just might come true.

5 "A New Day Breaking" in the City and the South

The Decline of the Crump Machine and the Rise of New Leadership, 1946–1954

In the postwar years, Memphis saw the growing political independence of its citizens. Black Memphians joined forces with white unionists and reformers to hand Edward H. Crump his first electoral defeat in decades in 1948. Their effort resulted in the Crump machine's decline, a more democratic political environment, and local government reforms. Robert R. Church Jr. carried on his battle to make the Republican Party embrace civil rights, while a new generation of black activists bolstered civil rights efforts in Memphis and the South. In order to increase voter registration, politicize African Americans, and ultimately break the Jim Crow system, more black Memphians began running for public office than at any time since the 1910s. Whereas black men generally held more visible roles, such as by bidding for office and doing public speaking, women mainly engaged in crucial behind-the-scenes work.[1] The year 1954 saw the *Brown v. Board of Education* decision, a victory for the black Memphians and southerners who had long pushed for an end to the Jim Crow system.

By ruling the white primary unconstitutional in its 1944 *Smith* decision, the Supreme Court spurred "a political revolution in the urban South."[2] Driven by the efforts of black veterans, NAACP branches, labor unions, and others, southern black voter registration shot up from less than 5 percent of those eligible before the ruling to 20 percent by 1952, even with obstacles such as violence, harassment, and legal efforts against the ruling. African Americans in urban areas of the Upper South and large cities of the Deep South made up the largest proportion of the black vote. In Mississippi, the state with arguably the most

175

intransigent system of white supremacy, black voter registration numbers increased from twenty-five hundred in 1946 to twenty thousand in 1950. Black voter clubs rose in number across southern states, and African Americans ran for public office, making bids in more than forty municipalities, and winning positions as significant as school board or city council seats in at least fifteen communities. African Americans held important appointive offices in many cities and increasingly held the balance of power in elections. Although black southerners held less than 5 percent of elective and appointive offices, the postwar environment signified more hope and potential for politics than at any time since Reconstruction.[3] The *Brown* decision remains the most remembered and recognized civil rights decision, but the impact of *Smith* on black political activism cannot be overestimated.

The postwar environment was ripe for economic change as well. Southern industrial workers had risen in number from 1.6 to 2.4 million during the war, and the federal government had forced many employers to provide higher wages and other union concessions. With labor union membership at an all-time high, the largest ever number of strikes took place in 1945 and 1946. The CIO embarked on an initiative called Operation Dixie to organize more unions in the South in 1946 and met with some success in workplaces with large numbers of black workers.[4]

Anticommunist hysteria swept the country, however, and hurt efforts for social and economic justice. By 1946, Operation Dixie declined because of white racism, police and company violence, and anticommunist propaganda. Congress passed the Taft-Hartley Bill in 1947; its antiunion provisions included prohibiting strikes by federal employees and requiring union officials to swear that they were not Communists. Victims of red baiting, both the Southern Conference for Human Welfare and the National Committee to Abolish the Poll Tax ended their operations in 1948.[5]

In Memphis, the immediate years after World War II saw labor activism intertwined with formal political efforts. With about 20 percent of its workers belonging to a union, Memphis was the most organized city in the Deep South. Even though most white workers remained uncommitted to interracial organizing, a small group of white Communists and leftists opposed segregation and engaged in biracial CIO work. Black unionists agitated for better working conditions, challenged discriminatory practices in the workplace, and undertook voter registration drives and other civil rights efforts in the community. In 1947, eighteen thousand labor activists—of the AFL, CIO, and railroad unions—marched in an integrated Labor Day parade in which they carried signs that urged everyone to vote, expressed support for the Fair Employment Practices Commission (FEPC), and opposed the Taft-Hartley Bill. The march began a number of joint efforts of these unions to lobby state legislators and support progressive candidates for office.[6]

Black Memphians also became increasingly outspoken against Crump. Remembering the harassment of A. Philip Randolph and J. B. Martin, they opposed the police brutality that continued with impunity, the area's lack of black police officers, and the machine's exile of its adversaries from Memphis.[7] They opposed Crump's pressure on blacks and black complicity with Crump. Two high school principals would tell teachers: "You better vote as Mr. Crump says; your job is at stake." If residents of public housing projects did not vote for his candidates, then they would be pressured to move out.[8] The city's refusal to allow the Freedom Train in late 1947 further angered them. Making stops in more than three hundred communities, the train reached 3.5 million people across the country from 1947 to 1949. Supported by the federal government, businesses, foundations, and unions, it carried documents related to the American heritage such as the Bill of Rights. Because local officials opposed the train's policy forbidding segregated viewing of its exhibits, Memphis was the first city to have its stop canceled.[9]

Fueled by their anger at Crump, and building on their wartime activism, black Memphians experienced a rising tide of protest. Along with whites, they spoke out against their exclusion from the Freedom Train. The LeMoyne College NAACP branch, which had seen the wartime draft of most of its male members, gained new strength. The adult NAACP chapter, which attracted veterans and working-class men and women, saw its membership rise to 4,120 in 1946 and experienced overflowing crowds at its meetings. Black ministers became increasingly politically active; even Bishop Charles H. Mason of the Church of God in Christ, which had traditionally shied away from politics, invited the African American congressman William Dawson of Chicago to speak at its annual convocation in 1949 and the governor of Tennessee the next year. Local leaders and groups also conducted a campaign for the hiring of black police officers. None had served in Memphis since 1919 even though other southern cities had begun to appoint them. Black Memphians argued that the hiring of black police officers would reduce racially biased police violence, effectively suppress black crime, and give blacks recognition for their wartime service. They called for black police officers in light of the sexual assault of two young, working-class black women by two white police officers in August 1945. The assaults and the officers' acquittal spurred protests of black Memphians, including by ministers and NAACP members, against the machine.[10]

When A. Philip Randolph returned to Memphis in 1947, he saw "a new day breaking" in the city. He spoke at the Memphis Labor Conference sponsored by the Brotherhood of Sleeping Car Porters. The Reverend G. A. Long hosted this public meeting at his Beale Street Baptist Church.[11] The "Crump machine is conspicuous by its silence," Randolph wrote Bob Church, reporting that the meeting generated no trouble and that "Memphis appears to be much more civilized now" than when he was there last.[12] Even so, most black ministers, professionals, and businesspeople were too afraid to attend; working-class men and women predominated. One was the young Reverend Dwight Kyle, who led a movement to set up a local FEPC council.[13] Since forming the National Council for a Permanent Fair Employment Practices Commission in 1943, Randolph had been founding local councils across the country. He called the Memphis chapter's founding "miraculous." Predicting that Memphis "may yet become one of the most liberal cities in the South because Crumpism is crumbling," he remarked: "I think the sun of decency, freedom and justice will shine in Memphis in the not distant future. An awakened Negro and white citizen [sic] will bring it about."[14]

Just as Randolph forecast, African Americans joined with white unionists and reformers in 1948 to back the first candidates to seriously challenge Crump in decades: Estes Kefauver and Gordon Browning, who ran in the Democratic primaries for the junior senatorial seat and the gubernatorial seat, respectively. Men and women of all economic levels participated in the rebellion. Crump supported the incumbent, Jim McCord, for governor and John A. Mitchell for the Senate. A little-known circuit court judge, Mitchell advocated states rights and opposed the FEPC. The incumbent senator, Tom Stewart, had lost Crump's favor but refused to leave the race. If voters split their ballots between Mitchell and Stewart, Kefauver could win.[15]

Both Kefauver and Browning conducted spirited campaigns that attacked Crump. A Democratic congressman from East Tennessee since 1939, Kefauver held liberal views that put him to the left of Crump and most of his southern counterparts. Although against a permanent FEPC and antilynching legislation, he supported abolishing the poll tax and had opposed the Taft-Hartley Bill. When Crump compared Kefauver to a pet coon, Kefauver began wearing a coonskin cap when on the campaign trail. Browning, a World War II veteran, announced his candidacy by saying that he had fought a war against a dictator and now wanted to rid his native state of Crump's dictatorship. Elected governor with Crump's support in 1936, Browning had been defeated two years later after displeasing him. In 1948, Browning made some three hundred speeches across Tennessee, focusing on Crump's negative influence on the state.[16]

In Memphis, a group of seven white businessmen and professionals publicly announced their support for Kefauver. They united around the book *Union Now* (1940) by Clarence Streit; it advocated the creation of an association of Western democracies in order to promote world peace and personal freedom as a safeguard against communism. Kefauver offered to sponsor a congressional resolution supporting the idea. By working against Crump, the group also promoted a more democratic political system locally. The first woman on the team, Frances Coe, acted as the group's office manager, and two other women eventually joined the committee. Coe worked ten- to sixteen-hour days for the campaign, leading to tension in her marriage because she sacrificed time that she might have devoted to her husband and children.[17]

The *Memphis Press-Scimitar* editor, Ed Meeman, along with the lawyer Lucius Burch, spearheaded the small group's campaign. A lonely public voice against Crump over the last decade and a half, Meeman had been limited in his opposition: Crump verbally attacked him, and the city charged him with property violations. Meeman and his committee met every day in a suite at the Peabody Hotel.[18] "This small Kefauver group attracted very few . . . people of any stature in the community," Coe recalled. "In fact, we knew only 200 people who would sign an advertisement that they were supporting Kefauver."[19]

The AFL and the CIO worked with the white reformers in order to oppose Crump and support Kefauver, who was friendly to unions. Previously, Memphis labor unions had made a strong showing in the

1944 presidential election. Union officials estimated that members of the AFL, the CIO, and four independent railroad brotherhoods were responsible for about thirty-five thousand of the sixty thousand votes cast; Crump had called these estimates high, perhaps not wanting to acknowledge the strength of a potential opposition group. In 1946, the CIO had made the first open political challenge of labor unions against the machine by backing non-Crump-supported candidates for the gubernatorial and senatorial seats. Labor activists registered to vote, became informed voters, and worked as poll watchers. However, their candidates lost by large margins, and many unionists did not vote. Still, this effort made the activists more determined to defeat Crump at the polls as they saw voting irregularities and gained electoral experience.[20]

In 1948, the interracial Local 19 of the CIO-affiliated Food, Tobacco, Agricultural and Allied Workers Union was one of the labor unions conducting voter registration drives; its members canvassed door-to-door in black neighborhoods.[21] LeRoy Boyd, an African American member, waited in line for four hours to register. "I remember that line was a long line," he recalled. "You know, they can use psychology on you. They can register you real slow and make the people in line get tired . . . and leave . . . but I got registered. And a lot of people were wanting to . . . register, and they wanted to exercise their right to do it."[22]

A variety of black Memphians, some of whom had long been politically active, championed the Kefauver-Browning ticket; their work intersected with that of the reformers and unionists. They raised campaign funds, held rallies, registered and organized voters, and encouraged poll tax payment. The Reverend James McDaniel, the head of the local Urban League, spoke to African Americans from a CIO sound truck. Minerva Johnican, who later became an elected official in the city, helped him pass out handbills. At a voters' school sponsored by the local League of Women Voters at the black Vance Avenue Young Women's Christian Association chapter, the white reformer Lucius Burch spoke. Black businessmen who supported the anti-Crump candidates included Taylor C. D. Hayes, who had railed against the machine in letters to his pastor ten years earlier, and J. E. Walker, who headed the black Democratic club, now independent from the machine. Neither the black Democrats nor the white reformers received any campaign funds from the Democratic state headquarters, so they raised funds on their own. Not all black Democrats supported the Kefauver-Browning ticket, however. Blair Hunt offered to campaign for Crump. One black political activist later observed that Hunt had been so integral to Crump's operation for so long that he did not think that Hunt could have gotten out of it, that he was caught in it.[23]

Crump's support for the Dixiecrats inspired African American opposition to the machine. President Harry S. Truman had begun a new course in the Democratic Party by calling for civil rights measures following the surge of black activism in the postwar years and the necessity of black votes for his reelection. During the war, the black population had grown by 40 percent in the North; African Americans held the balance of power in key states. Truman created the President's Committee on Civil Rights and endorsed its 1947 report, *To Secure These Rights,* which was the most far-reaching statement for civil rights of any US president or government agency since Reconstruction. Its proposals included eliminating the poll tax, making lynching a federal offense, and establishing a permanent FEPC. The Democratic national convention commended Truman for his civil rights stand but stopped short of endorsing any specific proposals; instead, general statements against racial discrimination were in the first-ever civil rights plank in the party platform. The Dixiecrats, a splinter group dedicated to the maintenance of segregation, walked out of the convention.[24] Contending that Truman's proposals intended "to force upon people of Tennessee and the South a deplorable social condition repugnant" to their "ideals, principles and tradition," the Shelby County Democratic Executive Committee issued a resolution against Truman's candidacy and his civil rights program.[25]

The local committee's statement was just one part of an election season filled with "extreme bitterness."[26] Through full-page newspaper advertisements, Crump vilified Kefauver and Browning; he smeared Kefauver as a Communist sympathizer. Browning suspected that Crump considered killing him, while some Kefauver supporters feared for the senator's life. Every member of the small group of white reformers faced pressure to stop their campaign.[27]

Frances Coe remembered that the "hardest thing was convincing people that they could vote freely and their vote would be known." To combat these fears, the reformers conducted both word-of-mouth and advertising campaigns to assure Memphians that their votes would count. The League of Women Voters chapter engaged in a similar effort and organized a "School for Watchers." When the August primaries arrived, one thousand poll watchers were on duty to prevent election fraud. The anti-Crump contingent armed itself with that many given, two years earlier, two hundred CIO-trained watchers had dissipated to two by the end of primary day. Some failed to show up, while others were chased away or put in jail. In 1948 middle-class women worked as poll watchers along with businessmen, unionists, and, apparently, FBI officials.[28] The machine could not easily intimidate poll watchers because of their strength in numbers and the presence of women.

On the primary day in August, African Americans joined with liberal whites to lift the "iron curtain of fear."[29] Organized twenty thousand strong, unionists came out in full force; especially those black voters associated with the labor movement opposed Crump. Both Kefauver and Browning won the Democratic nomination, ensuring their victory in November. Browning received 56 percent of the vote, while Kefauver received 42 percent, winning by a plurality. Although neither candidate carried Memphis or Shelby County, both got enough ballots there to hand them a victory, cracking the machine's control of the state.[30] "Everywhere are seen smiling faces of people who have broken the spell of fear—it's like Joe Louis winning a prize [fi]ght," the *Washington Afro American* reported.[31] Congratulating Kefauver on his victory, Bob Church, a friend of his, said: "Your courage . . . has done more to put hope into the heart of the 'Man on Street,' than anything that has been done during my generation."[32] Lieutenant Lee later called the defeat "the beginning of the gradual deterioration of the great Crump organization"; the black Memphian Emogene Wilson recalled that Crump's power declined because he could no longer "call the shots."[33] The black unionist George Holloway added: "Things changed completely when Senator Kefauver beat the Crump machine. . . . [I]t was like a new Memphis. People began to see that they could protest what was happening, and they weren't afraid."[34]

In September, Crump acceded to African American demands to employ black police officers, prompting celebration on Beale Street. Although African Americans were not allowed to arrest whites, thirteen began training as officers in October, and more were employed by the early 1950s. Furthermore, Crump retired Attorney General Will Gerber, who had played a crucial role in the machine's actions against J. B. Martin and A. Philip Randolph, and he replaced Mayor James E. Pleasants, who had come under fire during the Freedom Train incident, with Watkins Overton, who had a better record of working with African Americans.[35] All these tangible effects so soon after the primaries revealed the increased leverage that African Americans had won as a result of their political activity.

In 1948, some black Memphians demonstrated their independence from Crump by backing Republican candidates. Black Republicans encouraged voter registration, poll tax payment, and going to the polls. As vice president of the Shelby County Republican Campaign Committee, Lieutenant Lee recruited Roscoe Conkling Simmons to speak: the journalist, orator, and nephew of Booker T. Washington had mobilized black voters at political rallies in the city since 1916. Locally, the Republican primary yielded few votes compared to the Democratic one. In the primary's largest vote, Lee received only 975 votes in his successful bid for the state Republican Executive Committee.[36]

As industrialists had come to hold more influence in the party and white Republicans had concentrated on battling anticommunism, the Grand Old Party had become less supportive of civil rights and fair employment than in years past. After the party lost the black vote in 1944, one party official admitted that, while its platform plank in favor of a permanent FEPC had been chiefly an effort to win black support, African Americans had voted for Roosevelt anyway. He said that the party could not afford to support an FEPC law because New England and Midwestern industrialists would stop their campaign contributions. Republicans regained congressional control in the 1946 election for the first time in sixteen years but did not make any civil rights or fair employment efforts, leading to rebukes from the NAACP and Church's Republican American Committee. In 1948, the Republican presidential candidate, Thomas Dewey, the New York governor, had the strongest civil rights record of any governor in the country, but he hardly campaigned for the black vote and did not stress his civil rights achievements. Because Republicans lacked strength at the local, regional, and national levels, some black Memphians joined other black southerners in aligning with the Democratic Party. Moreover, many African Americans disapproved of the Republican Party's growing conservatism on major racial issues. The Memphis black press, for instance, condemned the Republican senatorial candidate Carroll Reece for endorsing states' rights and opposing the FEPC and Truman's civil rights proposals. Previously, Reece had voted for antilynching and anti–poll tax legislation as well as for the FEPC.[37]

Still, the Republican Party retained a degree of racial liberalism in 1948 that demonstrated that Democrats had not completely gained the upper hand when it came to civil rights. In its platform, the party called for the abolition of the poll tax and the enactment of antilynching legislation and also declared its opposition to racial segregation in the armed services. Church had, once again, helped persuade the party to include these statements.[38] He and other African Americans knew the platform was no guarantee of action; after all, such statements in previous years had been largely symbolic. But the party continued to afford them an element of recognition by including these demands and showing that it valued their votes, even if to a limited degree, unlike the many Democrats who opposed such statements and supported black disenfranchisement.

In Memphis, some African Americans took a different political track that election season by backing the Progressive Party. They attended the interracial gatherings of some two thousand to twenty-five hundred attendees that occurred when the party's presidential candidate, Henry Wallace, stopped in the city in September and when the famed black singer and activist Paul Robeson sang folk songs there a month later. Wallace unequivocally favored civil rights. Making the first bid by a black Memphian for public office in decades, the Reverend Dwight Kyle ran for the state legislature on the Progressive Party ticket with a white woman. The pastor of the Avery African Methodist Episcopal Chapel, a West Virginia native, and northern educated, he had moved to Memphis in 1946 and had become the local NAACP Executive Committee chairman. In addition to heading the Memphis FEPC Council, he was a member of Local 19 and participated in its voter registration efforts.[39] On the campaign trail, Kyle declared that he was for "total equality for the Negro" and "complete integration."[40] He had reason for hope: in Winston-Salem, North Carolina, white and black unionists and NAACP branch members backed the Reverend Kenneth Williams in his bid for a seat on the board of aldermen in 1947; he became the first African American to win public office against a white candidate in the twentieth-century South.[41]

After the primary election, black Democrats urged support for Truman, pointing to Crump's endorsement of the Dixiecrat presidential candidate, Strom Thurmond. The black Democratic club sponsored rallies in black wards and at black schools and also recruited white reformers to speak at a large meeting at the Labor Temple on Beale. Some African Americans who had voted in the Republican primary threw their support behind Democratic candidates, while black labor groups made a strong show of support for the Browning-Kefauver ticket. The Reverend James McDaniel estimated that 100 percent of black Democrats backed Browning and Kefauver, although some preferred Dewey over Truman.[42]

Crump not only made some concessions after the primary but also reasserted his power by harassing black activists. Police officers ordered three black ministers to leave a Republican rally. The ministers refused, and the police left them alone. But the police forced African Americans to leave other rallies for the Republican candidates and the Kefauver-Browning ticket. The black unionist Lonnie Jones reported that policemen with clubs chased him and sixty to seventy other black Memphians from a Kefauver-Browning meeting. Not yielding to fear, Jones publicly declared that he still planned to vote for the Democratic candidates.[43]

Browning and Kefauver won in the general election, and the Dixiecrats were defeated, dealing another blow to Crump's credibility. Kyle lost but received 3,760 votes, many of which came from predominantly white precincts. In Memphis, white Democrats split their votes between Truman and Thurmond, with each capturing around 40 percent. More than half of black voters supported Truman. Thirty percent of black voters and 18 percent of white voters backed Dewey. Fewer than two thousand Memphians voted for Wallace.[44] That so many white Memphians supported Thurmond revealed Crump's continuing influence and their opposition to civil rights reform.

The year 1948 shook the foundation of the political system in both Memphis and the South. Similar to how Crump's one-man rule had been broken, the one-party system in the region cracked as the Democratic Party splintered and four Deep South states went for the Dixiecrats. Black political activists and white labor activists formed coalitions in Memphis as well as Richmond, where a black lawyer, Oliver Hill, won a seat on the city council.[45] The *Chicago Defender* reported that more African Americans won office nationwide "than at any time in our memory."[46] In addition, African Americans engaged in direct action against segregation. A. Philip Randolph conducted protests at the Democratic national convention for the desegregation of the armed forces. The previous year, the Congress of Racial Equality sponsored interracial bus rides throughout the South to protest transportation segregation.[47] In 1948, Truman desegregated the military and established a nondiscriminatory fair employment policy for the federal government, providing two major victories for the freedom struggle.[48]

Although his machine was irrevocably damaged, Crump remained the most dominant political figure in Memphis and Shelby County after the 1948 elections. "His iron hand wrapped in velvet" continued to operate in local and state politics, the *Memphis World* observed.[49] He selected and appointed local officials, his candidates won elections, and his ward and precinct organizations remained active. Local government employees campaigned for him, and he relied on his long-standing tactics to manipulate some black voters. His supporters, for instance, would go to black neighborhoods and, through announcements over microphones, urge citizens to come out and vote. They would give black voters watermelons to take home from truckloads strategically stationed near polling stations.[50]

The white reformers kept up their battle against Crump. In 1949, they formed the nonpartisan Civic Research Committee (CRC) to promote greater citizen involvement in politics and local government and election reforms. The fifty charter members included labor leaders but mostly consisted of housewives, attorneys, businessmen, physicians, and others who had campaigned for Kefauver. Within a year, 250 people had joined the group. Wanting to stay away from controversial issues, the CRC avoided taking a position on segregation. It did not accept its first African American members until two years after its formation. Nonetheless, J. E. Walker and other black Memphians backed the CRC's initiatives. Memphis and Shelby County used paper ballots for elections, and citizens had to reregister annually to remain eligible for voting. The CRC's goals included pushing for voting machines and permanent registration and raising awareness of alternative structures of local government. Claiming that the CRC was not "anti-administration," the reformers pointed out that it did not support candidates, but Crump and Mayor Overton saw the organization for what it was—an obvious effort to challenge the machine and work against voter fraud and manipulation. CRC officials invited Overton to serve on a subcommittee, but he refused and denounced the association as "a strictly political move to discredit the city government."

He and Crump opposed the group's ideas and considered the reformers enemies.[51]

In order to retain political legitimacy, Crump was forced to accept some of the CRC's ideas. The group involved civic clubs, the chamber of commerce, and the media in a communitywide campaign for voting machines, which the city purchased in 1952 and used in 1954 for the first time. The CRC spearheaded voter registration drives and succeeded in having polling places changed from unstable locations such as tents to secure venues such as schoolhouses. It also successfully pressed Memphis officials to develop a comprehensive plan in order to keep the city's public services in pace with its growth; the plan directly connected with the recurring demand of black Memphians for better public services.[52]

Governor Browning's administration oversaw legislation that further changed the local political landscape and benefited African Americans. In 1949, the Tennessee legislature exempted women and veterans from the poll tax and abolished the requirement for primary elections. Other legal reforms included establishing permanent registration, outlawing the poll tax in 1951, and prohibiting public employees from being election officers. Browning appointed three CRC members to the Shelby County Election Commission to enforce these changes. By making examinations for civil service positions open to all and requiring that test scores determine job placement, the state legislature opened doors for African Americans. Browning granted university status to the Tennessee State Agriculture and Industrial College as well.[53]

While the CRC did not endorse candidates, its members played key roles in backing the first local ticket independent of Crump in twenty years in 1950. Eleven candidates sought state, congressional, and local offices, although Overton was not challenged as mayor. At least one hailed from the labor movement, and Crump included a labor representative on his ticket as a concession to 1948 developments. Black industrial workers especially backed the anti-Crump slate. Although no independent candidates beat Crump-backed office seekers in Memphis for the rest of his life, they challenged his control and contributed to a more democratic city.[54]

In the new political environment, the machine modified its long-standing practice of ward and precinct work. In the 1950 election, the white campaign worker Boyd Harte reported to the Crump organization on a poll tax payment and voter registration effort by city and county employees. He was careful about telling the employees that their work was "voluntary" and avoiding "the oldtime [*sic*] business of 'insisting that they work or else.'" Warning the workers that they would "find some enemies of the Administration, and some who might be biased by the *Press-Scimitar*," Harte instructed them "not to be overconfident" and to "WORK, WORK, WORK and sell Mr. Crump's leadership."[55] In the predominantly black Fiftieth Ward, Harte collaborated with J. Ashton Hayes, the principal of Manassas High School and the president of the local civic club. Hayes recruited workers to supplement city and county workers, both black and white, urging poll tax payment and voter registration, but he found some African Americans unwilling to support the Crump-backed candidates.[56]

Some black Memphians continued to back the machine out of their own free will and to see benefits firsthand in their lives. Blondale Clady Cross, who started voting in 1950, supported Crump's candidates because she could see improvements from one election to the next.[57] At a 1950 campaign rally, some three hundred black Memphians applauded Mayor Overton for meeting the requests of black delegations for street improvements. "Your curbs and gutters and street lights [*sic*] really, really helped," Boyd Harte told Overton.[58] The city bettered its educational services for African Americans and equalized black and white teacher pay.[59] The machine also erected a monument and dedicated a park to Tom Lee at the foot of Beale Street near the Mississippi River in 1954. In 1925, even though unable to swim, this black man single-handedly rescued thirty-two whites from a shipwreck. The monument described Lee as a "very worthy negro."

While Memphis achieved greater political independence as a result of the 1948 developments, its labor movement suffered from the wave of anticommunism spreading across the country. Antiracist actions made labor activists susceptible to charges of communism, a reason that interracial organizing in Memphis declined. In 1951, Senator James Eastland of Mississippi, a staunch segregationist and member of the Senate Internal Security Subcommittee, the Senate's equivalent of the House Un-American Activities Committee, conducted hearings in Memphis that targeted black unions. While union organizers faced harassment and brutality at the hands of the police and management, the city's CIO and AFL unions eliminated all their black organizers except one by 1954. All this opposition did not mean that the activism of black unionists ended: they continued to demand better working conditions and to participate in voter registration efforts both within and outside their plants.[60]

The local NAACP saw a waning of its activism as well. After surpassing more than 3,500 members per year from 1946 to 1948, the chapter declined to 880 members in 1949 and usually did not exceed 1,000 over the next five years. Collectively, the state's branches saw membership decline by nearly two-thirds from 1947 to 1950. Nationwide, NAACP membership declined from 350,000 in 1948 to 150,000 two years later. The Memphis branch faced financial difficulties, which hurt its ability to recruit new members and conduct programming. Utillus Phillips, the president of both the Memphis NAACP branch and the Tennessee State Conference of Branches, thought that the expense of the $2.00 membership fee drove away members and urged the national office to reduce it to $1.00, to no avail. Nationally, NAACP membership dropped for that same reason. In 1948, the national office had raised the membership fee to $2.00 from $1.00; it was experiencing financial troubles of its own and could not always provide the funding that it usually gave to branches. The Memphis chapter's troubles were also self-inflicted. In 1948, when experiencing high membership levels, the branch opened a downtown office. The increased overhead expense came at a time when memberships began to decline. The chapter could not afford to send a delegate to the national convention for a couple of years, and some Memphis NAACP members spent their own money to keep its activities going.[61] In a memorandum to the Tennessee State Conference in 1950, Lucille Black, the membership secretary of the national organization, said the "primary weakness" of the NAACP was due to "[its] failure to inject new blood into the life-stream of the Association," explaining: "We have depended too long on the *same officers*, the *same workers*, the *same members*." She continued: "There are thousands of people in the State who have never been members and who have never been drawn into our program. These people offer an untapped reservoir which must be capitalized upon."[62] In her advice for recruiting new members, the southeast regional secretary of the NAACP, Ruby Hurley, emphasized that the organization "must reach all classes of people."[63]

The Memphis branch was further limited by the continuing power of Crump. In 1950, Phillips observed that it had experienced difficulty for "quite a number of years" in "getting substantial citizens to take an active part in its affairs," commenting: "Without any apparent sound reason, the City Board of Education frowns upon the Organization, which is a definite handicap." He continued: "This linked with those who have an unfounded fear of 'Boss' Crump, cripples our efforts for the type of organization we should have."[64] Given the inadequate health services for black Memphians, the chapter supported the machine's plans for a new black public hospital despite the national organization's policy against segregation. At a 1952 meeting, branch leaders said that they felt that the black community so badly needed a new hospital that they could not go against Crump's plan. The hospital project came to fruition in 1956 when the E. H. Crump Memorial Hospital opened its doors.[65] In a letter to the national office reporting on the branch's support for the hospital, Ruby Hurley characterized the chapter as suffering from a "conservative influence," "little action," and a lack of inspiration; she contrasted it with one in Indianola, Mississippi, where World War II veterans were registering voters, holding public meetings, and reaching out to sharecroppers.[66]

The Memphis branch did not let the machine stand in the way of carrying out many of its civil rights activities, however. The young attorney H. T. Lockard became a member in 1951. At branch meetings, he found very few people "but nonetheless a solid core of mostly men who seemed to be interested and determined to addressing some of the existing problems and in fact doing something about it."[67] While the chapter conducted membership and fund-raising campaigns, it also undertook voter registration efforts. Its lawyers provided legal protection for black tenant farmers from unscrupulous employment practices throughout the tristate area. In 1953, the chapter voted to cooperate in all efforts to implement recent Supreme Court decisions ruling restrictive covenants and racial zoning in housing illegal. It raised funds for a lawsuit to integrate the University of Tennessee. Under Phillips's leadership, the Tennessee State Conference passed resolutions urging its members to register African Americans to vote and calling on state officials to remedy the denial of voting rights in some Tennessee counties, especially Fayette and Haywood, the majority-black counties in rural West Tennessee.[68]

In the meantime, George W. Lee, J. E. Walker, and four other black men issued a call to one hundred black leaders to join forces in a voter registration campaign in the spring of 1951. Taking advantage of the legal end of the poll tax that year, they wanted to extend to the black community the registration efforts of the CRC, which sought to qualify enough independent voters to overcome the Crump machine's grip in the area. A group of one hundred African American leaders, mainly men, formed the Citizens Nonpartisan Registration Committee. In a show of partisan unity, Lee and Walker, the area's leading black Republican and Democrat, respectively, cochaired the committee, which included representatives of the NAACP, black Republican and Democratic organizations, and civic clubs.[69]

Lee was well suited to start this grassroots organization. He maintained a Republican ward and precinct organization called the Lincoln League, which was not officially connected with Bob Church's former group of the same name. Whereas Church was nationally focused in his political work, Lee was locally focused. "When I succeeded Bob Church as political leader here, I found out that I had to develop a different approach. Church had developed his strength from the top through personal acquaintance with men on the echelon of the Republican Party," Lee recalled in the mid-1960s. "He was able to neutralize a great deal of his [local] opposition [by] commands down from the top but I had developed no such contact, and if I was to survive, I knew that I had to find my strength in the 'grassroots.'"[70] Under his leadership, local black Republicans built a ward and precinct organization that bolstered his own strength as a leader and acted as a venue for political education and mobilization. From a low of thirteen precinct clubs after Church and Martin left Memphis in 1940, the black Republicans had organized groups in twenty wards and at least sixty precincts by 1951.[71]

Lee used his organizational skills to ensure that the nonpartisan committee hit the ground running. "We are turning the town over to register Negroes," Lee wrote to Church, who remained in Chicago.[72] Lee and Walker helped recruit about 125 ministers to assist with voter registration, signaling how times had changed from the height of the Crump era, when many preachers had either shied away from politics or backed the machine. At "citizenship Sundays," ministers urged voter registration and educated their parishioners about civic responsibility. While civic clubs and churches competed for prizes for registering the most voters, nonpartisan committee members held rallies, raised and contributed funds, and canvassed door-to-door. The committee rented buses to transport people—congregated at the doorsteps of churches around town—to and from the courthouse to register.[73]

A few weeks into the campaign, Lee wrote to Church: "People are beginning to get a little afraid since Rev. [Dewitt] Alcorn was so brutally assaulted. . . . This situation should have stimulated registration but . . . it has had the opposite effect."[74] After accusing Alcorn, a member of the nonpartisan committee, of being a Communist, two white police officers kicked and beat him at the segregated Greyhound bus station. Charging him with loitering and resisting arrest, they transported him to a hospital for treatment. The Inter-Denominational Ministers' Alliance and the NAACP branch protested the police brutality to local authorities. Lucius Burch, the white reformer, defended Alcorn, only to see a city judge dismiss the charges against the police officers; Mayor Overton supported this decision.[75]

Nevertheless, Lee worked to recruit a black candidate for the school board and consulted Church about the matter. He explained to Church that he did not want to offer himself as a candidate because he feared that lily whites would use the opportunity to seize control of the local Republican organization and he wanted to become collector of customs in Memphis in the event of a Republican president. J. E. Walker was willing to run if he had Lee's support. Knowing that Walker, who headed both the Tri-State Bank and Universal Life Insurance Company, had the money to fund his own bid, Lee agreed to back him. Church did not support the choice of Walker because he thought that a black Republican should be selected to run. He feared and suspected that black Democrats were dominating the local black political scene and believed that Lee's credibility as a Republican leader would be hurt if he did not ensure that a Republican bid for office.[76]

In late July, Walker, who was around seventy years old, announced his candidacy for the school board. He became the first African American to seek local office in Memphis since the early twentieth century. The only candidate to run against Crump's ticket, Walker wanted his bid to spur African Americans to register to vote and saw many black community groups, including the NAACP branch and the Negro Junior Chamber of Commerce, increase their voter registration efforts.[77] Walker's very act of running for office struck "a major blow for racial equality," Benjamin L. Hooks, the future leader of the national office of the NAACP, recalled. "To the black community, this was an act of defiance of an old order. It was a clarion call for African Americans to rise up politically. To the white community, Walker's candidacy was a testament to the reality that things were forever changed."[78]

Walker may have received funds from the local white reformers and Governor Browning for his campaign. The white liberals had urged him to run because of their opposition to Crump; Walker apparently had not entered the race without their approval. Although the CRC did not endorse candidates, two prominent whites in the group, Edmund Orgill and O. D. Bratton, made radio appeals for Walker, while several members backed him. Orgill, a successful businessman, demonstrated the limits to his support, however, by saying that Walker's election might lessen black Memphians' demands that their children attend the same schools as whites.[79]

The campaign brought together new and long-standing black leaders. Ms. Tweze Twyman worked as its director of voter registration, and H. T. Lockard, the young black lawyer, NAACP branch member, and World War II veteran, campaigned for Walker. Women, including Walker's wife, Lelia, formed a "Women for Walker" club. They contacted women citywide about the campaign, held a luncheon, and declared a "Women for Walker Day." In addition to working as secretary of the nonpartisan registration organization, Benjamin Hooks, at age twenty-six, was chosen by Walker to comanage his campaign along with T. C. D. Hayes, who had followed in the footsteps of his father, T. H. Hayes Sr., to become one of the city's most prominent black undertakers. A Memphis native and World War II veteran, Hooks had personally experienced the indignity of guarding prisoners of war who could eat in restaurants where black soldiers could not have a meal.[80] He attended LeMoyne College and Howard University as an undergraduate and, after the war, DePaul University Law School in Chicago. While in Chicago, Hooks observed the freedoms enjoyed by African Americans and the existence of black public officials. He became convinced that "one of the keys to social change was the exercise of the ballot." After J. B. Martin offered to open doors for him professionally in Chicago, Hooks decided to accept his offer. However, as he recalled more than fifty years later: "Almost immediately, something told me this was not the thing to do. . . . [S]ome inextricable force urged me to return to Memphis. I cannot explain this somewhat mystical experience. All I know is that I saw, in my mind's eyes, black police officers and detectives, black lawyers and judges." He envisioned African American city and county commissioners as well as an integrated society. Hooks returned to Memphis shortly after receiving his law license in late 1948 and moved back in with his parents, who lived in the Foote Homes public housing project. One of only three black lawyers practicing in the city, he became as active as possible in civic affairs, joining the Memphis Negro Chamber of Commerce, the NAACP branch, and the Lincoln League.[81]

More than any other political effort up to that point, the Walker campaign allowed Hooks the opportunity to make his vision a reality.[82] Walker ran against four candidates. The four who received the most votes would win spots on the school board. If African Americans voted only for him and not for the other candidates, Walker had a greater chance of winning, so Hooks and other supporters urged black Memphians to engage in "single shot" voting.[83] Saying "a voteless people is a hopeless people," the campaign employed fund-raisers, rallies, and voter registration and education efforts.[84] "Interest in the campaign was high. There was a new pride in the black community in the city," Hooks recalled. "Everywhere, people were talking about the Walker candidacy. In beauty parlors, barbershops, offices, at church and social club meetings, on street corners, and around dinner tables, the talk was about the election."[85]

Walker explained his motivations for running in newspaper articles, radio addresses, speaking engagements, and campaign flyers.[86] Pledging honesty and fairness to all, he said: "I am not running just for my race, but I am running to serve the city and people of the great City of Memphis."[87] Noting that other southern cities had black school board members and elected officials, Walker argued that African Americans deserved representation because they made up 40 percent of the population; a black member would be sensitive to the concerns of black students and teachers.[88] In this time of the Korean War, he said that it would be a "righteous act" for a black school board member to serve in a system that trained young black men who enlisted in the military. Pointing to the Cold War context, his campaign said that his election would be "an example to the North and Russia that democracy works in the South."[89] The *Memphis World* added that black political representation would eventually cause the "walls of discrimination" to crumble and lead to "brotherhood, equality, and true democracy."[90]

The Crump machine opposed Walker's bid because he ran as an independent candidate, he was connected to the white reformers, and he challenged the social order. In radio ads, Overton warned that "a racial issue" had entered the election. The administration distributed voter instruction sheets that featured photographs of the five school board candidates—with Walker's picture unusually dark—to predominantly white neighborhoods, whereas it gave sheets with no photographs to predominantly black neighborhoods. Crump had Blair Hunt tell Walker that he would be forced to leave the area if he did not withdraw his bid, but Walker stayed.[91]

Walker lost the election in November. Despite the flurry of campaign activity, less than one-third of the city's registered voters participated in the election, with less than half the ballots of the twenty-three majority-black precincts going for Walker. Some African Americans were committed to another candidate, while others did not know about him or heard very little about his bid. Attesting to Crump's continuing dominance, some black teachers feared reprisals if Walker was elected.[92] Initially, Lieutenant Lee had tried to find someone else to run, partly because he considered Walker not "generally popular among the average run," but Hooks later characterized the candidate as having "universal respect among the black community."[93]

Walker had said: "Whether I'm elected or not, I still can't lose."[94] Indeed, the number of black registered voters rose from 7,000 at the campaign's start to 19,608 by the election.[95] Although Walker faced hostile tactics from the Crump machine and Reverend Alcorn was attacked, the opposition to the bid, all in all, was less intense than the violence and intimidation of 1940 in which African American activists were beaten or run out of town. Lee had not dared show his face at Republican meetings taking place then in opposition to Crump's orders, but he now felt free to openly challenge the political boss. The *Chicago Defender* named him to its "Honor Roll of Democracy" for rallying black Memphians to register and vote.[96] After the election, Walker's campaign managers, Hooks and Hayes, declared: "Progress has been made in Memphis. When a Negro can openly oppose the city administration without incrimination of any sort, it proves that Democracy is not a myth but exists in our Southland."[97] Hooks later recalled that the campaign gave him citywide recognition and propelled him into a leadership position in Memphis.[98]

Elsewhere in the South, black political efforts provided a foundation for civil rights advances. In Georgia, officials did not comply with the *Smith v. Allwright* decision until the Supreme Court struck down the state's white primary in *Chapman v. King* in 1946, the same year the poll tax was abolished in the state. John Wesley Dobbs, the leading black Republican of Atlanta and a member of Church's Republican American Committee, wrote Church: "Negroes are registering to vote in large numbers all over the state. There is a new day breaking for us in this state."[99] Along with black Democratic leaders and local NAACP and Urban League officials, he formed the All Citizens Registration Committee. Driven by the grassroots work of women, it launched a voter registration drive that year that eventually led to the founding of the Atlanta Voters League, an African American political organization, in 1949 and the election of three African Americans to public office in the 1950s. In 1949 and 1953, black voters held the balance of power in the election of Mayor William Hartsfield.[100]

In Memphis, hundreds of representatives of the twenty existing black civic clubs formed the Bluff City and Shelby County Council of Civic Clubs in July 1951; the idea for this new organization originated from Lincoln League members who were inspired by the nonpartisan committee's registration campaign. The council's initial goals were to form more civic clubs and register African Americans to vote.[101] In a letter to Walker, the group praised him for his "courage to run for office with the odds against" him; it said: "The Negroes of Memphis are appreciative of the . . . sacrifices made by you and . . . the intelligent manner in which your campaign was conducted. . . . [Y]ou are to be congratulated upon your contribution to the history of the South and America."[102] Professional and working-class black men and women, including unionists, educators, and businessmen, joined the council. Hooks acted as its founding legal adviser, and Walker became its president by 1954. In addition to conducting voter registration drives, civic clubs pushed for public service improvements and spoke out against urban renewal and residential segregation. Along with the NAACP and other black community organizations, it protested the bombing of a home purchased by an African American in a white neighborhood in 1953. It endorsed the CRC's voting machines initiative and pressed for black firefighters; the city hired the first ones since the late nineteenth century in 1955.[103]

By 1952, the council had grown to represent thirty-one civic clubs. In a report to municipal officials, it spotlighted the poor state of recreational facilities for African Americans, including broken swings, a pool filled with sticks, and no bathrooms at some locations. Noting that African Americans paid tax dollars for public services, the council protested their exclusion from some recreational and cultural facilities and the restrictions on their use of others. Calling on black

Memphians to take action by registering and voting, the council asked for improvements to existing recreational facilities and the admittance of African Americans to white facilities.[104] A. A. Branch, a professor at LeMoyne College; James T. Walker, a unionist; and Willa McWilliams, the council's assistant secretary, authored the report. Like other civil rights activists, they used anticommunist rhetoric to further their ends by exposing the contradiction of the United States battling communism abroad while engaging in undemocratic practices domestically. In light of the "deplorable" state of park services and the city's failure to meet their past requests for improvements, they said: "We cannot in all fairness to our children teach them the democratic principles of our government and ask them to go along with us." They submitted the report "to fight . . . the foe of democracy, communism."[105]

The city's response to the report was mixed. The administration promised new funding of $68,000 for black recreational facilities, yet Overton also decried the report, saying that the city had continually provided African Americans with better recreational facilities since he first became mayor in 1928.[106] "Nowhere in the entire South do our colored citizens have better facilities for their children, both schools and parks, than in the City of Memphis," he claimed.[107]

Another important part of black community and political life was the local radio station, WDIA, the first in the South with all-black programming. At a time when many African Americans were illiterate, it could hold more influence than the local black newspapers. The radio station began broadcasting in October 1948 and included political, educational, religious, and cultural programming. Nat D. Williams, the black newspaper columnist and Booker T. Washington High School history teacher, became a radio personality and hosted "Brown America Speaks," one of the first programs in the country where African Americans discussed local, national, and international issues of interest to the black community. WDIA promoted black political action as well. During the 1952 election season, deejays registered voters and campaigned on air for candidates. The station offered an award to the radio personality who had the most listeners attend a political rally sponsored by the nonpartisan registration committee.[108]

The early 1950s proved to be a momentous time for the Republican Party in Memphis. Since Martin and Church left the city in 1940, Lee and his black-and-tan group served as the regular Republican Party organization in the area. Black Republicans exerted the most influence as leaders and members and maintained the group. Along with Lee, Church's former political associates Drs. W. O. Speight and A. N. Kittrelle were leaders.[109] The lily-white faction—the all-white organization that had rivaled the black-and-tan group—had not been consistently active in decades. Raymond Lymon, the local black Republican activist, later said: "There were[n't] many so-called white Republicans. . . . They didn't think it was respectable at that time to work in the Republican party because it was actually dominated by Negroes. . . . [I]t was dominated by Negroes because we participated and we worked." He recalled that some whites worked for the party only during national election time.[110] Some black Republicans believed that many white Republican leaders had decided not to become active in the party until a Republican administration came into place so that they could profit from patronage; some white Republicans had previously involved themselves in the local party in order to receive post office jobs.[111]

Although African Americans constituted most of the Republican primary voters until the late 1950s, Lee's black-and-tan faction faced a serious challenge in early 1952. A "New Guard" Republican movement developed, especially powered by white housewives and businessmen and largely consisting of upper-middle-class people. A key leader, the white attorney Millsaps Fitzhugh, had been one of the three CRC members that Governor Browning had appointed as a local election officer. The New Guard Republicans attracted disgruntled white Democrats as well as whites who were economically conservative and antiunion. Opposed to Roosevelt's New Deal, wealthy white businessmen had come to make up a large number of Republican leaders throughout the region.[112] The year 1952 was an opportune time for the emergence of more white Republicans, locally and elsewhere, because of the possibility of the victory of the presidential candidate Dwight Eisenhower, the popular World War II general.

White housewives handled most of the grassroots, organizational work involved in building the New Guard movement. They arranged "Republican workshops" in precincts where local Republicans recruited party members by explaining the importance of a two-party South. They then formed a precinct organization for educating citizens about issues and mobilizing voters. "My wife and fifteen other Republican women built that precinct organization just themselves, with personal visits and phone calls and meetings," recalled Lewis Donelson III, a white attorney involved in these efforts. "They'd call up . . . somebody in the precinct and say, 'How'd you like to have a Republican workshop?' They'd find somebody and they'd say, 'Now you get as many of your friends as you can to come and we'll come and give you a lecture and all,' and we'd sign up Republicans."[113]

The New Guard Republicans vied with Lieutenant Lee's "Old Guard" Republicans for control of the local party throughout the 1950s; they hardly collaborated with each other. Although Donelson claimed in a 2004 oral history that no one in the New Guard group was racist, the New Guard Republicans remained mainly white throughout the 1950s, and many, though not all, opposed civil rights measures.[114] Lee later assessed the New Guard as having "drawn its strength almost all together from racial prejudice."[115]

Nationally, the Republican Party shied away from civil rights stances, while a wing of the party aligned with conservative southern Democrats. The alliance stemmed from a shared concern about the growth of the government, and its members accused the New Deal and Truman's Fair Deal—which advocated for further social welfare measures—of veering toward socialism. The Republican Party, after all, was the one of the anticommunist crusader Joseph McCarthy, and the Democratic Party's influential southern wing had hampered Truman's civil rights and social welfare proposals. The alliance members opposed the establishment of a permanent FEPC: Republicans saw it as a threat to the party's business interests, while conservative southern Democrats saw it as a threat to the Jim Crow system. Similarly to how he had spoken out against the lily-white movement, Bob Church railed against the Dixiecrat-Republican alliance during the late 1940s and early 1950s.[116]

In January 1952, the New Guard Republicans made their first major push to become the regular Republican organization locally. Some 150 whites showed up for a New Guard gathering, the most whites to attend a Republican meeting in recent memory. They decided to try to unseat Lee's faction at the next Shelby County Republican convention by arriving early in hopes of outnumbering them. The meeting always came to order at 2:00 P.M. in the Shelby County Criminal Court Room. Receiving word of their plans, Lee invited hundreds of black Republicans to a free breakfast at the Elks lodge on Beale Street and then transported them in chartered buses to the meeting four hours ahead of time. Ironically, he attracted a large crowd partly because some black Republicans told recruits that Church might return to Memphis to take over the local party's leadership from Lee. Four hundred members of Lee's group packed the room, with two hundred remaining outside. Just a few New Guard Republicans squeezed in; one called for the meeting to be moved to a larger room. George Klepper, the white attorney belonging to Lee's group and the long-standing chairman of these meetings, denied the request. The black Republicans dominated the meeting—in part by shouting down the white Republicans—and maintained their control of the local party.[117]

Calling the Old Guard actions "disgraceful," the New Guard Republicans urged Tennessee Republican leaders to expel Lee's group from the state party and recognize them as the regular Republicans. Carroll Reece, a longtime ally of Lee and the party boss, refused the request. After Church and Martin left Memphis in 1940, Lee had formed a working relationship with Reece. At the time, Lee had felt like he was in the middle of "a political ocean without a life preserver."[118] He was high in the councils of the state party by 1952; Reece and his associates saw him as a dependable ally. Whereas the New Guard Republicans backed Eisenhower, Reece and Lee supported Senator Robert Taft, who was also vying for the presidential nomination. Reece acted as Taft's southern campaign manager.[119]

The New Guard Republicans were not the only ones opposing Lee. Church disapproved of Lee's leadership of the local party and decided to return to Memphis in 1952 and offer himself as a candidate for Lee's position on the state Republican Executive Committee. Planning to run on the New Guard ticket, he wanted to regain control of the area's Republican Party. Since leaving Memphis in 1940, he had maintained ties to the local political scene. Local black Republicans asked him for political advice, he claimed that he knew more about the local party than anyone else, and a Shelby County Democratic official accused two white Republican leaders of receiving orders by telephone from him. Although Church had returned to Memphis on occasion after his exile in 1940, he had continued to operate out of Chicago and Washington, DC. He remained eligible to run because he owned a small piece of property in Memphis and considered the city his official residence. When he traveled to Memphis in October 1951, he expressed a desire to recruit more members, including young people, to the party. He believed that the black-and-tan faction had declined in strength under Lee's leadership; Raymond Lymon, who was active in the group under both Church and Lee, later agreed with his comment. Church feared that black Democrats were dominating the local black political scene.[120]

Church also wanted to head the party to inspire local Republicans to support Eisenhower for the presidency. He believed that the general was the strongest Republican candidate when it came to civil rights and disagreed with Lee's endorsement of Taft. Aligned with the party's conservative wing, Taft was for states' rights and opposed the New Deal, the FEPC, and some civil rights policies, although he backed antilynching legislation and the abolition of the poll tax. Reece had assured Lee that Taft's conservatism concerned fiscal policy, not civil rights. "[As] [m]uch as I loved and respected Church and as much as I was devoted to him over a long period of years, I thought it was politically right and proper since he had left the state to go along with [Reece]," Lee later explained. "Reece stood with me against 'lily whiteism' [and] stood with me in my ascendancy to leadership in the Ninth District over many outstanding ambitious whites." While Eisenhower displayed little knowledge of racial matters and opposed the FEPC, he received the backing of liberal members of the party and appeared more racially progressive than Taft. He favored antilynching legislation, the abolition of the poll tax, the desegregation of Washington, DC, and the elimination of segregation in areas under the authority of the federal government. He repudiated South Carolina newspaper statements characterizing him as for states' rights and opposed to desegregation.[121]

Some black Republicans, whom Church had previously influenced to become active in the party, did not support his goal to formally rejoin the local political scene; he suspected that they feared antagonizing Crump, who kept a file on his national activities.[122] Church apparently ran into Crump only once after leaving Memphis. He spotted him at the Kentucky Derby in the late 1940s. According to Church, when he approached Crump, Crump's hands began to tremble. Church expressed his disapproval of the city changing the name of Church's Park to Beale Avenue Park. "My father was a wonderful man, and he did a great deal for Memphis," he said. "And I certainly don't think it was proper and I don't appreciate the city changing the name of that park in view of . . . his contributions to the city." Crump professed unawareness of the name change and said that he would look into it, but no action was taken. When in Memphis in 1951, Church tried to schedule a meeting with him, to no avail.[123]

Despite his exile from Memphis, Church always saw it as his home, and African Americans there were not far from his mind. He had spent "many, many years . . . unceasingly fighting in order that colored citizens of Memphis should share equally in participation and representation on both the local and national political scenes," he remarked in 1951. "This political activity for the benefit of others was sustained by enormous sums of money spent from my personal funds."[124] He wrote Charles Browning of the *Tri-State Defender*, a local black newspaper founded that year: "There are no finer Colored people anywhere in America, than are in Memphis. I know them. If you[,] and those associated with you, intend to publish a newspaper of character . . . fighting the many injustices against them, those Memphis Colored people will support your paper, but if you do not, they will let your paper drop like a hot brick."[125]

In April 1952, Church traveled to Tennessee to recruit support for Eisenhower after meeting with his southern campaign manager in Washington, DC. Wearing a gold lapel pin that simply said "Ike," he attended the state Republican convention in Nashville.[126] "Just his presence there seemed to change the convention when he walked in," remembered Lymon, who observed that delegates, including white elected officials, deferred to him.[127] Despite this show of respect, Church failed to convince the convention to support Eisenhower. Out of loyalty to Reece, Lee ensured that his delegation unanimously backed Taft even though Lee personally supported the FEPC and was skeptical of Taft's conservative political philosophy. While Lee became a delegate to the Republican national convention, Church did not succeed in his attempt. He was dismayed when the state convention went on record against the FEPC despite one-third of its participants being black. All these matters made him more determined to regain local party control in Memphis.[128]

Lee dreaded the face-off with Church, who had given him his political start and mentored him, in the race for the state Republican Executive Committee. "I spent long hours in sorrow to think that I would have to come face-to-face against a man I had admired so many years and I had followed so long," he recalled. "It was a tremendous problem, an emotion[al] problem."[129] But the battle between the two political lions never occurred. Shortly after attending the state convention, Church died unexpectedly in Memphis on 17 April 1952. While on the phone with the longtime Mayor of Beale Street Matthew Thornton, he suffered a heart attack in his room at the Lumpkin Hotel; he died en route to the hospital. Church was telling Thornton that he thought Eisenhower could win and that Congress had a chance of passing civil rights legislation because some of Eisenhower's backers supported civil rights.[130]

Church was prescient: under Eisenhower's administration, the first civil rights legislation since Reconstruction became law. The Civil Rights Act of 1957 created the Civil Rights Division of the Department of Justice, authorized the attorney general to seek court orders enforcing voting rights, and established the US Civil Rights Commission, an investigative body that conducted hearings on voting rights violations. Although limited in effect, the act created a legal framework for combating voting rights discrimination.[131] Within a decade, Congress would pass the Voting Rights Act of 1965, which removed barriers to black voting and led to a dramatic increase in the number of black registered voters and black elected officials in the region. Church's hopes for greater black political participation would become a reality in a way that he never saw during his lifetime.

Roberta Church suspected that the strain of leaving Memphis in 1940 led to her father's death. She thought his departure from the city "was a quite devastating experience for him" but observed: "He always presented a calm outward appearance, and he threw himself into activities . . . that kept him before the public."[132] Like other men of that time, Church kept his emotions to himself. Roberta recalled that he never discussed or complained about his exile even though he suffered financially, professionally, and personally.

Right after Church died, J. B. Martin saw Roberta and Church's sister, Annette, in Chicago. "[Martin] was a big man, about six feet two, weight about 200 pounds . . . broad shoulders and so forth, very masculine," Roberta recalled. "He lost his composure and he wept." Martin escorted them to the funeral in Memphis and stood by them during it. The women did not ask Lee to be a pallbearer because they did not think Church would have approved.[133] Martin was both an active and an honorary pallbearer, while Church's local political associates W. O. Speight, O. D. Braithwaithe, and Bert Roddy were active pallbearers. A. Philip Randolph, Blair T. Hunt, the Reverend S. A. Owen, and Matthew Thornton were among the honorary pallbearers at the funeral, which thousands from all walks of life, both black and white, attended.[134] Shortly after Church died, Randolph, who apparently was very upset by Church's sudden death, said that Church had been one of his best friends and "a relentless fighter for the Brotherhood . . . [who] never failed to champion [its] cause . . . among his powerful and influential political and business friends."[135]

Church's death led to local and national tributes, and most every major black newspaper covered his funeral. The *Journal of Negro History* ran a lengthy obituary, national officials of the NAACP praised Church, and the *New York Times* called him one of the country's most influential black Republicans.[136] Calling him "the gentleman from Memphis," the *Pittsburgh Courier* asked: "Who is there in the party to take his place?" Local white and black newspapers ran flattering obituaries as well. "White people knew him and his family as a contradiction to the backward pictures of the Negro they had been conditioned to accept," the *Tri-State Defender* editorialized. "The Church family could rank with the best any group could offer in America. They were ambitious, energetic, aggressive and successful. They combined all the ingredients which Americans regard as great in folks."[137] The *Memphis Review,* a black publication, observed: "Church had the philosophy that the Negro's best opportunity lay with the Republican party, and he was a Republican during good years and bad." It noted that he had "fought an unceasing battle with the White Republicans of Memphis to keep Negroes in the party machinery and to control the local offices" and that "his strategy, wisdom and acumen were widely conceded to have kept him in control and to have made it possible for Negroes to obtain many of the benefits bestowed on them during Republican administrations."[138] A white man who attended his funeral said: "He was a man among men—He stood for a principle and if Bob Church had been a White Man he could have easily become President of the United States."[139]

After Church died, Theodore E. Brown of the Brotherhood of Sleeping Car Porters, who was an honorary pallbearer, wrote Roberta that "the task of hastening the obtaining of full civil rights for the American Negro . . . happily brought me together with your father" and that he had worked closely with him in the fight for a permanent FEPC. He called Church a "tireless worker" who "did much to hasten the day when a strong FEPC statute will be the law of our land."[140] Indeed, if Church had lived a dozen more years, he would have seen his objectives realized with the Civil Rights Act of 1964, which banned discrimination based on "race, color, religion, sex, or national origin" by labor unions, employers, and employment agencies and established the Equal Employment Opportunity Commission for enforcement purposes.[141]

Church's funeral procession went by his former Memphis residence on the way to his burial at Elmwood Cemetery. Within a few years, however, the house would be no more. The city selected it ostensibly to test firefighting equipment and burned it to the ground.[142] The *Tri-State Defender* called the action an "act of infamy."[143] "To me it was almost a lynching of the Negroes of Memphis," said Raymond Lymon when interviewed some thirty years later. The act "sticks in the craws [of] a lot of Negroes today," he said. Roberta Church, who was present when Lymon was being interviewed, called the burning a "psychological attempt to . . . intimidate the black population."[144]

To carry on her father's torch, Roberta, who was thirty-seven, made a bid for the state Republican Executive Committee after his friends asked her to do so. Lonnie Briscoe, whom Church had mentored, mobilized voters on her behalf in the Orange Mound neighborhood. Roberta and Lee were the only two African Americans to run for the committee; she implied that he had turned against African Americans by backing Taft.[145] She ran as a New Guard Republican on a slate with three white candidates. In making their appeal, they billed themselves as the "Eisenhower Ticket" and called for votes in order to forward a two-party system in the South and to protest "the corrupt and socialistic taints of the present Democratic Party."[146] She appeared in the first integrated television broadcast locally and in rallies and photograph sessions with members of her party faction. On the campaign trail, she discussed her family's past contributions to the city and her desire to continue her father's work for civil rights. At rallies, black lawyers from out of town spoke on her behalf and praised her father for his courage and his efforts to liberalize the party. Following the wishes of A. Philip Randolph, the local branch of the Brotherhood of Sleeping Car Porters campaigned for her.[147]

Roberta won one of the two spots for state committeewoman, while Lee was reelected as state committeeman. The only successful New Guard Republican candidate in the primary, Roberta became the first African American woman in the South elected to a state party committee. She believed that African Americans and whites voted for her as a tribute to her father. Not everyone backed her, however. During the campaign, she received an anonymous letter saying that her father would have disapproved of her association with the New Guard faction.[148]

Roberta met with Eisenhower's campaign officials in Denver and Washington, DC, and the *Memphis Press-Scimitar* published a photo of Eisenhower conversing with her.[149] After his win, Eisenhower appointed her the minority groups consultant for the US Department of Labor, so she resigned her state committee position. She was selected in part as a tribute to her father. "The people at the White House told me I had enough endorsements to carry me to heaven," she recalled.[150] One of a select group of women and African Americans appointed by Eisenhower, she held responsibility for promoting equal employment in the public and private sectors and enforcing the federal government's fair employment policy. Because of her prominence as a black, female political appointee and as the daughter of Bob Church, she made speeches around the country and was nationally recognized. W. C. Handy, the blues musician and longtime Church family friend, kept up with her through the newspapers.[151]

Lieutenant Lee also won Eisenhower's respect. At the Republican national convention, Lee led the delegates in the reciting of the Pledge of Allegiance and gave the speech seconding the nomination of Taft for the presidency, receiving much acclaim for the latter. After Eisenhower became the Republican nominee, Lee conferred with him and promised his utmost support. When he returned to Memphis, six hundred African Americans gathered at Booker T. Washington Stadium to give him a watch and pronounce a George W. Lee Day in the city.[152]

Billing Eisenhower as the best candidate for civil rights, Lee developed campaign literature and mobilized his Lincoln League, placing 150 paid workers in precincts. He condemned the Democratic Party for "fathering Jim Crow." Following the lead of the former presidential candidate Thomas Dewey, he spoke out against the Democratic vice presidential candidate, John Sparkman of Alabama, for voting against civil rights legislation twenty-three times. Lee accused Truman of insincerity, noting his comments to an Alabama Democrat that he pursued his civil rights agenda only to win votes. When Eisenhower made a campaign stop in Memphis, he rode down Beale and spotted Lee in front of his Atlanta Life Insurance office. The candidate stopped his limousine, and the two men shook hands and talked. Passersby looked on in awe.[153]

The New Guard and Old Guard Republicans joined together in the local campaign organization for Eisenhower, but their apparent unity was only a facade. White Republicans did not put a single African American on the reception committee coordinating Eisenhower's visit to Memphis, so Lee successfully maneuvered to place two African Americans, including Ben Hooks, on it. Black Democrats faced tensions with white Democrats as well. H. T. Lockard, J. E. Walker, and James T. Walker—the unionist and vice president of the black civic club council—refused to sit on the platform with white Democrats at a campaign event because of the segregated seating. Lockard chaired the black Democratic club, now called the Shelby County Democratic Club.[154]

When election day arrived, 54 percent of white Memphians supported Eisenhower, while 80 percent of black Memphians backed the Democratic candidate, Adlai Stevenson, even though he did not champion civil rights. Neither candidate came close to Truman in promoting civil rights. With many white southerners voting Republican for the first time, enough supported Eisenhower to lead to his victory in Tennessee and three other southern states. Tennessee had not gone for a Republican presidential candidate since 1928, the last time a Republican won the presidency. Republicans, with their turn away from civil rights, opposition to New Deal programs, and emphasis on big business, held little appeal for most black voters.[155]

Because of the greater voting support for Eisenhower among white Memphians than among black Memphians, the New Guard Republicans assumed control of patronage. But, at the insistence of Lee, Reece ensured that black Republicans, who had traditionally dispensed it, regained control of patronage the next year; Lee became the patronage referee. As a result, Raymond Lymon, an active member of the Lincoln League, became the first black deputy marshal in Tennessee since the nineteenth century, and Evelyn C. Stuart, the president of the Lincoln League of Republican Women, was appointed to the Shelby County Primary Board. Jim Crow signs were removed from the restrooms of the postal service, African Americans received better employment opportunities there, and a new postal station was built that Carroll Reece and others insisted carry Lee's name, marking the first time that the US Postal Service named a station for an African

American. It opened in 1956 with the fanfare of a community dedication ceremony that included a band concert at Mason Temple of the
Church of God in Christ.[156]

In 1954, three black candidates, including Benjamin Hooks, ran
as Republicans for the state legislature. The other two office seekers
were Bill Weathers, a Lincoln League member and political associate
of Lieutenant Lee, and T. L. Spencer, a Union Protective Life Insurance Company executive. Although they, like other black Memphians,
did not win public office in the 1950s, local black political appointments were common in southern communities with black political
influence: Mayor Overton appointed Dr. B. F. McCleave to chair the
Negro Hospital Advisory Committee in 1952. The next mayor, Frank
Tobey, appointed the real estate agent Edward R. Kirk to the Mayor's
Urban Rehabilitation Study Committee in 1953.[157]

With the election of Eisenhower, Crump's power declined even
further. His business associates had supported Eisenhower, whereas
Crump himself had endorsed Stevenson. He no longer had control over patronage or as much influence on the local, state, or national scenes.[158] He told the press that he felt like a "golf ball in tall
grass."[159] In 1952, he endorsed Frank Clement in the governor's race,
and Clement defeated Gordon Browning. Yet, on the campaign trail,
Clement often did not call attention to Crump's endorsement. When
Kefauver successfully ran for reelection two years later, the white reformers, along with African Americans, supported him through running an integrated campaign. Crump largely ignored the effort.[160] By
then, his heart was failing, and he died at age eighty in October 1954.

Thousands of Memphians, young and old, black and white, fa-
mous and ordinary, friend and foe, paid their respects to Crump.
About ten thousand passed by his bronze casket, and the Shelby
County Courthouse lowered its flag to half-mast. Past and present
Tennessee governors and local politicians were among those who attended Crump's funeral, the largest in the memory of Memphians.
At Elmwood Cemetery, the same place where Robert R. Church Sr.
and Robert R. Church Jr. were buried, thousands passed by Crump's
grave in the days that followed.[161] "It is almost impossible for residents
of Memphis and Shelby County to believe E. H. Crump is dead," editorialized the *Collierville Herald*. "Citizens came to see that while Mr.
Crump definitely was 'the boss' he loved Memphis and Shelby County
and instigated many progressive projects that aided the standing of

both the city and the county." The paper noted that he left no political heir to take his place and commented: "The death of Mr. Crump ends a colorful era of politics that possibly will never be duplicated."[162] Not everyone exuded praise. "Crump bribed Memphis with good government at low cost and Memphis has not functioned as a real democracy for half a century," one observer said.[163]

As Crump neared death, he had seen not only his political power greatly weakened but also his views on race relations increasingly challenged. In Baton Rouge, Louisiana, African Americans conducted the first successful bus boycott of the decade in 1953, foreshadowing the Montgomery bus boycott a few years later, which catapulted Dr. Martin Luther King Jr. to national leadership and sparked a mass civil rights movement across the South. Rosa Parks, like many civil rights activists at this time, had previously engaged in formal political efforts. She had pressed for voting rights through her work with Montgomery's NAACP chapter and the city's branch of the Progressive Democratic Association, an organization of black Democrats in Alabama. In May 1954, the Supreme Court issued its *Brown v. Board of Education* ruling, declaring segregated schools unconstitutional, and overturning the separate but equal doctrine of *Plessy v. Ferguson* (1896). Although Robert Church Jr. did not live to see *Brown*, his half-sister Mary Church Terrell did. Despite her old age, she had continued her lifelong quest against the Jim Crow system into the 1950s. She became a plaintiff in a successful lawsuit to desegregate eating facilities in Washington, DC, and participated in pickets, boycotts, and sit-ins protesting segregation. On at least one occasion, she stood at the head of a picket line with her cane in hand.[164] Terrell died at age ninety in 1954, two months after the *Brown* decision.

The years from 1946 to 1954 had been a momentous and democratizing time in Memphis and the South. As more and more African Americans across the South secured the right to vote after the *Smith* decision, they ran for office and otherwise used politics as a means to pursue civil rights. They won offices, received political appointments, and held the balance of power in elections. These developments helped break the stranglehold of conservative white Democrats in the region and helped lead to the mass-based civil rights movement that started in Montgomery. In Memphis, African Americans joined forces with white reformers and unionists to create a more democratic city of their own as they caused Crump's power to decline significantly. Although Crump's local candidates continued to win elections until his death, the 1948 rebellion led to the appointment of black police officers, the outlawing of the poll tax, and election reforms to combat voter fraud and manipulation. White politicians were elected who took steps for racial advancement, and a white leadership group developed that yielded some gains for African Americans even though it did not fully include them. Moreover, the rebellion resulted in an atmosphere conducive to Walker's bid for public office and Church's return to Memphis. The New Guard Republicans had a mixed record when it came to race relations, but they and the Old Guard Republicans made a two-party system more viable in the region.

When Walker ran in 1951, his campaign served as a bridge between longtime and new black political leaders in Memphis. All along, Church and his political allies had ultimately sought the dismantling of the Jim Crow system. Hooks, Lockard, and other young leaders would take advantage of the *Brown* decision to further press for freedom and equality. Hooks and Lockard would go on to help make the local NAACP branch a more powerful force and to stand in the forefront of the legal, political, and civil rights changes to come. They would win public office themselves. These young activists and their counterparts would be the heirs to Church and his associates as well as all the other black Memphians who had challenged Crump and the Jim Crow system, sought a better life for themselves and their children, and battled to make the promises of American democracy a reality.

Conclusion

For black Memphians, the *Brown v. Board of Education* ruling was a call to action. A new generation of leaders, including Maxine and Vasco Smith, Jesse Turner Sr., A. W. Willis Jr., and Russell and Laurie Sugarmon, joined Benjamin Hooks and H. T. Lockard in giving new life to the black freedom struggle in Memphis. With no appointed successor to Crump, a leadership vacuum existed in the city, and they took advantage of this environment to pursue political power and civil rights.[1] They joined the Bluff City and Shelby County Council of Civic Clubs and the local NAACP branch, which rose in membership from a low of 818 in 1954 to 2,418 in 1959. While these leaders supported lawsuits seeking the desegregation of Memphis, they engaged in sustained political mobilization as well. Black voter registration increased to 57,109 in 1959—more than eight times the number in 1951. The Reverend W. Herbert Brewster, the longtime follower of Robert R. Church Jr., contributed to these political efforts by staging a massive religious pageant to register hundreds of black voters in 1958. Memphis also became the center of the development of rock and roll, with Elvis Presley making his first hit recordings at Sun Studio in 1954. He had been inspired by the music he heard on Beale Street, including at the East Trigg Baptist Church, where Reverend Brewster preached. Sun Studio, with African Americans and whites recording, foreshadowed the integration that would occur in Memphis over the next decade.[2]

In the 1959 election, four black men made bids for public office as a unity slate called the Volunteer Ticket. African Americans represented one-third of the vote. Russell B. Sugarmon Jr., Benjamin Hooks, the Reverend Roy Love of Mount Nebo Baptist Church, and the Reverend Henry Bunton of Mount Olive Christian Methodist Episcopal Church made up the ticket. Hooks had been ordained as a Baptist minister in 1956, while Sugarmon had a law degree from

Harvard and was a Korean War veteran. Because the University of Tennessee Law School had refused to accept Sugarmon because he was African American, the state of Tennessee had paid his Harvard expenses. Love, a former day laborer and popular local minister who headed a working-class congregation, had nearly won a spot on the school board in 1955. As head of the Ministers and Citizens League, formed that year at the Pentecostal Temple Church of God in Christ in order to help increase the number of black Memphians registered to vote, Bunton had supported Reverend Love's campaign. A World War II veteran, Bunton had arrived in Memphis in 1953 with a prestigious graduate degree from Denver's Iliff School of Theology. He was a member of the Southern Christian Leadership Conference, the civil rights organization formed by Dr. Martin Luther King Jr. following the Montgomery bus boycott.[3]

In 1959, because each Volunteer Ticket candidate faced three or more white opponents, a unified black vote and split white vote could result in victory. The Volunteer Ticket organization formed for the campaign; its ward and precinct network included members of the Shelby County Democratic Club (the black Democratic organization) and the Lincoln League. The "thinking heart" behind the Volunteer Ticket, Lee took part in every stage of the campaign.[4] J. E. Walker had died the year before, so his son, A. Maceo Walker, also a successful businessman, cochaired the steering committee with Lee. Maxine Smith and other women made up the majority of the grassroots workers supporting the candidates.[5] More than a political campaign, the endeavor was a milestone in the freedom struggle of black Memphians and generated widespread interest. "What Negroes have in mind is to fight until hell freezes over and if necessary skate across on ice to freedom," Lieutenant Lee proclaimed at the ticket's largest political rally.[6] Martin Luther King Jr. spoke in Memphis on behalf of the Volunteer Ticket, as did the Little Rock civil rights leader Daisy Bates. In addition to extensive local press coverage, the campaign received attention from national media, including the *New York Times*, the *Pittsburgh Courier*, and the *Washington Post*.[7]

When election day arrived, a record number of African Americans and whites cast ballots. White Memphians had countermobilized against the candidates, especially Sugarmon, given that he was running for the most powerful position and had the greatest chance of winning.[8] All the Volunteer Ticket candidates came in second. Nonetheless, Sugarmon said: "We won everything but the election."[9] "It was a democratic activity," he recalled. "There were more people expressing themselves than ever. What we won was a politicized group who didn't want to stop."[10] After the election, he and other leaders made the Volunteer organization permanent by restructuring the Shelby County Democratic Club and turning it into a solid, precinct-based organization. Along with the NAACP branch, it became one of the two most powerful civil rights organizations in Memphis. The Democratic club mobilized support for black candidates and white office seekers willing to meet the organization's demands. As a result, African Americans received more political appointments, and whites were elected who took action to further civil rights. In 1960, Jesse Turner Sr. won a spot on the Shelby County Democratic Executive Committee, cracking white control of the party organization, and meriting *New York Times* coverage.[11] In 1961, Blair Hunt became the first African American appointed to the Shelby County School Board. The next year, Sugarmon and his associates formed the Tennessee Voters Council, which mobilized African Americans statewide in senatorial, gubernatorial, and presidential races.

College students conducted the first sit-ins in Memphis in March 1960, just seven months after the 1959 election and one month after Greensboro, North Carolina, students started the wave of sit-ins across the South. The Memphis students' actions sparked a twenty-month direct-action campaign. Local African Americans from all walks of life conducted marches, boycotts, sit-ins, and pickets in order to end segregation and employment discrimination. The ward and precinct organization of the Democratic club facilitated communication and mobilization, and political and direct-action leaders and activists overlapped. Maxine Smith coordinated the protests through the office of the NAACP chapter, which became the largest in the South with fifty-two hundred members in May 1960. The protests led to the desegregation of public and private facilities and better employment opportunities for African Americans. Elementary schools underwent token integration in 1961. By 1965, all legal barriers to integration were removed in the city.[12]

While black Memphians engaged in political activism in their own community, they also played a crucial role in the voting rights campaign in nearby Fayette and Haywood Counties that attracted the attention of the federal government, the national media, and national civil rights organizations. Beginning in 1959, these rural African Americans, most of whom worked as agricultural laborers, stepped up voter registration efforts and formed the Fayette County Civic and Welfare League in order to combat their nearly total exclusion from the voting rolls. They experienced fierce resistance from local whites, including evictions, which forced some to form a tent city, and the denial of loans and health services. The Memphis NAACP branch provided them with food and clothing and also helped them file complaints with the federal government and register to vote. In its 1960 annual report, the Memphis branch noted that its "outstanding achievement" that year was providing this assistance. Lee raised money for the evicted families, and the Tennessee Voters Council organized voters in the Fayette-Haywood area. H. T. Lockard was nearly lynched in Brownsville, the county seat of Haywood County, when he defended a voting rights activist, and Russell B. Sugarmon Jr., A. W. Willis Jr., and Benjamin Hooks were shot at when riding in a car in the Fayette–Haywood County area following their civil rights activism there. The Justice Department, empowered by the Civil Rights Act of 1957, filed legal actions against the civil rights violations experienced by African Americans in Fayette and Haywood Counties.[13] The voting rights activism in these rural areas reflected the increase in such action throughout the South: spurred by the sit-in movement, the Student Nonviolent Coordinating Committee formed in 1960, and it, along with other civil rights organizations, undertook voter registration efforts in rural areas in the region.

In Memphis, most young civil rights activists embraced the Democratic Party. While Lee's Lincoln League had fifty-six precinct clubs by 1963, it declined in power and came to represent an older generation of black Memphians. Local African Americans increasingly turned to the Democratic Party, while the New Guard Republicans became the most influential Republican group in Memphis. At the Republican national convention in 1964, Lee was not seated, despite his protests. The party's presidential candidate, Barry Goldwater, advocated states' rights and did not support the Civil Rights Act of 1964, which outlawed racial discrimination in public accommodations, provided greater protection for black voting rights, and prohibited racial discrimination by employers, employment agencies, and labor unions. The Democratic Party spearheaded its passage, and it became effective in July.[14]

Black electoral mobilization in Memphis peaked in influence in 1964. More than 99 percent of black Memphians voted for Democrats in state and national elections, while white Memphians voted more than two-to-one for Goldwater and the Republican candidate for Congress. Black Memphians provided the balance of power to force the incumbent congressman out of office in favor of the Democratic candidate supportive of integration and to elect an all-Democratic delegation to the state legislature, including A. W. Willis Jr., who became the first African American state legislator in Tennessee in the twentieth century. In the first successful African American bid for local office in the Memphis area in more than fifty years, H. T. Lockard won a seat on the Shelby County Court, the forerunner of the county commission.[15] "Shelby County political traditions, which once seemed as indestructible as the pyramids, are beginning to teeter in the shockwave of [the] awesome Negro vote," said the *Commercial Appeal*.[16] The Tennessee Voters Council provided the structure for the black vote statewide to be the decisive factor in the election of Democrats in the presidential and senatorial races. President Lyndon B. Johnson and the Democratic-controlled Congress would go on to back the Voting Rights Act of 1965, which enabled a majority of eligible black southerners to become registered voters and led to a dramatic rise in black elected officials across the region. That same year, Tennessee governor Frank Clement appointed Benjamin Hooks as a Shelby County Criminal Court judge, the highest judicial post ever achieved by an African American in the state.[17] In 1966, Hooks kept his seat in a countywide election.

The *New York Times* reported in April 1964 that Memphis had "made more progress toward desegregation with less strife than any other major city in the Deep South."[18] Yet the NAACP chapter president, Jesse Turner, remarked that most of the civil rights gains in the city had been token and halfhearted. The branch worked through a combination of litigation, political and direct action, negotiation, and letter writing to eradicate remaining discriminatory practices and press for more economic opportunities for African Americans. Taking advantage of the Civil Rights Act's Title VII provision, which banned racial discrimination by employers and unions, the chapter, along with black unionists, filed complaints with the federal government. The mid-1960s saw increased black labor activism and antipoverty organizing as well. African Americans achieved some economic gains, with more entering customary white jobs and supervisory positions than ever before.[19] Maxine Smith observed, however, that "covert resistance in the form of tokenism and appeasement has in many instances thwarted our [employment] efforts."[20]

While black political achievements continued to occur in the mid-1960s, a new run-off law proved to be restrictive. Russell B. Sugarmon Jr. was elected to the state legislature, and other black Memphians won public office. In 1967, A. W. Willis Jr. became the first black mayoral candidate in a major city in the South, although he lost. That year, the NAACP chapter and Shelby County Democratic Club supported the change of city government to a mayor-council system in which seven of the council seats were district positions and six were at-large seats. Two African Americans were elected to the city council from majority-black districts, and one was elected from a nearly majority-black district. Despite black opposition, however, Memphis voters passed a run-off law in 1967 requiring that candidates for city offices receive the majority of the vote. It precluded African Americans from holding many of these positions because not enough whites, who made up most of the population, were willing to vote for African Americans.[21]

The limits to civil rights victories were epitomized by the sanitation strike of 1968. Martin Luther King Jr. came to Memphis to support sanitation workers protesting poor working conditions, low pay, and racist supervisors. Their strike mobilized black Memphians, who, in the words of the historian Laurie Green, saw in them "a reflection of their own rage about ongoing racial injustice and their own quest for liberation."[22] But King was shot to death in the city on 4 April 1968, and Memphis and other urban areas throughout the country burst into riots. Mayor Henry Loeb, who had been elected with hardly any black support, reached a settlement with the strikers only after the murder. The murder hit the black community like a "heart attack," according to Sugarmon, and Democratic club efforts suffered as a result.[23]

Black Memphians did not give up hope. The next year, the Memphis NAACP achieved a major victory in the fight for educational equality. To protest the slow pace of school integration, Maxine Smith and Laurie Sugarmon led the "Black Monday" movement in 1969. In a controversial move, black students stayed home from school on Mondays. Because school funding was based on average daily attendance, these actions proved quite effective, resulting in the seating of black school board representatives, black administrators, and, eventually, the first black superintendent. After her supporters persuaded her to run, Smith became the first black woman elected to a city position when she won a school board seat in 1971. She served on the board until retiring in 1995.[24]

Black and white Memphians saw the continuation of economic and social divisions over the next few decades. Many white Memphians responded to the advent of busing in the 1970s by fleeing to the suburbs and forming private academies. In 2010, Memphis public schools remained overwhelmingly black, while county schools continued to be predominately white. African Americans made up a majority of the city population, and whites made up a majority of the county population. African Americans entered white-collar professions and graduated from high school and college in increasing numbers but were both in poverty and affected by crime in numbers disproportionate to the percentage of the population that they represented. In 2006, the city was the metropolitan area with the highest violent crime rate in the United States.[25]

From the 1970s forward, black Memphians continued to politically mobilize despite obstacles. The Harold Ford family became a dominant force in local politics. Yet only two African Americans won positions citywide by 1991 because of the run-off measure and ongoing racial tensions. It took the repeal of the run-off law that year for the city's first black mayor, Willie Herenton, to be elected. Receiving few white votes, he won with the help of Maxine Smith and other longtime activists. Herenton was reelected to a record fifth term in 2007, but the race was compared to that of 1991 because of its racial polarization. He did not receive a majority of votes, and he received scant white support even though a substantial number of whites had come to back him in previous elections. Those who did not support him were critical of the lack of economic development, the high rate of crime, and the corruption of local officials plaguing the city. At least sixty-six Memphis lawmakers, judges, council members, and public employees faced corruption charges from 2000 to 2007, casting a negative light on black and white city officials alike.[26] Herenton stepped down as mayor in 2009 and made an unsuccessful bid for a seat in the US House of Representatives.

The political gains of black Memphians should not be underestimated, however, despite the limits. In the first decade of the twenty-first century, it was common for black men and women to hold the majority of the seats on the city council and the school board. In contrast to previous years, when whites ensured that no African Americans became public officials, they now often had to choose which one to elect. The run-off repeal, a majority-black population, and ongoing black electoral mobilization helped explain these black political achievements. Whites held the most seats on the county council and the county school board, but young citizens of Shelby County were more likely to vote for someone of a different race. A. C. Wharton was elected the first African American mayor of Shelby County in 2002, and he stayed in the office until 2009, when he successfully ran to be Memphis's mayor. In 2011, the city school board members Tomeka Hart and Martavious Jones, part of a new generation of black political activists in Memphis, spearheaded the initiative to merge the city and the county school systems. The merger, the largest consolidation of school districts in US history, took place in 2013.[27]

The election of Barack Obama as the first black president was a milestone for civil rights activists in Memphis and elsewhere. In 2008, the majority of Memphis and Shelby County voters threw their support behind him.[28] Maxine and Vasco Smith, H. T. Lockard, Russell Sugarmon, and other heirs to Church Jr. and his supporters had lived to see this landmark election. While the media spotlighted the civil rights activism of the 1950s and 1960s in relation to Obama's victory, the deep roots of his election—the work of Church and others previously—cannot be ignored.

Indeed, the story of black political activists in Memphis shines a spotlight on the significance of southern black political mobilization in the Jim Crow era. To be sure, Church and other black political actors were flawed. By supporting Edward Crump and the candidates he endorsed, black Memphians shored up a machine government that provided them with some benefits but ultimately served as a barrier to their quest for civil rights. By cleaving to the Republican Party, Church fell out of step with the masses of African Americans who had turned to the Democratic Party. He and other African Americans who continued to support the party missed the opportunity to jump on the Democratic bandwagon and to use their political skills to bolster a party that improved the lives of African Americans in an unprecedented way through its passage of social welfare legislation and, eventually, civil rights legislation.

Yet the political efforts of black southerners in the Jim Crow era held more advantages than disadvantages. By engaging in sustained political mobilization, black southerners carved out a political space for themselves, exerting their right to participate in the political system, and sometimes succeeding in pressuring the government to serve their needs. In doing so, they cultivated the civic and personal pride that can come with political participation. They secured better public services and employment opportunities for African Americans, all of which made a significant difference at a time when most African Americans were poor and held low-level positions. By holding the balance of power in elections, they elected candidates who promised to be a better choice for them than their opponents. They also used politics as a public venue to declare their opposition to the Jim Crow system. They gave hope to ordinary African Americans in a time of segregation, disenfranchisement, and racial violence. By aligning with the NAACP, labor groups, and other organizations in pressing for civil rights and economic opportunities, black political activists made the black freedom struggle a stronger force and the United States a more democratic country. In all these ways, they forwarded the civil rights movement of the 1950s and 1960s.

By participating in the Republican Party, Church and other black southerners took advantage of the one party in the two-party system that allowed them a significant presence until the New Deal. They inspired local black Memphians to become politically active and encouraged their participation in organizations aligned with the Republican Party. Ordinary black Memphians ensured that Church rose to political power to the point where he could have an official voice in Republican circles, whether that be at the White House or in local, state, or national committees and organizations. He and other black Republicans served as voices for civil rights and greater black political participation in party councils and succeeded in opening up jobs and political opportunities for African Americans. By achieving political leadership positions and working on an equal footing with whites, they challenged stereotypes of African Americans as subservient and inferior. They called on white Republicans to live up to the party's historical ideals of freedom and equality and to adopt policies that adhered to the party's official statements denouncing lynching and affirming the constitutional rights of all citizens. In so doing, they served as a vital force against lily whitism and prevented the party from excluding African Americans to the extent that the Democratic Party did. It would have been tragic for both major parties to have denied African Americans participation, and it was important that Church remain a Republican as a voice for black concerns in the party after most African Americans switched to the Democratic Party. Those black Republicans who did switch to the Democratic Party, such as J. E. Walker, used their political skills to push the party to become more racially inclusive and to take civil rights and social welfare steps. All these efforts laid the foundation for the more democratic South that emerged in the 1960s.

The political efforts of black southerners in the Jim Crow era were part of the black freedom struggle that continues to this day. Most of these politically active black southerners probably would be amazed at the changes in society today: the election of the first black president and the rise of black public officials, the abolition of de jure segregation and intolerance for overt racism, and the integration that exists in the South and the nation as a whole. Yet most also would likely continue to battle for racial justice. After Obama was elected in 2008, Congressman John Lewis and other civil rights activists of the 1960s commented that his election represented a victory but not the end of the black freedom struggle. Just as Church and his Lincoln League members looked to the past history of black political achievements during the Reconstruction era as an inspiration for their struggle for freedom and democracy, current civil rights activists can look at their story and that of other politically active black southerners for inspiration in today's continuing battle for racial justice.

Acknowledgments

It is appropriate to begin by thanking my dissertation committee. My appreciation especially goes to my adviser, Jacquelyn Dowd Hall, for all the time and intellectual energy that she poured into shaping this book. A remarkably gifted writer and editor, she generously provided a wealth of perceptive comments, writing suggestions, and excellent ideas that immeasurably improved this work, molded me into a better historian, and made this project more enriching and enjoyable. I am blessed to have had such a dedicated, gracious, and exceptional adviser. I thank her for opening doors for me and believing in me. W. Fitzhugh Brundage served as the second reader. He suggested that I focus on black politics in the first place, and this work bears his imprint as well. Throughout my graduate career, he always generously provided me with excellent ideas for my work, and the papers that I did for his seminars helped me further my research. I thank him for his support, help, and confidence in me during my graduate school journey. William R. Ferris's unwavering enthusiasm and support made this book project and my graduate career more pleasurable. His suggestions enhanced this book, especially his advice to incorporate cultural details and engaging quotes. I also thank his assistant, Dana DiMaio, for his help. Larry J. Griffin and Genna Rae McNeil were the other two committee members. My conversations with them, their comments on my work, and their enthusiasm forwarded this book.

It has been an honor to work with Steven Lawson as well. He reviewed my dissertation proposal and two conference papers and also provided me with invaluable suggestions for books on Republican Party politics. He solicited my manuscript for this series and served as an excellent editor, reliably providing feedback, encouragement, and guidance. He was patient and prodding, and it is a pleasure to know him. At the University Press of Kentucky, my thanks goes to Anne Dean Watkins, the senior acquisitions editor, and her assistant, Bailey

Johnson, for all the hard work and time they spent on the project. Anne Dean's advocacy of and enthusiasm for this project as well as her kindness and competence meant a lot. My copyeditor, Joseph Brown, meticulously edited the manuscript, and his changes and corrections very much improved it. Three readers reviewed this manuscript; my thanks go to Carroll Van West, Eric Arnesen, and the reader who decided to remain anonymous for their serious and thoughtful evaluations, which greatly improved this manuscript. I thank Dr. Van West particularly for his suggestion to focus more on the role of ministers and the church. I especially wish to thank Eric Arnesen not only for his meticulous, thorough, and insightful report but also for his support and encouragement of my research and for our intellectual exchanges throughout the years. He generously dug through his files and provided me with long pdfs of new research material for this manuscript and urged and inspired me to mine databases of recently digitized black newspapers.

A number of people deserve my thanks in Washington, DC, where I received my undergraduate education at American University, and where this book had its genesis as a course project. It has been one of the most wonderful honors of my life to know Julian Bond, whom I had as a professor at American University. I could not have had a better teacher for learning in depth about the civil rights movement for the first time. My course project for his oral histories of the civil rights movement class turned into my senior honors thesis, which he generously agreed to advise. This book is an outgrowth of that thesis. While in graduate school, I took his University of Virginia bus tour on the history of the civil rights movement. He and his wife, Pam Horowitz, the coleader of the trip, made this experience possible and provided good company; in addition, he answered all my research questions during the trip. All in all, I thank Professor Bond for his kindness and support over the years. The American University Honors Program provided funding for my 2000 trip to Memphis. Its former director, Professor Michael Mass, has been particularly kind and supportive over the years, as has Paula Warrick, the director of the American University Office of Merit Awards. She recruited me to compete for a Harry S. Truman Scholarship and poured a lot of time and energy into helping me with the application process. I am grateful to the Harry S. Truman Foundation for this award, which enabled me to focus on my Memphis research during my senior year in college. I especially thank the foundation's former director, the distinguished Louis Blair. Always one to send a kind word my way, Mr. Blair has honored me by remaining supportive of and interested in my career path since the time we met and by being cheerfully willing to be of assistance when necessary. Thanks, too, to John Tambornino, a former colleague of mine at the US Department of Health and Human Services, for his mentorship and friendship.

I spent most of my time turning my dissertation into this book when working as a visiting assistant professor in the History Department at Middle Tennessee State University in Murfreesboro, Tennessee. My faculty mentor, Pippa Holloway, thoroughly and perceptively reviewed my dissertation and provided excellent suggestions for turning it into a book that greatly benefited this project. One of the best things about ending up in the History Department at Middle Tennessee State University was the opportunity to work with her. I also especially wish to thank the following faculty members in the History Department for their support of the project: Derek Frisby, Mary Hoffschwelle, Mark Doyle, Susan Myers-Shirk, and Kris McCusker. My thanks to my colleague Rebecca Cawood McIntyre and her husband, Steve McIntyre, for their support, career advice, and good company; they are two of the nicest and most considerate people in the world. In addition, Louis Woods's advice to work on the book manuscript at least forty-five minutes a day, five days a week, enabled me to get done with this project sooner than I probably would have otherwise. James Beeby, the department chair, not only was supportive of the project but also generously took the time to be a mentor and provide advice and insights to me in my position as a junior faculty member. My time at Middle Tennessee State University also benefited from the encouragement and support of the historians Ken Scherzer, Becky Bruce, Mike Paulauskas, Martha Norkunas, Amy Sayward, Brian Ingrassia, Lorne McWatters, Thomas Bynum, Lisa Pruitt, Emily Baran, Yuanling Chao, Jan Leone, Louis Haas, Lynn Nelson, and Antoinette G. van Zelm. Thanks also to Tara Hayes, the office manager of the History Department, for her assistance and to Virgil Statom, a graduate student, who provided me with important research information. In the School of Communication, my appreciation goes to Tom Neff, founder of the Documentary Channel and an Emmy Award–winning filmmaker. I am honored by his willingness to work on turning my Memphis research into a documentary film.

I would like to single out a number of other people who aided this project. David Godshalk generously offered to serve as an outside reader for my dissertation. He reviewed drafts of all five chapters and provided me with an abundance of suggestions. The many that I utilized significantly improved the writing and analysis of this work. He shared his own scholarship with me and provided me with constructive comments after my conference presentation on the 1959 election in Memphis at the 2006 Southern Association for Women Historians meeting in Baltimore, Maryland. My mom, Ruth Gritter, and aunt, Cynthia Gargagliano, were proofreaders, and I thank them for their time and diligence. They provided me with thoughtful comments to improve the writing and analysis and also carefully examined drafts for typos and grammatical errors. My mom, in particular, reviewed chapters. In addition, my friend and former American University roommate Jennifer L. Stair generously proofread a chapter and did an excellent job, applying analytic skills that she has honed as a lawyer in Baltimore. At Indiana University Southeast in New Albany, Indiana, where I am now an assistant professor of history, I thank Joe Wert, dean of the Social Sciences Division; Brigitte Adams, the faculty secretary; and the history professors Yu Shen, Kelly Ryan, Angelika Hoelger, and Quinn Daver for their support.

Nearly all my archival research in Memphis was done in the Memphis–Shelby County Room of the Memphis–Shelby County Public Library and Information Center and in the Special Collections Department of the University of Memphis Library. The resources and research assistance are exceptional at both places, and I express my appreciation to the staff as well as for the permissions granted to use photographs from both archives. At the Memphis Public Library, G. Wayne Dowdy, the curator of the Memphis–Shelby County Room and a prolific author on the subject of Memphis history, always answered any questions that I had over the course of this project; the insights and information that he shared with me helped give me a roadmap of what topics to explore. I also especially appreciated the enthusiasm, support, and research assistance of Jim Johnson, Patricia LaPointe, and Marilyn Umfress. At the University of Memphis, Edwin G. Frank, Sharon Banker, Christopher Ratliff, Brigitte Billeaudeaux, and Jim Montague not only provided me with excellent assistance in general but also went above and beyond the call of duty in compassionately helping me out when I ran into some research difficulties. I particularly thank the curator, Ed Frank, for answering all my queries, leading me to important collections, and taking the time to support my work in a kind and encouraging manner over the years.

This project further benefited from research conducted outside Memphis. My thanks goes to the staff at both the Harvard University Archives at Harvard University in Boston, Massachusetts, and the Manuscript Division of the Library of Congress in Washington, DC. Thanks, too, to Scott Sanders at Antioch College Archives, Charles Ransom at the University of Michigan Library, and Louisa Hoffman at the Oberlin College Archives. I am grateful to the Center for the Study of the American South (CSAS) at the University of North Carolina (UNC) at Chapel Hill and the John F. Kennedy Library in Boston, Massachusetts, for financial support for my research. Headed by Harry Watson, who has been kindly supportive of my work, the CSAS awarded me two summer research grants that allowed me to travel to Memphis in 2004 and 2007 and the Kennedy Library in 2007. I appreciate Barb Call's handling of the logistics for these grants. In addition, the CSAS's journal, *Southern Cultures,* published my interview with the civil rights activist H. T. Lockard; I thank the editors, Dave Shaw and Ayse Erginer, for their assistance. The Southern Oral History Program, a division of the CSAS, gave me a transcribing grant and allowed me to work on my Memphis oral histories while I was a research assistant there. The program's head, Jacquelyn Dowd Hall, as well as Beth Millwood and Joe Mosnier provided significant assistance in these respects. Finally, Stephen Plotkin and Sharon Kelley at the John F. Kennedy Library provided excellent assistance.

In Memphis, I benefited from the generosity and friendship of a number of local people. First of all, Susan B. Dynerman, a friend from my Washington, DC, days, generously let me stay in her home for two months in 2004 and five and a half weeks in 2007 while I conducted oral histories and collected archival research for this project. She provided good insights into my work and other assistance. I enjoyed reconnecting with her son, the creative and talented Max Dynerman, as well. I thank Susan for interesting me in examining Memphis in the first place and inspiring and enabling me to take my first research trip there in 2000. During that visit, Calvin Turley helped me conduct an oral history of Vasco Smith, provided accommodations, and otherwise provided assistance. His cotton museum downtown is well worth a visit. Calvin provided good company during that trip as well as my subsequent visits to Memphis, as did Henry and Lynne Turley. I enjoyed conversing with them about civil rights and politics in the city and was touched by Henry's presence at a talk that I gave on my research at Rhodes College. In addition, Beauty Macklin and the late Cordelia Turley were unforgettably kind during my 2000 visit. And Steve Cohen, who is now the US congressman from Memphis, was immensely helpful in putting me in touch with my interview subjects in 2000 and 2004. I am grateful for his continued interest in my research. James B. Jalenak sent me a copy of his outstanding 1961 senior thesis on Beale Street politics, and it was a great pleasure to have lunch with him during my 2004 trip to Memphis. Finally, I immensely thank Terry Thompson, a talented researcher and photographer, who generously provided me with outstanding research assistance during my 2007 visit to Memphis.

UNC at Chapel Hill History Department faculty and students also contributed to making my dissertation project and graduate career more enriching and enjoyable. My book benefited from the input of Professors William L. Barney, John Sweet, Donald J. Raleigh, Roger Lotchin, Kathleen DuVal, and Lloyd Kramer. I particularly remembered Professor Kramer's advice to think about what my subjects would say to me about my portrait of them. A number of other people made the graduate school journey easier through their support and kindness. Those who particularly come to mind are Professor John Kasson and the graduate students Josh Davis, Georgina Gajewski, Matt Harper, Kimberly Hill, Mike Huner, Cecelia Moore, Katie Otis, Aidan J. Smith, and Tomoko Yagyu. I also thank Tomoko for her advice to focus on primary sources. In one way or another, the graduate students Bruce Baker, Barbara Hahn, Kerry Taylor, David Sehat, Brian Turner, Catherine Conner, Ken Zogry, and Sarah Barksdale were supportive of this project and/or my graduate career. Finally, the History Department allowed me to present a paper at its research colloquium for graduate students, where Professor Genna Rae McNeil delivered excellent comments.

In particular, I thank my fellow UNC at Chapel Hill history graduate students Hilary N. Green and Dwana Waugh. A dedicated scholar and wonderful friend, Hilary provided suggestions for my research. I have appreciated our conversations about the dissertation and book process, graduate school, life as junior faculty members, and everything else. The conference paper that I did for the New Perspectives on the Black South Conference at UNC at Chapel Hill in 2007, which she helped organize, was beneficial to the book project. Dwana Waugh, my writing partner for a dissertation design course taught by my adviser, generously provided me with excellent, in-depth suggestions. A talented teacher, she went above and beyond what she had to do, especially considering how busy she was. She also is a warm and compassionate friend.

A number of other offices and personnel affiliated with the UNC at Chapel Hill forwarded this project. The UNC Graduate School awarded me a Smith Grant for transcribing my oral histories; Deborah G. Mitchum did an excellent and efficient job as the transcriber. Beverly Wyrick and Sandra Hoeflich of the Graduate School, Sarah Jonczak and Pamela Locklear of the Office of the Assistant Vice Chancellor for Student Affairs, and Virginia Carson of the Campus Y all generously provided me with funding so that I could take the bus tour on the civil rights movement in the South led by Julian Bond and sponsored by the University of Virginia's Travel and Learn Program, headed by Joan Gore. Professor Doug Eyre, the former chair of the Geography Department, was particularly enthusiastic about and supportive of this project. African and Afro-American Studies Professor Charlene Regester gave me excellent career advice and generously served as a mentor. Finally, I thank the staff at Davis Library. Sellers Lawrence, the interlibrary borrowing coordinator, and Kenny Jones, his assistant, did an excellent job fulfilling all my interlibrary loan requests. Joe Mitchem, Thomas Nixon, and the other circulation and reference desk staff were helpful as well.

While in graduate school, I was particularly involved with the Southern Association of Women Historians, and my thanks go to both this organization and several of its leaders and members in particular. Glenda Gilmore invited me to serve as the graduate student representative on the executive council and as a member of the graduate student committee. She, along with Laura Edwards, Cindy Kierner, and Melissa Walker, was president of the organization during my time of official service to it. Cita Cook headed the graduate student committee and provided me with suggestions for my research as well as great advice in general about the world of academia. I also enjoyed getting to know Megan Shockley, the indefatigable former secretary of the organization. One of the best parts about being involved with the Southern Association of Women Historians was having an article on the 1959 election in Memphis published as part of the organization's anthology, *Entering the Fray: Gender, Politics, and Culture in the New South* (University of Missouri Press, 2010). The article was an outgrowth of my master's thesis, dissertation research, and seminar paper for Claudia Koontz's course at Duke University on gender and ethnic conflict. I thank Professor Koontz, the anthology's editors, Jonathan D. Wells and Sheila R. Phipps, and the anonymous reviewers of the article for their comments on my work. I am grateful to the University of Missouri Press for allowing me to draw heavily on the article for my conclusion.

I was privileged to interact with other scholars during my time in graduate school and as a prospective graduate student. The following historians served as chairs or commentators for my conference presentations and/or conversed with me afterward about these talks: Elsa Barkley Brown, Ann Chirhart, Jane Dailey, Devin Fergus, Catherine Fosl, Adam Green, Blair Kelley, Elizabeth Jacoway, Kevin Kruse, Steven Lawson, Charles McKinney, Robert E. McGlone, and Sarah Wilkerson-Freeman. Dr. Fergus, in particular, gave me valuable advice concerning citations. I am grateful to C. Fred Williams and David Chappell for inviting me to present my work at the Little Rock School Desegregation Crisis Fiftieth Anniversary International Conference in Little Rock, Arkansas, in 2007. Delivering a conference paper at that event was a great honor. My appreciation goes to the following professors for their support in general and/or suggestions for my work: Manfred Berg, William Chafe, Catherine Clinton, Deborah A. Cohen, Karen Cox, Charles Crawford, Pete Daniel, John Dittmer, David Goldfield, Michael K. Honey, Ben Houston, Tracy E. K'Meyer, Steve Kantrowitz, Robert Korstad, Adriane Lentz-Smith, Sally Lineback, Danielle McGuire, Gail Murray, Kathryn Nasstrom, Robert J. Norrell, Margaret O'Mara, Phil Rubio, Diane Singerman, Harvard Sitkoff, Joe Soss, Timothy Tyson, Brian Ward, and especially Heather A. Thompson.

A special word of thanks goes to three scholars in particular. Elizabeth Jacoway generously served as a mentor and provided me with research information even while finishing up her own book on the Little Rock school desegregation crisis of 1957. She advised me to begin writing as soon as possible. Matt Clavin, whom I first met when he was my teaching assistant at American University, has always stood out for his enthusiasm for history. I am grateful for his unflagging mentorship, support, and kindness over the years. Finally, Timothy P. McCarthy is a joy to know, was generous in providing me with direction about career matters, and served as a source of moral support during the dissertation process.

Several other people deserve my appreciation. Charlie Byrd, my landlord in Chapel Hill, helped during my 2007 trip to Memphis by generously watching over my house. Emily Johnson, whom I met at a party in Philadelphia, recommended the Web site of the academic writing coach Gina Hiatt. I benefited from Ms. Hiatt's advice about writing and her generosity in making these communications and documents free. I especially thank Laura Rice, Jennifer L. Stair, Sean Coleman, Jennifer K. Costanza, Joan E. Gildemeister, and Bobby Blankenship for their friendship and support. The late Reverend Willie L. and Ruth Patterson, my neighbors when I grew up in Grand Rapids, Michigan, both shared with me their memories of living in Memphis before moving to the North in the mid-1950s. Thanks also to Ted Rayburn, the editorial page editor of the *Tennessean*, for publishing three op-ed columns that I wrote on the black freedom struggle in Memphis. My friend and "Murfreesboro Mom," Jane Blakey, took me to Nashville to peruse used bookstores for writings or works on Tennessee history. She and her husband, Bob, have been kind, supportive, and delightful.

I thank my family for their support as well, especially my parents, Robert D. and Ruth Gritter, my brother and sister-in-law, Thomas R. and Sarah Gritter, my niece, Emma Elizabeth Gritter, my nephew, James Thomas Gritter, my grandparents, Gladys Gritter and the late George E. Gritter, my aunt, Cynthia Gargagliano, and my late (great-)uncle, Raymond Kooi. My grandpa and grandma's interest in the civil rights movement inspired mine. My mom and dad have always been supportive of my goals and willing to lend a helping hand. They have sacrificed much to let me pursue my dreams. In addition, my dad traveled to Chapel Hill to assist me with my preparations for my 2004 trip to Memphis, and my mom provided particularly sound advice about the dissertation process. My parents have always been interested in my work, even to the point of listening attentively when I went on about the minutiae of graduate school and my dissertation and book project, even though they are not academics. My brother, Tom, helped make possible a research trip to the University of Michigan Library. I further thank my parents and brother for their compassion and support during stressful times with this project. As I was revising my dissertation into a book, my first-ever niece or nephew, Emma Elizabeth, was born to Tom and Sarah. She has been an inspiration. I am saddened that my late Uncle Ray did not live to see this book. An academic, he always was encouraging and supportive of me and my career as well as unfailingly enthusiastic and proud.

Finally, I thank all the Tennesseans who generously allowed me to interview and/or conduct oral histories of them; sadly, some are no longer living. John L. Seigenthaler shared with me his perspectives on Memphis and Tennessee politics in two lengthy phone interviews in which he discussed the relationship of black Memphians to the John F. Kennedy campaign and administration. His assistant, Gay Campbell, at Vanderbilt University helped make these discussions possible; I thank William R. Ferris for introducing me to Mr. Seigenthaler. Benjamin L. Hooks generously granted me two interviews, and his wife, Frances Hooks, helped make these conversations possible. A large number of Memphians allowed me to conduct oral histories of them, and all these interviews are housed in both the Everett Cook Collection of the Memphis–Shelby County Public Library and Information Center and the Southern Oral History Program Collection at UNC at Chapel Hill. These Memphians are Jennie M. Betts, Josephine Burson, Fred L. Davis, Lewis R. Donelson III, Jimmie W. Farris, John T. Fisher, Samuel B. Hollis, James Hunter Lane Jr., H. T. Lockard, Henry Gregg Loeb, William N. Morris Jr., Charlie S. Peete, Johnnie Mae Peters, Thomas R. Prewitt Sr., Anne W. Shafer, Thomas E. "Pete" Sisson, Maxine A. Smith, Vasco A. Smith, Russell B. Sugarmon Jr., Helen G. Wax, and Lillie J. Wheeler.

I especially thank the civil rights leaders Russell B. Sugarmon Jr. and the late H. T. Lockard as well as the late Maxine Smith and her late husband, Vasco Smith. They trusted me enough to tell me about their experiences during my first trip to Memphis in 2000, which turned out to be a life-changing experience. It was an honor and privilege to meet them, and they were as helpful as possible while I worked on this project. They all were willing to answer any questions and let me conduct a number of oral histories and interviews of them. Thanks, too, to Gina Sugarmon, the wife of Russell B. Sugarmon Jr., for her kindness, assistance, and friendship. Although I did not get to interview Dr. Miriam DeCosta-Willis for this project, I thank her for her support and encouragement of my work. My appreciation goes to Ida Lockard, the late wife of H. T. Lockard, for her kindness as well. This book is my way of giving back to these Memphians and all those civil rights activists who shared with me their memories of the black freedom struggle.

Notes

The following abbreviations are used throughout the notes:

AA	*Afro-American*
ADW	*Atlanta Daily World*
BTV	Behind the Veil: Documenting African American Life in the Jim Crow South Collection, Special Collections, Duke University
CA	*Commercial Appeal*
CD	*Chicago Defender*
Kennedy Library	John F. Kennedy Library, Boston
mfm	microfilm
MPS	*Memphis Press-Scimitar*
MSC	Memphis–Shelby County Room, Memphis–Shelby County Public Library and Information Center
MT	*Memphis Triangle*
MW	*Memphis World*
NYAN	*New York Amsterdam News*
NYT	*New York Times*
PC	*Pittsburgh Courier*
SC	Special Collections Department, Ned McWherter Library, University of Memphis
SOHP	Southern Oral History Program Collection, Southern Historical Collection, University of North Carolina at Chapel Hill
TSD	*Tri-State Defender*
UMOH	University of Memphis Oral History Research Office Collection
WTHSP	*West Tennessee Historical Society Papers*

Introduction

1. I interchangeably use *electoral action/activity* and *political action/ activity* to refer to formal politics throughout this book.

2. The Peripheral South is defined as Arkansas, Florida, North Carolina, Tennessee, Texas, and Virginia and the Deep South as Alabama, Georgia, Louisiana, Mississippi, and South Carolina. Henry Lee Moon, *Balance of Power: The Negro Vote* (Garden City, NY: Doubleday, 1948), 176; Michael J. Klarman, *From Jim Crow to Civil Rights: The Supreme Court and the Struggle for Racial Equality* (New York: Oxford University Press, 2004), 103.

3. Scholarship that looks at southern black political mobilization from the late nineteenth century until 1944 includes Paul Lewinson, *Race, Class, and Party: A History of Negro Suffrage and White Politics in the South* (1932; reprint, New York: Russell & Russell, 1963); Ralph J. Bunche, *The Political Status of the Negro in the Age of FDR*, ed. Dewey W. Grantham (Chicago: University of Chicago Press, 1973); Darlene Clark Hine, *Black Victory: The Rise and Fall of the White Primary in Texas*, 2nd ed. (Columbia: University of Missouri Press, 2003); Klarman, *From Jim Crow to Civil Rights;* Paul Ortiz, *Emancipation Betrayed: The Hidden History of Black Organizing and White Violence in Florida from Reconstruction to the Bloody Election of 1920* (Berkeley and Los Angeles: University of California Press, 2005); Manfred Berg, *Ticket to Freedom: The NAACP and the African American Right to Vote* (Gainesville: University Press of Florida, 2005); and Lorraine Gates Schuyler, *The Weight of Their Votes: Southern Women and Political Leverage in the 1920s* (Chapel Hill: University of North Carolina Press, 2006).

4. Michael J. Klarman, "The White Primary Rulings: A Case Study in the Consequences of Supreme Court Decisionmaking," *Florida State University Law Review* 29, no. 55 (Fall 2001): 55–107; Donald R. Matthews and James W. Prothro, *Negroes and the New Southern Politics* (New York: Harcourt, Brace & World, 1966), 18. For the post–World War II years, civil rights historiography primarily emphasizes legal and direct action and, increasingly, labor activism. Other scholarly works that examine sustained black political mobilization in the urban South include Steven F. Lawson, *Black Ballots: Voting Rights in the South, 1944–1969* (New York: Columbia University Press, 1976), *Running for Freedom: Civil Rights and Black Politics in America since 1941*, 2nd ed. (New York: McGraw-Hill, 1997), and *Civil Rights Crossroads: Nation, Community, and the Black Freedom Struggle* (Lexington: University Press of Kentucky, 2003); Kathryn L. Nasstrom, "Down to Now: Memory, Narrative, and Women's Leadership in the Civil Rights Movement in Atlanta, Georgia," *Gender and History* 11, no. 1 (April 1999): 113–44; J. Mills Thornton III, *Dividing Lines: Municipal Politics and the Struggle for Civil Rights in Montgomery, Birmingham, and Selma* (Tuscaloosa: University of Alabama Press, 2002); and Robert Korstad, *Civil Rights Unionism: Tobacco Workers and the Struggle for Democracy in the Mid-Twentieth-Century South* (Chapel Hill: University of North Carolina Press, 2003).

5. Matthews and Prothro, *Negroes and the New Southern Politics*, 176;

Julian Bond, "MLK in Memphis" (paper presented as part of the University of Virginia's Civil Rights South bus tour program, Memphis, 13 March 2010, copy in author's possession), 19. To understand southern black politics in the Jim Crow era, it is crucial to delve into the immense body of work written by social scientists in the 1950s and 1960s. Hundreds of studies speculated on the impact of increased black political activity following the *Smith v. Allwright* (1944) decision. In addition to Matthews and Prothro's *Negroes and the New Southern Politics,* see Hugh D. Price, *The Negro in Florida Politics: A Chapter of Florida History* (New York: New York University Press, 1957); Harry A. Bailey Jr., ed., *Negro Politics in America* (Columbus: Charles E. Merrill, 1967); William R. Keech, *The Impact of Negro Voting: The Role of the Vote in the Quest for Equality* (Chicago: Rand McNally, 1968); and Harry Holloway, *The Politics of the Southern Negro: From Exclusion to Big City Organization* (New York: Random House, 1969).

6. Klarman, "White Primary Rulings," 96–101, and *From Jim Crow to Civil Rights,* 32, 103; Lewinson, *Race, Class, and Party,* 132–52; Matthews and Prothro, *Negroes and the New Southern Politics,* 177; Lawson, *Black Ballots,* 129–30.

7. For examples of how scholars have underscored the limits of black involvement in the Republican Party, see Simon Topping, *Lincoln's Lost Legacy: The Republican Party and the African American Vote, 1928–1952* (Gainesville: University Press of Florida, 2008); Nancy J. Weiss, *Farewell to the Party of Lincoln: Black Politics in the Age of FDR* (Princeton, NJ: Princeton University Press, 1983); Harvard Sitkoff, *A New Deal for Blacks,* 30th anniversary ed. (New York: Oxford University Press, 2009), 3–25; and Hanes Walton Jr., *Black Republicans: The Politics of the Black and Tans* (Metuchen, NJ: Scarecrow, 1975).

8. For a good analysis of these points, see Neil McMillen, *Dark Journey: Black Mississippians in the Age of Jim Crow* (Urbana: University of Illinois Press, 1990), 70–71.

9. See, e.g., Weiss, *Farewell to the Party of Lincoln;* and Sitkoff, *New Deal for Blacks.*

10. Patricia Sullivan, *Days of Hope: Race and Democracy in the New Deal Era* (Chapel Hill: University of North Carolina Press, 1996).

11. This book builds on and challenges Topping's *Lincoln's Lost Legacy.* Topping analyzes the relationship of African Americans to the Republican Party from 1928 to 1952 and makes a strong case for recognizing the complex process of their realignment to the Democratic Party. Yet, like other scholars, he largely focuses on the northern black vote and national politics and does not recognize the degree to which black southerners participated in politics. He dismisses black participation in the Republican Party before 1928 and takes a top-down approach that focuses on leaders and not ordinary African Americans.

12. Leslie Brown, e.g., complicates the idea of the nadir period by showing a black business elite flourishing in Durham, North Carolina. See Leslie Brown, *Upbuilding Black Durham: Gender, Class, and Black Community Development in the Jim Crow South* (Chapel Hill: University of North Carolina Press, 2008). Similarly, Story Matkin-Rawn argues that more black activism was going on in the nadir period than scholars have acknowledged. See Story Matkin-Rawn, "From Land Ownership to Legal Defense: The World War I Watershed in Black Arkansan Organizing" (paper presented at the Conference on Race, Labor and Citizenship in the Post-Emancipation South, Charleston, SC, 11–13 March 2010). On ways in which African Americans endured and resisted the Jim Crow South, see William H. Chafe, Raymond Gavins, and Robert Korstad, eds., *Remembering Jim Crow: African Americans Tell about Life in the Segregated South* (New York: New Press, 2001).

13. Steven Hahn, *A Nation under Our Feet: Black Political Struggles in the Rural South from Slavery to the Great Migration* (Cambridge, MA: Harvard University Press, 2003).

1. "To Regain the Lost Rights of a Growing Race"

1. New Castle was on the border of Fayette and Hardeman Counties. W. Herbert Brewster Sr., interview by Charles W. Crawford, Memphis, 6 July 1983, transcript, p. 2, UMOH.

2. Ibid., 5–6 (quote 6). On Simmons, see Andrew Kaye, "Roscoe Conkling Simmons and the Significance of African American Oratory," *Historical Journal* 45, no. 1 (2002): 79–102; and "Roscoe Simmons Dies," *PC*, 5 May 1951, 1.

3. "Precious Memories of Rev. Dr. William Herbert Brewster, Sr., 1897–1987," funeral program, 20 October 1987, p. 2, Notable Black Memphians—Funeral Programs Collection, SC; Miriam DeCosta-Willis, *Notable Black Memphians* (Amherst, NY: Cambria, 2008), 52.

4. "Platform of the Lincoln Republican League of Tennessee," 8 September 1916, folder 24, box 3, and "Report on Feb. 1, 1916, Meeting of the Lincoln League," February 1916, folder 25, box 3, Robert R. Church Family Papers, SC.

5. The decision was *Guinn v. United States*. The grandfather clause was adopted by some southern states in an attempt to disenfranchise African Americans and limit voting rights to whites; it exempted men whose ancestors could vote before 1867 from voting restrictions. Klarman, *From Jim Crow to Civil Rights*, 103; Moon, *Balance of Power*, 176; Lewinson, *Race, Class, and Party*, 136–37, 146–53; Glenda Gilmore, *Gender and Jim Crow: Women and the Politics of White Supremacy in North Carolina, 1896–1920* (Chapel Hill: University of North Carolina Press, 1996), 147–48, 172–74; Tera W. Hunter, *To 'Joy My Freedom: Southern Black Women's Lives and La-*

bors after the Civil War (Cambridge, MA: Harvard University Press, 1999), 138; R. Volney Riser, *Defying Disfranchisement: Black Voting Rights Activism in the Jim Crow South, 1890–1908* (Baton Rouge: Louisiana State University Press, 2010), esp. 1–2, 6, 151–52, 188; Alton Hornsby, *Black Power in Dixie: A Political History of African Americans in Atlanta* (Gainesville: University Press of Florida, 2009), 35; Peter F. Lau, *Democracy Rising: South Carolina and the Fight for Black Equality since 1865* (Lexington: University Press of Kentucky, 2006), 26–33.

6. Brewster interview, p. 6.

7. Willard B. Gatewood, *Aristocrats of Color: The Black Elite, 1880–1920* (Fayetteville: University of Arkansas Press, 2000); Annette E. Church and Roberta Church, *The Robert R. Churches of Memphis* (Ann Arbor, MI: Edwards Bros., 1974), 3–6; Mary Church Terrell, *A Colored Woman in a White World* (1940; reprint, with an introduction by Nellie Y. McKay, New York: G. K. Hall, 1996), 2–5; Gloria Brown Melton, "Blacks in Memphis, Tennessee, 1920–1955: A Historical Study" (Ph.D. diss., Washington State University, 1982), 59 n. 62.

8. Roberta Church and Annette Church, interview by Charles W. Crawford, Memphis, 4 January 1973, interview no. 1, transcript, p. 12, UMOH; "Robert R. Church, Memphis' Wealthiest Man, Dead," *AA,* 15 September 1912, 6; Paul R. Coppock, "Bob Church: An Early Believer in Memphis," *CA,* 1 July 1973, sec. 6, p. 7; Roberta Church and Ronald Walter, *Nineteenth Century Memphis Families of Color, 1850–1900,* 3rd ed., ed. Charles Crawford (Memphis: Murdock Printing, 2002), 16; obituary of Robert R. Church Sr. from a white Memphis newspaper, n.p., n.d., folder 54, box 1, Church Family Papers.

9. Melton, "Blacks in Memphis," 3; Christopher Caplinger, "Conflict and Community: Racial Segregation in a New South City, 1860–1914" (Ph.D. diss., Vanderbilt University, 2003), 29–33, 132–33; Lester C. Lamon, *Blacks in Tennessee, 1791–1970* (Knoxville: University of Tennessee Press, 1981), 39; Church and Walter, *Nineteenth Century Memphis Families,* 16; Terrell, *Colored Woman,* 7.

10. Terrell, *Colored Woman,* xix; G. P. Hamilton, *The Bright Side of Memphis* (1908; reprint, LaVergne, TN: Lightning Source, 2003), 99; Melton, "Blacks in Memphis," 33; Church and Church, *Robert R. Churches,* 13, 21–24; Charles W. Crawford, "Memphis' First Black Capitalist," *Daily News,* 3 June 1976, folder 68, box 1, Church Family Papers; S. Davidson Hill, "The Self-Defined African American Community of Jim Crow Memphis" (senior thesis, Princeton University, 2000), 31; George W. Lee, *Beale Street: Where the Blues Began* (New York: Robert O. Ballou, 1934), 24–26; obituary of Robert R. Church Sr.; Walter P. Adkins, "Beale Street Goes to the Polls" (master's thesis, Ohio State University, 1935), 69; "[Ex-?]Slave's Gift:

Church Donates $1,000 to [Confederate?] Reunion Fund," *CA*, 30 January 1901, folder 31, box 1, and "Souvenir Programme, Dr. Booker T. Washington, Memphis, Tenn.," 24 November 1909, p. 2, folder 33, box 2, Church Family Papers; Church and Walter, *Nineteenth Century Memphis Families,* 18; "Wealthy Colored Men," *Chicago Tribune,* 25 May 1890, folder 31, box 1, Church Family Papers.

11. For more information on Louisa Ayres Church, see Terrell, *Colored Woman.*

12. Church and Church interview, 4 January 1973, interview no. 1, pp. 2–3, 6–7; Roberta Church and Annette Church, interview by Charles W. Crawford, Memphis, 10 July 1973, transcript, p. 8, UMOH; "[Ex-?]Slave's Gift," *CA;* Bessie Blanden, "Our Colored Society," 5 April 1890, [*CA?*], folder 9, box 1, Church Family Papers; "Wealthy Colored Men," *Chicago Tribune.*

13. From the late 1860s through the early years of the twentieth century, African Americans served in the following positions in and from Memphis and Shelby County: city councilman, county school board member, city school board member, constable, justice of the peace, assistant attorney general, wharfmaster, coal inspector, county registrar, state legislator, US deputy marshal, Shelby County commissioner, federal customs collector, circuit county clerk, whiskey inspector, police officer, and firefighter. Caplinger, "Conflict and Community," 33–34; Mingo Scott, *The Negro in Tennessee Politics and Governmental Affairs, 1865–1965* (Nashville: Rich, 1964), 14; Lamon, *Blacks in Tennessee,* 35–36, 45; Joseph H. Cartwright, *The Triumph of Jim Crow: Tennessee Race Relations in the 1880s* (Knoxville: University of Tennessee Press, 1976), 2; Melton, "Blacks in Memphis," 15; David M. Tucker, *Black Pastors and Leaders: Memphis, 1819–1972* (Memphis: Memphis State University Press, 1975), 13–14, 26–27, 30; Joe Walk, *A History of African-Americans in Memphis Government* (Memphis: Joe Walk, 1996), 8; Lee, *Beale Street,* 240; Adkins, "Beale Street," 11–12; Church and Church, *Robert R. Churches,* 50–51; Clark Porteous, "A Vow to Citizens by Negro Winners," *MPS,* 4 November 1964, vertical file 1964 Elections, MSC; Church and Walter, *Nineteenth Century Memphis Families,* 17; Roberta Church and Annette Church, interview by Charles W. Crawford, Memphis, 5 January 1973, interview no. 1, transcript, pp. 1–3, UMOH; Annette E. Church to William E. Miller, 4 September 1961, folder 21, box 12, Church Family Papers.

14. Hahn, *Nation under Our Feet,* 208–11, 219–20, 237, 249–51; Eric Foner and Olivia Mahoney, *America's Reconstruction: People and Politics after the Civil War* (New York: HarperPerennial, 1995), 95, 97; Hunter, *To 'Joy My Freedom,* 85–88.

15. Church and Church, *Robert R. Churches,* 37–39, 42; Church and Church interview, 5 January 1973, interview no. 1, pp. 5–8; Church and

Walter, *Nineteenth Century Memphis Families,* 114–16; Church and Church interview, 4 January 1973, interview no. 1, pp. 9–12. For more on Bruce and Lynch, see Stephen Middleton, ed., *Black Congressmen during Reconstruction: A Documentary Sourcebook* (Westport, CT: Praeger, 2002), 1–37, 145–225.

16. Lee, *Beale Street,* 27; Terrell, *Colored Woman,* 36–37; Gerald M. Capers Jr., *The Biography of a River Town: Memphis: Its Heroic Age* (Chapel Hill: University of North Carolina Press, 1939), 188, 200; Robert R. Church Jr., "Material for the Carnegie Corporation of New York—Requested by Dr. Bunche," [1938?], p. 1, folder 45, box 6, and Annette E. Church and Roberta Church, "Robert R. Church, Sr., Memphis' First Black Capitalist," Memphis Sesquicentennial Commission, 1969, folder 68, box 1, Church Family Papers.

17. Church and Church, "Robert R. Church, Sr., Memphis' First Black Capitalist."

18. W. Fitzhugh Brundage, *Lynching in the New South: Georgia and Virginia, 1880–1930* (Urbana: University of Illinois Press, 1993); Lee, *Beale Street,* 25–26; Caplinger, "Conflict and Community," 50–51.

19. Lawson, *Black Ballots,* 10–15; John David Smith, foreword to Middleton, ed., *Black Congressmen during Reconstruction,* ix; J. Morgan Kousser, *The Shaping of Southern Politics: Suffrage Restriction and the Establishment of the One-Party South, 1880–1910* (New Haven, CT: Yale University Press, 1974), 12.

20. The secret ballot made the voting process more difficult for illiterate voters, affecting African Americans in particular. As late as 1900, nearly 50 percent of black Tennesseans were illiterate, compared to 14 percent of whites. Caplinger, "Conflict and Community," 46–47; Lamon, *Blacks in Tennessee,* 59–60; Michael Perman, *Struggle for Mastery: Disfranchisement in the South, 1888–1908* (Chapel Hill: University of North Carolina Press, 2001), 59; Porteous, "A Vow to Citizens"; Lee, *Beale Street,* 240; Adkins, "Beale Street," 16.

21. Lamon, *Blacks in Tennessee,* 46–47, 58–59; Caplinger, "Conflict and Community," 78, 83, 105; Adkins, "Beale Street," 14; Mary Frances Berry, *My Face Is Black Is True: Callie House and the Struggle for Ex-Slave Reparations* (New York: Knopf, 2005), 28. For a broader look at the segregation of railroad travel in the South, see Edward Ayers, *The Promise of the New South: Life after Reconstruction* (New York: Oxford University Press, 1992).

22. Preston Valien, "Expansion of Negro Suffrage in Tennessee," *Journal of Negro Education* 26, no. 3 (Summer 1957): 362–68, 363; Caplinger, "Conflict and Community," 55; Melton, "Blacks in Memphis," 9.

23. Caplinger, "Conflict and Community," 20, 56–57; Hill, "Self-Defined African American Community" (thesis), 10; Beverly G. Bond, "Every

Duty Incumbent upon Them: African American Women in Nineteenth-Century Memphis," in *Trial and Triumph: Essays in Tennessee's African American History*, ed. Carroll Van West (Knoxville: University of Tennessee Press, 2002), 203–26, 220.

24. Hamilton, *Bright Side*, 24.

25. "News of Bygone Days: 75 Years Ago, Jan. 5, 1898," *CA*, 5 Jan. 1973, vertical file 1898 Election, MSC.

26. Caplinger, "Conflict and Community," 47, 56–57, 73–74 n. 87.

27. Hamilton, *Bright Side*, 24–25. For a profile of Hamilton, see DeCosta-Willis, *Notable Black Memphians*, 148–49.

28. John H. Grant, *Defense of the Negro; or, A Review of the "Commercial Appeal's" Attack on the Negro* (Memphis: LeMoyne, 1903), 6–8, copy in box 1, folder 37, Church Family Papers. The *Commercial Appeal* editorial appeared on 16 February 1903, and Grant's response appeared on 22 February 1903.

29. Grant, *Defense of the Negro*, 9 (quote), 25, 12 (quote), 13–14, 16 (quote), 19 (quote), 21 (quote).

30. Donald J. Lisio, *Hoover, Blacks, and Lily-Whites: A Study of Southern Strategies* (Chapel Hill: University of North Carolina Press, 1985), 36–37; Richard B. Sherman, *The Republican Party and Black America from McKinley to Hoover, 1896–1933* (Charlottesville: University Press of Virginia, 1973); V. O. Key, *Southern Politics* (New York: Vintage, 1949), 292; Walton, *Black Republicans*, 43.

31. These men were J. N. Ruffin and W. J. Yerby. Lisio, *Hoover, Blacks, and Lily-Whites*, 36–37; Adkins, "Beale Street," 12; Lewinson, *Race, Class, and Party*, 110–11; Walton, *Black Republicans*, 38–40; Melton, "Blacks in Memphis," 38–39; Church and Walter, *Nineteenth Century Memphis Families*, 17; Church and Church, *Robert R. Churches*, 51–52. On the complexities of Republican factional politics, see Key, *Southern Politics*, 292, 294–97.

32. Sherman, *Republican Party*, 23–112; Berg, *Ticket to Freedom*, 44; Garna L. Christina, "Brownsville Raid of 1906," *Handbook of Texas Online*, Texas State Historical Association, 1997–2002, http://www.tshaonline. org/handbook/online/articles/pkb06; James Leiker, "Brownsville Affray, 1906," BlackPast.org: Remembered and Reclaimed, http://www.blackpast. org/?q=aaw/brownsville-affray-1906; Edward O. Frantz, *The Door of Hope: Republican Presidents and the First Southern Strategy, 1877–1933* (Gainesville: University Press of Florida, 2011), 209.

33. Paul G. Partington, "The Moon Illustrated Weekly—the Precursor of the *Crisis*," *Journal of Negro History* 48, no. 3 (July 1963): 206–16.

34. Gatewood, *Aristocrats of Color*, 95. For an analysis of the response of the black elite to the imposition of Jim Crow, see ibid., 300–322.

35. Booker T. Washington to Robert R. Church Sr., 20 February 1911,

folder 50, box 1, and "Life Membership: National Negro Business League," folder 10, box 1, Church Family Papers; Church and Church interview, 5 January 1973, interview no. 1, pp. 5–7.

36. Tucker, *Black Pastors and Leaders*, 46–47, 52–54, 153; Fred L. Hutchins, *What Happened in Memphis* (Kingsport, TN: Kingsport, 1965), 37, 39; Wells to Church, n.d. (postmarked 22 February 1904), and Wells-Barnett to Church, 30 August 1918, folder 26, box 1, Church Family Papers; Terrell, *Colored Woman*, xix, 197–208. For recent biographies of Wells, see Paula Giddings, *Ida: A Sword among Lions: Ida B. Wells and the Campaign against Lynching* (New York: Amistad, 2009); and Mia Bay, *To Tell the Truth Freely: The Life of Ida B. Wells* (New York: Hill & Wang, 2009).

37. Roscoe Conkling Simmons, "Robert R. Church," *Illinois Chronicle*, 14 September 1912, folder 58, box 1, Church Family Papers; obituary of Robert R. Church Sr.; Church and Walter, *Nineteenth Century Memphis Families*, 18; C. R. Bowles to Robert R. Church Sr., 30 November 1906, folder 26, box 1, Church Family Papers; Hutchins, *What Happened in Memphis*, 100; Ron Walter, "Business/Leaders Provide a Mix of Talent," *CA*, 1981, folder 5, box 3, African-American Culture and Life Collection, MSC; Church and Church interview, 4 January 1973, interview no. 2, p. 17.

38. Church and Church, "Robert R. Church, Sr., Memphis' First Black Capitalist." See also William N. Jones, "Day by Day: The R. R. Church Dynasty," *AA*, 16 April 1938, 4.

39. William A. Gordon, Letter to the Editor, *Washington Post*, 29 May 1901; D. H. K. Bingham to Robert R. Church Sr., 16 May 1904, folder 4, box 1, Church Family Papers; obituary of Robert R. Church Sr.

40. "[Ex-?]Slave's Gift," *CA*.

41. Church gave the chairman his "best wishes for complete success." Church to A. B. Pickett, 28 June 1901, folder 34, box 1, Church Family Papers.

42. "[Ex-?]Slave's Gift," *CA*. This quote is reprinted in William A. Gordon, Letter to the Editor, *Washington Post*, 29 May 1901.

43. Hutchins, *What Happened in Memphis*, vii, 103.

44. The "antebellum Eden" quote is from Carl H. Nightingale, "How Lynchings Became High-Tech, and Other Tales from the Modern South," *Reviews in American History* 27, no. 1 (1999): 140–48, 141. I also drew from Grace Elizabeth Hale, *Making Whiteness: The Culture of Segregation in the South, 1890–1940* (New York: Pantheon, 1998); W. Fitzhugh Brundage, *The Southern Past: A Clash of Race and Memory* (Cambridge, MA: Belknap Press of Harvard University Press, 2005); Joel Williamson, *The Crucible of Race: Black/White Relations in the American South since Emancipation* (New York: Oxford University Press, 1984).

45. Lee, *Beale Street*, 27–28; Church and Church interview, 4 January

1973, interview no. 2, p. 10; Melton, "Blacks in Memphis," 30; Church and Church, "Robert R. Church, Sr., Memphis' First Black Capitalist"; Simmons, "Robert R. Church"; Howard N. Rabinowitz, "From Exclusion to Segregation: Southern Race Relations, 1865–1890," *Journal of American History* 63, no. 2 (September 1976): 325–50, 338. The quote is from "[Ex-?]Slave's Gift," *CA.*

46. Church and Church interview, 4 January 1973, interview no. 2, pp. 6–16; Pink Palace Museum, *Historic Black Memphians* (Memphis: Foundation of Memphis Pink Palace Museum, 1978), 9; Annette and Roberta Church to Henry Loeb, 30 January 1970, folder 3, box 16, ser. 2, Henry Loeb III Papers, MSC; W. C. Handy, *Father of the Blues: An Autobiography* (New York: Da Capo, 1991), 254; Hutchins, *What Happened in Memphis,* 101.

47. Handy, *Father of the Blues,* 278.

48. Church and Church to Loeb, 30 January 1970 (folder 3, box 16, ser. 2, Loeb Papers) contains a copy of the program at Church's Auditorium. For more on the event, see Church and Walter, *Nineteenth Century Memphis Families,* 17, 51, 80; and Carol Lynn Yellin and Janann Sherman, *The Perfect 36: Tennessee Delivers Woman Suffrage* (Memphis: Wilson Graphics, 1998), 68.

49. No record exists of Anna Wright enrolling at, taking classes at, or graduating from Antioch College. Many records of the school's music institute are, however, missing from the college archive, so it remains possible that she did study there. Scott Sanders, archivist, Antioch College, phone conversation and email correspondence with the author, September 2012. While Wright's attendance at Oberlin has been confirmed, she did not receive a degree. Louisa Hoffman, archival assistant, Oberlin College, email message to the author, 24 September 2012. For more on Anna Wright Church, see Church and Church, *Robert R. Churches,* 27–36; and James M. Trotter, *Music and Some Highly Musical People* (Boston: Lee & Shepherd; New York: Charles T. Dillingham, 1881), 331, http://www.gutenberg.org/files/28056/28056-h/28056-h.htm#. On Lucy Jane Wright, see Church and Walter, *Nineteenth Century Memphis Families,* 114–16.

50. Church and Church, *Robert R. Churches,* 35; "[Ex-?]Slave's Gift," *CA;* Church and Walter, *Nineteenth Century Memphis Families,* 14, 20; Church and Church interview, 5 January 1973, interview no. 2, pp. 5, 6.

51. Church and Church interview, 5 January 1973, interview no. 1, p. 6.

52. Adkins, "Beale Street," 69–70. For an analysis of the education of the black elite during this time, see Gatewood, *Aristocrats of Color,* 247–71.

53. Church and Walter, *Nineteenth Century Memphis Families,* 100; Church and Church interview, 10 July 1973, interview no. 3, p. 8; Church and Church interview, 4 January 1973, interview no. 1, pp. 6–7.

54. Church, "Material for the Carnegie Corporation," 1. On the streetcar segregation law, see Caplinger, "Conflict and Community," 112; Melton, "Blacks in Memphis," 12–13; and Church and Walter, *Nineteenth Century Memphis Families*, 4–5. For a discussion of streetcars in Memphis, see Hutchins, *What Happened in Memphis*, 23–30. For a broader discussion of streetcar laws in the South, see Rabinowitz, "From Exclusion to Segregation," 325–50.

55. Church, "Material for the Carnegie Corporation," 1.

56. Adkins, "Beale Street," 70; Church and Church, *Robert R. Churches*, 64; Church and Church interview, 5 January 1973, interview no. 1, p. 6.

57. Hamilton, *Bright Side*, 91–92; "Memphis Solvent Savings Bank and Trust Co.," *The Moon Illustrated Weekly*, 2 March 1906, 3, folder 10, box 2, Church Family Papers; DeCosta-Willis, *Notable Black Memphians*, 80; Delta Center for Culture and Learning, "The Mound Bayou Story" (Cleveland, MS: Delta State University, n.d.), 2; McMillen, *Dark Journey;* Church and Church interview, 4 January 1973, interview no. 2, p. 12; Simmons, "Robert R. Church"; Melton, "Blacks in Memphis," 30; Hutchins, *What Happened in Memphis*, 100.

58. Hamilton, *Bright Side*, 100–101 (quote 101); Clarence L. Kelly, "Robert R. Church, a Negro Tennessean in Republican, State, and National Politics from 1912 to 1932" (master's thesis, Tennessee A&I State University, 1954), 11–13; Church and Walter, *Nineteenth Century Memphis Families*, 58; Church and Church, *Robert R. Churches*, 65–66, 97; Church and Church interview, 5 January 1973, interview no. 2, pp. 1–2, 6–7; Mr. and Mrs. W. E. B. Du Bois to Robert and Sara Church, 23 August 1911, folder 44, box 2, Church Family Papers.

59. Simmons, "Robert R. Church"; "Old Land Mark Removed by Death," *Broad Axe*, 7 September 1912, 1; "Robert R. Church, Memphis' Wealthiest Man, Dead," *AA;* "Robert R. Church in His Later Years," folder 13, box 38, Church Family Papers, available at http://catalogquicksearch. memphis.edu/iii/cpro/DigitalItemViewPage.external?lang=eng&sp=10 00099&sp=T&sp=1&suite=def; Church and Church interview, 5 January 1973, interview no. 1, pp. 5–6; "Resolution upon the Death of Mr. R. R. Church," Solvent Savings Bank & Trust Co., 1912, folder 58, box 1, Church Family Papers; Church and Church interview, 4 January 1973, interview no. 1, pp. 7–8; James G. Carter to Robert R. Church Jr., 30 October 1912, folder 15, box 2, Church Family Papers; Kelly, "Robert R. Church," 11; DeCosta-Willis, *Notable Black Memphians*, 81; Church and Church interview, 10 July 1973, interview no. 2, p. 3. The newspaper quote is from Church and Church, "Robert R. Church, Sr., Memphis' First Black Capitalist."

60. William D. Miller, *Mr. Crump of Memphis* (Baton Rouge: Louisiana State University Press, 1964), 33–38, 41; G. Wayne Dowdy, *Mr. Crump*

Don't Like It: Machine Politics in Memphis (Jackson: University Press of Mississippi, 2006), ix–x; G. Wayne Dowdy, "Biography," finding aid to Edward Crump Papers, mfm, p. 1, Edward H. Crump Papers, MSC.

61. Miller, *Mr. Crump*, 42; Dowdy, *Mr. Crump*, xi–xii. See also Hutchins, *What Happened in Memphis*, 66.

62. Handy, *Father of the Blues*, x, xiv, 80, 93–94, 232; Dowdy, *Mr. Crump*, 5–6, 102; David Robertson, *W. C. Handy: The Life and Times of the Man Who Made the Blues* (New York: Knopf, 2009), 118–20, 123–25; Lee, *Beale Street*, 133–34; Caplinger, "Conflict and Community," 59; Loyal Tennesseans League, *Edward H. Crump: Public Enemy No. 1* (Memphis: Loyal Tennesseans League, 1932), 8, folder 44, box 4, Church Family Papers.

63. Miller, *Mr. Crump*, 41, 97–98.

64. Hill, "Self-Defined African American Community" (thesis), 10; Laurie B. Green, "Battling the Plantation Mentality: Consciousness, Culture, and the Politics of Race, Class and Gender in Memphis, 1940–1968" (Ph.D. diss., University of Chicago, 1999), 331; Lamar Whitlow Bridges, "Editor Mooney versus Boss Crump," *WTHSP* 20 (1966): 77–107, 78, 82–83, 85; Dowdy, *Mr. Crump*, 4–5; Loyal Tennesseans League, *Edward H. Crump*, 7–8.

65. Allen H. Kitchens, "Ouster of Mayor Edward H. Crump, 1915–1916," *WTHSP* 19 (1965): 105–20, 118.

66. Ibid., 118–20; "Official Record of Edward H. Crump, during His Incumbency as Mayor of Memphis, Covering a Period of Five Years, Ten Months, and Two Days," n.d., pp. 2–3, mfm 000998-9, folder Biography 1917, box 44, ser. 2, Crump Papers; Dowdy, *Mr. Crump*, x, 7–11, 18–19; Hutchins, *What Happened in Memphis*, 67; William D. Miller, *Memphis during the Progressive Era, 1900–1917* (Memphis: Memphis State University Press, 1957), 166, and *Mr. Crump*, 2; Nat D. Williams, interview by Ronald Anderson Walter, Memphis, 13 September 1976, transcript, p. 20, Everett R. Cook Collection, MSC.

67. Hill, "Self-Defined African American Community" (thesis), 10; Caplinger, "Conflict and Community," 62; Dowdy, *Mr. Crump*, 19–20; Thomas H. Hayes Sr. et al., Petition from Negro Undertakers to Edward H. Crump and Board of Commissioners, [1910], mfm 002231, folder City Business 1910, box 15, ser. 1, J. T. Settle Sr. to Crump, mfm 000987, folder Politics "S" 1915, box 32, ser. 1, F. W. Watson to Crump, 11 November 1911, mfm 001792-4, folder Politics "T" 1911, box 33, ser. 1, and Colored Men's Civic League, Petition to E. H. Crump, 8 April 1914, mfm 000623, folder "Mc" City Business 1914, box 22, ser. 1, Crump Papers. See also Crump to Thomas H. Hayes Sr., 7 July 1916, mfm 001776, and Crump to A. A. Kincannon, 7 July 1916, mfm 001775, folder Politics 1916, box 47, ser. 2, Central Committee of the Colored Voters to Various Candidates of Shelby County,

Tennessee, [1914], mfm 000424, and Eleventh Ward Improvement Club to E. H. Crump, 25 July 1914, mfm 000422, folder Politics "N" 1914, box 26, ser. 1, and T. O. Fuller to Crump, 13 November 1912, mfm 000528, T. O. Fuller to Crump, 1 May 1912, mfm 000529, and Crump to T. O. Fuller, 14 November 1912, mfm 000564, folder "F" City Business 1912, box 11, ser. 1, Crump Papers.

68. G. Wayne Dowdy, "Scope and Content Notes," finding aid to Crump Papers, p. ix, Crump Papers.

69. This assessment is based on my review of numerous documents in the Crump Papers.

70. The letter does not indicate why they met. Church to Crump, 9 July 1915, folder Personal "C," box 7, ser. 1, Crump Papers.

71. The title was later changed to "Memphis Blues." Robertson, *W. C. Handy,* 128–30.

72. Church and Church interview, 10 July 1973, interview no. 3, p. 8; Kelly, "Robert R. Church," 7–9; Adkins, "Beale Street," 19.

73. Adkins, "Beale Street," 88; Church, "Material for the Carnegie Corporation," 2.

74. Church, "Material for the Carnegie Corporation," 2.

75. Church and Church, *Robert R. Churches;* "Souvenir Programme, Dr. Booker T. Washington"; Hamilton, *Bright Side,* 72–75, 92, 130–31; Partington, "The Moon Illustrated Weekly"; Church and Walter, *Nineteenth Century Memphis Families,* 40–42, 74–75; Hutchins, *What Happened in Memphis,* 76–80; DeCosta-Willis, *Notable Black Memphians;* Robertson, *W. C. Handy;* Roger Didier, "Harry Pace Lists 'Depression Cure,'" *ADW,* 6 December 1934, 1.

76. Church to George W. Lee, 22 June 1951, folder 41, box 4, Church Family Papers.

77. Memphis had embarked on a park-building plan in 1899 but had not allowed African Americans access to any parks or built a park for African Americans. Pace to Crump, 8 July 1911, mfm 000888-9, folder City Business 1911, box 27, ser. 1, Crump Papers; Caplinger, "Conflict and Community," 60–61; Melton, "Blacks in Memphis," 37; DeCosta-Willis, *Notable Black Memphians,* 12; Board of Trade, *Cost of Living in American Towns* (London: Darling & Son, 1911), 245.

78. Caplinger, "Conflict and Community," 61.

79. W. M. Melton to E. H. Crump, 21 October 1911, mfm 002450-1, folder Politics "M," box 25, ser. 1, Crump Papers.

80. Caplinger, "Conflict and Community," 61; Dowdy, "Scope and Content Notes," p. ix; E. H. Crump to P. P. Van Vleet, 6 March 1911, mfm 002450, folder "V" City Business 1911, box 35, ser. 1, and "Can We Afford to Re-Elect Mr. Crump," *Bluff City News,* n.d., mfm 002452, and "Pub-

lic Sentiment Reacts against Mayor Crump," *Bluff City News,* 22 October 1911, mfm 002453, folder Politics "M" 1911, box 25, ser. 1, Crump Papers.

81. Technically, the commission was known at this time as the county court, and Purnell was seeking to be elected a magistrate. Hamilton, *Bright Side,* 135, 217–18; H. C. Purnell and O. W. Williams to E. H. Crump, 28 October 1911, mfm 000722, folder Politics "W" 1911, box 36, ser. 1, Crump Papers.

82. Campaign Committee of H. C. Purnell to Crump, 20 July 1912, mfm 002136-8, folder Politics 1912, box 29, ser. 1, Crump Papers.

83. Bridges, "Editor Mooney," 85–86; Loyal Tennesseans League, *Edward H. Crump,* 9; Acting Secretary to E. H. Crump [name not given] to T. Harbert Taylor, 12 August 1912, mfm 002002, and E. H. Crump to John A. Tipton, 11 August 1912, mfm 002004, folder Politics "T" 1914, box 34, ser. 1, Crump Papers.

84. W. Hatchman to C. W. Schuyler, 11 December 1915, mfm 001022, folder Politics "S" 1915, box 32, ser. 1, Crump Papers.

85. Bridges, "Editor Mooney," 92–94; Loyal Tennesseans League, *Edward H. Crump,* 8–9; Kitchens, "Ouster of Mayor Edward H. Crump." For a look at how the Democratic machine in Cincinnati, Ohio, manipulated black voters in ways similar to the Crump machine, see Nikki Taylor, "The Democratic Machine as a Vehicle for African-American Civil Rights? The Politics of Peter H. Clark, 1882–1888" (paper presented at the Conference on Race, Labor and Citizenship in the Post-Emancipation South, Charleston, SC, 11–13 March 2010).

86. Kelly, "Robert R. Church," 4, 13–17; Adkins, "Beale Street," 54–55; Berg, *Ticket to Freedom,* 44; Sherman, *Republican Party;* Walton, *Black Republicans,* 152; McMillen, *Dark Journey,* 57; Church to Simmons, 23 October 1915, and Church to Simmons, 3 December 1915, folder R. R. Church, 1915–19, box 2, Roscoe Conkling Simmons Papers, Harvard University Archives, Boston.

87. David M. Tucker, *Lieutenant Lee of Beale Street* (Nashville: Vanderbilt University Press, 1971), 81–82; Roscoe Conkling Simmons, *The Republican Party and American Colored People, 1856–1936* (Chicago: Republican National Committee, 1936), 22–30; Sherman, *Republican Party;* Robert S. McElvaine, *The Great Depression* (New York: Times Books, 1984), 188.

88. Woman's National Republican Campaign Committee, *Reasons Why You Should Work for Republican Candidates* (New York: National Woman's Campaign Committee, 1916), folder 6, box 4, Church Family Papers; Sherman, *Republican Party,* 113–18.

89. Some 90 percent of African Americans lived in the South from 1890 to 1910. Despite the Great Migration, 79 percent still lived in the South in 1930. Thomas Maloney, "African Americans in the Twentieth Century,"

EH. Net Encyclopedia, http://eh.net/encyclopedia/article/maloney.african. american.

90. Frantz, *Door of Hope,* 3.

91. Woman's National Republican Campaign Committee, *Reasons Why You Should Work for Republican Candidates.*

92. Sherman, *Republican Party,* 121–22.

93. Kelly, "Robert R. Church," 20, 26, 34.

94. Church, "Material for the Carnegie Corporation," 2.

95. Church and Church, *Robert R. Churches,* 88.

96. Ibid.; Scott, *Negro in Tennessee Politics,* 90; Kelly, "Robert R. Church," 15; Church and Church, *Robert R. Churches,* 89. See also Robert R. Church Jr. to Roscoe Conkling Simmons, 26 January 1916, 21 February 1916, and 26 August 1916, folder R. R. Church, 1915–19, box 2, Simmons Papers.

97. Church and Church, *Robert R. Churches,* 88.

98. Robert R. Church Jr., "Remarks at First Meeting [of the] Lincoln League, Church's Park and Auditorium," 1 February 1916, pp. 1–2, folder 23, box 3, Church Family Papers; Robert R. Church Jr. to Roscoe Conkling Simmons, 26 January 1916, 2 February 1916, and 16 March 1916, folder R. R. Church, 1915–19, box 2, Simmons Papers. Roberta and Annette Church later commented that by 1917 the league had become a statewide organization called the Lincoln League of Tennessee, but it is unclear exactly when and how the Lincoln League mobilized African Americans elsewhere in Tennessee. See Church and Church, *Robert R. Churches,* 102.

99. "The Lincoln League: What It Is," [November 1916?], and "Directors, Lincoln Republican League," [24 January 1916], folder 25, box 3, Church Family Papers; Robert R. Church Jr. to Roscoe Conkling Simmons, 26 January 1916, folder R. R. Church, 1915–19, box 2, Simmons Papers.

100. "R. R. Church, Jr., Heads Big Movement," *Beacon Light,* 5 February 1916, 1, folder R. R. Church, 1915–19, box 2, Simmons Papers.

101. Lymus Wallace was elected to the board of public works (which was part of the city legislature) in 1882 and served until 1890. In addition, he was appointed a member of the school board. Another league member was Fred Savage Jr. His late father, Fred Savage Sr., had been a school board member in the late nineteenth century. "Directors, Lincoln Republican League"; Hamilton, *Bright Side,* 283; Church and Walter, *Nineteenth Century Memphis Families,* 77–78, 100–101.

102. Flyer for 1 February 1916 meeting, folder R. R. Church, 1915–19, box 2, Simmons Papers.

103. Church, "Remarks at First Meeting [of the] Lincoln League"; "Report on Feb. 1, 1916, Meeting of the Lincoln League"; Church and Church interview, 5 January 1973, interview no. 2, p. 10; Robert R. Church Jr. to Roscoe Conkling Simmons, 2 February 1916, folder R. R. Church, 1915–

19, box 2, Simmons Papers; "R. R. Church, Jr., Heads Big Movement," *Beacon Light*, 1. The Griggs quote is from "Robert R. Church, Jr.," *Washington Bee*, 12 February 1916, 2.

104. "R. R. Church, Jr., Heads Big Movement," *Beacon Light*. See also "The Lincoln League: What It Is," 3.

105. "The Lincoln League: What It Is," 1.

106. "Constitution of the Lincoln Republican Club of Tennessee," January 1916, folder 25, box 3, Church Family Papers; DeCosta-Willis, *Notable Black Memphians*, 378.

107. Church to Simmons, 26 November 1915, folder R. R. Church, 1915–19, box 2, Simmons Papers. On intraracial divisions, see also "R. R. Church, Jr., Heads Big Movement," *Beacon Light*.

108. "R. R. Church, Jr., Heads Big Movement," *Beacon Light*.

109. "The Lincoln League: What It Is," 1. See also Brown, *Upbuilding Black Durham*; and Evelyn Brooks Higginbotham, *Righteous Discontent: The Women's Movement in the Black Baptist Church, 1880–1920* (Cambridge, MA: Harvard University Press, 1993).

110. "The Lincoln League: What It Is," 2.

111. The Lincoln League ticket was composed of the following candidates: Wayman Wilkerson ran for US Congress; H. H. Bomar and Bert Roddy ran for state senator; T. H. Hayes Sr. ran for floterial senator; G. W. Atkins, Nat Bowles, Arthur E. Clouston, N. F. Clowers, Ed Lewis, J. T. Settle Jr., O. W. Williams, and J. B. Willis ran for state representative. Church, "Remarks at First Meeting [of the] Lincoln League"; Kelly, "Robert R. Church," 15–19, 26–28; Church, "Material for the Carnegie Corporation," 2; Church to Simmons, 26 August 1916, folder R. R. Church, 1915–19, box 2, Simmons Papers; Church and Walter, *Nineteenth Century Memphis Families*, 118; Tucker, *Lieutenant Lee*, 70.

112. Simmons had been friends with Robert R. Church Sr. Roscoe Conkling Simmons to Robert R. Church Sr., 30 March 1911, folder 10, box 1, Church Family Papers; Simmons, "Robert R. Church"; Church and Church interview, 10 July 1973, interview no. 3, p. 7; Tucker, *Lieutenant Lee*, 70–71. The national Republican Party may have sent Simmons to Tennessee to speak on behalf of the Lincoln League. See Church to Simmons, 3 October 1916, folder R. R. Church, 1915–19, box 2, Simmons Papers.

113. Kelly, "Robert R. Church," 29.

114. Ibid., 22–25, 28; Church to Simmons, 3 October 1916, folder R. R. Church, 1915–19, box 2, Simmons Papers; Adkins, "Beale Street," 54; Church to Roosevelt, 8 August 1916, and 28 August 1916, folder 14, box 2, telegram, Church to Roosevelt, 7 November 1916, folder 15, box 2, and Church to Roosevelt, 7 July 1917, and Roosevelt to Church, 12 July 1917, folder 26, box 3, Church Family Papers.

115. Church, "Remarks at First Meeting [of the] Lincoln League," 3.

116. Church to Simmons, 9 September 1916, folder R. R. Church, 1915–19, box 2, Simmons Papers. The quotes are from "Platform of the Lincoln Republican League of Tennessee."

117. "Platform of the Lincoln Republican League of Tennessee."

118. Terrell to Church, 29 January 1910, folder 35, box 2, Church Family Papers. Terrell makes a similar argument in a 1912 article that she wrote for the *Crisis* titled "The Justice of Woman Suffrage." It is reprinted in Yellin and Sherman, *Perfect 36*, 61–62.

119. Church and Church, *Robert R. Churches*, 97.

120. Kelly, "Robert R. Church," 26–27.

121. Ibid.

122. Ibid., 26, 30, 33; Melton, "Blacks in Memphis," 40–41; "The Lincoln League: What It Is," 4; Church, "Material for the Carnegie Corporation," 2.

123. Church and Church interview, 5 January 1973, interview no. 2, pp. 10–13.

124. "Robert R. Church and the Lincoln League," *Champion Magazine*, January 1917, 238, folder 25, box 3, Church Family Papers. *Champion Magazine* was a black publication based in Chicago.

125. Church and Walter, *Nineteenth Century Memphis Families*, 118.

126. Kelly, "Robert R. Church," 31–32.

127. Church, "Material for the Carnegie Corporation," 2.

128. Robert R. Church Jr., "Material Requested by Mr. Clarence Kelly for Thesis," [1952?], p. 9, folder 45, box 6, Church Family Papers.

2. "The Fight . . . to Make America Safe for Americans"

1. Steven A. Reich, "The Great War, Black Workers, and the Rise and Fall of the NAACP in the South," in *The Black Worker: A Reader*, ed. Eric Arnesen (Urbana: University of Illinois Press, 2007), 147.

2. Chad L. Williams, *Torchbearers of Democracy: African American Soldiers in the World War I Era* (Chapel Hill: University of North Carolina Press, 2010); Adriane D. Lentz-Smith, *Freedom Struggles: African Americans and World War I* (Cambridge, MA: Harvard University Press, 2009); Steven A. Reich, "Soldiers of Democracy: Black Texans and the Fight for Citizenship, 1917–1921," *Journal of American History* 82, no. 4 (March 1996): 1478–1504, and "The Great War."

3. Melton, "Blacks in Memphis," 50–51.

4. My account of the Ell Persons lynching is drawn from "Memphis: May 22, A.D., 1917," supplement to the *Crisis* 14, no. 3 (July 1917), folder 28, box 3, and James Weldon Johnson, "The Burning of Ell Person at Memphis: A Report Made for the National Association for the Advancement of

Colored People," 1917, folder 28, box 3, Church Family Papers; and Patricia Sullivan, *Lift Every Voice: The NAACP and the Making of the Civil Rights Movement* (New York: New Press, 2009), 65–66. For more information on NAACP investigations into racial violence, see Julie Buckner Armstrong, *Mary Turner and the Memory of Lynching* (Athens: University of Georgia Press, 2011). On African American efforts against lynching during this time, including those of the NAACP, see Sherman, *Republican Party;* Berg, *Ticket to Freedom;* Brundage, *Lynching in the New South;* Sullivan, *Lift Every Voice.*

5. Armstrong, *Mary Turner and the Memory of Lynching,* 70–71; Handy, *Father of the Blues,* 159; Church and Church, *Robert R. Churches,* 101–2; Jeffrey B. Ferguson, *The Harlem Renaissance: A Brief History with Documents* (Boston: Bedford/St. Martin's, 2008), 4.

6. Sullivan, *Lift Every Voice,* 66; Melton, "Blacks in Memphis," 46–51; Church and Church interview, 5 January 1973, interview no. 2, pp. 14–15; "Application for Charter of the Memphis Branch of the National Association for the Advancement of Colored People," 11 June 1917, folder 28, box 3, Church Family Papers; DeCosta-Willis, *Notable Black Memphians,* 270; Brewster interview, p. 20; Church and Walter, *Nineteenth Century Memphis Families,* 120–21; William N. Jones, "Day by Day: The R. R. Church Dynasty," *AA,* 16 April 1938, 4; Church and Church, *Robert R. Churches,* 67–70; Tucker, *Lieutenant Lee,* 41; Church to Roosevelt, 7 July 1917, and Roosevelt to Church, 12 July 1917, folder 26, box 3, and Church to *New York World,* 15 September 1921, folder 50, box 3, Church Family Papers.

7. Reich, "The Great War," 147, 158; Johnson to Church, 29 October 1918, folder 28, box 3, and Robert R. Church Jr., "Material for the Carnegie Corporation of New York—Requested by Dr. Bunche," [1938?], p. 2, folder 45, box 6, Church Family Papers; Church and Church interview, 5 January 1973, interview no. 2, pp. 13–15; "Board Notes," *Crisis,* January 1919, 122, folder 31, box 3, Church Family Papers; "Our New National Board Member," *Branch Bulletin* 3, no. 1 (January 1919): 12, folder 32, box 3, Church Family Papers.

8. "Board Notes," *Crisis;* "Our New National Board Member," *Branch Bulletin* (quote).

9. Church and Church, *Robert R. Churches,* 102.

10. Brewster interview, pp. 10–12, 4.

11. Schuyler, *Weight of Their Votes;* David Godshalk, *Veiled Visions: The 1906 Atlanta Race Riot and the Reshaping of American Race Relations* (Chapel Hill: University of North Carolina Press, 2005), 248–51; Hornsby, *Black Power in Dixie,* vi, 51.

12. Church to Simmons, 3 August 1918, folder R. R. Church, 1915–19, box 2, Simmons Papers; Kelly, "Robert R. Church," 37.

13. "Bob Church Takes His Seat," *CD,* 18 September 1918, 3; "Our New National Board Member," *Branch Bulletin;* Kelly, "Robert R. Church," 37.

14. "Our New National Board Member," *Branch Bulletin;* Anita Shafer Goodstein, "A Rare Alliance: African American and White Women in the Tennessee Elections of 1919 and 1920," *Journal of Southern History* 64, no. 2 (May 1998): 219–46; Kelly, "Robert R. Church," 38; Church and Church, *Robert R. Churches,* 35.

15. Gilmore, *Gender and Jim Crow;* Schuyler, *Weight of Their Votes;* Lau, *Democracy Rising,* 31–33.

16. "Lincoln League Sample Ballot," 1919, folder 24, box 3, Church Family Papers; Lee, *Beale Street,* 241; Bunche, *Political Status,* 495; Walk, *History of African-Americans,* 27–28.

17. Robert R. Church Jr., "Material Requested by Mr. Clarence Kelly for Thesis," [1952?], p. 3, folder 45, box 6, Church Family Papers.

18. Anna Wright Church to Robert R. Church Jr., 5 May 1920, folder 14, box 2, and telegram, Wayman Wilkerson to Church, 4 June 1920, telegram, R. F. Lewis to Church, 5 June 1920, telegram, Matthew Thornton to Church, 4 June 1920, telegram, J. D. M. and J. H. Eiland to Church, 4 June 1920, and telegram, Jacob D. Woods Jr. to Church, 7 June 1920, box 4, folder 14, Church Family Papers.

19. See, e.g., "Bob Church Takes His Seat," *CD.*

20. Tucker, *Lieutenant Lee,* 74. See also John W. Farley, *Statistics and Politics* (Memphis: Memphis Linotype Printing Co., 1920).

21. Lee, *Beale Street,* 251; Kelly, "Robert R. Church," 35; Church and Church interview, 10 July 1973, interview no. 3, p. 18; Church and Walter, *Nineteenth Century Memphis Families,* 120–21.

22. Melton, "Blacks in Memphis," 96; Church to George W. Lee, 12 May 1921 (quote), folder 13, box 9, George W. Lee Papers, MSC.

23. Sherman, *Republican Party,* 124, 132–33, 143–44.

24. J. Will Taylor to Robert R. Church Jr., 31 October 1918, folder 10, box 4, Church Family Papers. See also J. Will Taylor to Robert R. Church Jr., 7 November 1918, folder 10, box 4, Church Family Papers.

25. Church, "Material for the Carnegie Corporation," 2.

26. J. E. Hansell, *Hill-Billy Bill: A Biography of Hon. J. Will Taylor of Tennessee* (LaFollette, TN: LaFollette, 1932), 118–20, folder 12, box 4, Church Family Papers; David D. Lee, *Tennessee in Turmoil: Politics in the Volunteer State, 1920–1932* (Memphis: Memphis State University Press, 1979), 15, 18; Eugene Travis, "Bob Church—Tennessee's 'Man of Destiny,'" *PC,* national ed., 23 April 1932, sec. 2, p. 1; "Tennessee G.O.P. Are Kluxers," *CD,* 6 September 1924, 1; "Bob Church Winning Fight for Recognition in Dixie," *CD,* 4 October 1924, A3; Tucker, *Lieutenant Lee,* 80–81, 84. See also the

communications between Church and Taylor in folders 10 and 11, box 4, Church Family Papers.

27. Church to Taylor, 1 November 1928, folder 10, box 4, Church Family Papers.

28. G. Michael McCarthy, "Smith vs. Hoover—the Politics of Race in West Tennessee," *Phylon* 39, no. 2 (2nd Quarter 1978): 154–68.

29. "The South Republican? Never!" *CA*, n.d., folder 18, box 4, Church Family Papers.

30. Lillian Smith, "Addressed to White Liberals," 18 September 1944, in *Gonna Sit at the Welcome Table* (2nd ed.), ed. Julian Bond and Andrew Lewis (New York: American Heritage, 1995), 161–63; John F. Marzsalek, *A Black Congressman in the Age of Jim Crow: South Carolina's George Washington Murray* (Gainesville: University Press of Florida, 2006), xv.

31. Wayne Dowdy, "E. H. Crump and the Mayors of Memphis," *WTH-SP* 53 (1999): 78–99, 83–85; Edwin Frank, finding aid to R. E. Johnson Papers, p. 2, SC; Dowdy, *Mr. Crump,* 32–33; Schuyler, *Weight of Their Votes,* 104, 108; Tucker, *Lieutenant Lee,* 19; Church and Church interview, 10 July 1973, interview no. 1, p. 16; Adkins, "Beale Street," 24–25. See also "List of Unions, and Their Officers," mfm 002067-9, "Barbers," mfm 002071-3, and other documents in folder Voters List 1920, box 47, ser. 2, and "President Parent-Teachers Ass'n of Colored Schools," mfm 001332, "List of All Negro Preachers," mfm 001347, "Lady Workers [by Ward]," mfm 001358, and other documents in folder Election 1923, box 47, ser. 2, Crump Papers.

32. Church and Church, *Robert R. Churches,* 102; Church, Cohen, and Simmons, form letter, n.d., folder 23, box 3, Church Family Papers.

33. "Lincoln League Stirs South," *CD*, 28 June 1919, 1.

34. Ibid.; Church and Church, *Robert R. Churches,* 103–4; Williams, *Torchbearers of Democracy,* esp. 214.

35. "Lincoln League Postpones Meeting," *CD*, 30 August 1919, 19.

36. Church and Church, *Robert R. Churches,* 106–7; Kelly, "Robert R. Church," 40; "Americanism Is Endorsed by Lincoln League," *CD*, 21 February 1920, 1; "Hays at the Lincoln League," *AA*, 6 February 1920, 4.

37. "The Weaning Process," *AA*, 30 January 1920, 2.

38. Church and Church, *Robert R. Churches,* 106–7.

39. "Sidelights on the Lincoln League," *CD*, 28 February 1920, 2. See also Church and Church, *Robert R. Churches,* 109.

40. "Lincoln League Holds Monster Meeting," *CD*, 14 February 1920, 1; "Americanism Is Endorsed by Lincoln League," *CD;* "The Lincoln League Convention," *CD*, 28 February 1920, 20; "Sidelights on the Lincoln League," *CD;* Church and Church, *Robert R. Churches,* 108.

41. These three speakers were John R. Lynch, J. C. Napier, former regis-

trar of the US Treasury, and Ralph W. Tyler, former auditor of the US Navy. "Delegates Attending Lincoln Meeting: South Park M.E. Church, Chicago Feb. 11," *CD*, 14 February 1920, 1.

42. Kelly, "Robert R. Church," 41–42; "Wood Stampedes Lincoln League," *AA*, 20 February 1920, 1; "Wood Believes in the 'All Men Up' Policy," *AA*, 5 March 1920, 4; "Lowden Speech Fell Flat on Race Question," *AA*, 10 September 1927, 3.

43. "Sidelights on the Lincoln League," *CD;* Church and Church, *Robert R. Churches,* 107–8; "Lincoln League Holds Monster Meeting," *CD;* "Hays Denounces Lynching," *Washington Post,* 12 February 1920, 2.

44. "Hays at the Lincoln League," *AA*.

45. "Wood Stampedes Lincoln League," *AA*. See also "Lowden Speech Fell Flat on Race Question," *AA*.

46. "Wood Stampedes Lincoln League," *AA;* Church and Church, *Robert R. Churches,* 109; "Americanism Is Endorsed by Lincoln League," *CD*.

47. "Americanism Is Endorsed by Lincoln League," *CD;* "Hays at the Lincoln League," *AA*.

48. "Lincoln League Opens Chicago Headquarters," *CD*, 22 May 1920, 12.

49. Travis, "Bob Church"; Church and Church, *Robert R. Churches,* 110, 199, 201–3; Robert R. Church Jr., "The American Republic," *Tomorrow: A Magazine of Racial Problems,* April 1920, 80–82, reprinted in Church, "Material Requested by Mr. Clarence Kelly," 12, 17.

50. "Lincoln League Worth While," *CD*, 19 June 1920, 9.

51. "G.O.P.—Living or Dying," *CD*, 5 June 1920, 11.

52. George W. Lee, "Church Names Postmaster," *MT*, 25 June 1927, 1; Church, "Material Requested by Mr. Clarence Kelly," 5; Tucker, *Lieutenant Lee,* 75 (quote).

53. Lee, *Beale Street,* 259.

54. A. B. Fields, "Fight for Seats at G.O.P. Meet," *CD*, 5 June 1920, 1; "Lincoln League Worth While," *CD*.

55. Sherman, *Republican Party,* 145–47; Robert R. Moton to George W. Lee, 17 September 1923, folder 13, box 9, Lee Papers.

56. Kelly, "Robert R. Church," 59–61; Schuyler, *Weight of Their Votes,* 72, 97, 100, 218; Melton, "Blacks in Memphis," 95; Charles T. Magill, "Nation's Capital Is Ready for Harding," *CD*, 5 March 1921, 1.

57. Kelly, "Robert R. Church," 43–45.

58. James C. Dickerson, "Tennessee State News," *CD*, 2 May 1936, 23.

59. Lee, *Beale Street,* 251; Church and Church interview, 5 January 1973, interview no. 2, p. 18.

60. Sherman, *Republican Party,* 147–51.

61. Ibid., 149–73.

62. For more information on Garvey, see Lawrence W. Levine, "Marcus Garvey and the Politics of Revitalization," in Bond and Lewis, eds., *Gonna Sit at the Welcome Table*, 83–103; Tony Martin, *Race First: The Ideological and Organizational Struggles of Marcus Garvey and the Universal Negro Improvement Association* (Westport, CT: Greenwood, 1976); US House Committee on the Judiciary, *Mail Fraud Charges against Marcus Garvey*, 100th Cong., 1st sess., 28 July 1987; Judith Stein, *The World of Marcus Garvey: Race and Class in Modern Society* (Baton Rouge: Louisiana State University Press, 1986); Deborah Gray White, *Too Heavy a Load: Black Women in Defense of Themselves, 1894–1994* (New York: Norton, 1999), 110–41; Steven Hahn, *The Political Worlds of Slavery and Freedom* (Cambridge, MA: Harvard University Press, 2009), 115–62; Mary G. Rolinson, *Grassroots Garveyism: The Universal Negro Improvement Association in the Rural South, 1920–1927* (Chapel Hill: University of North Carolina Press, 2007); and Claudrena N. Harold, *The Rise and Fall of the Garvey Movement in the Urban South, 1918–1942* (New York: Routledge, 2007).

63. The founding and activities of the Memphis chapter remain obscure. Rolinson, *Grassroots Garveyism*, 3–4, 103, 200.

64. Sherman, *Republican Party*, 200–223.

65. Ibid., 195–96, 199, 201; "Chicago Prepares for Lincoln League," *CD*, 2 February 1924, 4.

66. The point about Church financing his own political efforts shows up commonly in primary and secondary sources. See, e.g., Kelly, "Robert R. Church," 41–42; Church and Church interview, 5 January 1973, interview no. 2, pp. 16–17, 19; Lee, *Beale Street*, 254–55; "National Affairs: G.O.P., South," *Time*, 18 February 1929, 10; Travis, "Bob Church"; and Church and Walter, *Nineteenth Century Memphis Families*, 21.

67. "Tennessee G.O.P. Are Kluxers," *CD*.

68. Kelly, "Robert R. Church," 63, 68; C. J. Lilley, "Bob Church, Colored Politician, at Home in Memphis, as in Washington," newspaper clipping, 17 May 1927, folder 14, box 5, Church Family Papers; "Bob Church Is Visitor at White House," *CD*, 3 October 1925, 1; Church and Church, *Robert R. Churches*, 77, 209–10; Church to J. Will Taylor, 4 July 1926, folder 11, box 4, Church Family Papers; Louis R. Lautier, "Coolidge Names Cobb for Judge," *PC*, 20 February 1926, 1; Lee, *Tennessee in Turmoil*; Arthur M. Evans, "South Seen as Ripe for an Effective Republican Party," *Washington Post*, 16 September 1927, 4.

69. Lee, *Beale Street*, 250; Travis, "Bob Church"; Annette E. Church to Miller, 4 September 1961, folder 21, box 12, Church Family Papers; Kelly, "Robert R. Church," 38, 71; Melton, "Blacks in Memphis," 94.

70. Kelly, "Robert R. Church," 44, 61–67; Lee, *Beale Street*, 267–68; Roberta Church, "J. Will Taylor—Tennessee," folder 10, box 4, Church Family

Papers; Church and Church, *Robert R. Churches,* 21, 114, 173, 216; Hays to Harding, 27 April 1921, folder 25, box 3, Church Family Papers; Tucker, *Lieutenant Lee,* 75–77; Lee, *Beale Street,* 266; W.O.W., "Down the Big Road," *Cleveland Call and Post,* 24 March 1934, 4; Matthew Thornton, "As I Saw Bob Church," *ADW,* 6 May 1952, 4. See also the communications between Church and Taylor in folders 10 and 11, box 4, Church Family Papers.

71. According to Church, the Quinn incident was the only case on record of the revocation of a postmaster appointment before the appointee reached his destination. Church, "Material Requested by Mr. Clarence Kelly," 1; Kelly, "Robert R. Church," 44, 64–65; Church and Church, *Robert R. Churches,* 74, 175; Lee, *Beale Street,* 260–61; "Bob Church Shows His Political Power," *PC,* 2 July 1927, 9; Lee, "Church Names Postmaster." For a history of the relationship between African Americans and the US Postal Service, see Philip F. Rubio, *There's Always Work at the Post Office: African American Postal Workers and the Fight for Jobs, Justice, and Equality* (Chapel Hill: University of North Carolina Press, 2010).

72. Adkins, "Beale Street," 75–76; Church and Church, *Robert R. Churches,* 211; Church, "Material Requested by Mr. Clarence Kelly," 2; Kelly, "Robert R. Church," 76–77; Lee, *Beale Street,* 265–66; Evans, "South Seen as Ripe."

73. Lee, *Beale Street,* 250.

74. "R. R. Church, a Leader," *Memphis Times,* 26 March 1921, folder 19, box 4, Church Family Papers.

75. Church continued to reside in his childhood home in his adulthood. L. Raymond Lymon, interview by Charles W. Crawford, Memphis, 6 July 1983, transcript, pp. 1–2 (quote), 16 (quote), 3–4, UMOH. Lymon also recalled: "We . . . actually loved the Republican Party. We felt it was our salvation." He pointed out that his and other black Memphians' ancestors had been born in slavery and that Lincoln had freed them. Ibid., 1–2. For remarks by Lonnie Briscoe that are similar to Lymon's, see chapter 3.

76. Nettie George Speedy, "Lincoln League in Session," *CD,* 16 February 1924, 1.

77. Ibid.; Morris Brown, press release, 15 February 1924, folder 25, box 3, Church Family Papers. (The Brown article is stapled to the Constitution and By Laws of the Lincoln League of America.)

78. "Chicago Prepares for Lincoln League," *CD,* 2 February 1924, 4; Speedy, "Lincoln League in Session"; untitled press release, 18 February 1924, pp. 2–3, folder 25, box 3, Church Family Papers. (The press release is stapled to the Constitution and By Laws of the Lincoln League of America.)

79. Roscoe Simmons, "The Week," *CD,* 16 February 1924, A1. For more on Lethia Fleming, see "Fleming, Lethia Cousins," *The Encyclopedia of Cleveland History,* http://ech.cwru.edu/ech-cgi/article.pl?id=FLC.

80. "Lincoln League in Stormy Session," *PC,* 23 February 1924, 9.

81. "Lincoln League Hears Simmons, Abbott, Church," *CD*, 8 September 1923, 2; Kaye, "Roscoe Conkling Simmons," 88, 94; "One Delegate Allowed for Each Dist.," *AA*, 14 December 1923, A1; "Chicago Prepares for Lincoln League," *CD*; "Nation Pays Tribute to Henry Lincoln Johnson," *CD*, 19 September 1925, 1; Adkins, "Beale Street," 53–54; Schuyler, *Weight of Their Votes*, 115–16; Ann Field Alexander, *Race Man: The Rise and Fall of the "Fighting Editor," John Mitchell, Jr.* (Charlottesville: University of Virginia Press, 2002); Bunche, *Political Status*, 547–48, 554.

82. The *Chicago Defender* had given the league extensive coverage in part because its editor, Robert Abbott, served on its executive committee. "Lincoln League Holds Its Inaugural Meeting," *CD*, 14 March 1925, A5; "Lincoln League Drafts Political Program," *CD*, 14 March 1925, 3; "Colored Citizens Plan Inaugural Week Program," *Washington Post*, 2 March 1925, 1; "Secret G.O.P. [Caucus] Has Failed to Name a Leader," *AA*, 31 December 1927, 3; "W. L. Cohen Dies; Was G.O.P. Chief," *NYAN*, 31 December 1930, 1.

83. Sherman, *Republican Party*, 224; "Political Attitude of Race Uncertain as Election Time Nears," *PC*, 28 July 1923, 4; "W. L. Cohen Dies," *NYAN*.

84. "The Two Conventions," *PC*, 23 February 1924, 16.

85. McMillen, *Dark Journey*, 69; Lisio, *Hoover, Blacks, and Lily-Whites*, 100–101; Weiss, *Farewell to the Party of Lincoln*, 78.

86. Moton to Lee, 17 September 1923, folder 13, box 9, Lee Papers; Wilkerson to Simmons, 21 August 1923, folder Lincoln League "W-Z," box 4, Simmons Papers.

87. Wilkerson to Simmons, 10 January 1924, folder Lincoln League "W-Z," box 4, Simmons Papers.

88. "Political Attitude of Race Uncertain," *PC*.

89. Simmons to Wilkerson, 30 January 1924, folder Lincoln League "W-Z," box 4, Simmons Papers.

90. William N. Jones, "Day by Day," *AA*, 15 February 1924, 9.

91. Lilley, "Bob Church, Colored Politician." For more discussion of these photographs, see Travis, "Bob Church."

92. Church, "Material for the Carnegie Corporation," 3.

93. Tucker, *Lieutenant Lee*, 76–77.

94. Melton, "Blacks in Memphis," 94–109; Tucker, *Lieutenant Lee*, 53–54, 79; Lilley, "Bob Church, Colored Politician"; Lee, *Beale Street*, 250; Church and Church interview, 10 July 1973, interview no. 3, p. 5; Travis, "Bob Church"; Brewster interview, p. 10.

95. George W. Lee, interview by Aaron Boom, Memphis, 17 April 1966, transcript, pp. 10–14, 16–17, 20, UMOH; Tucker, *Lieutenant Lee*, 31–33; McMillen, *Dark Journey*, 30; Williams, *Torchbearers of Democracy*, 223–25,

232–40; DeCosta-Willis, *Notable Black Memphians,* 213; George W. Lee, interview by Aaron Boom, Memphis, 24 May 1966, transcript, pp. 4–7, UMOH.

96. Lee interview, 17 April 1966, p. 19.

97. Ibid.; Tucker, *Lieutenant Lee,* 40.

98. Lee interview, 17 April 1966, p. 19.

99. Tucker, *Lieutenant Lee,* 53; George Schuyler, "Aframerica Today: Memphis—Cotton Metropolis," *PC,* national ed., 27 February 1926, 3; Church and Church interview, 10 July 1973, interview no. 3, p. 21.

100. Lee interview, 17 April 1966, pp. 24–25.

101. Harry S. New to George W. Lee, 3 November 1920, William M. Butler to George W. Lee, 3 November 1924, and William C. Matthews to George W. Lee, 7 November 1924, folder 13, box 9, Lee Papers; Tucker, *Lieutenant Lee,* 79–83; George W. Lee to Roscoe Conkling Simmons, 22 August 1923, folder Lincoln League "W-Z," box 4, Simmons Papers; "Political Leaders Who Are Working for a Republican Victory," *CD,* 1 November 1924, A2.

102. Tucker, *Lieutenant Lee,* 79–80; Adkins, "Beale Street," 39; Lee to Simmons, 22 August 1923, folder Lincoln League "W-Z," box 4, Simmons Papers; Melton, "Blacks in Memphis," 96–99. For a profile of the Memphis Klan during these years, see Kenneth Jackson, *The Ku Klux Klan in the City, 1915–1930* (New York: Oxford University Press, 1967). For a broader look at the Klan, see Kathleen M. Blee, *Women of the Klan: Racism and Gender in the 1920s* (Berkeley and Los Angeles: University of California Press, 1991).

103. "News of Bygone Days: 50 Years Ago, October 19, 1923," *CA,* 19 October 1973, vertical file 1923 Election, MSC; Adkins, "Beale Street," 39; Melton, "Blacks in Memphis," 96, 99; Schuyler, "Aframerica Today."

104. Kelly, "Robert R. Church," 99; Lee, *Beale Street,* 256, 263–64.

105. Jones, "Day by Day," *AA,* 1938.

106. Lee, *Beale Street,* 251–52, 281–82.

107. Lee, "Church Names Postmaster."

108. Brewster interview, p. 9.

109. Lee, *Beale Street,* 251; Brewster interview, pp. 8–10.

110. Williams interview, 13–14. For more discussion of these distinctions based on color of skin in the black community in Memphis, see Marsha Hunt, *Repossessing Ernestine: A Granddaughter Uncovers the Secret History of Her American Family* (New York: HarperCollins, 1996).

111. I have found no evidence that Church engaged in any romantic relationships after his wife's death. "All Memphis in Grief," *CD,* 8 July 1922, 2; "Mrs. Church Dies in Washington, Capital Mourns," *CD,* 8 July 1922, 2; Church and Church interview, 5 January 1973, interview no. 2, p. 8; Kelly, "Robert R. Church," 10–11; Travis, "Bob Church."

112. Melton, "Blacks in Memphis," 74–75; Tucker, *Lieutenant Lee*, 120; Reich, "The Great War," 167–70; Stein, *World of Marcus Garvey*, 162; Mrs. H. F. Wilkerson to Mr. Robert W. Bagwell, 12 April 1924, and 13 December 1925, folder Memphis, Tenn. 1924–1930, box G199, Group 1, NAACP Papers, Manuscript Division, Library of Congress, Washington, DC; Schuyler, "Aframerica Today."

113. Lee, *Beale Street*, 211; Yellin and Sherman, *Perfect 36*, 72.

114. Gunnar Myrdal, *An American Dilemma: The Negro Problem and Modern Democracy*, 2 vols. (New York: Harper & Bros., 1944), 2:842–50; Jacquelyn D. Hall, *Revolt against Chivalry: Jessie Daniel Ames and the Campaign against Lynching*, rev. ed. (New York: Columbia University Press, 1993), 59, 62–65, 102; Sitkoff, *New Deal for Blacks*, 18–19; Glenda Gilmore, *Defying Dixie: The Radical Roots of Civil Rights, 1919–1950* (New York: Norton, 2008).

115. Memphis Inter Racial League, *The Inter Racial Blue Book* (Memphis: Inter Racial League, 1926), 1–4, 9; Melton, "Blacks in Memphis," 44, 65, 67, 68; Mary S. Hoffschwelle, *The Rosenwald Schools of the American South* (Gainesville: University Press of Florida, 2006), 222, 226–30; DeCosta-Willis, *Notable Black Memphians*, 299.

116. Memphis Inter Racial League, *Inter Racial Blue Book*, 3; Tucker, *Lieutenant Lee*, 58–59, and *Black Pastors and Leaders*, 64; "Directors, Lincoln Republican League," [24 January 1916], folder 25, box 3, Church Family Papers; Finnie D. Coleman, *Sutton E. Griggs and the Struggle against White Supremacy* (Knoxville: University of Tennessee Press, 2007), 26; Carroll Van West and Jen Stoecker, "Thomas Oscar Fuller," 1 January 2010, *Tennessee Encyclopedia of History and Culture*, http://www.tennesseeencyclopedia. net/entry.php?rec=528; Randolph Meade Walker, "The Role of the Black Clergy in Memphis during the Crump Era," *WTHSP* 33 (1979): 42.

117. Tucker, *Black Pastors and Leaders*, 55–56, 65–66; LeRae Umfleet, "The Wilmington Race Riot—1898," *Ncpedia*, 2010, http://www.ncpedia .org/history/cw-1900/wilmington-race-riot; Van West and Stoecker, "Thomas Oscar Fuller."

118. Fuller to Church, 31 January 1907, folder 4, box 1, Church Family Papers; Van West and Stoecker, "Thomas Oscar Fuller"; Walker, "Role of Black Clergy," 36; Melton, "Blacks in Memphis," 18–20; T. O. Fuller, *The Story of Church Life among Negroes in Memphis* (Memphis: T. O. Fuller, 1938), 39; August Meier, *Negro Thought in America, 1880–1915: Racial Ideologies in the Age of Booker T. Washington* (Ann Arbor: University of Michigan Press, 1963); Laurie B. Green, *Battling the Plantation Mentality: Memphis and the Black Freedom Struggle* (Chapel Hill: University of North Carolina Press, 2007), 34; Tucker, *Lieutenant Lee*, 58, and *Black Pastors and Leaders*, 55–56, 65–66; Umfleet, "The Wilmington Race Riot—1898."

119. Caplinger, "Conflict and Community," 59; Van West and Stoecker, "Thomas Oscar Fuller."

120. Walker, "Role of Black Clergy," 44.

121. Green, *Battling the Plantation Mentality,* 34–35; Fuller to Crump, 23 April 1942, vertical file T. O. Fuller, MSC. For examples of Fuller's mayoral correspondence, see Fuller to Crump, 13 November 1912, mfm 000528, and Fuller to Crump, 1 May 1912, mfm 000529, folder "F" City Business 1912, box 11, ser. 1, Crump Papers.

122. Sutton E. Griggs, *The Hindered Hand* (Nashville: Orion, 1905).

123. For biographical information on Griggs, see Coleman, *Sutton E. Griggs;* Tucker, *Lieutenant Lee,* 60–63, and *Black Pastors and Leaders,* 71–86; Green, *Battling the Plantation Mentality,* 33–36; Wilson Jeremiah Moses, *The Golden Age of Black Nationalism, 1850–1925* (Hamden, CT: Archon, 1978); Walker, "Role of Black Clergy," 42–44; James W. Byrd and David M. Tucker, "Sutton Elbert Griggs," *Handbook of Texas Online,* Texas State Historical Association, 1997–2002, http://www.tshaonline.org/handbook/online/articles/fgr85; and DeCosta-Willis, *Notable Black Memphians,* 145–47.

124. Tucker, *Black Pastors and Leaders,* 80–81; Coleman, *Sutton E. Griggs,* x, 74, 112, 135–36.

125. "Date of Lyric Meeting," n.d., folder 1923 Election, box 45, ser. 2, Crump Papers; Melton, "Blacks in Memphis," 43–44, 66–67, 71–73; Sherman, *Republican Party,* 130; Memphis Inter Racial League, *Inter Racial Blue Book,* 17; Tucker, *Black Pastors and Leaders,* 82–85; Coleman, *Sutton E. Griggs,* 110; Walker, "Role of Black Clergy," 43. See also Sutton E. Griggs, *Guide to Racial Greatness; or, The Science of Collective Efficiency* (Memphis: National Public Welfare League, 1923).

126. Tucker, *Lieutenant Lee,* 59. See also Coleman, *Sutton E. Griggs,* 26–27.

127. Memphis Inter Racial League, *Inter Racial Blue Book,* 39.

128. Tucker, *Lieutenant Lee,* 59–64, and *Black Pastors and Leaders,* 64; Melton, "Blacks in Memphis," 64, 73–74; DeCosta-Willis, *Notable Black Memphians,* 134.

129. "Memphis Negroes Win Great Victory!" *Houston Informer,* 19 November 1927, folder 10, box 5, and Randolph to Church, 6 August 1928, folder 4, box 9, Church Family Papers.

130. Lee to T. O. Fuller, 7 June 1923, folder 32, box 4, Church Family Papers.

131. Alain Locke, ed., *The New Negro* (1925; reprint, with a preface by Robert Hayden, New York: Atheneum, 1968).

132. Melton, "Blacks in Memphis," 64–73.

133. Memphis Inter Racial League, *Inter Racial Blue Book,* 1–2; George W. Lee, interview by unidentified individual, n.p., n.d., transcript, pp. 1–2,

Cook Collection, MSC; Lee, *Beale Street*, 245; Green, *Battling the Plantation Mentality*, 36.

134. Melton, "Blacks in Memphis," 101; Adkins, "Beale Street," 42–45; Lee, *Beale Street*, 245–46; Schuyler, "Aframerica Today"; "Memphis Mayor Declines to Heed Demands," *CD*, 24 September 1927, 4.

135. Lee, *Beale Street*, 245–46; Tucker, *Lieutenant Lee*, 93; "Startling Facts about Mr. High-Tax Pain's Extravagant Government," folder 11, box 2, Watkins Overton Papers, SC; "Sink or Swim: The Ballot Box in Memphis, the People's Only Hope," *MT*, 13 August 1927, 1, folder 17, box 5, Church Family Papers.

136. "Sink or Swim," *MT*.

137. Lee, *Tennessee in Turmoil;* Miller, *Mr. Crump*, 130–31; "News of Bygone Days: 50 Years Ago, Jan. 14, 1927," *CA*, 14 January 1977, vertical file 1926 Election, MSC; Melton, "Blacks in Memphis," 100; Loyal Tennesseans League, *Edward H. Crump*, 15–16.

138. Tucker, *Lieutenant Lee*, 99–100; Adkins, "Beale Street," 36; Lee interview, n.d., pp. 1–2; "Mayor's Statement Dealing with Negro Political Issue," *MT*, 13 August 1927, 1, folder 17, box 5, Church Family Papers.

139. See Brown to Crump, 1 September 1927, mfm 001043, and Crump to Brown, 2 September 1927, mfm 001044, folder General Correspondence "B" 1927, box 106, ser. 4, Crump Papers.

140. "Overton-Davis Platform—Progressive for a Big City," 1927, newspaper clipping, folder 11, box 2, Overton Papers, SC; Tucker, *Lieutenant Lee*, 95; Adkins, "Beale Street," 42–43.

141. Tucker, *Lieutenant Lee*, 95–96.

142. "Bob Church on Warpath," *PC*, 10 October 1927, excerpts in Adkins, "Beale Street," 21.

143. Schuyler, "Aframerica Today."

144. Lee, *Beale Street*, 246–48; Tucker, *Lieutenant Lee*, 94–95.

145. "8,000 Voters Defeat Mayor in Memphis," *AA*, 19 November 1927, 1.

146. "Negrophobist Ousted from Mayor's Office at Memphis Election," *The Light*, 19 November 1927, 19; Church and Church interview, 10 July 1973, interview no. 3, pp. 18–19; "Bomb Thrown in Memphis School," *NYAN*, 16 November 1927, 2; "Bob Church Names Overton as Mayor of Memphis, Tenn.," *CD*, 19 November 1927, 1; "8,000 Voters Defeat Mayor in Memphis," *AA*.

147. "Mayor's Statement Dealing with Negro Political Issue," *MT*.

148. "Memphis Mayor Declines to Heed Demands," *CD*.

149. Ibid.; Adkins, "Beale Street," 41–42; "Negrophobist Ousted," *The Light;* Roberta Church, "Summary by Roberta Church Re: Robert R. Church Jr. and Edward Hull Crump," 14 July 1992, finding aid folder of

Church Family Papers, Church Family Papers; Annette E. Church and Roberta Church, "Robert R. Church, Sr., Memphis' First Black Capitalist," Memphis Sesquicentennial Commission, 1969, folder 68, box 1, Church Family Papers

150. Tucker, *Lieutenant Lee*, 94.
151. Green, *Battling the Plantation Mentality*, 36.
152. "8,000 Voters Defeat Mayor in Memphis," *AA*.
153. Lee, *Beale Street*, 246.
154. Melton, "Blacks in Memphis," 102–3; Lee, *Beale Street*, 247.
155. "Sink or Swim," *MT*.
156. "Bomb Thrown in Memphis School," *NYAN*.
157. Melton, "Blacks in Memphis," 102–3.
158. "Memphis and Harlem," *NYAN*, 23 November 1927, 20.
159. "Recognizing Our Political Power," *PC*, 26 November 1927, 20.
160. "Memphis Negroes Win Great Victory!" *Houston Informer*.
161. Adkins, "Beale Street," 44; Melton, "Blacks in Memphis," 84–89.

3. "Come . . . and See What a Negro Democrat Looks Like"

1. Adkins, "Beale Street," 26, 89; Melton, "Blacks in Memphis," 103–4; Roberta Church, "Summary by Roberta Church Re: Robert R. Church Jr. and Edward Hull Crump," 14 July 1992, finding aid folder of Church Family Papers, Church Family Papers; Lewinson, *Race, Class, and Party*, 138–41; Bunche, *Political Status*, 499; Loyal Tennesseans League, *Edward H. Crump*, 17; Moon, *Balance of Power*, 176; untitled newspaper clipping, *MT*, 13 October 1928, folder 22, box 5, Church Family Papers; Tucker, *Lieutenant Lee*, 99–100; Lee interview, 17 April 1966, p. 32.

2. Lamon, *Blacks in Tennessee*, 89; Tucker, *Lieutenant Lee*, 64–65; Melton, "Blacks in Memphis," 84, 87–89.

3. Melton, "Blacks in Memphis," 88.

4. Walker, "Role of Black Clergy," 41.

5. Ibid., 33; Lee interview, n.d., pp. 5–6.

6. Lee to Watkins Overton, 2 November 1931, folder 31, box 7, Overton Papers, SC. For evidence of Lee's observations, see "Public Improvements Sponsored by City of Memphis for Colored Citizens: January 1, 1928–June 1, 1937," n.d., folder 1940 Race Relations, box 14, Walter Chandler Papers, MSC.

7. Adkins, "Beale Street," 45.

8. See, e.g., Dammons to Crump, 3 December 1933, mfm 002153, and Charlie Gates to Crump, 3 February 1933, mfm 002154, folder Watkins Overton, 1933, box 84, ser. 3, Crump Papers.

9. Bunche, *Political Status*, 499; Campbell to Church, 30 July 1934, folder 20, box 6, and Hale to Church, 14 November 1934, folder 2, box 6,

Church Family Papers; G. Wayne Dowdy, interview by author, Memphis, 20 June 2007, typed notes in author's possession.

10. Lee interview, n.d., p. 8.

11. Tucker, *Lieutenant Lee,* 100; Lisio, *Hoover, Blacks, and Lily-Whites,* 36–37.

12. Michael K. Honey, *Black Workers Remember: An Oral History of Segregation, Unionism, and the Freedom Struggle* (Berkeley and Los Angeles: University of California Press, 1999), 65.

13. Hill, "Self-Defined African American Community" (thesis), 14; Loyal Tennesseans League, *Edward H. Crump,* 14. For a description of the underworld, see Lee, *Beale Street,* 62–65.

14. Walker, "Role of Black Clergy," 34, 35, 38; Tucker, *Black Pastors and Leaders,* x, 24, 97, 99; Melton, "Blacks in Memphis," 17.

15. Honey, *Black Workers Remember,* 66.

16. Walker, "Role of Black Clergy," 42, 44; Dammons to Crump, 3 December 1933, mfm 002153, folder Watkins Overton, 1933, box 84, ser. 3, Crump Papers.

17. Walker, "Role of Black Clergy," 42; Honey, *Black Workers Remember,* 66.

18. Church and Church interview, 10 July 1973, interview no. 1, pp. 14–15.

19. Walker, "Role of Black Clergy," 34–39, 45; Myrdal, *American Dilemma,* 2:872–78; Tucker, *Black Pastors and Leaders,* 14, 97–99.

20. Walker, "Role of Black Clergy," 37, 38.

21. Bunche, *Political Status,* 501.

22. Tucker, *Black Pastors and Leaders,* 154.

23. Walker, "Role of Black Clergy," 42.

24. For more details, see chapters 1 and 2.

25. Estimates differ as to how many African Americans registered and voted overall because of the lack of consistent records. Official registration statistics, separated by race, were not kept until 1951, and no permanent registration existed—blacks and whites had to reregister annually to remain eligible. Lewinson, *Race, Class, and Party,* 138; Walker, "Role of Black Clergy," 33; James B. Jalenak, "Beale Street Politics" (senior honors thesis, Yale University, 1961), 27; Melton, "Blacks in Memphis," 137; Loyal Tennesseans League, *Edward H. Crump,* 15; "The Week," *CD,* 12 September 1931, 1.

26. Walker, "Role of Black Clergy," 33, 45; Loyal Tennesseans League, *Edward H. Crump,* 14.

27. Florence McCleave to Robert Bagnall, 5 August 1932, folder Memphis NAACP 1932, box G199, Group 1, NAACP Papers.

28. Melton, "Blacks in Memphis," 137. For biographical information on Venson, see DeCosta-Willis, *Notable Black Memphians,* 380.

29. Lewinson, *Race, Class, and Party,* 138.

30. Marie Fort, interview by Charles W. Crawford, Memphis, 23 August 1989, transcript, pp. 1, 42–43 (quotes), UMOH. See also Green, *Battling the Plantation Mentality,* 201, 221.

31. Adkins, "Beale Street," 28, 34; Key, *Southern Politics,* 47–48; Church and Church interview, 10 July 1973, interview no. 3, pp. 16–17; Loyal Tennesseans League, *Edward H. Crump,* 15.

32. James D. Squires, *The Secrets of the Hopewell Box: Stolen Elections, Southern Politics, and a City's Coming of Age* (New York: Times Books, 1996), 41, 51–52, 56–58, 61, 69–70, 173–74, 176; Key, *Southern Politics,* 60–61, 65, 67, 72–73, 75, 78–79.

33. Lee, *Tennessee in Turmoil,* 106–7, 111.

34. Johnson's political positions included Shelby County relief commissioner and deputy inspector in the State Department of Finance and Taxation. Edwin Frank, p. 2, finding aid to R. E. Johnson Papers, SC; Loyal Tennesseans League, *Edward H. Crump,* 30–31.

35. Loyal Tennesseans League, *Edward H. Crump,* 5, 6–7 (quotes).

36. Ibid., 18.

37. Adkins, "Beale Street," 29.

38. Loyal Tennesseans League, *Edward H. Crump,* 19–20.

39. Moon reported that African Americans in the Twenty-ninth Ward were considering running candidates for the constable position and the county commission. Ibid., 26.

40. Lee, *Beale Street,* 251–52; Kelly, "Robert R. Church," 79–82.

41. Owen to Church, 22 March 1928, folder 8, box 5, Church Family Papers. For biographical information on Owen, see Pink Palace Museum, *Historic Black Memphians,* 29; Tucker, *Black Pastors and Leaders,* 107, 116–17; and DeCosta-Willis, *Notable Black Memphians,* 255–57. For a tribute to Owen by Howard Thurman, a friend of Owen and a mentor of Dr. Martin Luther King Jr., see Howard Thurman, "Dr. S. A. Owen Eulogy," folder Dr. S. A. Owen Eulogy, box 100, Howard Thurman Papers, Howard Gotlieb Archival Research Center, Boston University, Boston, MA.

42. Taylor to Church, 2 April 1928, folder 17, box 4, Church Family Papers. For biographical information on Taylor, see Fred L. Hutchins, "Frank Street," n.d., Fred Hutchins Papers, SC; Susie Peebles Hightower, interview by Ronald Anderson Walter, Memphis, 14 September 1976, transcript, p. 4, Cook Collection, MSC; and DeCosta-Willis, *Notable Black Memphians,* 298–99.

43. "Memphis Resents Attack on Bob Church," *CD,* 31 March 1928, 1.

44. See "Beat Bob Church," campaign handbill, 1928, "Vote for Henry Horton," campaign handbill, 1928, and "R. R. CHURCH Must Be Eliminated," campaign flyer, 1928, folder 24, box 4, Church Family Papers.

45. "Bob Church Has a Machine Also," *Memphis Evening Appeal*, 3 August 1928, 4, folder 22, box 5, Church Family Papers; Lee, *Beale Street*, 281–82; Lee, *Tennessee in Turmoil*, 92; "Bob Church Wins Again," *PC*, 11 August 1928, A8; "Church Swamps Tenn. Lily-Whites Despite Threats," *AA*, 11 August 1928, 2.

46. Lee, *Tennessee in Turmoil*, 91.

47. "Church Swamps," *AA*; "Bob Church Wins Victory in Tennessee," *CD*, 11 August 1928, 2; Travis, "Bob Church."

48. Tucker, *Lieutenant Lee*, 98.

49. "The Ludicrous Attempt to Create a Jim Crow Republican Party," *CA*, 6 October 1928, folder 23, box 5, Church Family Papers.

50. "The Week," *CD*, 20 October 1928, A1. See also "Other Papers Say," *CD*, 27 October 1928, A2; and "Memphis Paper Comes Out for Bob Church," *CD*, 27 October 1928, 2.

51. "Damning with Faint Praise," *PC*, 27 October 1928, A8.

52. Lisio, *Hoover, Blacks, and Lily-Whites*; Walton, *Black Republicans*, 151, 154, 159–60; McMillen, *Dark Journey*, 58.

53. "Negroes Hitch Dry Idea to Suffrage," *New York World*, 10 June 1928, folder 2, box 4, Church Family Papers; "Bob Church Wins Fights with Whites," *CD*, 16 June 1928, 1; Lisio, *Hoover, Blacks, and Lily-Whites*, 99–100.

54. Lisio, *Hoover, Blacks, and Lily-Whites*, 100–101, 106; Kelly Miller, "The Political Desert," *NYAN*, 15 April 1928, 16, and "Behold the 'Lily Whites,'" *NYAN*, 15 August 1928, 16; "Church's Letter Stirs G.O.P.," *CD*, 25 August 1928, 1; "Lesser of Two Evils," *CD*, 3 November 1928, 2; "An Illinois Candidate," *CD*, 30 January 1932, 14; Travis, "Bob Church"; Dan Burley, "Declares Southern Race Man Determines Status in North," *CD*, 6 March 1937, 4; Jacob Anderson, "Will Hays, Movie Czar, Tells of Negro Politicians, Picture Stars and Future," *NYAN*, 30 November 1935, 11; "Leadership of Late Henry 'Linc' Johnson Lauded Here at Service in His Honor," *NYAN*, 1 October 1930, 3.

55. "Church's Letter," *CD*; Lisio, *Hoover, Blacks, and Lily-Whites*, 102–7; "Leaders Look Askance at Church's Stand," *PC*, 1 September 1928, 1.

56. "Bob Church Rumor Bursts Like Bubble under Sweep of Scott Facts," *PC*, 22 September 1928, 3.

57. R. R. Church, "Why I Am for Hoover," *CD*, 3 November 1928, 3; "National Affairs," *Time*, 18 February 1929, 10; Lisio, *Hoover, Blacks, and Lily-Whites*, 111.

58. "National Affairs," *Time*.

59. Church, "Why I Am for Hoover."

60. Chicago, like Memphis, had a long history of black political mobilization; black Chicagoans also worked with local white politicians by using

their votes as leverage for improvements such as increased job opportunities. See Beth Tompkins Bates, *Pullman Porters and the Rise of Protest Politics in Black America, 1925–1945* (Chapel Hill: University of North Carolina Press, 2001), esp. 55–58.

61. G. Michael McCarthy, "Smith vs. Hoover—the Politics of Race in West Tennessee," *Phylon* 39, no. 2 (2nd Quarter 1978): 157–59.

62. "'Bob' Church Congratulates Hoover," *CD*, 10 November 1928, 1.

63. Lisio, *Hoover, Blacks, and Lily-Whites*, 120–21; "Bob Church Forces Colonel Horace A. Mann to Resign," *CD*, 16 March 1929, 1; "Bird in the Hand," *NYAN*, 20 March 1929, 16.

64. "Bird in the Hand," *NYAN*.

65. Hoover's aides replaced black-and-tan leaders with lily whites in Georgia, South Carolina, and Mississippi; these black-and-tan factions had been investigated for corruption. In Georgia, his aides secretly experimented with a new faction that included lily whites and African Americans who had influence. Although on occasion Hoover publicly said that he did not favor purging African Americans from the party, he never gave a public explanation for his southern reform strategy and, thus, never publicly clarified that his political vision encompassed African American leadership and membership in the party. Lisio, *Hoover, Blacks, and Lily-Whites*, 121–27, 131, 134, 178, 180, 276; Tucker, *Lieutenant Lee*, 86; Kelly Miller, "Mr. Hoover Speaks Out," *NYAN*, 3 April 1929, 20; Sherman, *Republican Party*, 172–76, 238–39; Lee, *Beale Street*, 273; McMillen, *Dark Journey*, 66–68.

66. Miller, "Mr. Hoover Speaks Out."

67. Kelly Miller, "End of Co-Racial Politics," *NYAN*, 18 September 1929, 20.

68. "Congressmen Get Letters from Robert R. Church," *CD*, 27 April 1929, 1; "Verdict Expected Today in Howard's Job Selling Trial," *NYAN*, 24 April 1929, 1.

69. Church to Hoover, 6 November 1929, folder 7, box 4, Church Family Papers.

70. Sherman, *Republican Party*, 234–35; Lisio, *Hoover, Blacks, and Lily-Whites*, 175–77.

71. Travis, "Bob Church."

72. Handy, *Father of the Blues*, 178–85; Hutchins, *What Happened in Memphis*, 74, 79; Handy to Annette Church, 19 December 1956, folder 16, box 12, Church Family Papers; "Beale Street's Hero," *Time*, 25 May 1936, 54–55; Robertson, *W. C. Handy*, 175–76; Lee interview, n.d., pp. 3–5; Lee, *Beale Street*, 242; "Dedicate New Park in Memphis," *CD*, 28 March 1931, 13; T. J. Johnson, "Memphis Names Park for Handy," *CD*, 4 April 1931, 13.

73. Lisio, *Hoover, Blacks, and Lily-Whites*, 205–31; Sullivan, *Lift Every*

Voice, 138–42; Weiss, *Farewell to the Party of Lincoln,* 15–17; Topping, *Lincoln's Lost Legacy,* 9–28; Sherman, *Republican Party,* 224–59.

74. Sherman, *Republican Party,* 238–39, 252–53; Lisio, *Hoover, Blacks, and Lily-Whites,* 135–37, 177, 261, 278; McMillen, *Dark Journey,* 65; Milton L. Randolph, "Bob Church Lands on Hoover," *ADW,* 19 June 1932, 1.

75. Sherman, *Republican Party,* 254–55; Sitkoff, *New Deal for Blacks,* 65–66.

76. "The Party in Power," *CD,* 20 October 1928, A2.

77. Topping, *Lincoln's Lost Legacy,* 26; Weiss, *Farewell to the Party of Lincoln,* 18–21; Lewinson, *Race, Class, and Party,* 175–76; Sitkoff, *New Deal for Blacks,* 30–32; Lisio, *Hoover, Blacks, and Lily-Whites,* 271–73; Simmons, *Republican Party,* 30 (quotes); Sherman, *Republican Party,* 252–54; Tucker, *Lieutenant Lee,* 88–89.

78. "R. R. Church Opens Offices to Aid Hoover," *CD,* 22 October 1932, 4; "Bob Church through with Hoover," *AA,* 8 October 1932, 15; "Talk Up and Talk Down," *AA,* 12 November 1932, 6; "Colored Republi-Crats in Tennessee May Swing State to Roosevelt Next Month," *AA,* 22 October 1932, 1.

79. Melton, "Blacks in Memphis," 138–39.

80. "Associated Negro Press Begins Annual Survey on Race," *ADW,* 26 December 1932, 2.

81. Dowdy, *Mr. Crump,* 71; Roger Biles, *Memphis in the Great Depression* (Knoxville: University of Tennessee Press, 1986), 52–53, 93.

82. Walker, "Role of Black Clergy," 31; Tucker, *Black Pastors and Leaders,* 85–86; Lamon, *Blacks in Tennessee,* 96; Brian D. Page, "Sutton E. Griggs," *The Tennessee Encyclopedia of History and Culture,* 4 January 2010, http://tennesseeencyclopedia.net/entry.php?rec=1605.

83. "Public Improvements Sponsored by City of Memphis," n.d.; Biles, *Memphis,* 84–85, 95; Harvard Sitkoff, "The Impact of the New Deal on Black Southerners," in Bond and Lewis, eds., *Gonna Sit at the Welcome Table,* 113–24, and *New Deal for Blacks,* 51–58; "Registration for Dixie Homes 523, Association Told," *ADW,* 25 October 1937, 2.

84. Biles, *Memphis,* 55, 59, 69, 79, 93, 95–96; Dowdy, *Mr. Crump,* 59; Green, *Battling the Plantation Mentality,* 20, 25; Lamon, *Blacks in Tennessee,* 89–93; David R. Goldfield, *Black, White, and Southern: Race Relations and Southern Culture, 1940 to the Present* (Baton Rouge: Louisiana State University Press, 1990), 29; Adkins, "Beale Street," 30–31; Emogene Wilson, interview by Mausiki Stacey Scales, Memphis, 5 July 1995, tape recording, BTV; W. H. Foote to E. H. Crump, 1 January 1937, mfm 002034, folder Wm Foote, box 138, ser. 4, Crump Papers; Hill, "Self-Defined African American Community" (thesis), 20–21; Melton, "Blacks in Memphis," 159; Van West and Stoecker, "Thomas Oscar Fuller."

85. Weiss, *Farewell to the Party of Lincoln,* 50–58, 175–79; Jacquelyn

Dowd Hall, "The Long Civil Rights Movement and the Political Uses of the Past," *Journal of American History* 91, no. 4 (March 2005): 1240–41; Sitkoff, *New Deal for Blacks*, 32–43.

86. Weiss, *Farewell to the Party of Lincoln;* Sitkoff, *New Deal for Blacks*, 57–58, 248.

87. Weiss, *Farewell to the Party of Lincoln;* Sitkoff, *New Deal for Blacks*, xv, 45–49, 59–62, 248.

88. Bunche, *Political Status,* 76–77, 94–100; Scott, *Negro in Tennessee Politics,* 98–99; Weiss, *Farewell to the Party of Lincoln,* 78–95, 234; Sitkoff, *New Deal for Blacks,* 66–67; Topping, *Lincoln's Lost Legacy,* 2.

89. Robert J. Norrell, *The House I Live In: Race and the American Century* (New York: Oxford University Press, 2005), 115–17; Sitkoff, *New Deal for Blacks,* 74–75; Bunche, *Political Status;* Amelia Boynton Robinson, *Bridge across Jordan* (Washington, DC: Schiller Institute, 1991); Hornsby, *Black Power in Dixie,* 52; Julian Bond, interview by author, Birmingham, 6 March 2008, typed notes in author's possession; Lau, *Democracy Rising,* 100–106.

90. Sullivan, *Days of Hope;* Hall, "Long Civil Rights Movement," 1245–48.

91. In the late 1920s, Memphis had the most unionized workers of any city in Tennessee, but African Americans made up only 1 percent of union members, and they generally faced racial friction with the white members. Melton, "Blacks in Memphis," 151, 153; Michael K. Honey, *Southern Labor and Black Civil Rights: Organizing Memphis Workers* (Urbana: University of Illinois Press, 1993), 19, 93–116; Adkins, "Beale Street," 103.

92. Adkins, "Beale Street," 36, 53, 92–96, 101–12; Honey, *Southern Labor,* 55, and *Black Workers Remember,* 177–79; Melton, "Blacks in Memphis," 18–21, 152–53; Dowdy, *Mr. Crump,* 61; Sitkoff, *New Deal for Blacks,* 56–57, 67.

93. Key, *Southern Politics,* 59; Silliman Evans to V. O. Key, 10 November 1949, folder Comments 1 of 2, box 58, V. O. Key Papers, Kennedy Library; Paul Coppock, "Crump Ticket Rides into City's Offices on Confidence Vote," *CA,* 10 November 1939, vertical file 1939 Election, MSC; Dowdy, *Mr. Crump,* 75; J. Morgan Kousser, *Colorblind Injustice: Minority Voting Rights and the Undoing of the Second Reconstruction* (Chapel Hill: University of North Carolina Press, 1999), 143, 146.

94. Church and Church interview, 10 July 1973, interview no. 2, pp. 2–3.

95. Ibid., 5–12; "Party Out of Power—Taxes," *NYAN,* 3 April 1937, 11; "Ask Sale of Bob Church Property in Memphis to Collect $55,000 Taxes," *NYAN,* 5 March 1938, 4; "Bob Church Pays Taxes," *PC,* 10 April 1937, 24; "Property May Be Sold for Taxes," *ADW,* 5 March 1938, 1; "Bob Church Sued for Unpaid Taxes," *PC,* 5 March 1938, 1; William N. Jones, "Day by Day: The R. R. Church Dynasty," *AA,* 16 April 1938, 4; Church and Church

interview, 10 July 1973, interview no. 2, pp. 3, 11; "Church Property Sold," *PC,* 17 February 1940, 1. See also Robert R. Church Jr. to Howard B. Shofner, 2 November 1934, and Robert R. Church Jr. to J. Will Taylor, 2 November 1934, folder 11, box 4, Church Family Papers.

96. Clark Porteous, "The Two Eds of Memphis—Meeman and Crump," *WTHSP* 45 (1991): 140–52; Edward J. Meeman, *The Editorial We: A Posthumous Autobiography* (Memphis: Memphis State University Press, 1976).

97. Evans to Key, 10 November 1949, folder Comments 1 of 2, box 58, V. O. Key Papers, Kennedy Library. For more on Evans, see Squires, *Secrets of the Hopewell Box.*

98. David M. Tucker, *Memphis since Crump: Bossism, Blacks, and Civic Reformers, 1948–1968* (Knoxville: University of Tennessee Press, 1980), 54, 56; Wayne Dowdy, email to author, 12 April 2005, copy in author's possession; Melton, "Blacks in Memphis," 154–55; Honey, *Southern Labor;* Green, *Battling the Plantation Mentality,* 30–32; Biles, *Memphis,* 81–87; Sullivan, *Days of Hope,* 4, 5, 61, 100; Sitkoff, *New Deal for Blacks,* 77–104; Virginia Emerson Lewis, "Fifty Years of Politics in Memphis, 1900–1950" (Ph.D. diss., New York University, 1955), 138; Watkins Overton, "Statement," 14 March 1938, folder 11, box 10, Overton Papers, SC; Honey, *Black Workers Remember.*

99. Perre Magness, "Lee Loses Position as Blacks' Spokesman," *CA,* 15 February 1990, vertical file George W. Lee, MSC; Tucker, *Lieutenant Lee,* 100–101, 120; Charles W. Crawford, "History of the Robert R. Church Family: Interview with Lonnie Briscoe" (Memphis: Oral History Research Office, Memphis State University, 1991), 20–21; Lee, *Beale Street,* 212; Ralph Picard to E. H. Crump, 12 February 1935, mfm 000722, folder Walter Chandler 1936, box 111, ser. 4, Crump Papers; Bunche, *Political Status,* 499–500; Lee interview, n.d., p. 5.

100. Lee interview, n.d., p. 8.

101. Tucker, *Lieutenant Lee,* 109–12; Church and Church interview, 10 July 1973, interview no. 3, p. 22; Lee interview, 24 May 1966, pp. 11–12; George W. Lee, *Beale Street: Where the Blues Began* (New York: Robert O. Ballou, 1934).

102. For biographical information on Walker, see Pink Palace Museum, *Historic Black Memphians,* 18–19; McMillen, *Dark Journey,* 106, 184–86, 275–76, 298; Jalenak, "Beale Street Politics," 39–40; "Tennessee's $6,000,000 Negro Business," *Color,* March 1950, folder 7, box 2, African-American Culture and Life Collection; Hutchins, *What Happened in Memphis,* 86–89; "Hard Work Brings Success to Head of Universal Life," *ADW,* 25 September 1932, 1A; and "Dr. Walker Resigns Political Club Office," *ADW,* 17 May 1944, 2.

103. Adkins attributed their tension to similar ambitions, although he did

not specify what he meant by this statement. Adkins, "Beale Street," 111–12. See also Melton, "Blacks in Memphis," 135, 143; and Tucker, *Lieutenant Lee*, 121–22.

104. Lamon, *Blacks in Tennessee*, 95.

105. "Negro Business Given Government Help," *NYAN*, 10 October 1936, 2.

106. Melton, "Blacks in Memphis," 136, 170–71; Tucker, *Lieutenant Lee*, 121–22; "Vote, Civic Problems Discussed," *ADW*, 4 August 1932, 2A; Adkins, "Beale Street," 111; "Tennessee Democrats Forced to Recognize Negro's Vote," *ADW*, 26 July 1932, 1.

107. "Tennessee Democrats Forced to Recognize Negro's Vote," *ADW*.

108. Melton, "Blacks in Memphis," 126, 132–34, 172; "Tennessee State News," *CD*, 20 August 1932, 11; "Tennessee State News," *CD*, 12 November 1932, 12; "Head of Business League Honored," *CD*, 7 October 1939, 6; "Memphis Expresses Pride in Dr. Walker's Election," *CD*, 16 September 1939, 19.

109. Melton, "Blacks in Memphis," 142–50; Tucker, *Lieutenant Lee*, 122; "Seeks Admission to Tenn. U. Grad School," *CD*, 9 May 1936, 3; Sullivan, *Lift Every Voice*, 205–13.

110. Melton, "Blacks in Memphis," 141–43; "Cites N.A.A.C.P. Membership Boost," *NYAN*, 6 January 1932, 3; "Robert R. Church Quits N.A.A.C.P.," *CD*, 30 January 1932, 13; Walter White, Letter to the Editor, *CD*, 13 February 1932, 15; Robert R. Church to Roscoe Conkling Simmons, 9 January 1932, and Robert R. Church to Walter White, 2 January 1932, folder R. R. Church, 1920–1939, box 2, Simmons Papers.

111. Adkins, "Beale Street," 107.

112. Ibid., 94–95; Weiss, *Farewell to the Party of Lincoln*, 78–80, 229–32; Kelly Miller, "G.O.P. 'Heading for the Last Roundup' Kelly Miller Writes as Election Nears," *PC*, 31 October 1936, A2; "DeWitt Alcorn Heads Club as President," *Memphis Journal*, 30 November 1934, mfm 000724, and Ralph Picard to E. H. Crump, 12 February 1935, mfm 000722, folder Walter Chandler 1936, box 111, ser. 4, Crump Papers.

113. Jalenak, "Beale Street Politics," 40; Adkins, "Beale Street," 112; McElvaine, *Great Depression*, 188.

114. Adkins, "Beale Street," 67, 80; "Republican Primary Is Orderly," *ADW*, 9 August 1932, 2A; "Record Vote for Primary Predicted," *ADW*, 3 August 1932, 2A; "Tennessee Democrats Forced to Recognize Negro's Vote," *ADW*; "Negroes' Ballots Decide Tennessee Primary," *PC*, 13 August 1932, A8; "346 Work in Tenn. Primary," *AA*, 20 August 1932, 8.

115. "Republican Primary Is Orderly," *ADW*.

116. Ibid.; "Bob Church Faction Is Recognized," *ADW*, 26 September 1932, 1.

117. "Negroes' Ballots Decide Tennessee Primary," *PC;* "346 Work in Tenn. Primary," *AA;* "Tennessee Election Contest Thrown Out," *ADW,* 29 August 1932, 1A; "'Lily-Whites' in Tenn. Defeated," *PC,* 19 November 1932, 4; T. J. Johnson, "Election in Memphis to Be Spirited," *CD,* 30 July 1932, 13; "The Week," *CD,* 10 September 1932, 1; "The Week," *CD,* 22 October 1932, 1; Bessie Thornton, "Tennessee State News," *CD,* 30 July 1932, 11; Kelly, "Robert R. Church," 93; "35,000 Negroes in Memphis Prepare for Election," *ADW,* 18 July 1932, 1A; "Voters Rallying to Support of 'Bob' Church," *PC,* 30 July 1932, 4; "Record Vote for Primary Predicted," *ADW;* "Colored Republi-Crats in Tennessee," *AA.*

118. "35,000 Voters Register in Tenn. County," *AA,* 23 July 1932, 7.

119. "Tennessee Democrats Forced to Recognize Negro's Vote," *ADW.*

120. "Colored Republi-Crats in Tennessee," *AA.*

121. Scott, *Negro in Tennessee Politics,* 93; Church and Church, *Robert R. Churches,* 215–16; Roger Biles, "Robert R. Church, Jr. of Memphis: Black Republican Leader in the Age of Democratic Ascendancy, 1928–1940," *Tennessee Historical Quarterly* 42 (1983): 362–82; George W. Lee, "Inside the Memphis Report," program, 14 July 1963, folder 1, box 2, Lee Papers; Topping, *Lincoln's Lost Legacy,* 29–33.

122. Jalenak, "Beale Street Politics," 39–40; Adkins, "Beale Street," 112; James C. Dickerson, "Tennessee State News," *CD,* 2 May 1936, 23; Travis, "Bob Church"; Biles, "Robert R. Church," 368, 370; Lee, *Beale Street,* 279, 284; Crawford, "Interview with Lonnie Briscoe," 9–10; Wilson interview; "National Affairs," *Time,* 28 May 1934, folder 26, box 6, Church Family Papers; "Robert Church Is on Executive GOP Committee," *CD,* 19 September 1936, 5; Williams interview, pp. 13–14. On the black-and-tan and lily-white battles, see, e.g., "Lily-Whites Continue Open Warfare on Church's Faction," *CD,* 16 April 1932, 1; "Lily-Whites, 'Bob' Church Clash in Tenn.," *PC,* 31 March 1934, 6; "Foil Effort of Whites to Rule Memphis Confab," *CD,* 7 April 1934, 4; "Bob Church Wins Again in Memphis," *CD,* 8 September 1934, 4; "Tenn. GOP in Convention at Nashville: Bob Church Defeats the 'Lily-Whites,'" *CD,* 16 May 1936, 9; and "Bob Church Wins Convention Seat After Contest," *Cleveland Call and Post,* 11 June 1936, 1.

123. Travis, "Bob Church."

124. Williams interview, p. 14.

125. "Political Mob 'Crucifies' Bob Church; Jealous Whites End Long Regime of Tennessee's Renowned G.O.P. Leader," *PC,* 26 May 1934, 2. For more criticism from McCall, see "Bob Church and McCall Still at Odds," *ADW,* 17 July 1934, 1.

126. "Forces of Bob Church Win in Tenn. Feud," *PC,* 22 December 1934, 2; "State Convention Recognizes Robert R. Church Faction," *ADW,* 9 May 1936, 5.

127. "Even His Enemies Pay Tribute," *PC*, 26 May 1934, 2.

128. The *Commercial Appeal* editorial, published on May 17, 1934, is quoted in Nat D. Williams, "Down on Beale," *Memphis World*, 22 May 1934, folder 18, box 4, Church Family Papers.

129. See Owen to Church, 21 May 1934, and Church to Owen, 28 May 1934, folder 2, box 6, Church Family Papers.

130. George W. Lee, "Church Names Postmaster," *MT*, 25 June 1927, 1.

131. Crawford, "Interview with Lonnie Briscoe," 3–5.

132. Ibid., 6–10, 14, 17, 28 (quotes 9–10, 14; see also 33).

133. Ibid., 19–20, 29–32 (quotes 31, 19, 29, 30, 31–32).

134. Ibid., 9, 30–33 (quotes 32, 30, 33, 9, 31).

135. Ibid., 14; Nannie H. Burroughs to Church, 23 February 1935, folder 47, box 4, Church Family Papers; Hornsby, *Black Power in Dixie*, 54; Tomiko Brown-Nagin, *Courage to Dissent: Atlanta and the Long History of the Civil Rights Movement* (Oxford: Oxford University Press, 2011), 45.

136. Dobbs to Church, 22 June 1935, folder 3, box 6, Church Family Papers.

137. Robert M. Ratcliff, "Dobbs to Head Civic League," *ADW*, 13 February 1932, 1.

138. Adkins, "Beale Street," 88, 103, 88, 87. Unfortunately, Adkins does not provide additional information or more specific information about Church's views of the New Deal. I have found little information, in general, on this topic; Church's avoidance of giving interviews and making public statements helps explain this.

139. Weiss, *Farewell to the Party of Lincoln*, 216–28, 229–32; Miller, "G.O.P. 'Heading for the Last Roundup.'"

140. Weiss, *Farewell to the Party of Lincoln*, 231. See also Simmons, *Republican Party*.

141. Sitkoff, *New Deal for Blacks*, 77–84.

142. Weiss, *Farewell to the Party of Lincoln*, 185–204; Sitkoff, *New Deal for Blacks*, 69–71; Topping, *Lincoln's Lost Legacy*, 40–45; Simmons, *Republican Party*; "Gov. Alf M. Landon Outspoken on Lynch Question at Conference," *CD*, 17 October 1936, 4.

143. Melton, "Blacks in Memphis," 171; Walker to E. W. Hale, 1 May 1944, folder Negroes 1944, box 66, Chandler Papers; "Invited to Look at 'a Negro Democrat,'" *CD*, 31 October 1936, 22 (quote); "Colored Demo Club Looks to '38 Election," *MW*, 13 August 1937, 1, folder R. R. Church, 1920–39, box 2, Simmons Papers; "Demo Club Holds Big Opening," *ADW*, 2 November 1936, 1; "J. E. Walker Now Demo Pilot," *ADW*, 18 August 1937, 3A; "Meanderings around Memphis, Tennessee," *CD*, 7 November 1936, 19; "Meanderings around Memphis, Tennessee," *CD*, 14 November 1936, 19.

144. "With Landon G.O.P. Begins Its Recovery," *CD*, 1 August 1936, 1. On the enthusiasm of black Republicans for the Landon ticket, see "Knox Ceremony Attracts Many," *NYAN*, 8 August 1936, 2; "Landon's Notification Draws Negro Leaders," *NYAN*, 1 August 1936, 5; and "Memphis Business Men Plan to Work for GOP Cause," *ADW*, 12 September 1936, 7.

145. Simmons, *Republican Party;* "Landon Greets Little and Church," *CD*, 17 October 1936, 1; "Gov. Alf M. Landon," *CD;* "Gov. Landon Takes Stand on Lynching," *CD*, 10 October 1936, 9; "Landon Backs Law to End Lynching," *NYAN*, 10 October 1936, 1; Roscoe Simmons, "The Week," *CD*, 17 October 1936, 1; "Roosevelt Attacked Lynching as Murder," *NYAN*, 10 October 1936, 1; "R. R. Church at Landon Ceremony," *ADW*, 1 August 1936, 4; "Negro Notables of Nation Attend Landon Notification Ceremonies," *PC*, 1 August 1936, 6; "Landon Says Lynch Law Must Go," *ADW*, 7 October 1936, 2; "Landon Hits at U.S. Mobs," *AA*, 10 October 1936, 1.

146. Kelly Miller, "Solicitude of Landon for Race Is Very Sudden," *PC*, 31 October 1936, 7. See also Miller, "G.O.P. 'Heading for the Last Roundup.'"

147. "G.O.P. National Committee Turns 'Lily White,'" *PC*, 31 October 1936, 2.

148. "Robert Church Is on Executive GOP Committee," *CD*.

149. "Bob Church Helps Shape Policies of Landon's Forces," *PC*, 19 September 1936, 2.

150. Simmons, *Republican Party*, 14–18 (quotes 14, 15, 17–18).

151. Weiss, *Farewell to the Party of Lincoln*, 211–12; "Negro Demo Club Draws 4,000 Solid Voters to Polls," *ADW*, 6 November 1936, 1.

152. Topping, *Lincoln's Lost Legacy*, 3; Church and Church, *Robert R. Churches*, 133, 250–55; "Robert R. Church Demands U.S. Control of National Elections," *CD*, 18 December 1937, 1; "Bob Church Hurls Bombshell at G.O.P.," *PC*, 20 August 1938, 1. For a scholarly view critical of Church, see Biles, "Robert R. Church."

153. "Citizens Greet Mrs. F. D. Roosevelt at Tenn. School," *ADW*, 26 November 1937, 1; "Power of Colored Vote Recognized in Memphis, Tenn.," *PC*, 23 July 1938, 6.

154. Bunche, *Political Status*, 493–94; Green, *Battling the Plantation Mentality*, 32; Honey, *Southern Labor*, 1–5, 61; Church and Church interview, 10 July 1973, interview no. 3, pp. 17–18; Melton, "Blacks in Memphis," 144–45; Honey, *Black Workers Remember*, 23–28; Owen to Church, 3 February 1938, folder 2, box 6, Church Family Papers. For a personal perspective on the conduct of the police toward black Memphians, see Honey, *Black Workers Remember*, 64.

155. Bell to Church, 3 February 1938, folder 2, box 6, Church Family Papers.

156. Melton, "Blacks in Memphis," 175; "Inauguration for Beale St. Mayor Nov. 6," *CD*, 5 November 1938, 7.

157. L. O. Swingler and Norman E. Jones to Walter Chandler, 9 March 1940, folder 1940 Public Improvements Colored Citizens, box 13, Chandler Papers.

158. Williams interview, p. 17; Watkins Overton, "To the 'Mayor and Commissioners of Beale Street,'" 5 November 1938, folder 1940 Public Improvements Colored Citizens, box 13, Chandler Papers; Hutchins, *What Happened in Memphis,* 68–69; Church and Walter, *Nineteenth Century Memphis Families,* 95–97; DeCosta-Willis, *Notable Black Memphians,* 308; Robertson, *W. C. Handy,* 106–7, 112–13; Bunche, *Political Status,* 87.

159. "Chicago Defender's Ace Reporter Interviews Interesting Memphis Personalities," *CD,* 6 March 1937, 4.

160. Hayes to Grant, 17 July 1938, folder 44, box 4, Church Family Papers. See also the 29 July 1938 issue of the *Southern Journal,* a copy of which is in folder 36, box 7, Church Family Papers.

161. Church and Church interview, 10 July 1973, interview no. 1, pp. 13–15.

162. "Political Renaissance in Memphis," *PC,* 27 August 1938, 10.

163. Grant to Hayes, 12 July 1938, box 4, folder 44, box 4, Church Family Papers. This letter was misdated; it was written on receipt of the July 17 letter.

164. Hayes to Grant, 19 July 1938, folder 44, box 4, Church Family Papers.

165. Bunche, *Political Status,* 496–97, 499; Tucker, *Lieutenant Lee,* 124–25; Green, *Battling the Plantation Mentality,* 32–33; "Political Renaissance," *PC;* "Negroes Flock to State Convention at Knoxville," *PC,* 24 September 1938, 4.

166. Dowdy, "E. H. Crump," 87–89; Robert Lasch, "Boss Crump Makes Hague Look Like Mere Amateur," *Chicago Sun,* 6 August 1944, folder 36, box 7, Church Family Papers; Honey, *Southern Labor,* 1–5, 93–116; Green, *Battling the Plantation Mentality,* 32; "Tom Watkins Flees amid Police Bullets," [*MPS*], 27 May 1939, mfm 19:001006, Utillus R. Phillips to Thurgood Marshall, 20 July 1939, mfm 19:001011, and Grace T. Hamilton to Walter White, 27 May 1939, mfm 19:001007, folder Memphis, Tenn. 1939, box C367, Group 2, NAACP Papers, microfilm version (Bethesda, MD: University Publications of American, 1982–1995).

167. Phillips to Murphy, 27 May 1939, mfm 19:001005, folder Memphis, Tenn. 1939, box C367, Group 2, NAACP Papers.

168. Bunche, *Political Status,* 500.

4. "As Un-American as Any Dictator-Ridden Country in Europe"

1. Harry Woodbury to Roberta Church, 15 April 1986, folder 19, box 1, Roberta Church Papers, MSC.

2. Robert Lasch, "Boss Crump Makes Hague Look Like Mere Amateur," *Chicago Sun,* 6 August 1944, folder 36, box 7, Church Family Papers.

3. Arthur Evans, "Bosses Come, Bosses Go, but Not Mr. Crump," *Chicago Tribune,* 15 July 1947, 11, folder 7, box 7, James Pleasants Papers, MSC.

4. Ibid.

5. Key, *Southern Politics,* 62, 68–69. For more on Crump's political partnership with East Tennessee Republicans, see chapter 3.

6. Estes Kefauver, "How Boss Crump Was Licked," *Colliers,* 16 October 1948, excerpts reprinted in Church and Church, *Robert R. Churches,* 191–93; Thomas F. Doyle, "Gestapo in Memphis," *Crisis,* May 1941, 152, folder 17, box 7, Church Family Papers; Lasch, "Boss Crump"; Wayne Dowdy, "'We Engaged in a Hard Campaign': Primary Sources Related to the 1940 and 1944 Presidential Elections in Shelby County," *Tennessee Librarian* 54, no. 1 (2004), copy in author's possession.

7. Lasch, "Boss Crump."

8. Evans, "Bosses Come, Bosses Go."

9. Lasch, "Boss Crump."

10. Lowell Mellett, "'On the Other Hand': Finds Memphis Boss Confused concerning Meaning of a Word," newspaper clipping, 1944, folder 36, box 7, Church Family Papers.

11. Evans, "Bosses Come, Bosses Go."

12. Mellett, "'On the Other Hand.'"

13. Lasch, "Boss Crump."

14. Robert S. Allen, ed., *Our Fair City* (New York: Vanguard, 1947), 229.

15. Tucker, *Lieutenant Lee,* 127. Indeed, Hague and Pendergast displayed similarities to Crump. See Thomas F. X. Smith, *The Powerticians* (Secaucus, NJ: L. Stuart, 1982); and Lawrence H. Larsen and Nancy J. Hulston, *Pendergast!* (Columbia: University of Missouri Press, 1997).

16. Topping, *Lincoln's Lost Legacy,* 202; Sitkoff, *New Deal for Blacks,* 228–29.

17. Scott, *Negro in Tennessee Politics,* 129; Church and Church interview, 10 July 1973, interview no. 3, pp. 2–3; J. B. Martin, "Memorandum regarding Police Persecution of Dr. J. B. Martin of Memphis, Tennessee, because of Political Activities in 1940 Presidential Election," n.d., p. 1, folder 17, box 1, Roberta Church Papers; "Dr. J. B. Martin Goes to Cleveland to G.O.P. Meet," *PC,* 13 June 1936, 5; Roi Ottley, "Memphis Row Is Boon to Chicago," *Chicago Tribune,* 28 September 1954, sec. 3, p. 15, mfm 000307, folder Newspaper Articles, Magazine Clippings, 1954, box 308, ser. 4, Crump Papers; M. S. Stuart to Walter Chandler, 1 November 1940, folder Race Relations, 1940, box 14, Chandler Papers; US Department of Justice,

transcript of deposition of J. B. Martin, Washington, DC, 12 March 1941, p. 20, folder 11, box 7, Church Family Papers. For more on the Memphis Red Sox, see Hill, "Self-Defined African American Community" (thesis), 58–74.

18. Church to Kenneth D. McKellar, 25 May 1945, folder 9, box 8, Roberta Church Papers.

19. Church and Church interview, 10 July 1973, interview no. 1, p. 3; Tucker, *Lieutenant Lee*, 127; US Department of Justice, transcript of deposition of J. B. Martin, pp. 10–12.

20. Clapp to Guy Joyner, 22 October 1940, folder Negroes Election Data 1940, box 179, ser. 4, Crump Papers. For a personal perspective on the Reverend Gibson, see Bill Weathers, interview by Marjean Kremer and Selma Lewis, Memphis, 17 May 1978, transcript, p. 26, Selma S. Lewis Collection, MSC. George Albert Long is more commonly referred to as G. A. Long; I have referred to him as such subsequently.

21. In his extensive memorandum, Martin just puts in quotes that he was told that his store would be "policed." He does not indicate that more details were provided about what this policing would entail. Martin faced the harassment even though he had served as a notary public for more than twenty years, an appointment made after the Shelby County Court certified his moral character. Moreover, he had served on a federal jury, had been named a special officer of the police department, and had been permitted to work as an unlicensed bondsman. In a lawsuit against the city of Memphis a year later, Atkinson insisted that he had not acted illegally and that the harassment had been politically motivated. Church and Church interview, 10 July 1973, interview no. 1, pp. 4–5; Martin, "Memorandum," 1–5; Church and Church, *Robert R. Churches*, 182; Green, *Battling the Plantation Mentality*, 39, 45; "Both Races Reported Disturbed over 'Insult' to Negro Leader," *ADW*, 18 December 1940, 1; US Department of Justice, transcript of deposition of J. B. Martin, pp. 22–23; Tucker, *Lieutenant Lee*, 127.

22. Church and Church interview, 10 July 1973, interview no. 1, pp. 3–4.

23. Scott, *Negro in Tennessee Politics*, 129.

24. Lee interview, 17 April 1966, pp. 37–39.

25. Scott, *Negro in Tennessee Politics*, 129; Church and Church interview, 10 July 1973, interview no. 2, pp. 3–6; Melton, "Blacks in Memphis," 188, 232 n. 5; "Sell Bob Church Estate for Taxes," *CD*, 10 February 1940, 1; "Bob Church's Property Sold at Auction," *CD*, 17 February 1940, 9; "Church Property Sold," *PC*, 17 February 1940, 1; "Church's Property Sold for Back Taxes," *ADW*, 19 February 1940, 2; James H. Purdy Jr., "File Another Suit against Bob Church," *CD*, 20 April 1940, 1.

26. Beale St. was sometimes called Beale Ave. The *Memphis World* reported the name change on 22 November 1940. Kelly, "Robert R. Church," 93–97; Church and Church interview, 10 July 1973, interview no. 2, pp.

5–6, 12–13; Melton, "Blacks in Memphis," 195; Church and Church, *Robert R. Churches*, 53–54, 184; Patricia M. LaPointe, finding aid to Roberta Church Collection, p. 17, Roberta Church Papers; "Another Tradition Passes from Beale Street," *ADW*, 22 November 1940, 2; James H. Purdy Jr., "Bob Church Home Sold in Memphis," *CD*, 6 December 1941, 1.

27. Lee interview, 17 April 1966, p. 33.

28. "Church Property Sold," *PC*; Church and Church interview, 10 July 1973, interview no. 2, pp. 4–5.

29. Church and Church interview, 10 July 1973, interview no. 2, pp. 5–6, 8–9, 14–15; Church and Church, *Robert R. Churches*, 184.

30. W. S. Martin to E. H. Crump, 1 November 1940, mfm 000472, folder "Ma" 1940, box 177, ser. 4, Crump Papers; Walker to Hale, 1 May 1944, folder Negroes 1944, box 66, Chandler Papers; Roosevelt Democratic Headquarters, Memphis, TN, "To the Colored Voters of Memphis and Shelby County," mfm 001817, folder Negroes Election Data 1940, box 179, ser. 4, Crump Papers; Colored Democratic Club, "Attention Colored Voters," 1940, folder 1940—Public Improvements for Colored Citizens, box 13, Chandler Papers; "Governor Cooper Gets Protests on Lynching," *ADW*, 12 July 1940, 1; Mack Lofton to John Vesey, 21 September 1940, Lyda Graham-Binns to E. W. Hale, 22 November 1940, and Walker to E. W. Hale, 21 October 1940, folder Election 1940–41, box 19, E. W. Hale Papers, MSC. See also "Facts Every Negro Should Know about Roosevelt and the Democratic Administration," "Mass Meeting, Oct. 29," and "Grand Jubilee—Rally and Festival, Oct. 31, 1940," Colored Democratic Club flyers, folder Election 1940–41, box 19, Hale Papers.

31. Johnson to Chandler, 3 November 1940, folder Race Relations 1940, box 14, Chandler Papers.

32. Grant to Chandler, 7 September 1940, folder Roosevelt Democratic Club, box 9, Chandler Papers.

33. King to E. W. Hale, 19 October 1940, folder Election 1940–41, box 19, Hale Papers.

34. King to Chandler, 29 July 1940, folder 1940—Public Improvements for Colored Citizens, box 13, Chandler Papers.

35. Chandler to G. A. Long, 5 November 1940, folder Race Relations—1940, box 14, Chandler Papers.

36. Walter Chandler, form letter to ministers, n.d., mfm 001816, folder Negroes Election Data 1940, box 179, ser. 4, Crump Papers.

37. Hunt to Chandler, 4 November 1940, folder Race Relations 1940, box 14, Chandler Papers. See also W. H. Winston to Chandler, 4 November 1940, Arthur W. Womack to Chandler, 7 November 1940, W. A. Johnson to Chandler, 4 November 1940, G. H. Howard to Chandler, 4 November 1940, D. Morrison to Chandler, 4 November 1940, W. C. Paine to Chan-

dler, 3 November 1940, and J. H. Johnson to Chandler, 3 November 1940, folder Race Relations 1940, box 14, Chandler Papers.

38. Tucker, *Lieutenant Lee,* 135. I found no other record of such a letter in the Chandler Papers. For an analysis of why some black ministers supported Crump, see chapter 3.

39. Long to Chandler, 4 November 1940, and Chandler to Long, 5 November 1940, folder Race Relations 1940, box 14, Chandler Papers.

40. Melton, "Blacks in Memphis," 191–92, 233 n. 12.

41. Green, *Battling the Plantation Mentality,* 26, 39–41; Honey, *Southern Labor,* 165–67.

42. Martin, "Memorandum," 7. This branch was organized earlier in 1940 by the Memphis Ministerial Association and was affiliated with the Atlanta-based Commission on Interracial Cooperation. It is unclear whether a connection existed between it and the city's Inter Racial League chapter that was prominent in the 1920s.

43. Ibid., 6–7; Green, *Battling the Plantation Mentality,* 41; Tucker, *Lieutenant Lee,* 129; Doyle, "Gestapo in Memphis," 152; Daniel D. Carter to Walter Chandler, 26 November 1940, folder Negroes Election Data 1940, box 179, ser. 4, Crump Papers.

44. Martin, "Memorandum," 7.

45. The *Globe* is quoted in both Martin, "Memorandum," 8; and Church and Church interview, 10 July 1973, interview no. 3, p. 13.

46. Stuart to Chandler, 1 November 1940, folder Race Relations 1940, box 14, Chandler Papers.

47. Martin, "Memorandum," 3–4; Tucker, *Lieutenant Lee,* 130–31; Melton, "Blacks in Memphis," 196–97; Green, *Battling the Plantation Mentality,* 39.

48. Green, *Battling the Plantation Mentality,* 41; Martin, "Memorandum," 9–10.

49. I have not been able to find the specific dates when Martin and Robert and Annette Church left Memphis. Elmer Atkinson also left the city and sold his business. Martin to George M. Klepper, 18 April 1942, folder 19, box 7, Church Family Papers; Lee interview, 17 April 1966, pp. 34–37 (quote 35); Green, *Battling the Plantation Mentality,* 41; Melton, "Blacks in Memphis," 195, 235 n. 30; Church and Church, *Robert R. Churches,* 182.

50. Ottley, "Memphis Row."

51. Church apparently helped Martin with his 1942 race. Ibid.; Benjamin L. Hooks and Jerry Guess, *The March for Civil Rights: The Benjamin Hooks Story* (Chicago: American Bar Association, 2003), 46; Church and Church, *Robert R. Churches,* 182; "Memphians Witness Inaugural Ceremony for Dr. J. B. Martin," *ADW,* 10 December 1946.

52. Ottley, "Memphis Row"; "Both Races Reported Disturbed," *ADW;*

Church and Church, *Robert R. Churches,* 184; Martin, "Memorandum"; Church and Church interview, 10 July 1973, interview no. 1, pp. 11–12; Church to George W. Lee, 9 February 1948, folder 41, box 6, Church to Carroll Reece, 29 February 1944, folder 4, box 8, Church to James R. Wright, 26 October 1943, folder 27, box 7, and Marie Wathen to Church, 31 October 1943 and 12 March 1944, and Matthew Thornton to Church, 10 June 1943, folder 1, box 7, Church Family Papers.

53. Martin to Church, 20 March 1941, folder 12, box 7, Church Family Papers.

54. Martin to Church, 25 March 1941, folder 12, box 7, Church Family Papers.

55. Thornton to Church, 10 June 1943, folder 1, box 7, and Church to Wright, 26 October 1943, folder 27, box 7, Church Family Papers.

56. Church to Wright, 26 October 1943, folder 27, box 7, Church Family Papers.

57. Walker, "Role of Black Clergy," 31.

58. Lymon interview, pp. 23–24. See also Honey, *Black Workers Remember,* 77, 138.

59. Weathers interview, p. 29.

60. Lymon interview, pp. 24–26.

61. Ibid., 24. See also Robert R. Church to James R. Wright, 18 November 1943, p. 3, folder 27, box 7, Church Family Papers.

62. Blair T. Hunt, interview by Ronald Anderson Walter, Memphis, 8 September 1976, transcript, p. 18, Cook Collection, MSC.

63. Martin to Klepper, 18 April 1942, folder 19, box 7, Church Family Papers; US Department of Justice, transcript of deposition of J. B. Martin, pp. 1–10, 26–27. See also Church and Church interview, 10 July 1973, interview no. 3, pp. 1–5; and Lee interview, 17 April 1966, pp. 37, 39.

64. Tucker, *Lieutenant Lee,* 131–33 (quote 131); Green, *Battling the Plantation Mentality,* 43; Lee to Crump, 19 November 1940, folder 1940—Public Improvements for Colored Citizens, box 13, Chandler Papers.

65. Tucker, *Lieutenant Lee,* 123, 131, 133.

66. Crawford, "Interview with Lonnie Briscoe," 21.

67. Honey, *Black Workers Remember,* 65; Tucker, *Lieutenant Lee,* 155; Lymon interview, 25–26; Melton, "Blacks in Memphis," 225, 265, 320; Dowdy, "'We Engaged in a Hard Campaign'"; "At a Meeting Held . . . April 22, 1944," 1944, folder 11: Election Misc. 1944, box 19, Hale Papers; Key, *Southern Politics,* 73; Woodbury to Church, 15 April 1986, folder 19, box 1, Roberta Church Papers; "Lt. Lee Responsible for Packed GOP Meeting," *MPS,* 6 February 1952, vertical file George W. Lee, MSC; Church and Church, *Robert R. Churches,* 227–28.

68. Walker, "Role of Black Clergy," 33; Mary E. Murphy and Jennie S.

Broadnax to Chandler, 1 August 1942, folder Negroes 1942, box 39, Chandler Papers; Marie L. Adams et al. to Chandler, 3 February 1945, folder Negroes 1945, box 79, Chandler Papers; DeCosta-Willis, *Notable Black Memphians,* 308. On the Mayor of Beale Street contest, see "Mayor Chandler Commissions Beale St. Mayor," *ADW,* 16 August 1940, 1; and "Americanism Day on Beale Draws 500 to Church Park," *ADW,* 16 August 1940, 2.

69. Memphis Negro Chamber of Commerce and Housewives League to White Rose Laundry-Cleaners, 5 October 1942, folder Negroes 1942, box 39, Chandler Papers.

70. See L. J. Searcy to Chandler, 13 October 1942, and Walter Chandler to Walter Klyce and Arnold Klyce, 6 October 1942, folder Negroes 1942, box 39, Chandler Papers. For more on this matter, see Green, *Battling the Plantation Mentality,* 63–64.

71. Walker to E. W. Hale, 1 May 1944, and Walker to Walter Chandler, 20 April 1944, folder Negroes 1944, box 66, Chandler Papers; "Named Chairman of Democratic Club," *ADW,* 13 August 1937, 3.

72. "Dr. Walker Resigns Political Club Office," *ADW,* 17 May 1944, 2.

73. George W. Lee, interview by Aaron Boom, Memphis, 19 May 1966, transcript, pp. 1–2, UMOH; Melton, "Blacks in Memphis," 251.

74. George W. Lee, interview by Aaron Boom, Memphis, 17 May 1966, transcript, p. 18, UMOH.

75. See, e.g., Fuller to Crump, 8 January 1942, mfm 002378, and Fuller to Crump, 23 March 1942, mfm 002372, folder "Fu" 1942, box 192, ser. 4, Crump Papers.

76. Fuller to Crump, 16 April 1942, mfm 002368, folder "Fu" 1942, box 192, ser. 4, Crump Papers.

77. Fuller to Crump, 9 March 1942, mfm 002375, folder "Fu" 1942, box 192, ser. 4, Crump Papers.

78. Fuller to Crump, 23 April 1942, vertical file T. O. Fuller, MSC.

79. "Dr. T. O. Fuller, Negro Leader, Son of Slave Parents, Dies," *CA,* 22 June 1942, vertical file T. O. Fuller, MSC.

80. Pink Palace Museum, *Historic Black Memphians,* 13; DeCosta-Willis, *Notable Black Memphians,* 181–83; Hunt, *Repossessing Ernestine,* esp. 12–13, 49; Williams interview; Ada Gilkey, "$650 Investment Inspired by 33-Year-Old Failure," *MPS,* 26 March 1947, Perre Magness, "Hunt Gave Blacks a Political 'Ear,'" *CA,* 14 February 1991, and Mantri Sivanada, "Blair T. Hunt: A Resourceful and an Illustrious Black Memphian 1887–1976," January 2000, vertical file Blair Hunt, MSC.

81. Hunt, *Repossessing Ernestine,* 13; Maxine Smith, interview by author, Memphis, 26 June 2007, typed notes in author's possession.

82. See, e.g., E. W. Hale to Hunt, 27 December 1944, Hunt to E. W. Hale, 8 November 1944, and Hunt to E. W. Hale, 2 August 1946, folder 13,

box 32, Hale Papers. See also Hunt and Earl Allen to Crump, 21 December 1933, mfm 001509, and Crump to Hunt, 5 January 1934, mfm 001508, folder Greetings 1934, box 59, ser. 2, Crump Papers.

83. Hunt to Walter Chandler, 22 May 1942, folder Negroes 1942, box 39, Chandler Papers.

84. Hunt to E. W. Hale, 30 October 1944, folder 12, box 19, Hale Papers; Hunt to Walter Chandler, 30 October 1944, and Hunt, "Cold Facts and Figures on Why Negroes Should Vote for President Roosevelt," 1944, folder 1944 Presidential Campaign, box 66, Chandler Papers.

85. Magness, "Hunt Gave Blacks a Political 'Ear.'"

86. Chandler to Kemper G. McComb, 28 July 1943, folder Negroes 1943, box 52, Chandler Papers.

87. See, e.g., George W. Lee to Chandler, 11 December 1940, Chandler to T. O. Fuller Jr., 10 June 1940, T. O. Fuller Jr. to Chandler, 8 June 1940, and J. L. Campbell to Chandler, 11 September 1940, folder 1940—Public Improvements for Colored Citizens, box 13, Chandler Papers.

88. Chandler to Thornton, 10 June 1940, and Lewis O. Swingler to Chandler, 31 July 1940, folder 1940—Public Improvements for Colored Citizens, box 13, Chandler Papers.

89. This assessment is based on my review of numerous documents in the Chandler Papers.

90. Doyle, "Gestapo in Memphis," 152.

91. Honey, *Southern Labor,* 204.

92. B. E. Booth to Chandler, 11 September 1942, folder Negroes 1942, box 39, Chandler Papers.

93. Mrs. E. C. Felts to Chandler, 24 September 1942, S. Toof Brown to Chandler, 22 September 1942, anonymous to Draft Board, 17 September 1942, and "From several weman [*sic*] of city" to Chandler, 20 September 1942, folder Negroes 1942, box 39, Chandler Papers; Green, *Battling the Plantation Mentality,* 92.

94. Honey, *Southern Labor,* 145–47; Benjamin Quarles, "A. Philip Randolph: Labor Leader at Large," in Bond and Lewis, eds., *Gonna Sit at the Welcome Table,* 136; Louis Kesselman, *The Social Politics of FEPC: A Study in Reform Pressure Movements* (Chapel Hill: University of North Carolina Press, 1948), 93–94.

95. Honey, *Southern Labor,* 177–82; Green, *Battling the Plantation Mentality,* 49, 50–51, 56, 61–62.

96. Honey, *Southern Labor,* 155–63, 170–71, 209; Tucker, *Memphis since Crump,* 55; Green, *Battling the Plantation Mentality,* 40.

97. Green, *Battling the Plantation Mentality,* 304 n. 67.

98. Tucker, *Memphis since Crump,* 54–56; Honey, *Southern Labor,* 170, 187–91, 208–9, and *Black Workers Remember,* 49, 132, 134.

99. Honey, *Black Workers Remember,* 132; Green, *Battling the Plantation Mentality,* 79.

100. Honey, *Black Workers Remember,* 63 n. 13, 127, and *Southern Labor,* 203–4; Green, *Battling the Plantation Mentality,* 46, 54, 92; Utillus R. Phillips to Ella J. Baker, 25 October 1944, mfm 19:00785, folder Tennessee State Conference, 1944–47, box C187, Group 2, NAACP Papers; E. B. Cowan, forward to "Souvenir Booklet and Program: Third Annual Conference N.A.A.C.P. Branches of Tennessee," 14 July 1949, mfm 19:00061, folder Tennessee State Conference, 1948–50, box C187, Group 2, NAACP Papers.

101. Green, *Battling the Plantation Mentality,* 152–54; A. B. Clapp to Walter Chandler, 3 October 1942, folder Negroes 1942, box 39, Chandler Papers; Gilmore, *Defying Dixie,* 373.

102. In addition to Sheriff Oliver Perry and Attorney General Gerber, the Crump lieutenants were E. W. Hale, the Shelby County Commission chairman; Joe Boyle, the city commissioner; and Charles Cabtree, the county attorney. Anonymous Report of Meeting of Black Leaders with Crump Lieutenants, n.d., pp. 1–2, folder 1, box 7, Church Family Papers; Tucker, *Lieutenant Lee,* 140–41; Green, *Battling the Plantation Mentality,* 74; Walker, "Role of Black Clergy," 46.

103. "Notes on Telephone Call from A. Philip Randolph, Monday, November 29, 1943," 1943, mfm 23:00846, folder Randolph A. Philip, 1942–55, box A507, Group 2, NAACP Papers; Tucker, *Lieutenant Lee,* 141; Green, *Battling the Plantation Mentality,* 74–75; A. Philip Randolph, "Speech at Memphis, Tennessee, First Baptist Church," 31 March 1944, pp. 1–2, folder 44, box 4, Church Family Papers; "William Green and the Memphis Free Speech Meeting," *Black Worker* 10, no. 5 (April 1944): 4; "Randolph Denounces Crump Machine in Memphis," press release, n.p., 10 November 1943, Green to Randolph, 17 January 1944, and Randolph to R. R. Church, 24 January 1944, folder 1, box 7, Church Family Papers.

104. Church to Roy Wilkins, 15 March 1944, folder 1, box 7, Church Family Papers. See also Church to Wright, 18 November 1943, Church to Wilkins, 15 March 1944, and R. R. Church to Roy Wilkins, 22 March 1944, folder 28, box 3, Church Family Papers; Walter White to Cordell Hull, 3 December 1943, mfm 23:00850, folder Randolph A. Philip, 1942–55, box A507, Group 2, NAACP Papers; "Notes on Telephone Call," 1943; and Randolph to Church, 10 March 1944, Randolph to Church, 24 November 1943, Church to Marshall Field, 24 November 1943, Church to Randolph, 20 December 1943, Wilkins to Francis Biddle, 23 March 1944, and Wilkins to Church, 23 March 1944, folder 1, box 7, Church Family Papers.

105. The senator was William Langer (R-ND). See *Congressional Record,* Friday, November 26, 1943, 10093. See also Church to Field, 24 November

1943, and Church to Marshall Field, 18 December 1943, folder 1, box 7, Church Family Papers.

106. Lee to Church, 23 March 1944, folder 41, box 6, Church Family Papers. See also Fay Young, "Randolph Speaks; Defies 'Boss' Crump," *CD*, 8 April 1944, 1.

107. Randolph to Church, 24 November 1943, folder 1, box 7, Church Family Papers.

108. L. J. Sullivan to Chandler, 23 November 1943, folder Negroes 1943, box 52, Chandler Papers; Tom C. Clark to Randolph, 27 November 1943, and Randolph to Francis Biddle, 10 March 1944, folder 1, box 7, Church Family Papers.

109. Lane to Chandler, n.d. (received 22 November 1943), folder Negroes 1943, box 52, Chandler Papers. For an analysis of the international dimension of the Randolph controversy, see Green, *Battling the Plantation Mentality*, 74–76.

110. Beale Avenue Baptist Church was also known as First Baptist Church and Beale Street Baptist Church. Young, "Randolph Speaks" (quote); Green, *Battling the Plantation Mentality*, 75; Honey, *Southern Labor*, 206; Church and Church, *Robert R. Churches*, 187; "William Green," *Black Worker;* untitled newspaper clipping, 6 April [1944 or 1945], folder 1, box 7, Church Family Papers.

111. Randolph, "Speech at Memphis," 6–11 (quotes 7–8, 6, 6–7, 8, 10).

112. Church and Church, *Robert R. Churches*, 186.

113. Randolph, "Speech at Memphis," 7, 10–11.

114. Ibid., 16.

115. Ibid., 15–16, 18–19, 21 (quotes 18, 15, 18, 18, 21).

116. Sarah Wilkerson-Freeman, "The Second Battle for Woman Suffrage: Alabama White Women, the Poll Tax, and V. O. Key's Master Narrative of Southern Politics," *Journal of Southern History* 68, no. 2 (May 2002): 333–74; Gilmore, *Defying Dixie*, 336–41; Randolph, "Speech at Memphis," 18; G. Wayne Dowdy, "General Correspondence 1925–1954," p. xv, finding aid to Crump Papers, Crump Papers.

117. Randolph to Church, 12 April 1944, folder 44, box 4, Church Family Papers.

118. Robert J. Norrell, *Reaping the Whirlwind: The Civil Rights Movement in Tuskegee,* rev. ed. (Chapel Hill: University of North Carolina Press, 1998); Sullivan, *Days of Hope,* 116; Lawson, *Black Ballots,* 66; "Message to the Republican and Democratic Conventions; From the Negroes of America!" *NYT,* 24 June 1944, folder 11, box 19, Hale Papers.

119. Green, *Battling the Plantation Mentality,* 75–76 (quote 76).

120. Randolph to Church, 12 April 1944, folder 44, box 4, Church Family Papers.

121. Randolph to Crump, 6 April 1944, folder 1, box 7, Church Family Papers.

122. News release, n.p., 24 April 1944, folder 1, box 9, Church Family Papers.

123. Honey, *Southern Labor*, 206; "Negro-Baiting in Memphis Laid to Police," newspaper clipping, 16 June 1944 (quote), mfm 23:00872, folder Randolph, A. Philip, 1942–55, box A507, Group 2, NAACP Papers.

124. "Negro-Baiting," 1944; Gilmore, *Defying Dixie*, 315.

125. Green, *Battling the Plantation Mentality*, 76–77.

126. Tucker, *Lieutenant Lee*, 142–43; Honey, *Southern Labor*, 206; Walker, "Role of Black Clergy," 47; Tucker, *Black Pastors and Leaders*, 106; "Negro-Baiting," 1944; George W. Lee, "Inside the Memphis Report," program, 14 July 1963, folder 1, box 2, Lee Papers; Church to Long, 10 May 1945, Long to Church, 18 May 1945, Randolph to Church, 26 May 1944, and Long, "Defense of Dr. G. A. Long," Waco, TX, 19–20 February 1947, p. 4, folder 1, box 7, Church Family Papers.

127. James C. Dickerson to R. R. Church, 22 October 1941, folder 10, box 7, Church Family Papers.

128. Church and Church, *Robert R. Churches*, 227–28.

129. Church to Wright, 18 November 1943, folder 28, box 3, Church Family Papers.

130. Church and Church, *Robert R. Churches*, 228; Lee, "Inside the Memphis Report"; Melton, "Blacks in Memphis," 240; Reece to George W. Lee, 8 March 1944, folder 23, box 7, Church Family Papers.

131. Church and Church interview, 10 July 1973, interview no. 3, pp. 23–24; Church and Church interview, 10 July 1973, interview no. 2, p. 20; Church and Church, *Robert R. Churches*, 79–86; Robert R. Church Jr., "Material for the Carnegie Corporation of New York—Requested by Dr. Bunche," [1938?], p. 2, folder 45, box 6, Church Family Papers.

132. Church and Church, *Robert R. Churches*, 80–86; "What Other Editors Say," *Cleveland Call and Post*, 27 August 1949, 4B.

133. Church and Church, *Robert R. Churches*, 83–84; Topping, *Lincoln's Lost Legacy*, 98; Harry S. McAlpin, "Un-Covering Washington: GOP Plans on the Negro," *ADW*, 5 July 1944, 1; Republican Party Platform of 1944, 26 June 1944, Political Party Platforms, American Presidency Project, http://www.presidency.ucsb.edu/ws/?pid=25835; Democratic Party Platform of 1944, 19 July 1944, Political Party Platforms, American Presidency Project, http://www.presidency.ucsb.edu/ws/?pid=29598.

134. Topping, *Lincoln's Lost Legacy*, 97–105.

135. R. R. Church to the Members of the Republican National Committee, 8 January 1945, folder R. R. Church, 1906–1945, box 2, Simmons Papers. See also Ernest E. Johnson, "Dissension Splits Race Ranks of GOP; Breach

Is Widening," *ADW,* 29 October 1944, 1; "Church Says GOP 'Missed the Boat,'" *AA,* 27 January 1945, 15; "GOP Has Not Won since Negroes Quit Party, Church Warns Heads," *ADW,* 28 January 1945, 5.

136. Topping, *Lincoln's Lost Legacy,* 109–11; Church and Church, *Robert R. Churches,* 84–86; "GOP Action on Promises Urged," *ADW,* 7 September 1947, 4; "GOP Leaders Tell Wherry Party Must Put FEP Vote," *ADW,* 1 December 1949, 1.

137. Church and Church interview, 5 January 1973, interview no. 2, pp. 2–3.

138. Telegram, Church to Robert A. Taft, 14 January 1942, folder 1, box 4, Church Family Papers.

139. A. Philip Randolph, forward to Church and Church, *Robert R. Churches,* vi; Louis Lautier, "A. Philip Randolph Blamed for Failure of National FEPC Council," *Cleveland Call and Post,* 17 August 1946, 12B; P. L. Prattis, "Capital Confetti," *PC,* 15 February 1947, 24; "Russell Continues Fight against Negro Civic Advancement," *ADW,* 25 March 1948, 5; Louis Lautier, "Convention Spotlight," *Cleveland Call and Post,* 24 July 1948, 12A; Church and Church, *Robert R. Churches,* 77; Church and Church interview, 10 July 1973, interview no. 2, p. 19. For more on Church's FEPC advocacy, see Church and Church, *Robert R. Churches.*

140. A. Philip Randolph, foreword to Church and Church, *Robert R. Churches,* v.

141. The National Committee to Abolish the Poll Tax was formerly the anti–poll tax committee of the Southern Conference for Human Welfare. Church and Church, *Robert R. Churches,* 78; Church and Church interview, 10 July 1973, interview no. 2, p. 19; Clarence Mitchell, "Clarence Mitchell's Work Bench," *AA,* 3 May 1952, 22K; Virginia Durr to Church, 21 March 1944, Church to Katherine Shryver, 14 May 1945, and Church to Katherine Shryver, 16 May 1945, folder 8, box 8, Church Family Papers. Interestingly, Virginia Durr's grandfather, Josiah Patterson, had been a friend of Church's white grandfather, Colonel Church. When the colonel died, Patterson had become the executor of Church's grandfather's estate and the legal guardian of Church's father. Hollinger F. Barnard, ed., *Outside the Magic Circle: The Autobiography of Virginia Foster Durr* (New York: Simon & Schuster, 1987), 159–60.

142. *Benefits and Opportunities for Colored Citizens of Memphis: Civic Progress 1940–44* (Memphis: City of Memphis, 1944).

143. My analysis is based on the numerous documents pertaining to this booklet in folder Negroes 1944, box 66, and folder Negroes 1945, box 79, Chandler Papers.

144. Chandler to Jesse Cunningham, 17 October 1944, folder Negroes 1944, box 66, Chandler Papers. See also Chandler to E. H. Crump, 21 April 1944, folder Negroes 1944, box 66, Chandler Papers.

145. Walter Chandler, foreword to *Benefits and Opportunities*, i.

146. George S. Schuyler, "Views and Reviews," *PC*, 27 January 1945, folder Negroes 1945, box 79, Chandler Papers; G. Wayne Dowdy, interview by author, Memphis, 7 July 2007, typed notes in author's possession.

147. A. J. Garvy to Chandler, 16 February 1945, folder Negroes 1945, box 79, Chandler Papers.

148. Washburn to Chandler, 18 September 1944, folder Negroes 1944, box 66, Chandler Papers.

149. Stuart to Chandler, 14 February 1945, folder Negroes 1945, box 79, Chandler Papers.

150. Hunt to Chandler, 18 September 1944, and Walker to Chandler, 4 October 1944, folder Negroes 1944, box 66, Chandler Papers.

151. Stuart to Chandler, 31 January 1945, folder Negroes 1945, box 79, Chandler Papers.

152. Schuyler, "Views and Reviews."

153. Hartsfield to Chandler, 15 December 1944, folder Negroes 1944, box 66, Chandler Papers. See also Chandler to Hartsfield, 18 December 1944, folder Negroes 1944, box 66, Chandler Papers.

154. McKaine to Chandler, 12 February 1945, folder Negroes 1945, box 79, Chandler Papers.

155. McKaine to Chandler, 31 January 1945, folder Negroes 1945, box 79, Chandler Papers.

156. McLaurin to Chandler, 14 February 1945, folder Negroes 1945, box 79, Chandler Papers.

157. McLaurin to Chandler, 23 May 1945, folder Negroes 1945, box 79, Chandler Papers.

158. Ibid. On the Crump machine's censorship policy, see Green, *Battling the Plantation Mentality*, 145–63; and Whitney Strub, "Black and White and Banned All Over: Race, Censorship and Obscenity in Postwar Memphis," *Journal of Social History* 40, no. 3 (2007): 685–715.

159. I did not find any record of a response from Chandler. McLaurin to Chandler, 23 May 1945, folder Negroes 1945, box 79, Chandler Papers.

160. Doyle, "Gestapo in Memphis," 152.

161. Klarman, "White Primary Rulings," 55–107, and *From Jim Crow to Civil Rights*; Hine, *Black Victory*; Jennifer Brooks, *Defining the Peace: World War II Veterans, Race, and the Remaking of Southern Political Tradition* (Chapel Hill: University of North Carolina Press, 2004); Moon, *Balance of Power*, 194; Lau, *Democracy Rising*, 132–44; Chandler to Walker, 22 February 1945, and "'New Spirit of Leadership' Dr. Walker Tells Men's Day Audience, Salem Gilfield," unidentified newspaper clipping, n.d., folder Negroes 1945, box 79, Chandler Papers; "Memphis Leader Joins in Petitioning for Anti-Poll Tax Measure to U.S. Senate," *ADW*, 9 May 1944, 4.

5. "A New Day Breaking" in the City and the South

1. Benjamin L. Hooks, interview by author, Memphis, 29 June 2004, typed notes in author's possession; H. T. Lockard, interview by author, Memphis, 13 July 2004, typed notes in author's possession; H. T. Lockard, interview by author, Memphis, 19 July 2004, typed notes in author's possession; Kousser, *Colorblind Injustice,* 146; Hooks, *March for Civil Rights,* 49. For a sampling of the work on the political and civil rights work of women during the postwar era, see Joanne Meyerowitz, ed., *Not June Cleaver: Women and Gender in Postwar America, 1945–1960* (Philadelphia: Temple University Press, 1994); Pamela Tyler, *Silk Stockings and Ballot Boxes: Women and Politics in New Orleans, 1920–1963* (Athens: University of Georgia Press, 1996); Peter J. Ling and Sharon Monteith, eds., *Gender in the Civil Rights Movement* (New York: Garland, 1999); and Vicki L. Crawford, Jacqueline Anne Rouse, and Barbara Woods, eds., *Women in the Civil Rights Movement: Trailblazers and Torchbearers, 1941–1965* (Brooklyn, NY: Carlson, 1990).

2. Klarman, "White Primary Rulings," 107.

3. Matthews and Prothro, *Negroes and the New Southern Politics,* 18, 176; Lawson, *Black Ballots,* 129; Margaret Price, *The Negro Voter in the South* (Atlanta: Southern Regional Council, 1957); Numan V. Bartley, *The New South, 1945–1980* (Baton Rouge: Louisiana State University Press, 1995), 171–75; Harry A. Bailey Jr., ed., *Negro Politics in America* (Columbus: Charles E. Merrill, 1967), 29–30; Moon, *Balance of Power,* 188; Nasstrom, "Down to Now"; John N. Popham, "The Southern Negro: Change and Paradox," *NYT Magazine,* 1 December 1957, 27, 132–33; Holloway, *Politics of the Southern Negro;* Keech, *Impact of Negro Voting;* Klarman, "White Primary Rulings"; Tiffany M. Gill, *Beauty Shop Politics: African American Women's Activism in the Beauty Shop Industry* (Urbana: University of Illinois Press, 2010), 103–4, 109–11; Brown-Nagin, *Courage to Dissent,* 41–58; Lau, *Democracy Rising,* 175–81; Hornsby, *Black Power in Dixie,* 68–85.

4. Honey, *Southern Labor,* 214, 225–26, and *Black Workers Remember,* 133.

5. Honey, *Black Workers Remember,* 134–35, and *Southern Labor,* 235; Barnard, ed., *Outside the Magic Circle,* 186.

6. Michael K. Honey, review of *Battling the Plantation Mentality: Memphis and the Black Freedom Struggle,* by Laurie B. Green, *Journal of Southern History* 74, no. 4 (November 2008): 1023, *Black Workers Remember,* 134, and *Southern Labor,* 227, 233–34, 238; Green, *Battling the Plantation Mentality,* 139, 179–81; Melton, "Blacks in Memphis," 278.

7. John Jasper, "Minority Vote Helped Ruin 'Crump Machine,'" *Washington Afro-American,* 10 August 1948, folder 33, box 5, Church Family Papers; Church and Church interview, 10 July 1973, interview no. 3, p. 13; Green, *Battling the Plantation Mentality,* 81–141.

8. Jasper, "Minority Vote"; Tucker, *Lieutenant Lee,* 143; James Hunter Lane Jr., interview by author, Memphis, 14 July 2004, transcript, p. 7, SOHP.

9. Green, "Battling the Plantation Mentality," 228, and *Battling the Plantation Mentality,* 121; Melton, "Blacks in Memphis," 255.

10. Green, *Battling the Plantation Mentality,* 81–111, 113, 122–31, 129–37, 190; Tucker, *Black Pastors and Leaders,* 102–3, 154; "Nation-Wide Membership Campaign: Membership Status of Tennessee Branches as of November 6, 1947," n.d., mfm 19:00849, folder Tennessee State Conference, 1944–47, box C187, Group 2, NAACP Papers.

11. "Memphis Labor Conference, September 14–19, 1947," n.d., folder 4, box 9, and "Welcome Program and Reception Honoring A. Philip Randolph," 15 September 1947, folder 1, box 7, Church Family Papers.

12. Randolph to Church, 19 September 1947, and Randolph to Church, 16 September 1947, folder 1, box 7, Church Family Papers.

13. Randolph to Church, 19 September 1947, and Randolph to Church, 16 September 1947, folder 1, box 7, Church Family Papers; "Memphis Labor Conference," n.d.; "Welcome Program," 1947.

14. Randolph to Church, 19 September 1947, folder 1, box 7, Church Family Papers.

15. Tucker, *Memphis since Crump,* 40–60; Honey, *Southern Labor,* 248–52; Green, *Battling the Plantation Mentality,* 136–41; Sally Palmer Thomason, "The Three Eds: Memphis 1948," *WTHSP* 52 (1998): 150–58; Samuel B. Hollis, interview by author, Memphis, 14 June 2004, transcript, pp. 2–3; Jimmie W. Farris, interview by author, Memphis, 16 June 2004, tape recording, SOHP; Melton, "Blacks in Memphis," 263.

16. Honey, *Southern Labor,* 248; Melton, "Blacks in Memphis," 264; Key, *Southern Politics,* 58; Evans to Key, 10 November 1949, p. 14, folder Comments 1 of 2, box 58, V. O. Key Papers, Kennedy Library; Joseph H. Riggs, "Gordon Browning: An Oral Memoir" (Memphis: Memphis Public Library, 1966), 84–86, 125, box 16, Cook Collection, MSC.

17. Apparently, Coe was the most influential woman in the group, and her involvement was not publicly known at the time. All the women had graduated from Vassar College; Coe believed that their educational experience outside Memphis had contributed to their willingness to oppose Crump. Previously involved in interracial work, Coe had participated in a local Public Affairs Forum and earned the respect of the *Memphis Press-Scimitar* editor, Ed Meeman. He invited her to join the 1948 group. She had not previously involved herself in political campaigns. Tucker, *Memphis since Crump,* 40–52; James H. White, "Estes, Crump, Coonskin Caps, Etc.—the Colorful '48 Race in Retrospect," *MPS,* 20 March 1962, vertical file 1962 Election, MSC; Hollis interview, p. 3; Frances Coe, interviews by Aaron Boom, Memphis, 16, 20, 23 December 1965, transcript, pp. 21–22, UMOH (because the

transcript does not specify which parts were recorded on which dates, subsequent references will be to "Coe interview").

18. Tucker, *Memphis since Crump,* 40–50, 56; Evans to Key, 10 November 1949, pp. 14–15, folder Comments 1 of 2, box 58, V. O. Key Papers, Kennedy Library.

19. Coe interview, pp. 23–24.

20. Tucker, *Memphis since Crump,* 54, 56; Key, *Southern Politics,* 73–74; Coe interview, p. 25; "Labor Vote Estimate High, Crump Asserts," *CA,* 9 November 1944, mfm 002090, folder Election Data 1943, box 192, ser. 4, Crump Papers; Honey, *Southern Labor,* 231.

21. Honey, *Southern Labor,* 249–51.

22. Honey, *Black Workers Remember,* 129.

23. Jasper, "Minority Vote"; Melton, "Blacks in Memphis," 265; Honey, *Southern Labor,* 249; Green, *Battling the Plantation Mentality,* 137–38; Coe interview, p. 24; George W. Lee to R. R. Church, 25 July 1951, folder 41, box 6, Church Family Papers; Hunt to E. W. Hale, 14 May 1948, folder 13, box 32, Hale Papers; Hollis Price, interview by Marjean Kremer and Selma Price, Memphis, 1 September 1978, transcript, Lewis Collection, MSC.

24. Democratic Party Platform of 1948, 12 July 1948, Political Party Platforms, American Presidency Project, http://www.presidency.ucsb.edu/ws/?pid=29599. On the 1948 election and Truman's civil rights program, see Kari Frederickson, *The Dixiecrat Revolt and the End of the Solid South, 1932–1968* (Chapel Hill: University of North Carolina Press, 2001); Bartley, *New South,* 74–104; Key, *Southern Politics,* 58–59, 70–75; Tucker, *Memphis since Crump,* 40–60; Topping, *Lincoln's Lost Legacy,* 118–39; and Steven F. Lawson, ed., *To Secure These Rights: The Report of Harry S Truman's Committee on Civil Rights* (Boston: Bedford/St. Martin's, 2004).

25. Shelby County Democratic Executive Committee, Resolution against Truman and His Civil Rights Program, [1948], folder 27, box 9, Overton Papers, SC.

26. Coe interview, p. 23.

27. Tucker, *Memphis since Crump,* 50, 53; Key, *Southern Politics,* 68; Riggs, "Gordon Browning," 87; Coe interview, pp. 5–6, 26–27, 32–33; "News of Bygone Days: 25 Years Ago, July 12, 1948," *CA,* 12 July 1973, and "News of Bygone Days: 25 Years Ago, July 13, 1948," *CA,* 13 July 1973, vertical file 1948 Election, MSC.

28. Coe interview, p. 24; Estes Kefauver, "How Boss Crump Was Licked," *Colliers,* 16 October 1948, excerpts reprinted in Church and Church, *Robert R. Churches,* 191–94; Key, *Southern Politics,* 64; Tucker, *Memphis since Crump,* 58; Honey, *Southern Labor,* 249; Jasper, "Minority Vote."

29. Jasper, "Minority Vote."

30. Tucker, *Memphis since Crump,* 58–59; Honey, *Black Workers Remem-*

ber, 130; Kefauver, "How Boss Crump Was Licked"; Honey, *Southern Labor,* 249; Key, *Southern Politics,* 62; Melton, "Blacks in Memphis," 264.

31. Jasper, "Minority Vote."

32. Church to Kefauver, 6 November 1948, folder 11, box 7, Church Family Papers. See also Church and Church, *Robert R. Churches,* 191.

33. Lee interview, n.d., p. 7; Wilson interview.

34. Honey, *Black Workers Remember,* 155–56.

35. Green, *Battling the Plantation Mentality,* 109; Walk, *History of African-Americans,* 29–33; Melton, "Blacks in Memphis," 261–62, 269, 300; Tucker, *Memphis since Crump,* 59. For praise from black Memphians on Overton's return to office, see, e.g., Mimmie Smith to Overton, 17 January 1949, folder 21, box 6, and S. A. Owen to Overton, 14 January 1949, folder 23, box 6, Overton Papers, SC.

36. Green, *Battling the Plantation Mentality,* 140; Melton, "Blacks in Memphis," 265–66.

37. Topping, *Lincoln's Lost Legacy,* 106, 110–11, 113–15, 125–26, 132, 138, 203; Melton, "Blacks in Memphis," 262–63, 266; Louis Lautier, "Divided GOP," *ADW,* 10 April 1946, 1.

38. Republican Party Platform of 1948, 21 June 1948, Political Party Platforms, American Presidency Project, http://www.presidency.ucsb.edu/ws/?pid=25836; Robert R. Church Jr., "Material Requested by Mr. Clarence Kelly for Thesis," [1952?], p. 2, folder 45, box 6, Church Family Papers.

39. Green, *Battling the Plantation Mentality,* 100, 107–8, 127, 139; Honey, *Southern Labor,* 203, 249–51, and *Black Workers Remember,* 235; Melton, "Blacks in Memphis," 267–68; Topping, *Lincoln's Lost Legacy,* 132. For more on Henry Wallace's campaign, see Patricia Sullivan, "Henry Wallace's Campaign Foreshadowed the Movement as Well as the Rainbow," *Southern Changes* 10, no. 5 (1988): 11, 16–17.

40. Honey, *Southern Labor,* 251.

41. Korstad, *Civil Rights Unionism,* 306–10; Robert Korstad and Nelson Lichtenstein, "Opportunities Found and Lost: Labor, Radicals, and the Early Civil Rights Movement," *Journal of American History* 75, no. 3 (December 1988): 786–811.

42. Melton, "Blacks in Memphis," 266–67.

43. Jones made this statement in the *Memphis World.* Green, *Battling the Plantation Mentality,* 140; Melton, "Blacks in Memphis," 266.

44. Shortly after the election, Kyle moved away from Memphis, having been transferred to another congregation. Honey, *Southern Labor,* 251; Jalenak, "Beale Street Politics," 142–43.

45. Moon, *Balance of Power,* 156–65; Christopher Silver and John V. Moeser, *The Separate City: Black Communities in the Urban South, 1940–1968*

(Lexington: University Press of Kentucky, 1995), 59–60; Shockley, *We, Too, Are Americans: African American Women in Detroit and Richmond, 1940–54* (Urbana: University of Illinois Press, 2004), 126.

46. Topping, *Lincoln's Lost Legacy*, 158.

47. For a statement on Randolph's philosophy of direct action, see Randolph to Robert R. Church, 12 April 1949, folder 4, box 9, Church Family Papers.

48. Harry S. Truman, "Executive Order 9980—Regulations Governing Fair Employment Practices within the Federal Establishment," 26 July 1948, American Presidency Project, http://www.presidency.ucsb.edu/ws/?pid=78208#axzz2fve1Hv00.

49. Melton, "Blacks in Memphis," 330.

50. Tucker, *Memphis since Crump*, 61. For a personal perspective on black voter manipulation, see Blondale Clady Cross, interview by Paul Ortiz, Memphis, 23 June 1995, transcript, pp. 3–4, 28, BTV.

51. Tucker, *Memphis since Crump*, 63–64, 70 (quotes 63); John Terreo and James E. Montague, "Historical Sketch," finding aid to Civic Research Committee Records, May 2004, SC; Information Sheet on Civic Research Committee, n.d., pp. 1, 4, folder 36, box 4, Ed Meeman Papers, SC; Melton, "Blacks in Memphis," 315.

52. Tucker, *Memphis since Crump*, 61–62, 65–66, 69–71; Civic Research Committee, "Why Every Citizen Should Be a Member of CRC," brochure, n.d., folder 38, box 4, Meeman Papers.

53. Valien, "Expansion of Negro Suffrage," 364; Tucker, *Memphis since Crump*, 65; Melton, "Blacks in Memphis," 279, 324. For more on the elimination of the poll tax, see Valien, "Expansion of Negro Suffrage," 365; Melton, "Blacks in Memphis," 314–15.

54. Coe interview, 29; Melton, "Blacks in Memphis," 314; Tucker, *Memphis since Crump*, 59, 65.

55. Harte, "Memo to Commissioner Andrews," 30 May 1950, folder 39, box 2, Overton Papers, SC.

56. Ibid.; Harte to Hayes, 2 August 1950, folder 18, box 6, Overton Papers, SC. See also "Anti Activity 26/2," 1954, mfm 000920, folder Newspaper Clippings, Magazine Articles, 1954, box 308, ser. 4, Crump Papers.

57. Cross interview, 28.

58. Harte to Hayes, 2 August 1950, box 6, Overton Papers, SC. See also Overton to O. P. Williams, 31 March 1950, folder 39, box 2, and "Improvements Asked by Negro Civic Club," *CA*, 12 August 1949, folder 42, box 2, Overton Papers, SC.

59. Melton, "Blacks in Memphis," 280–81, 340.

60. Michael K. Honey, "Labour Leadership and Civil Rights in the South: A Case Study of the CIO in Memphis, 1935–1955." *Studies in History and Politics* 5 (1986): 97–120, *Southern Labor*, 263–77, and *Black Workers Re-*

member, 177–212, 288; Green, *Battling the Plantation Mentality,* 185–89, 213; Melton, "Blacks in Memphis," 279, 298, 300. For more on the East-land hearings, see Honey, *Black Workers Remember,* 213–36; and Barnard, ed., *Outside the Magic Circle,* 254–73.

61. Gloster B. Current to H. T. Lockard, 10 February 1955, folder Memphis NAACP, box C186, Group 2, NAACP Papers; Manfred Berg, "Black Civil Rights and Liberal Anticommunism: The NAACP in the Early Cold War," *Journal of American History* 94, no. 1 (June 2007): 93; "Record of Memberships Sent in and 40th Anniversary Quotas Paid, January 1 to August 15, 1949: Tennessee Branches," n.d., mfm 19:00057, Lucille Black, memorandum to Officers and Delegates—Tennessee State Conference NAACP, 24 August 1950, mfm 19:00037, "Comparative Study of Tennessee Branches: Memberships," n.d., mfm 19:00172, Current to Phillips, 2 November 1950, mfm 19:00166, Phillips to Roy Wilkins, 25 July 1950, mfm 19:00134, Roy Wilkins to Utillus R. Phillips, 16 December 1949, mfm 19:00102, Phillips to Gloster B. Current, 25 October 1950, mfm 19:00167, and Phillips to Roy Wilkins, 7 December 1949, mfm 19:00103, folder Tennessee State Conference, 1948–50, box C187, Group 2, NAACP Papers. See also Lucille Black to Ruby Hurley, 13 August 1951, mfm 19:00215, "Membership Status of Tennessee Branches, May 15, 1952," n.d., mfm 19:00232, and Phillips to Gloster B. Current, 22 May 1952, mfm 19:00259, folder Tennessee State Conference, 1951–55, box C187, Group 2, NAACP Papers.

62. Black, memorandum.

63. E. B. Cowan, "Memorandum to Branch Officers regarding Fifth Annual Conference of NAACP Branches in Tennessee," and "Summary of Minutes—Fifth Annual Conference NAACP Branches in Tennessee," 31 August 1951, mfm 19:00217-9, folder Tennessee State Conference, 1951–55, box C187, Group 2, NAACP Papers.

64. Utillus R. Phillips to Leah I. Brook, 7 February 1950, folder Memphis NAACP 1947–1950, box C185, Group 2, NAACP Papers.

65. Melton, "Blacks in Memphis," 272–77, 308–12; Green, *Battling the Plantation Mentality,* 189–90.

66. Green, *Battling the Plantation Mentality,* 189.

67. H. T. Lockard, interview by author, Memphis, 10 October 2000, transcript, p. 4, SOHP.

68. Hooks, *March for Civil Rights,* 49; Lockard interview, 13 July 2004; Melton, "Blacks in Memphis," 335–36; "Press Release: Local Branch Protests Bombing," 3 July 1953, folder Memphis NAACP 1951–55, box C186, Group 2, NAACP Papers; Utillus R. Phillips, memorandum to Branch Officers, Members and Fellow Citizens re: Annual Membership Campaign and Defense Fund, 27 March 1951, mfm 19:00181, E. B. Cowan, memorandum to Presidents and Secretaries of Tennessee Branches, N A A C P, n.d.

[received at NAACP national office 18 April 1951], mfm 19:00183, and "Resolutions Adopted at the Third Annual Conference of the Tennessee State Conference of Branches, NAACP, Jackson, Tennessee, August 25–6, 1949," n.d., mfm 19:00088, folder Tennessee State Conference, 1951–55, box C187, Group 2, NAACP Papers.

69. These four men were Hollis Price, the president of LeMoyne College; Roy Love, the pastor of Mount Nebo Baptist Church; A. A. Latting, a lawyer; and A. N. Kittrelle, a doctor, minister, and Republican associate of Church. "Negro Leaders Plan Registration Drive," CA, 23 May 1951, 21; Melton, "Blacks in Memphis," 315; Lee to R. R. Church, 12 July 1951, folder 41, box 6, Church Family Papers; "Lt. Lee Responsible for Packed GOP Meeting," MPS, 6 February 1952, vertical file George W. Lee, MSC; "Organizational Plans for Citizens Non-Partisan Voter Registration Campaign for 1962 in Memphis and Shelby County," folder 2, box 1, Russell B. Sugarmon Jr. Papers, SC.

70. Lee interview, 17 May 1966, p. 1.

71. Ibid.; "Lt. Lee Responsible," MPS; Lymon interview, pp. 21–22, 25–26.

72. Lee to Church, 4 June 1951, folder 41, box 6, Church Family Papers.

73. Melton, "Blacks in Memphis," 315–16; Lee interview, 17 May 1966, p. 2; Lee to Church, 28 June 1951, folder 41, box 6, Church Family Papers; "Lt. Lee Responsible," MPS; Tucker, Black Pastors and Leaders, 103–18.

74. Lee to Church, 28 June 1951, folder 41, box 6, Church Family Papers.

75. "Negro Leaders Plan Registration Drive," CA; G. Wayne Dowdy, "'Friends of the Organization': The Political Role of African Americans in Segregated Memphis," 1 July 2003, copy in author's possession.

76. See Lee to Church, 4, 28 June, 12, 25 July, and 7, 10 August 1951, and Church to Lee, 22 June, 6, 17, 24, 30 July, and 9, 13 August 1951, folder 41, box 6, Church Family Papers. Lee also wrote Church on 19 and 21 July 1951, but I have not found copies of these letters.

77. Clark Porteous, "Negro Civic Leader Running for Board of Education," MPS, 27 July 1951, folder 30, box 7, Overton Papers, SC; Kousser, Colorblind Injustice, 146; Melton, "Blacks in Memphis," 317.

78. Hooks, March for Civil Rights, 50.

79. Lee to Church, 10 August 1951, folder 41, box 6, Church Family Papers; Melton, "Blacks in Memphis," 317; Silver and Moeser, Separate City, 86–7; Tucker, Memphis since Crump, 64–65.

80. Hooks, March for Civil Rights, 48–51; H. T. Lockard, interview by author, Memphis, 29 July 2004, transcript, p. 4, SOHP; "Campaign for Walker's Candidacy Gains Momentum," ADW, 28 September 1951, 1. For more on Lockard, see Elizabeth Gritter, "Memories of H. T. Lockard," Southern Cultures 14, no. 3 (Fall 2008): 106–16.

81. Hooks, *March for Civil Rights,* 49, 46–47; Melton, "Blacks in Memphis," 279–80.

82. For a broader look at the new generation of activists across the South that Hooks represented, see Timothy B. Tyson, *Radio Free Dixie: Robert F. Williams and the Roots of Black Power* (Chapel Hill: University of North Carolina Press, 1999); Charles Payne, *I've Got the Light of Freedom: The Organizing Tradition and the Mississippi Freedom Struggle* (Berkeley and Los Angeles: University of California Press, 1991); and John Dittmer, *Local People: The Struggle for Civil Rights in Mississippi* (Champaign: University of Illinois Press, 1995). For a take on generational differences in the North, see Jack Doughtery, *More Than One Struggle: The Evaluation of Black School Reform in Milwaukee* (Chapel Hill: University of North Carolina Press, 2004).

83. Hooks, *March for Civil Rights,* 50; Melton, "Blacks in Memphis," 319.

84. Melton, "Blacks in Memphis," 317. The quote is from Ad for J. E. Walker, "Souvenir Program: The Second Annual Omega Showboat," Omega Psi Psi Fraternity, Inc., 24 September 1951, folder 1, box 4, African-American Culture and Life Collection.

85. Hooks, *March for Civil Rights,* 50–51.

86. "Dr. Walker Appeals for White Support," *CA,* 5 November 1951, 22. See also the flyer for the mass rally sponsored by the Twenty-fifth Ward Civic Club at Bethel A.M.E. Church on 11 October 1951: "Mass Rally," campaign flyer for J. E. Walker, folder 30, box 7, Overton Papers, SC.

87. "Walker to Take Plea to White Memphians," *CA,* 7 October 1951, 7. The quote is from Porteous, "Negro Civic Leader."

88. "Walker to Take Plea to White Memphians," *CA;* "Dr. Walker Appeals for White Support," *CA.*

89. "Walker to Take Plea to White Memphians," *CA.*

90. Melton, "Blacks in Memphis," 316.

91. Ibid., 318–19; Silver and Moeser, *Separate City,* 86; Hooks, *March for Civil Rights,* 49, 51; "Walker Makes Good Showing in Race for School Board Post," *ADW,* 13 November 1951, 2. See also the unissued Watkins Overton, Statement, 27 July 1951, folder 8, box 6, Overton Papers, SC.

92. Melton, "Blacks in Memphis," 319; Nat D. Williams, "Down on Beale," *PC,* 1 December 1951, 24.

93. Lee to Church, 7 August 1951, folder 41, box 6, Church Family Papers; Hooks, *March for Civil Rights,* 50. See also Lee to Church, 25 July and 10 August 1951, folder 41, box 6, Church Family Papers.

94. Melton, "Blacks in Memphis," 317.

95. Kousser, *Colorblind Injustice,* 146.

96. "Honor Roll of Democracy Includes Lt. George W. Lee," *MPS,* 31 December 1951, vertical file George W. Lee, MSC.

97. Mary T. Davis, "Walker's Campaign Hailed as Great 'Moral Victory,'" *ADW,* 13 November 1951, 1.

98. Hooks, *March for Civil Rights,* 51.

99. Dobbs to Church, 12 April 1946, folder 10, box 7, Church Family Papers.

100. Nasstrom, "Down to Now"; Hornsby, *Black Power in Dixie,* xvi, 79, 84.

101. Lymon interview, p. 22; "Council Is Formed by 20 Negro Clubs," *CA,* 9 July 1951, 22; Weathers interview, pp. 28–29.

102. A. A. Branch et al. to Walker, 8 December 1951, folder 29, box 7, Overton Papers, SC.

103. Green, *Battling the Plantation Mentality,* 200–207; "Press Release: Local Branch Protests Bombing," 1953; Wayne Dowdy, "'Something for the Colored People': Memphis Mayor Frank Tobey and the East Olive Bombing," *WTHSP* 51 (1997): 108–15; A. A. Branch et al., letter regarding the Bluff City and Shelby County Council of Civic Club's projects and objectives for 1952, n.d., folder 14, box 4, African-American Culture and Life Collection. For examples of black civic clubs pushing for public service improvements, see Henry F. Picher to O. P. Williams, 21 March 1952, and Henry F. Picher to Overton, 21 March 1952, folder Civic Clubs, 1952, box 32, ser. 2, Overton Papers, MSC.

104. Green, *Battling the Plantation Mentality,* 204; Ellis Moore, "Negroes, Worried about Youth, Present a Nine-Point Program," *CA,* 19 June 1952, "Need Responsibility, Too," *CA,* 22 June 1952, and Ellis Moore, "Some of Negro Parks Are Like Vacant Lots," *CA,* 20 June 1952, folder 14, box 4, African-American Culture and Life Collection.

105. Moore, "Negroes, Worried about Youth."

106. Ellis Moore, "City to Spend Extra $68,000 for Negroes' Play Facilities," *CA,* 21 June 1952, and "Negro Parks Works Lauded by Overton," *CA,* 20 June 1952, folder 14, box 4, African-American Culture and Life Collection.

107. "Negro Parks Works Lauded by Overton," *CA.*

108. Green, *Battling the Plantation Mentality,* 163–82, 206; Louis Cantor, *Wheelin' on Beale: How WDIA-Memphis Became the Nation's First All-Black Radio Station and Created the Sound That Changed America* (New York: Pharos, 1992). For a broad study of black radio, see Brian Ward, *Radio and the Struggle for Civil Rights in the South* (Gainesville: University Press of Florida, 2004).

109. R. R. Church to Guy G. Gabrielson, 7 November 1951, folder 44, box 9, Church Family Papers; Tucker, *Lieutenant Lee,* 155; Melton, "Blacks in Memphis," 320; Tucker, *Memphis since Crump,* 143–44; "Lt. Lee Responsible," *MPS.*

110. Lymon interview, p. 9.

111. Tucker, *Memphis since Crump,* 143; Lewis R. Donelson III, interview by author, Memphis, 25 June 2004, transcript, p. 2, SOHP; "Lt. Lee Responsible," *MPS.*

112. Donelson interview, pp. 7–8, 26, 38–39; Tucker, *Memphis since Crump,* 65, 144; William B. Street, "Lieutenant Lee, the Rise and Fall," *CA,* 3 October 1971, vertical file George W. Lee, MSC; Key, *Southern Politics,* 293–94. For a discussion of the types of white Republicans in the South, see Jack Bass and Walter DeVries, *Transformation of Southern Politics: Social Change and Political Consequence since 1945* (New York: Basic, 1976), 25.

113. Donelson interview, pp. 2–12, 38, 47 (quotes).

114. Ibid., 2–4, 9–11, 26; Tucker, *Memphis since Crump,* 143–51; Tucker, *Lieutenant Lee,* 155–57.

115. Lee, "Inside the Memphis Report."

116. Topping, *Lincoln's Lost Legacy,* 86–87, 106–8, 110–11, 144, 147, 157, 160, 170; Church and Church, *Robert R. Churches,* 221–26, 270–92; Kesselman, *Social Politics of FEPC,* 215–16; Francis P. Douglas, "Empty Room in Senate Building Turned Over to FEPC Lobbyist," *Washington Star,* 31 March 1948, A22, folder Bob Church, 1948, box 247, ser. 4, Crump Papers; "Church Gives GOP Vote Formula," *CD,* 13 August 1949, 3; "GOP Leaders Threaten to Bolt Party in Fight over Dixiecrats," *CD,* 26 May 1951, 1.

117. Tucker, *Memphis since Crump,* 156–57; Melton, "Blacks in Memphis," 320–21; "Lt. Lee Responsible," *MPS.*

118. George W. Lee, interview by Aaron Boom, Memphis, 26 April 1966, transcript, p. 1, UMOH.

119. Ibid., 5–6; Tucker, *Lieutenant Lee,* 155–57.

120. Melton, "Blacks in Memphis," 321, 355–56 n. 69; John Spence, "Miss Church Off to Washington for Talks about Ike's Drive in South," *MPS,* 8 August 1952, folder 3, box 4, Roberta Church Papers; "News of Bygone Days: 25 Years Ago, Oct. 9, 1948," *CA,* 9 October 1973, vertical file 1948 Election, MSC; Lymon interview, pp. 14, 26–27. See also Church to Lee, 17, 24, 30 July, 9, 13 August, folder 41, box 6, Church Family Papers.

121. Melton, "Blacks in Memphis," 321–22; Church and Church interview, 10 July 1973, interview no. 3, pp. 25–27; Tucker, *Lieutenant Lee,* 157; "Thousands Attend Final Rites for Memphis Political Leader," *ADW,* 22 April 1952, 1; Lee, "Inside the Memphis Report"; Topping, *Lincoln's Lost Legacy,* 124–25, 132, 164–70, 180, 182–84; Robert F. Burk, *The Eisenhower Administration and Black Civil Rights* (Knoxville: University of Tennessee Press, 1984), 16. The quote is from Lee interview, 26 April 1966, p. 7.

122. Church and Church, *Robert R. Churches,* 228–29; folder Bob Church, 1948, box 247, ser. 4, Crump Papers.

123. See the discussion of Robert R. Church Sr. in chapter 1. Church and Church interview, 10 July 1973, interview no. 2, pp. 22–23.

124. Church to Lee, 22 June 1951, folder 41, box 4, Church Family Papers.

125. Church subscribed to the *Tri-State Defender*. Church to Browning, 25 October 1951, folder 44, box 9, Church Family Papers.

126. Church and Church, *Robert R. Churches*, 147; Spence, "Miss Church Off to Washington."

127. Lymon interview, p. 7.

128. Lee interview, 26 April 1966, pp. 6–7; Melton, "Blacks in Memphis," 321–22; Lee to Church, 12 November 1951, folder 41, box 6, Church Family Papers; Church and Church, *Robert R. Churches*, 53.

129. Lee interview, 26 April 1966, pp. 7–8.

130. Church and Church, *Robert R. Churches*, 229; L. Alex Wilson, "Bob Church, GOP Head, Dead at 67," *CD*, 26 April 1951, 1; James H. Purdy Jr., "Thousands Came to Pay Their Final Respects to 'Bob' Church," *ADW*, 22 April 1952. See also Burk, *Eisenhower Administration*, 16.

131. For a history and analysis of the Civil Rights Act of 1957, see Lawson, *Black Ballots*, 140–249.

132. Church and Church interview, 10 July 1973, interview no. 2, pp. 15–16.

133. Church and Church interview, 10 July 1973, interview no. 3, pp. 24–25.

134. Wilson, "Bob Church, GOP Head, Dead at 67"; "Thousands Came to Pay Their Final Respects," *ADW*.

135. Church and Church interview, 10 July 1973, interview no. 3, p. 25. The quote is from Randolph to H. F. Patton, 27 May 1952, folder 4, box 9, Church Family Papers.

136. Church had been a life member of the Association for the Study of Negro Life and History and a friend of its founder, Carter G. Woodson. Reprint from *Journal of Negro History* 38, no. 2 (April 1953), folder 41, box 9, Church Family Papers; Church and Church interview, 5 January 1973, interview no. 2, pp. 16–18; Clarence Mitchell to family of Robert R. Church, 21 April 1952, folder 20, box 14, Church Family Papers; "Robert R. Church," *NYT*, 10 April 1952, 15; "Thousands Came to Pay Their Final Respects," *ADW*.

137. Church and Church, *Robert R. Churches*, 293–96; Church and Church interview, 10 July 1973, interview no. 3, pp. 35–36; "The Gentleman from Memphis," *PC*, 3 May 1952, 8; Joseph D. Bibb, "Gaps in GOP," *PC*, 10 May 1952, 9.

138. "Robert R. Church: The Great Republican Died in Memphis Where He Gained Fame," *Memphis Review*, 19 April 1952, 1, folder 9, box 10, Church Family Papers.

139. "Thousands Came to Pay Their Final Respects," *ADW*.

140. Brown to Church, 15 May 1952, folder 3, box 14, Church Family Papers.

141. Green, *Battling the Plantation Mentality*, 263.

142. Church and Church interview, 10 July 1973, interview no. 2, pp. 13–14; Lymon interview, pp. 16–19.

143. Church and Church interview, 10 July 1973, interview no. 2, p. 13.

144. Lymon interview, pp. 16–18 (quotes 17–18).

145. Church to Chauncey McCormick, 5 October 1953, folder 7, box 2, Roberta Church Papers; Crawford, "Interview with Lonnie Briscoe," 21; Tucker, *Lieutenant Lee*, 158.

146. Fitzhugh-Wellford Coalition, "Vote the Eisenhower Ticket," flyer for the 7 August 1952 Republican primary election, folder 2, box 2, Roberta Church Papers. See also "Bob Church's Daughter Out to Defeat Lieut. George Lee," *PC,* 9 August 1952, 19.

147. Church and Church interview, 10 July 1973, interview no. 3, p. 28; Melton, "Blacks in Memphis," 323; Tucker, *Lieutenant Lee,* 158; "A Tribute and Salute to Miss Church," *TSD,* n.d., folder 3, box 4, Roberta Church Papers; Randolph to Patton, 27 May 1952, folder 4, box 9, and Randolph to Church, 19 August 1952, and H. F. Patton to Church, 2 July 1952, folder 2, box 14, Church Family Papers.

148. Melton, "Blacks in Memphis," 324; Beverly Greene Bond, "Roberta Church: Race and the Republican Party in the 1950s," in *Portraits of African American Life since 1865,* ed. Nina Mjagkij (Wilmington, DE: Scholarly Resources, 2003), 187; Church and Church interview, 10 July 1973, interview no. 3, p. 29.

149. Spence, "Miss Church Off to Washington"; Church and Church, *Robert R. Churches,* 232.

150. Church and Church interview, 10 July 1973, interview no. 3, p. 31.

151. Church to McCormick, 5 October 1953, folder 7, box 2, Roberta Church Papers; Pamela Palmer, ed., *The Robert R. Church Family of Memphis: Guide to the Papers with Selected Facsimiles of Documents and Photographs* (Memphis: Memphis State University Press, 1978), 12; Bond, "Roberta Church," 187–95; Toko Schalk Johnson, "Partial List of Who's Who of American Women," *PC,* 3 January 1959, folder 2, box 4, Roberta Church Papers; Handy to Annette Church, 19 December 1956, p. 2, folder 16, box 12, Church Family Papers. For examples of national news coverage of Roberta Church, see Stanley Roberts, "Roberta Church Follows in Footsteps of Father," *PC,* 25 July 1953; William Gordon, "Miss Church, Minority Consultant Studies Employment," *ADW,* 4 May 1954; and "People's Similarities More Important Than Differences, NCC [North Carolina College] Audience Told," *Durham Morning Herald,* 19 February 1956. Copies of these and related articles are in folder 3, box 4, Roberta Church Papers.

152. Tucker, *Lieutenant Lee,* 158–62; Lee interview, 17 April 1966, pp. 43–45.

153. Topping, *Lincoln's Lost Legacy,* 178, 180–82, 186; Tucker, *Lieutenant Lee,* 162–63; Melton, "Blacks in Memphis," 325–26.

154. Lockard termed the Shelby County Democratic Club a "vest-pocket organization" in the early 1950s. Tucker, *Lieutenant Lee,* 162–63; Melton, "Blacks in Memphis," 325–26; Lockard interview, 19 July 2004.

155. Jalenak, "Beale Street Politics," 143; Topping, *Lincoln's Lost Legacy,* 191, 206.

156. Melton, "Blacks in Memphis," 328; Tucker, *Lieutenant Lee,* 163–65; Lee interview, 26 April 1966, pp. 10–11; Lee interview, 17 May 1966, p. 7.

157. Weathers interview, p. 30; Melton, "Blacks in Memphis," 328–29; Bartley, *New South,* 175; Bailey, ed., *Negro Politics in America,* 29–30. On the Kirk appointment, see Dowdy, "'Something for the Colored People.'"

158. Coe interview, pp. 37–38; Tucker, *Memphis since Crump,* 144.

159. Coe interview, p. 37.

160. I did not see any evidence in the Crump Papers to refute Coe's assertion that he ignored the effort. Coe interview, pp. 38–39; Melton, "Blacks in Memphis," 324.

161. "Thousands Pass Bier of Crump," 18 October 1954, *Nashville Tennessean,* mfm 000463, Clark Porteous, "Throngs Pay Their Last Respects to the Memory of E. H. Crump," *MPS,* 19 October 1954, mfm 000481, and James Gunter, "Throng Flows All Day Long around Grave of E. H. Crump," *CA,* 20 October 1954, mfm 000397, folder Obituaries, box 308, ser. 4, Crump Papers.

162. "Mr. E. H. Crump," *Collierville Herald,* 21 October 1954, mfm 000387, folder Obituaries, box 308, ser. 4, Crump Papers.

163. "'Boss' Crump, Who Cleaned Up Memphis but Became 'Benevolent' Dictator, Dies," newspaper clipping, October 1954, mfm 000608, folder Statements, box 309, ser. 4, Crump Papers.

164. Douglas Brinkley, *Rosa Parks* (New York: Viking, 2000), 54, 70; Danielle L. McGuire, *At the Dark End of the Street* (New York: Knopf, 2010), 12, 63; Roberta Church and Ronald Walter, "Mary Church Terrell (1863–1954)," n.d., http://ww2.tnstate.edu/library/digital/terrell.htm.

Conclusion

1. Laurie Sugarmon was later known as Miriam DeCosta-Willis. On this group of leaders, see Sherry L. Hoppe and Bruce W. Speck, *Maxine Smith's Unwilling Pupils: Lessons Learned in Memphis's Civil Rights Classroom* (Knoxville: University of Tennessee Press, 2007); and Elizabeth Gritter, "Local Leaders and Community Soldiers: The Memphis Desegregation Movement, 1955–1961" (senior honors thesis, American University, 2001).

2. Current to Lockard, 10 February 1955, folder Memphis NAACP, box C186, Group 2, NAACP Papers; "Meeting [Minutes] of the Executive Board, Memphis Branch NAACP," Memphis NAACP Branch, 5 May 1959, folder 2, box 3, Maxine Smith Papers, MSC; "Heavy Voting May Set Record," *MPS*, 20 August 1959, 1; DeCosta-Willis, *Notable Black Memphians*, 52–53; Pete Daniel, *Lost Revolutions: The South in the 1950s* (Chapel Hill: University of North Carolina Press for Smithsonian National Museum of American History, 2000), 121–47.

3. Tucker, *Black Pastors and Leaders*, 107–11; DeCosta-Willis, *Notable Black Memphians*, 64–65; Russell B. Sugarmon Jr., interview by author, Memphis, 13 October 2000, transcript, pp. 4–5, SOHP.

4. Nat D. Williams, "Dark Shadows," *TSD*, 8 August 1959, 7.

5. On women's participation in the campaign, see Elizabeth Gritter, "'Women Did Everything Except Run': Black Women's Participation in the 1959 Volunteer Ticket Campaign in Memphis, Tennessee," in *Entering the Fray: Gender, Politics, and Culture in the New South*, ed. Jonathan D. Wells and Sheila R. Phipps (Columbia: University of Missouri Press, 2010), 136–60.

6. "Dr. King Urges Memphians to Elect Negro Candidates," *MW*, 5 August 1959, 1. This article was published in the *Birmingham World* as well, and a copy is in the Martin Luther King Jr. Papers at Boston University. See also Burleigh Hines, "5000 Bury Uncle Toms at Rally," *TSD*, 8 August 1959, 1.

7. "National Interest in Our Election," *MPS*, 20 August 1959, 3; "Can Memphis Negroes Elect City Officials? Unprecedented Six Candidates Entered in August Election," *Jet*, 30 July 1959, 14; "Memphis Could Elect 4 Negroes," *PC*, 15 August 1959, 5; Robert E. Baker, "Memphis Negroes Find Voting Pays," *Washington Post*, 20 September 1959, A8; Trezzvant W. Anderson, "A Tale of Two Cities: The Memphis Story Heralds Race Votes," *PC Magazine*, 21 November 1959, 3; "Negro's Campaign Jars Memphis in Battle for Major City Post," *NYT*, 16 August 1959, 70.

8. Jalenak, "Beale Street Politics," 127–28; William E. Wright, *Memphis Politics: A Study in Racial Bloc Voting*, Eagleton Institute Cases in Practical Politics, no. 27 (New York: McGraw-Hill, 1962), 29–30, 32; Silver and Moeser, *Separate City*, 95.

9. L. F. Palmer Jr., "We Won Everything but the Election," *TSD*, 29 August 1959, 9.

10. Sugarmon interview, 13 October 2000, pp. 13–14.

11. Ibid., 14, 16–17, 28–32; Russell B. Sugarmon Jr., interview by author, Memphis, 25 June 2004, typed notes in author's possession; Jalenak, "Beale Street Politics," 16, 53–54, 92–97; Wright, *Memphis Politics*, 34–35; Holloway, *Politics of the Southern Negro*, 284–86; "Memphis Democrats Elect Negro," *NYT*, 6 August 1960, 8.

12. Gritter, "Local Leaders," 41–42, 47–74; Green, *Battling the Plantation Mentality*, 226, 232–50; Lucille Black to Maxine Smith, 19 May 1960, folder Memphis NAACP 1960, box C186, Group 3, NAACP Papers; Hoppe and Speck, *Maxine Smith's Unwilling Pupils;* Benjamin Muse, *Memphis* (Atlanta: Southern Regional Council, 1964), 7–8, 12, 45.

13. Green, *Battling the Plantation Mentality*, 217, 226–31; Lorene Thomas, "Annual Report of Branch Activities, 1960," Memphis NAACP Branch, n.d., mfm 17:00373, folder Tennessee, 1956–1965, box C194, Group 3, NAACP Papers; Lockard interview, 10 October 2000, pp. 21–23; Maxine Smith, interview by author, Memphis, 26 July 2004, transcript, pp. 22–24, 41, SOHP; US Commission on Civil Rights, "Civil Rights Calendar—July 16 to 31, 1963," Berl Bernhard Papers, Kennedy Library; Russell B. Sugarmon Jr., interview by author, Memphis, 30 July 2004, typed notes in author's possession; Hugh T. Love, "Special Report," 14–16 October 1964, and E. V. Braswell for the Citizen's Committee of Fayette County to A. W. Willis Jr. of Tennessee Voter's Council, 26 September 1964, Russell B. Sugarmon Jr. Personal Papers, Memphis, TN; "About the Tennessee Voters Council," [1964], folder 9: Tennessee Voters Council, 1964–1967, box 3, Sugarmon Papers. For a study of the long black freedom struggle in Haywood County, see Richard A. Couto, *Lifting the Veil: A Political History of Struggles for Emancipation* (Knoxville: University of Tennessee Press, 1993). See also Robert Hamburger, *Our Portion of Hell: Fayette County, Tennessee: An Oral History of the Struggle for Civil Rights* (New York: Links, 1973).

14. George W. Lee, "Inside the Memphis Report," program, 14 July 1963, folder 1, box 2, Lee Papers; Elizabeth Gritter, "'This Is a Crusade for Freedom': The Volunteer Ticket Campaign in the 1959 City Election in Memphis, Tennessee" (master's thesis, University of North Carolina at Chapel Hill, 2005), 66–67; Tucker, *Memphis since Crump*, 149–50; Jennie M. Betts, interview by author, Memphis, 28 June 2004, transcript, p. 36, SOHP.

15. "Analysis of the Negro Votes in Shelby County Received by Democratic Nominees, November 3, 1964," [1964], folder 7, box 1, Sugarmon Papers; Tucker, *Memphis since Crump*, 145, 149; Scott, *Negro in Tennessee Politics*, 187–95; Norman L. Parks, "Tennessee Politics since Kefauver and Reece: A 'Generalist' View," *Journal of Politics* 28, no. 1 (February 1966): 144–68; Maxine A. Smith, "Annual Report of Memphis Branch NAACP, 1964," 23 December 1964, folder Memphis NAACP 1963 to 1965, box C146, Group 3, NAACP Papers.

16. William Thomas, "Moment of History Lies Buried beneath Ballots," *CA*, 8 November 1964, vertical file Memphis—Elections, 1964, MSC.

17. "Analysis of the Negro Votes," [1964]; "Clement Names Negro Attorney to New Court," *CA*, 12 May 1965, vertical file Benjamin L. Hooks, MSC.

18. John Herbers, "Integration Gains in Memphis; Biracial Leadership Takes Hold," *NYT,* 5 April 1964, Schomburg Clipping Files, University of the District of Columbia, Washington, DC.

19. Muse, *Memphis,* 25, 36–42; Gritter, "'This Is a Crusade,'" 67–68; Smith, "Annual Report of Memphis Branch NAACP, 1964," pp. 8–9. On the NAACP's employment efforts, see, e.g., Maxine A. Smith, "Annual Report Memphis Branch NAACP 1965," 23 December 1965, pp. 11–13, and "Memphis Branch NAACP Annual Report 1967," [1967], pp. 4–8, folder Memphis Branch 1966–69, box C30, Group 4, NAACP Papers. On the efforts of black unionists and antipoverty activists, see Green, *Battling the Plantation Mentality,* 258–75. For a broader study, see Nancy MacLean, *Freedom Is Not Enough: The Opening of the American Workplace* (Cambridge, MA: Harvard University Press, 2006).

20. Smith, "Memphis Branch NAACP Annual Report 1967," 1.

21. Jonathan I. Wax, "Program of Progress: The Recent Change in the Form of Government in Memphis, Part 1," *WTHSP* 23 (1969): 81–109, and "Program of Progress: The Recent Change in the Form of Government in Memphis, Part 2," *WTHSP* 24 (1970): 74–96; Kousser, *Colorblind Injustice,* 173–80; Marcus D. Pohlmann and Michael P. Kirby, *Racial Politics at the Crossroads: Memphis Elects Dr. W. W. Herenton* (Knoxville: University of Tennessee Press, 1996), 111–15.

22. Green, "Battling the Plantation Mentality," 395.

23. Sugarmon interview, 25 June 2004.

24. Gritter, "Local Leaders," 92–93; Kira V. Duke, "'To Disturb the People as Little as Possible': The Desegregation of Memphis City Schools" (master's thesis, University of Tennessee at Knoxville, 2005), 26–32; Smith interview, 9 October 2000, pp. 25–26.

25. Jimmie Covington, "Census Snapshot—Poverty High Despite Gains," *CA,* 29 January 2004, B2; US Census Bureau, Census 2000 Summary Files 3, Memphis, www.census.gov; Chris Peck, "Why a Candidate's Past Matters," *CA,* 30 September 2007, V4.

26. Kousser, *Colorblind Injustice,* 193–95; Pohlmann and Kirby, *Racial Politics;* Walter Leavy, "New Black Mayors Take Charge; 'A New Beginning' in Memphis, a Big Victory in Cincinnati," *Ebony* 47, no. 5 (March 1992): 106–10; Jacinthia Jones, "Herenton Stays Strong in Black Precincts—Chumney, Morris Split Vote in Majority-White Areas," *CA,* 11 October 2007, A1; Tom Charlier, "Memphis Mayor Willie W. Herenton Seized a Record Fifth Term Thursday, but He Won It with His Lowest Support Level Ever," *CA,* 5 October 2007, A1; Jacinthia Jones, "Three-Way Race Provides Plurality for Incumbent," *CA,* 5 October 2007, A1; Blake Fontenay, "Coming Apart at the Polls—Election Results Seen as Crucial—Whoever Wins the Hotly Contested City Races, There Will Be Healing To Do," *CA,* 30 September 2007,

V1; "A Crossroads for Mayor Herenton," *CA,* 6 October 2007, A10; Peck, "Why a Candidate's Past Matters."

27. Pohlmann and Kirby, *Racial Politics,* 179–83, 198, 200; Thomas Jordan, "Voting along Racial Lines a Habit That's Hard to Break," *CA,* 30 June 2002, A1; Sam Dillon, "Merger of Memphis and County School Districts Revives Race and Class Challenges," *NYT,* 5 November 2011.

28. Zack McMillan, "Official Tally Is In: Obama Took 63.4 Percent of Shelby County Vote," *CA,* 17 November 2008.

Bibliography

Primary Sources

Archival Collections

The following abbreviations are used throughout this section:

Kennedy Library   John F. Kennedy Library, Boston
MSC   Memphis–Shelby County Room, Memphis–Shelby
    County Public Library and Information Center
SC   Special Collections Department, Ned McWherter
    Library, University of Memphis

AFL-CIO. Memphis Labor Council Records. SC.
African-American Culture and Life Collection. MSC.
Berl Bernhard Papers. Kennedy Library.
Josephine Burson Papers. MSC.
Walter Chandler Papers. MSC.
Robert R. Church Family Papers. SC.
Roberta Church Collection. MSC.
Civic Research Committee Records. SC.
Civil Rights Division Records of the 1960 Presidential Campaign. Democratic National Committee Papers. Kennedy Library.
Everett R. Cook Collection. MSC.
Edward H. Crump Papers. MSC.
Dedicated Citizens Association Papers. SC.
William Farris Papers. Parrish Library, Southwest Tennessee Community College, Memphis.
Gayoso Collection. MSC.
Goldsmith Papers. MSC.
Erwin Griswold Papers. Special Collections, Harvard Law Library, Boston.
E. W. Hale Papers. MSC.
T. H. Hayes Jr. Papers. MSC.
M. A. Hinds Papers. SC.
Blair T. Hunt Papers. MSC.

Fred Hutchins Papers. SC.

John F. Kennedy Pre-Presidential Papers, 1946–1961. Kennedy Library.

Robert F. Kennedy Attorney General Papers: General Correspondence Series. Kennedy Library.

Robert F. Kennedy Pre-Administration Papers. Kennedy Library.

George W. Lee Papers. MSC.

Selma S. Lewis Collection. MSC.

Henry Loeb III Papers. MSC.

Ed Meeman Papers. SC.

Benjamin Muse Papers. Special Collections, Duke University, Durham, NC.

NAACP Papers. Manuscript Division, Library of Congress, Washington, DC.

NAACP. Microfilm version. Bethesda, MD: University Publications of America, 1982–1995.

Notable Black Memphians—Funeral Programs Collection. SC.

Edmund Orgill Papers. SC.

Watkins Overton Papers. MSC.

Watkins Overton Papers. SC.

James Pleasants Papers. MSC.

Schomburg Clipping Files. University of the District of Columbia, Washington, DC.

Roscoe Conkling Simmons Papers. Harvard University Archives, Boston, MA.

Maxine Smith Papers. MSC.

Ted Sorenson Papers. Kennedy Library.

Russell B. Sugarmon Jr. Papers. SC.

Russell B. Sugarmon Jr. Personal Papers. Memphis, TN.

Howard Thurman Papers. Howard Gotlieb Archival Research Center, Boston University, Boston.

Dr. R. Q. & Ethel H. Venson Cotton Makers Jubilee Collection. MSC.

Vertical File Collection. MSC.

Lee White Papers. Kennedy Library.

A. W. Willis Jr. Papers. MSC.

Interviews

The following abbreviations are used throughout this section:

BTV	Behind the Veil: Documenting African American Life in the Jim Crow South Collection, Special Collections, Duke University
MSC	Memphis–Shelby County Room, Memphis–Shelby County Public Library and Information Center

SOHP   Southern Oral History Program Collection, Southern
                Historical Collection, University of North Carolina at
                Chapel Hill
UMOH   University of Memphis Oral History Research Office
                Collection

Betts, Jennie M. Interview by author. Memphis, 28 June 2004. Transcript.
    SOHP.
Bond, Julian. Interview by author. Birmingham, 6 March 2008. Typed notes
    in author's possession.
Booth, Alma Roulhac. Interview by Charles W. Crawford. Memphis, 11 Sep-
    tember 1991. Transcript. UMOH.
Boyd, Leroy. Interview by Paul Ortiz. Memphis, 19, 22 June 1995. Tran-
    script. BTV.
Brewster, W. Herbert. Interview by Charles W. Crawford. Memphis, 6 July
    1983. Transcript. UMOH.
Burson, Josephine. Interview by author. Memphis, 28 July 2004. Tape re-
    cording. SOHP.
Church, Roberta, and Annette Church. Interviews by Charles W. Crawford.
    Memphis, 4, 5 January, 10 July 1973. Transcripts. UMOH.
Coe, Frances. Interviews by Aaron Boom. 16, 20, 23 December 1965. Tran-
    script. UMOH. The transcript does not specify which parts were recorded
    on which dates.
Cross, Blondale Clady. Interview by Paul Ortiz. Memphis, 23 June 1995.
    Transcript. BTV.
Davis, Fred L. Interview by author. Memphis, 11 October 2000. Transcript.
    SOHP.
Donelson, Lewis R., III. Interview by author. Memphis, 25 June 2004.
    Transcript. SOHP.
Dowdy, G. Wayne. Interviews by author. Memphis, 20 June 2007, 7 July
    2007. Typed notes in author's possession.
Farris, Jimmie W. Interview by author. Memphis, 16 June 2004. Tape re-
    cording. SOHP.
Fisher, John T. Interview by author. Memphis, 16 June 2004. Transcript.
    SOHP.
Fort, Marie. Interview by Charles W. Crawford. Memphis, 23 August 1989.
    Transcript. UMOH.
Hightower, Susie Peebles. Interview by Ronald Anderson Walter. Memphis,
    14 September 1976. Transcript. Everett R. Cook Collection, MSC.
Hollis, Samuel B. Interview by author. Memphis, 14 June 2004. Transcript.
    SOHP.

Holloway, George. Interview by Michael Honey. Baltimore, 23 March 1990. Transcript. BTV.

Hooks, Benjamin L. Telephone interview by author. 11 October 2000. Typed notes in author's possession.

———. Interview by author. Memphis, 29 June 2004. Typed notes in author's possession.

Hunt, Blair T. Interview by Ronald Anderson Walter. Memphis, 8 September 1976. Transcript. Everett R. Cook Collection, MSC.

———. Interview by unidentified individual. N.p., n.d. Transcript. Everett R. Cook Collection, MSC.

Lane, James Hunter, Jr. Interviews by author. Memphis, 15 June, 14 July 2004. Transcripts. SOHP.

Lee, George W. Interviews by Aaron Boom. Memphis, 17, 26 April, 17, 19, 24, 26 May 1966. Transcripts. UMOH.

———. Interview by unidentified individual. N.p., n.d. Transcript. Everett R. Cook Collection, MSC.

Lockard, H. T. Interviews by author. Memphis, 10 October 2000, 29 July 2004. Transcripts. SOHP.

———. Interviews by author. Memphis, 13, 16, 19 July 2004. Typed notes in author's possession.

Loeb, Henry Gregg. Interview by author. Memphis, 21 June 2004. Tape recording. SOHP.

Lymon, L. Raymond. Interview by Charles W. Crawford. Memphis, 6 July 1983. Transcript. UMOH.

Morris, William N., Jr. Interview by author. Memphis, 24 June 2004. Transcript. SOHP.

Patton, William C. Interview by Tywanna Whorley. Birmingham, 14 June 1994. Transcript. BTV.

Peete, Charlie S. Interview by author. Memphis, 22 June 2004. Transcript. SOHP.

Peters, Johnnie Mae. Interview by author. Memphis, 29 June 2004. Transcript. SOHP.

Prewitt, Thomas R., Sr. Interview by author. Memphis, 18 June 2004. Transcript. SOHP.

Price, Hollis. Interview by Marjean Kremer and Selma Lewis. Memphis, 1 September 1978. Transcript. Selma S. Lewis Collection, MSC.

Seigenthaler, John L. Telephone interviews by author. 5 October 2004, 4 October 2007. Typed notes in author's possession.

Shafer, Anne W. Interview by author. Memphis, 28 June 2004. Transcript. SOHP.

Sisson, Thomas E. "Pete." Interview by author. Memphis, 25 June 2004. Transcript. SOHP.

Smith, Maxine A. Interviews by author. Memphis, 9 October 2000, 26 July 2004. Transcripts. SOHP.

———. Interview by author. Memphis, 26 June 2007. Typed notes in author's possession.

Smith, Vasco A. Interviews by author. Memphis, 9, 10, 12 October 2000, 12 July 2004. Transcripts. SOHP. Calvin Turley helped conduct the 9 October interview.

Sugarmon, Russell B., Jr. Interview by author. Memphis, 13 October 2000. Transcript. SOHP.

———. Telephone interviews by author. 10 April 2001, 9, 23 February, 11 March 2005, 7 October 2007. Typed notes in author's possession.

———. Interviews by author. Memphis, 19 June, 30 July 2004. Tape recordings. SOHP.

———. Interviews by author. Memphis, 25 June, 16 July 2004. Typed notes in author's possession.

Turley, Henry. Interview by author. Memphis, 1 August 2004. Typed notes in author's possession.

Turner, Elaine Lee. Interview by Laurie B. Green. Memphis, 22 August 1995. Tape recording. BTV.

Wax, Helen G. Interview by author. Memphis, 17 June 2004. Tape recording. SOHP.

Weathers, Bill. Interview by Marjean Kremer and Selma Lewis. Memphis, 17 May 1978. Transcript. Selma S. Lewis Collection, MSC.

Wheeler, Lillie J. Interview by author. Memphis, 28 June 2004. Transcript. SOHP.

Williams, Nat D. Interview by Ronald Anderson Walter. Memphis, 13 September 1976. Transcript. Everett R. Cook Collection, MSC.

Wilson, Emogene. Interview by Mausiki Stacey Scales. Memphis, 5 July 1995. Tape recording. BTV.

Secondary Sources

Adkins, Walter P. "Beale Street Goes to the Polls." Master's thesis, Ohio State University, 1935.

Alexander, Ann Field. *Race Man: The Rise and Fall of the "Fighting Editor," John Mitchell, Jr.* Charlottesville: University of Virginia Press, 2002.

Allen, Robert S., ed. *Our Fair City.* New York: Vanguard, 1947.

Armstrong, Julie Buckner. *Mary Turner and the Memory of Lynching.* Athens: University of Georgia Press, 2011.

Arnesen, Eric. "Civil Rights and the Cold War at Home: Postwar Activism, Anticommunism, and the Decline of the Left." *American Communist History* 11, no. 1 (2012): 4–44.

———. "The Final Conflict? On the Scholarship of Civil Rights, the Left and the Cold War." *American Communist History* 11, no. 1 (2012): 63–80.

———. "No 'Graver Danger': Black Anticommunism, the Communist Party, and the Race Question." *Labor: Studies in Working-Class Histories of the Americas* 3, no. 4 (2006): 13–52.

Ayers, Edward. *The Promise of the New South: Life after Reconstruction.* New York: Oxford University Press, 1992.

Bailey, Harry A., Jr., ed. *Negro Politics in America.* Columbus: Charles E. Merrill, 1967.

Baker, Paula. "The Domestication of Politics: Women and American Political Society, 1780–1920." In *Unequal Sisters: A Multi-Cultural Reader in U.S. Women's History* (2nd ed.), ed. Vicki L. Ruiz and Ellen Carol DuBois, 85–110. New York: Routledge, 1994. First published in the *American Historical Review* 89 (June 1984): 620–47.

Baker, Thomas Harrison. *The Memphis Commercial Appeal: A History of a Southern Newspaper.* Baton Rouge: Louisiana State University Press, 1971.

Barnard, Hollinger F., ed. *Outside the Magic Circle: The Autobiography of Virginia Foster Durr.* New York: Simon & Schuster, 1987.

Bartley, Numan V. *The New South, 1945–1980.* Baton Rouge: Louisiana State University Press, 1995.

Bass, Jack, and Walter DeVries. *The Transformation of Southern Politics: Social Change and Political Consequence since 1945.* New York: Basic, 1976.

Bates, Beth Tompkins. *Pullman Porters and the Rise of Protest Politics in Black America, 1925–1945.* Chapel Hill: University of North Carolina Press, 2001.

Bay, Mia. *To Tell the Truth Freely: The Life of Ida B. Wells.* New York: Hill & Wang, 2009.

Beifuss, Joan. *At the River I Stand: Memphis, the 1968 Strike, and Martin Luther King.* Brooklyn, NY: Carlson, 1989.

Benefits and Opportunities for Colored Citizens of Memphis: Civic Progress 1940–44. Memphis: City of Memphis, 1944.

Berg, Manfred. "Black Civil Rights and Liberal Anticommunism: The NAACP in the Early Cold War." *Journal of American History* 94, no. 1 (June 2007): 75–96.

———. *The Ticket to Freedom: The NAACP and the African American Right to Vote.* Gainesville: University Press of Florida, 2005.

Berry, Mary Frances. *My Face Is Black Is True: Callie House and the Struggle for Ex-Slave Reparations.* New York: Knopf, 2005.

Biles, Roger. *Memphis in the Great Depression.* Knoxville: University of Tennessee Press, 1986.

———. "Robert R. Church, Jr. of Memphis: Black Republican Leader in the Age of Democratic Ascendancy, 1928–1940." *Tennessee Historical Quarterly* 42 (1983): 362–82.

Blee, Kathleen M. *Women of the Klan: Racism and Gender in the 1920s.* Berkeley and Los Angeles: University of California Press, 1991.

Board of Trade. *Cost of Living in American Towns.* London: Darling & Son, 1911.

Bond, Beverly G. "Every Duty Incumbent upon Them: African American Women in Nineteenth-Century Memphis." In *Trial and Triumph: Essays in Tennessee's African American History,* ed. Carroll Van West, 203–26. Knoxville: University of Tennessee Press, 2002.

———. "Roberta Church: Race and the Republican Party in the 1950s." In *Portraits of African American Life since 1865,* ed. Nina Mjagkij, 181–98. Wilmington, DE: Scholarly Resources, 2003.

Bond, Julian. "Martin Luther King, Jr.—Origins." Paper presented as part of the University of Virginia's Civil Rights South bus tour program, Atlanta, 1 March 2008.

———. "MLK in Memphis." Paper presented as part of the University of Virginia's Civil Rights South bus tour program, Memphis, 13 March 2010. Copy in author's possession.

Bond, Julian, and Andrew Lewis, eds. *Gonna Sit at the Welcome Table.* 2nd ed. New York: American Heritage, 1995.

Bridges, Lamar Whitlow. "Editor Mooney versus Boss Crump." *West Tennessee Historical Society Papers* 20 (1966): 77–107.

Brinkley, Douglas. *Rosa Parks.* New York: Viking, 2000.

Brooks, Jennifer. *Defining the Peace: World War II Veterans, Race, and the Remaking of Southern Political Tradition.* Chapel Hill: University of North Carolina Press, 2004.

Brown, Leslie. *Upbuilding Black Durham: Gender, Class, and Black Community Development in the Jim Crow South.* Chapel Hill: University of North Carolina Press, 2008.

Brown-Nagin, Tomiko. *Courage to Dissent: Atlanta and the Long History of the Civil Rights Movement.* Oxford: Oxford University Press, 2011.

Brundage, W. Fitzhugh. *Lynching in the New South: Georgia and Virginia, 1880–1930.* Urbana: University of Illinois Press, 1993.

———. *The Southern Past: A Clash of Race and Memory.* Cambridge, MA: Belknap Press of Harvard University Press, 2005.

Bunche, Ralph J. *The Political Status of the Negro in the Age of FDR.* Edited by Dewey W. Grantham. Chicago: University of Chicago Press, 1973.

Burk, Robert Fredrick. *The Eisenhower Administration and Black Civil Rights.* Knoxville: University of Tennessee Press, 1984.

Byrd, James W., and David M. Tucker. "Sutton Elbert Griggs." *Handbook of Texas Online,* Texas State Historical Association, 1997–2002. http://www.tshaonline.org/handbook/online/articles/fgr85.

Cantor, Louis. *Wheelin' on Beale: How WDIA-Memphis Became the Nation's*

First All-Black Radio Station and Created the Sound That Changed America. New York: Pharos, 1992.

Capers, Gerald M., Jr. *The Biography of a River Town: Memphis: Its Heroic Age.* Chapel Hill: University of North Carolina Press, 1939.

Caplinger, Christopher. "Conflict and Community: Racial Segregation in a New South City, 1860–1914." Ph.D. diss., Vanderbilt University, 2003.

Cartwright, Joseph H. *The Triumph of Jim Crow: Tennessee Race Relations in the 1880s.* Knoxville: University of Tennessee Press, 1976.

Chafe, William H. *Civilities and Civil Rights: Greensboro, North Carolina, and the Black Struggle for Freedom.* New York: Oxford University Press, 1980.

Chafe, William H., Raymond Gavins, and Robert Korstad, eds. *Remembering Jim Crow: African Americans Tell about Life in the Segregated South.* New York: New Press, 2001.

Cha-Jua, Sundiata Keita, and Clarence Lang. "The 'Long Movement' as Vampire: Temporal and Spatial Fallacies in Recent Black Freedom Studies." *Journal of African American History* 92, no. 2 (2007): 265–88.

Chirhart, Ann Short. *Torches of Light.* Athens: University of Georgia Press, 2005.

Christina, Garna L. "Brownsville Raid of 1906." *Handbook of Texas Online,* Texas State Historical Association, 1997–2002. http://www.tshaonline.org/handbook/online/articles/pkb06.

Church, Annette E., and Roberta Church. *The Robert R. Churches of Memphis.* Ann Arbor, MI: Edwards Bros., 1974.

Church, Roberta, and Ronald Walter. "Mary Church Terrell (1863–1954)." N.d. http://ww2.tnstate.edu/library/digital/terrell.htm.

———. *Nineteenth Century Memphis Families of Color, 1850–1900.* 3rd ed. Edited by Charles W. Crawford. Memphis: Murdock Printing, 2002.

Cochran, Thomas C. "The 'Presidential Synthesis' in American History." *American Historical Review* 53, no. 4 (July 1948): 748–59.

Colburn, David R. *Racial Change and Community Crisis: St. Augustine, Florida, 1877–1980.* New York: Columbia University Press, 1985.

Coleman, Finnie D. *Sutton E. Griggs and the Struggle against White Supremacy.* Knoxville: University of Tennessee Press, 2007.

Couto, Richard A. *Lifting the Veil: A Political History of Struggles for Emancipation.* Knoxville: University of Tennessee Press, 1993.

Crawford, Charles W. "History of the Robert R. Church Family: Interview with Lonnie Briscoe." Memphis: Oral History Research Office, Memphis State University, 1991.

Crawford, Vicki L., Jacqueline Anne Rouse, and Barbara Woods, eds. *Women in the Civil Rights Movement: Trailblazers and Torchbearers, 1941–1965.* Brooklyn, NY: Carlson, 1990.

Dailey, Jane, Glenda E. Gilmore, and Bryant Simon, eds. *Jumpin' Jim Crow: Southern Politics from Civil War to Civil Rights*. Princeton, NJ: Princeton University Press, 2000.

Daniel, Pete. *Lost Revolutions: The South in the 1950s*. Chapel Hill: University of North Carolina Press for the Smithsonian National Museum of American History, 2000.

Dawson, Michael C. "A Black Counterpublic? Economic Earthquakes, Racial Agenda(s) and Black Politics." *Public Culture* 7 (1994): 195–223.

DeCosta-Willis, Miriam. "Between a Rock and a Hard Place: Black Culture in Memphis during the Fifties." In *Memphis: 1948–1958*, ed. J. Richard Gruber, 66–83. Memphis: Memphis Brooks Museum of Art, 1986.

———. *Notable Black Memphians*. Amherst, NY: Cambria, 2008.

Delta Center for Culture and Learning. "The Mound Bayou Story." Cleveland, MS: Delta State University, n.d.

Democratic Party Platform of 1944. 19 July 1944. Political Party Platforms, American Presidency Project. http://www.presidency.ucsb.edu/ws/?pid=29598.

Democratic Party Platform of 1948. 12 July 1948. Political Party Platforms, American Presidency Project. http://www.presidency.ucsb.edu/ws/?pid=29599.

Dittmer, John. *Local People: The Struggle for Civil Rights in Mississippi*. Champaign: University of Illinois Press, 1995.

Doughtery, Jack. *More Than One Struggle: The Evaluation of Black School Reform in Milwaukee*. Chapel Hill: University of North Carolina Press, 2004.

Dowdy, Wayne. "E. H. Crump and the Mayors of Memphis." *West Tennessee Historical Society Papers* 53 (1999): 78–99.

———. "'Friends of the Organization': The Political Role of African Americans in Segregated Memphis." 1 July 2003. Copy in author's possession.

———. *Mr. Crump Don't Like It: Machine Politics in Memphis*. Jackson: University Press of Mississippi, 2006.

———. "Sin in Memphis: Organized Crime and Machine Politics in a Southern City, 1935–1940." In *Crossroads: A Southern Culture Annual*, ed. Ted Olson, 171–93. Macon, GA: Mercer University Press, 2004.

———. "'Something for the Colored People': Memphis Mayor Frank Tobey and the East Olive Bombing." *West Tennessee Historical Society Papers* 51 (1997): 108–15.

———. "'We Engaged in a Hard Campaign': Primary Sources Related to the 1940 and 1944 Presidential Elections in Shelby County." *Tennessee Librarian* 54, no. 1 (2003). Copy in author's possession.

Duke, Kira V. "'To Disturb the People as Little as Possible': The Desegregation of Memphis City Schools." Master's thesis, University of Tennessee at Knoxville, 2005.

Eagles, Charles. "Toward New Histories of the Civil Rights Era." *Journal of Southern History* 66, no. 4 (2000): 815–48.

Egerton, John. *Speak Now against the Day: The Generation before the Civil Rights Movement in the South.* Chapel Hill: University of North Carolina Press, 1995.

Eskew, Glenn T. *But for Birmingham: The Local and National Movements in the Civil Rights Struggle.* Chapel Hill: University of North Carolina Press, 1997.

Fairclough, Adam. *Race and Democracy: The Civil Rights Struggle in Louisiana, 1915–1972.* Athens: University of Georgia Press, 1995.

Farley, John W. *Statistics and Politics.* Memphis: Memphis Linotype Printing Co., 1920.

Ferguson, Jeffrey B. *The Harlem Renaissance: A Brief History with Documents.* Boston: Bedford/St. Martin's, 2008.

Fields, Barbara. "Ideology and Race in American History." In *Race, Region, and Reconstruction: Essays in Honor of C. Vann Woodward,* ed. J. Morgan Kousser and James M. McPherson, 143–77. New York: Oxford University Press, 1982.

———. "Slavery, Race and Ideology in the United States of America." *New Left Review* 181 (1990): 95–117.

"Fleming, Lethia Cousins." *The Encyclopedia of Cleveland History.* http://ech.cwru.edu/ech-cgi/article.pl?id=FLC.

Flournoy, John Craig. "Reporting the Movement in Black and White: The Emmett Till Lynching and the Montgomery Bus Boycott." Ph.D. diss., Louisiana State University, 2003.

Foner, Eric, and Olivia Mahoney. *America's Reconstruction: People and Politics after the Civil War.* New York: HarperPerennial, 1995.

Frantz, Edward O. *The Door of Hope: Republican Presidents and the First Southern Strategy, 1877–1933.* Gainesville: University Press of Florida, 2011.

Frazier, E. Franklin. *Black Bourgeoisie: The Rise of a New Middle Class.* New York: Free Press, 1957.

Frederickson, Kari. *The Dixiecrat Revolt and the End of the Solid South, 1932–1968.* Chapel Hill: University of North Carolina Press, 2001.

Fredrickson, George M. *The Black Image in the White Mind: The Debate on Afro-American Character and Destiny, 1817–1914.* New York: Harper & Row, 1971.

———. *White Supremacy: A Comparative Study in American and South African History.* New York: Oxford University Press, 1981.

Fuller, T. O. *The Story of Church Life among Negroes in Memphis.* Memphis: T. O. Fuller, 1938.

Gaines, Kevin. "The Historiography of the Struggle for Black Equality since 1945." In *A Companion to Post-1945 America,* ed. Jean-Christophe Agnew and Roy Rosenzweig, 211–34. Malden, MA: Blackwell, 2002.

Garrow, David. *Protest at Selma: Martin Luther King, Jr., and the Voting Rights Act of 1965*. New Haven, CT: Yale University Press, 1978.

Gatell, Frank Otto, Paul Goodman, and Allen Weinstein, eds. *Readings in American Political History: A Modern Reader*. New York: Oxford University Press, 1972.

Gatewood, Willard B. *Aristocrats of Color: The Black Elite, 1880–1920*. Fayetteville: University of Arkansas Press, 2000.

Giddings, Paula. *Ida: A Sword among Lions: Ida B. Wells and the Campaign against Lynching*. New York: Amistad, 2009.

———. *When and Where I Enter: The Impact of Black Women on Race and Sex in America*. New York: Morrow, 1984.

Gill, Tiffany M. *Beauty Shop Politics: African American Women's Activism in the Beauty Shop Industry*. Urbana: University of Illinois Press, 2010.

Gillon, Steven M. "The Future of Political History." *Journal of Policy History* 9, no. 2 (1997): 240–53.

Gilmore, Glenda. *Defying Dixie: The Radical Roots of Civil Rights, 1919–1950*. New York: Norton, 2008.

———. *Gender and Jim Crow: Women and the Politics of White Supremacy in North Carolina, 1896–1920*. Chapel Hill: University of North Carolina Press, 1996.

Godshalk, David. *Veiled Visions: The 1906 Atlanta Race Riot and the Reshaping of American Race Relations*. Chapel Hill: University of North Carolina Press, 2005.

Goldfield, David R. *Black, White, and Southern: Race Relations and Southern Culture, 1940 to the Present*. Baton Rouge: Louisiana State University Press, 1990.

———. *Cotton Fields and Skyscrapers: Southern City and Region, 1607–1980*. Baton Rouge: Louisiana State University Press, 1982.

Goodstein, Anita Shafer. "A Rare Alliance: African American and White Women in the Tennessee Elections of 1919 and 1920." *Journal of Southern History* 64, no. 2 (May 1998): 219–46.

Gordon, Ann D., Bettye Collier-Thomas, John H. Bracey, Arlene Voski Arakian, and Joyce Avrech Berkman, eds. *African American Women and the Vote, 1837–1965*. Amherst: University of Massachusetts Press, 1997.

Graham, Hugh Davis. *Crisis in Print: Desegregation and the Press in Tennessee*. Nashville: Vanderbilt University Press, 1967.

Grantham, Dewey. *The Life and Death of the Solid South*. Lexington: University Press of Kentucky, 1988.

Green, Laurie Beth. "Battling the Plantation Mentality: Consciousness, Culture, and the Politics of Race, Class and Gender in Memphis, 1940–1968." Ph.D. diss., University of Chicago, 1999.

———. *Battling the Plantation Mentality: Memphis and the Black Freedom Struggle*. Chapel Hill: University of North Carolina Press, 2007.

Greene, Christina. *Our Separate Ways: Women and the Black Freedom Movement in Durham, North Carolina*. Chapel Hill: University of North Carolina Press, 2005.

Griggs, Sutton E. *Guide to Racial Greatness; or, The Science of Collective Efficiency*. Memphis: National Public Welfare League, 1923.

———. *The Hindered Hand*. Nashville: Orion, 1905.

Gritter, Elizabeth. "Interview with Julian Bond." *Southern Cultures* 12, no. 1 (Spring 2006): 76–91.

———. "Local Leaders and Community Soldiers: The Memphis Desegregation Movement, 1955–1961." Senior honors thesis, American University, 2001.

———. "Maxine A. Smith." In *African American National Biography* (8 vols.), ed. Henry Louis Gates Jr. and Evelyn B. Higginbotham, 7:290–91. New York: Oxford University Press, 2008.

———. "Memories of H. T. Lockard." *Southern Cultures* 14, no. 3 (Fall 2008): 106–16.

———. "'This Is a Crusade for Freedom': The Volunteer Ticket Campaign in the 1959 City Election in Memphis, Tennessee." Master's thesis, University of North Carolina at Chapel Hill, 2005.

———. "'Women Did Everything Except Run': Black Women's Participation in the 1959 Volunteer Ticket Campaign in Memphis, Tennessee." In *Entering the Fray: Gender, Politics, and Culture in the New South*, ed. Jonathan D. Wells and Sheila R. Phipps, 136–60. Columbia: University of Missouri Press, 2010.

Hadley, Charles D. "Presidential Address: Blacks in Southern Politics: An Agenda for Research." *Journal of Politics* 56, no. 3 (August 1994): 585–600.

Hahn, Steven. *A Nation under Our Feet: Black Political Struggles in the Rural South from Slavery to the Great Migration*. Cambridge, MA: Harvard University Press, 2003.

———. *The Political Worlds of Slavery and Freedom*. Cambridge, MA: Harvard University Press, 2009.

Hale, Grace Elizabeth. *Making Whiteness: The Culture of Segregation in the South, 1890–1940*. New York: Pantheon, 1998.

Hall, Jacquelyn Dowd. "The Long Civil Rights Movement and the Political Uses of the Past." *Journal of American History* 91, no. 4 (March 2005): 1233–63.

———. *Revolt against Chivalry: Jessie Daniel Ames and the Campaign against Lynching*. Rev. ed. New York: Columbia University Press, 1993.

Hamburger, Robert. *Our Portion of Hell: Fayette County, Tennessee: An Oral History of the Struggle for Civil Rights*. New York: Links, 1973.

Hamilton, G. P. *The Bright Side of Memphis*. 1908. Reprint, LaVergne, TN: Lightning Source, 2003.

Handy, W. C. *Father of the Blues: An Autobiography.* New York: Da Capo, 1991.

Harold, Claudrena N. *The Rise and Fall of the Garvey Movement in the Urban South, 1918–1942.* New York: Routledge, 2007.

Havel, Vaclav. "The Power of the Powerless." In *The Power of the Powerless: Citizens against the State in Central-Eastern Europe,* ed. John Keane, 23–96. Armonk, NY: M. E. Sharp, 1990.

Herenton, Willie W. "A Historical Study of School Desegregation in the Memphis City Schools, 1954–1970." Ph.D. diss., Southern Illinois University, 1971.

Hewitt, Nancy A., ed. *A Companion to American Women's History.* Malden, MA: Blackwell, 2002.

Higginbotham, Evelyn Brooks. *Righteous Discontent: The Women's Movement in the Black Baptist Church, 1880–1920.* Cambridge, MA: Harvard University Press, 1993.

Hill, S. Davidson. "The Self-Defined African American Community of Jim Crow Memphis." Senior thesis, Princeton University, 2000.

———. "The Self-Defined African American Community of Jim Crow Memphis." *West Tennessee Historical Society Papers* 54 (2000): 1–33.

Hine, Darlene Clark. *Black Victory: The Rise and Fall of the White Primary in Texas.* 2nd ed. Columbia: University of Missouri Press, 2003.

Hochschild, Jennifer. *Facing Up to the American Dream: Race, Class, and the Soul of the Nation.* Princeton, NJ: Princeton University Press, 1994.

Hoffschwelle, Mary S. *The Rosenwald Schools of the American South.* Gainesville: University Press of Florida, 2006.

Holloway, Harry. "Negro Political Strategy: Coalition or Independent Power Politics?" *Social Science Quarterly* 49, no. 3 (December 1968): 534–47.

———. *The Politics of the Southern Negro: From Exclusion to Big City Organization.* New York: Random House, 1969.

Holloway, Pippa. *Sexuality, Politics, and Social Control in Virginia, 1920–1945.* Chapel Hill: University of North Carolina Press, 2006.

Honey, Michael K. *Black Workers Remember: An Oral History of Segregation, Unionism, and the Freedom Struggle.* Berkeley and Los Angeles: University of California Press, 1999.

———. *Going Down Jericho Road: The Memphis Strike, Martin Luther King's Last Campaign.* New York: Norton, 2007.

———. "Labour Leadership and Civil Rights in the South: A Case Study of the CIO in Memphis, 1935–1955." *Studies in History and Politics* 5 (1986): 97–120.

———. Review of *Battling the Plantation Mentality: Memphis and the Black Freedom Struggle,* by Laurie B. Green. *Journal of Southern History* 74, no. 4 (November 2008): 1023–24.

————. *Southern Labor and Black Civil Rights: Organizing Memphis Workers.* Urbana: University of Illinois Press, 1993.

Hooks, Benjamin L., and Jerry Guess. *The March for Civil Rights: The Benjamin Hooks Story.* Chicago: American Bar Association, 2003.

Hoppe, Sherry L., and Bruce W. Speck. *Maxine Smith's Unwilling Pupils: Lessons Learned in Memphis's Civil Rights Classroom.* Knoxville: University of Tennessee Press, 2007.

Hornsby, Alton. *Black Power in Dixie: A Political History of African Americans in Atlanta.* Gainesville: University Press of Florida, 2009.

Hunt, Marsha. *Repossessing Ernestine: A Granddaughter Uncovers the Secret History of Her American Family.* New York: HarperCollins, 1996.

Hunter, Tera. *To 'Joy My Freedom: Southern Black Women's Lives and Labors after the Civil War.* Cambridge, MA: Harvard University Press, 1999.

Hutchins, Fred L. *What Happened in Memphis.* Kingsport, TN: Kingsport, 1965.

Jackson, Kenneth. *The Ku Klux Klan in the City, 1915–1930.* New York: Oxford University Press, 1967.

Jacobs, Meg, William J. Novak, and Julian E. Zelizer, eds. *The Democratic Experiment: New Directions in American Political History.* Princeton, NJ: Princeton University Press, 2003.

Jacoway, Elizabeth, and David R. Colburn, eds. *Southern Businessmen and Desegregation.* Baton Rouge: Louisiana State University Press, 1982.

Jalenak, James B. "Beale Street Politics: A Study of Negro Political Activity in Memphis, Tennessee." Senior honors thesis, Yale University, 1961.

Johnson, James Weldon. "The Burning of Ell Person at Memphis: A Report [M]ade for the National Association for the Advancement of Colored People." 1917. Folder 28. Box 3. Church Family Papers.

Kaplan, Temma. "Female Consciousness and Collective Action: The Case of Barcelona, 1910–1918." *Signs: Journal of Women in Culture and Society* 7, no. 3 (Spring 1982): 545–66.

Kaye, Andrew. "Roscoe Conkling Simmons and the Significance of African American Oratory." *Historical Journal* 45, no. 1 (2002): 79–102.

Keech, William R. *The Impact of Negro Voting: The Role of the Vote in the Quest for Equality.* Chicago: Rand McNally, 1968.

Kelly, Clarence L. "Robert R. Church, a Negro Tennessean in Republican, State, and National Politics from 1912 to 1932." Master's thesis, Tennessee A&I State University, 1954.

Kesselman, Louis. *The Social Politics of FEPC: A Study in Reform Pressure Movements.* Chapel Hill: University of North Carolina Press, 1948.

Key, V. O. *Southern Politics.* New York: Vintage, 1949.

Kinder, Donald R., and Lynn M. Sanders. *Divided by Color: Racial Politics and Democratic Ideals.* Chicago: University of Chicago Press, 1996.

Kitchens, Allen H. "Ouster of Mayor Edward H. Crump, 1915–1916." *West Tennessee Historical Society Papers* 19 (1965): 105–20.

Klarman, Michael J. *From Jim Crow to Civil Rights: The Supreme Court and the Struggle for Racial Equality.* New York: Oxford University Press, 2004.

———. "How Brown Changed Race Relations: The Backlash Thesis." *Journal of American History* 81, no. 1 (June 1994): 81–118.

———. "The White Primary Rulings: A Case Study in the Consequences of Supreme Court Decisionmaking." *Florida State University Law Review* 29, no. 55 (Fall 2001): 55–107.

Korstad, Robert. *Civil Rights Unionism: Tobacco Workers and the Struggle for Democracy in the Mid-Twentieth-Century South.* Chapel Hill: University of North Carolina Press, 2003.

Korstad, Robert, and Nelson Lichtenstein. "Opportunities Found and Lost: Labor, Radicals, and the Early Civil Rights Movement." *Journal of American History* 75, no. 3 (December 1988): 786–811.

Kousser, J. Morgan. *Colorblind Injustice: Minority Voting Rights and the Undoing of the Second Reconstruction.* Chapel Hill: University of North Carolina Press, 1999.

———. "The New Postmodern Southern Political History." *Georgia Historical Quarterly* 87, no. 3–4 (2003): 427–48.

———. *The Shaping of Southern Politics: Suffrage Restriction and the Establishment of the One-Party South, 1880–1910.* New Haven, CT: Yale University Press, 1974.

Kruse, Kevin M. *White Flight: Atlanta and the Making of Modern Conservatism.* Princeton, NJ: Princeton University Press, 2005.

Kuklinski, James H., Michael D. Cobb, and Martin Gilens. "Racial Attitudes and the 'New South.'" *Journal of Politics* 59, no. 2 (1997): 323–49.

Kuumba, M. Bahati. *Gender and Social Movements.* Walnut Creek, CA: AltaMira, 2001.

———. "'You've Struck a Rock': Comparing Gender, Social Movements, and Transformation in the United States and South Africa." *Gender and Society* 16, no. 4 (August 2002): 504–23.

Ladd, Everett C., Jr. *Negro Political Leadership in the South.* Ithaca, NY: Cornell University Press, 1966.

Lamis, Alexander P. *The Two-Party South.* New York: Oxford University Press, 1988.

Lamon, Lester C. *Blacks in Tennessee, 1791–1970.* Knoxville: University of Tennessee Press, 1981.

Larsen, Lawrence H., and Nancy J. Hulston. *Pendergast!* Columbia: University of Missouri Press, 1997.

Lau, Peter F. *Democracy Rising: South Carolina and the Fight for Black Equality since 1865.* Lexington: University Press of Kentucky, 2006.

Lawson, Steven F. *Black Ballots: Voting Rights in the South, 1944–1969.* New York: Columbia University Press, 1976.

———. *Civil Rights Crossroads: Nation, Community, and the Black Freedom Struggle.* Lexington: University Press of Kentucky, 2003.

———. "Freedom Then, Freedom Now: The Historiography of the Civil Rights Movement." *American Historical Review* 96, no. 2 (1991): 456–71.

———. *In Pursuit of Power: Southern Blacks and Electoral Politics, 1965–1982.* New York: Columbia University Press, 1985.

———. *Running for Freedom: Civil Rights and Black Politics in America since 1941.* 2nd ed. New York: McGraw-Hill, 1997.

———, ed. *To Secure These Rights: The Report of Harry S Truman's Committee on Civil Rights.* Boston: Bedford/St. Martin's, 2004.

Lawson, Steven F., and Charles Payne. *Debating the Civil Rights Movement, 1945–1968.* Lanham, MD: Rowman & Littlefield, 1998.

Lebsock, Suzanne. *Virginia Women, 1600–1945: "A Share of Honour."* Richmond: Virginia State Library, 1987.

Lee, David D. *Tennessee in Turmoil: Politics in the Volunteer State, 1920–1932.* Memphis: Memphis State University Press, 1979.

Lee, George W. *Beale Street: Where the Blues Began.* New York: Robert O. Ballou, 1934.

Leff, Mark H. "Revisioning U.S. Political History." *American Historical Review* 100, no. 3 (1995): 85–123.

Leiker, James. "Brownsville Affray, 1906." BlackPast.org: Remembered and Reclaimed. http://www.blackpast.org/?q=aaw/brownsville-affray-1906.

Lentz-Smith, Adriane D. *Freedom Struggles: African Americans and World War I.* Cambridge, MA: Harvard University Press, 2009.

Leuchtenberg, William E. "The Pertinence of Political History: Reflections on the Significance of the State in America." *Journal of American History* 73, no. 3 (December 1986): 585–600.

Lewinson, Paul. *Race, Class, and Party: A History of Negro Suffrage and White Politics in the South.* 1932. Reprint, New York: Russell & Russell, 1963.

Lewis, Selma S., and Marjean G. Kremer. *The Angel of Beale Street: A Biography of Julia Ann Hooks.* Memphis: St. Luke's, 1986.

Lewis, Virginia Emerson. "Fifty Years of Politics in Memphis, 1900–1950." Ph.D. diss., New York University, 1955.

Lineback, Sarah Casey. "African American Women in the Memphis Civil Rights Movement: The Intertwining Influences of Race, Class, and Gender." Senior thesis, Rhodes College, 2007.

Ling, Peter J., and Sharon Monteith, eds. *Gender in the Civil Rights Movement.* New York: Garland, 1999.

Lisio, Donald J. *Hoover, Blacks, and Lily-Whites: A Study of Southern Strategies.* Chapel Hill: University of North Carolina Press, 1985.

Locke, Alain, ed. *The New Negro* (1925). Reprint, with a preface by Robert Hayden, New York: Atheneum, 1968.

Loyal Tennesseans League. *Edward H. Crump: Public Enemy No. 1.* Memphis: Loyal Tennesseans League, 1932.

Lublin, David. *The Republican South: Democratization and Partisan Change.* Princeton, NJ: Princeton University Press, 2004.

MacLean, Nancy. *Freedom Is Not Enough: The Opening of the American Workplace.* Cambridge, MA: Harvard University Press, 2006.

———. "From the Benighted South to the Sunbelt: The South in the Twentieth Century." In *Perspectives on Modern America: Making Sense of the Twentieth Century,* ed. Harvard Sitkoff, 113–24. New York: Oxford University Press, 2001.

Maloney, Thomas. "African Americans in the Twentieth Century." *EH.Net Encyclopedia,* 14 January 2002. http://eh.net/encyclopedia/article/maloney.african.american.

Mansbridge, Jane, and Aldon Morris, eds. *Oppositional Consciousness: The Subjective Roots of Social Protest.* Chicago: University of Chicago Press, 2001.

Martin, Tony. *Race First: The Ideological and Organizational Struggles of Marcus Garvey and the Universal Negro Improvement Association.* Westport, CT: Greenwood, 1976.

Marzsalek, John F. *A Black Congressman in the Age of Jim Crow: South Carolina's George Washington Murray.* Gainesville: University Press of Florida, 2006.

Massey, Douglas S., and Nancy A. Denton. *American Apartheid: Segregation and the Making of the Underclass.* Cambridge, MA: Harvard University Press, 1993.

Matkin-Rawn, Story. "From Land Ownership to Legal Defense: The World War I Watershed in Black Arkansan Organizing." Paper presented at the Conference on Race, Labor and Citizenship in the Post-Emancipation South, Charleston, SC, 11–13 March 2010.

Matthews, Donald R., and James W. Prothro. *Negroes and the New Southern Politics.* New York: Harcourt, Brace & World, 1966.

McCarthy, G. Michael. "Smith vs. Hoover—the Politics of Race in West Tennessee." *Phylon* 39, no. 2 (2nd Quarter 1978): 154–68.

McElvaine, Robert S. *The Great Depression.* New York: Times Books, 1984.

McGirr, Lisa. *Suburban Warriors: The Origins of the New American Right.* Princeton, NJ: Princeton University Press, 2001.

McGuire, Danielle L. *At the Dark End of the Street.* New York: Knopf, 2010.

McMillen, Neil. *The Citizens' Council: Organized Resistance to the Second*

Reconstruction, 1954–1964. Rev. ed. Urbana: University of Illinois Press, 1994.

———. *Dark Journey: Black Mississippians in the Age of Jim Crow.* Urbana: University of Illinois Press, 1990.

Meeman, Edward J. *The Editorial We: A Posthumous Autobiography.* Memphis: Memphis State University Printing Services, 1976.

Meier, August. *Negro Thought in America, 1880–1915: Racial Ideologies in the Age of Booker T. Washington.* Ann Arbor: University of Michigan Press, 1963.

Melton, Gloria Brown. "Blacks in Memphis, Tennessee, 1920–1955: A Historical Study." Ph.D. diss., Washington State University, 1982.

Memphis Inter Racial League. *The Inter Racial Blue Book.* Memphis: Inter Racial League, 1926.

Meyerowitz, Joanne. "Beyond the Feminist Mystique: A Reassessment of Postwar Mass Culture, 1946–1958." *Journal of American History* 79, no. 4 (March 1993): 1455–82.

———, ed. *Not June Cleaver: Women and Gender in Postwar America, 1945–1960.* Philadelphia: Temple University Press, 1994.

Middleton, Stephen, ed. *Black Congressmen during Reconstruction: A Documentary Sourcebook.* Westport, CT: Praeger, 2002.

Miller, Kristie. *Ruth Hanna McCormick: A Life in Politics, 1880–1944.* Albuquerque: University of New Mexico Press, 1992.

Miller, William D. *Memphis during the Progressive Era, 1900–1917.* Memphis: Memphis State University Press, 1957.

———. *Mr. Crump of Memphis.* Baton Rouge: Louisiana State University Press, 1964.

Miller, Zane L. *Boss Cox's Cincinnati: Urban Politics in the Progressive Era.* New York: Oxford University Press, 1968.

Mitchell, Michele. "Silences Broken, Silences Kept: Gender and Sexuality in African-American History." *Gender and History* 11, no. 3 (1999): 433–44.

Moon, Henry L. *Balance of Power: The Negro Vote.* Garden City, NY: Doubleday, 1948.

Mooney, Jack, ed. *A History of Tennessee Newspapers.* Nashville: Tennessee Press Association, 1996.

Morris, Aldon D. *The Origins of the Civil Rights Movement: Black Communities Organizing for Change.* New York: Free Press, 1984.

Morrow, Martha Barret. "The Reaction of Tennessee to the Supreme Court Desegregation Decision of 1954: From May 1954 through December 1957." Master's thesis, Memphis State University, 1964.

Moses, Wilson Jeremiah. *The Golden Age of Black Nationalism, 1850–1925.* Hamden, CT: Archon, 1978.

Murray, Gail S. *Throwing Off the Cloak of Privilege: White Southern Women Activists in the Civil Rights Era.* Gainesville: University Press of Florida, 2004.

Muse, Benjamin. *Memphis.* Atlanta: Southern Regional Council, 1964.

Myrdal, Gunnar. *An American Dilemma: The Negro Problem and Modern Democracy.* 2 vols. New York: Harper & Bros., 1944.

Nasstrom, Kathryn L. "Down to Now: Memory, Narrative, and Women's Leadership in the Civil Rights Movement in Atlanta, Georgia." *Gender and History* 11, no. 1 (April 1999): 113–44.

———. "Women, the Civil Rights Movement, and the Politics of Historical Memory in Atlanta, 1946–1973." Ph.D. diss., University of North Carolina at Chapel Hill, 1993.

Nightingale, Carl H. "How Lynchings Became High-Tech, and Other Tales from the Modern South." *Reviews in American History* 27, no. 1 (1999): 140–48.

Norrell, Robert J. *The House I Live In: Race and the American Century.* New York: Oxford University Press, 2005.

———. *Reaping the Whirlwind: The Civil Rights Movement in Tuskegee.* Rev. ed. Chapel Hill: University of North Carolina Press, 1998.

Oberschall, Anthony. *Social Conflict and Social Movements.* Englewood Cliffs, NJ: Prentice-Hall, 1973.

O'Connor, Len. *Clout: Mayor Daley and His City.* Chicago: Henry Regnery, 1975.

Ortiz, Paul. *Emancipation Betrayed: The Hidden History of Black Organizing and White Violence in Florida from Reconstruction to the Bloody Election of 1920.* Berkeley and Los Angeles: University of California Press, 2005.

Page, Brian D. "Sutton E. Griggs." *The Tennessee Encyclopedia of History and Culture,* 4 January 2010. http://tennesseeencyclopedia.net/entry.php?rec=1605.

Palmer, Pamela, ed. *The Robert R. Church Family of Memphis: Guide to the Papers with Selected Facsimiles of Documents and Photographs.* Memphis: Memphis State University Press, 1978.

Parent, Keith. "Dr. Miriam DeCosta-Willis." Independent Study, African Americans at Hopkins Project, 2004. http://afam.nts.jhu.edu/people/decosta_willis/parent.pdf.

Parks, Norman L. "Tennessee Politics since Kefauver and Reece: A 'Generalist' View." *Journal of Politics* 28, no. 1 (February 1966): 144–68.

Partington, Paul G. "The Moon Illustrated Weekly—the Precursor of the *Crisis.*" *Journal of Negro History* 48, no. 3 (July 1963): 206–16.

Payne, Charles. *I've Got the Light of Freedom: The Organizing Tradition and the Mississippi Freedom Struggle.* Berkeley and Los Angeles: University of California Press, 1991.

Perman, Michael. *Struggle for Mastery: Disfranchisement in the South, 1888–1908*. Chapel Hill: University of North Carolina Press, 2001.

Pink Palace Museum. *Historic Black Memphians*. Memphis: Foundation of Memphis Pink Palace Museum, 1978.

Pohlmann, Marcus D., and Michael P. Kirby. *Racial Politics at the Crossroads: Memphis Elects Dr. W. W. Herenton*. Knoxville: University of Tennessee Press, 1996.

Porteous, Clark. "The Two Eds of Memphis—Meeman and Crump." *West Tennessee Historical Society Papers* 45 (1991): 140–52.

Price, Hugh D. *The Negro in Florida Politics: A Chapter of Florida History*. New York: New York University Press, 1957.

Price, Margaret. *The Negro and the Ballot in the South*. Atlanta: Southern Regional Council, 1959.

———. *The Negro Voter in the South*. Atlanta: Southern Regional Council, 1957.

Rabinowitz, Howard N. "From Exclusion to Segregation: Southern Race Relations, 1865–1890." *Journal of American History* 63, no. 2 (September 1976): 325–50.

———. *Race Relations in the Urban South, 1865–1890*. New York: Oxford University Press, 1978.

Reed, Adolph. *Stirrings in the Jug: Black Politics in the Post-Segregation Era*. Minneapolis: University of Minnesota Press, 1999.

Reich, Steven A. "The Great War, Black Workers, and the Rise and Fall of the NAACP in the South." In *The Black Worker: A Reader*, ed. Eric Arnesen, 147–77. Urbana: University of Illinois Press, 2007.

———. "Soldiers of Democracy: Black Texans and the Fight for Citizenship, 1917–1921." *Journal of American History* 82, no. 4 (March 1996): 1478–1504.

Republican Party Platform of 1944. 26 June 1944. Political Party Platforms, American Presidency Project. http://www.presidency.ucsb.edu/ws/?pid=25835.

Republican Party Platform of 1948. 21 June 1948. Political Party Platforms, American Presidency Project. http://www.presidency.ucsb.edu/ws/?pid=25836.

Riggs, Joseph H. "Gordon Browning: An Oral Memoir." Memphis: Memphis Public Library, 1966.

Riser, R. Volney. *Defying Disfranchisement: Black Voting Rights Activism in the Jim Crow South, 1890–1908*. Baton Rouge: Louisiana State University Press, 2010.

Robertson, David. *W. C. Handy: The Life and Times of the Man Who Made the Blues*. New York: Knopf, 2009.

Robinson, Amelia Boynton. *Bridge across Jordan*. Washington, DC: Schiller Institute, 1991.

Robinson, James H. "A Social History of the Negro in Memphis and in Shelby County." Ph.D. diss., Yale University, 1934.

Robnett, Brenda. *How Long? How Long? African-American Women in the Struggle for Civil Rights.* New York: Oxford University Press, 1997.

Rolinson, Mary G. *Grassroots Garveyism: The Universal Negro Improvement Association in the Rural South, 1920–1927.* Chapel Hill: University of North Carolina Press, 2007.

Royko, Mike. *Boss: Richard J. Daley of Chicago.* New York: Dutton, 1971.

Rubio, Philip F. *There's Always Work at the Post Office: African American Postal Workers and the Fight for Jobs, Justice, and Equality.* Chapel Hill: University of North Carolina Press, 2010.

Rushing, Wanda. *Memphis and the Paradox of Place: Globalization in the American South.* Chapel Hill: University of North Carolina Press, 2009.

Rustin, Bayard. "From Protest to Politics: The Future of the Civil Rights Movement." *Commentary* 39, no. 2 (February 1965): 25–31.

Scher, Richard K. *Politics in the New South: Republicanism, Race and Leadership in the Twentieth Century.* 2nd ed. Armonk, NY: M. E. Sharpe, 1997.

Schultz, Mark. *The Rural Face of White Supremacy: Beyond Jim Crow.* Urbana: University of Illinois Press, 2005.

Schuyler, Lorraine Gates. *The Weight of Their Votes: Southern Women and Political Leverage in the 1920s.* Chapel Hill: University of North Carolina Press, 2006.

Scott, James C. *Domination and the Arts of Resistance: Hidden Transcripts.* New Haven, CT: Yale University Press, 1998.

Scott, Mingo. *The Negro in Tennessee Politics and Governmental Affairs, 1865–1965.* Nashville: Rich Printing Company, 1964.

Shafer, Anne W. *History of the Memphis City Beautiful Commission and Its Impact on Our Lives.* Memphis: A. Shafer, 1996.

Shafer, Byron E., and Anthony J. Badger, eds. *Contesting Democracy: Substance and Structure in American Political History, 1775–2000.* Lawrence: University Press of Kansas, 2001.

Shannon, Samuel. "Tennessee." In *The Black Press in the South, 1865–1979,* ed. Henry L. Suggs. Westport, CT: Greenwood, 1983.

Sherman, Richard B. *The Republican Party and Black America from McKinley to Hoover, 1896–1933.* Charlottesville: University Press of Virginia, 1973.

Shockley, Megan T. *We, Too, Are Americans: African American Women in Detroit and Richmond, 1940–54.* Urbana: University of Illinois Press, 2004.

Silbey, Joel H. "The State and Practice of American Political History at the Millennium: The Nineteenth Century as a Test Case." *Journal of Policy History* 11, no. 1 (1999): 1–30.

Silver, Christopher, and John V. Moeser. *The Separate City: Black Communi-*

ties in the Urban South, 1940–1968. Lexington: University Press of Kentucky, 1995.

Simmons, Roscoe Conkling. *The Republican Party and American Colored People, 1856–1936.* Chicago: Republican National Committee, 1936.

Simon, Bryant. *A Fabric of Defeat: The Politics of South Carolina Millhands, 1910–1948.* Chapel Hill: University of North Carolina Press, 1998.

Sitkoff, Harvard. "The Impact of the New Deal on Black Southerners." In *Gonna Sit at the Welcome Table,* ed. Julian Bond and Andrew Lewis, 113–24. New York: American Heritage Custom Publishing, 1995.

———. *A New Deal for Blacks.* 30th anniversary ed. New York: Oxford University Press, 2009.

Sivananda, Mantri. "Blair T. Hunt: A Resourceful and an Illustrious Black Memphian, 1887–1976." January 2000. A copy is in the Blair Hunt Vertical File of the Memphis–Shelby County Public Library and Information Center.

———. "Controversial Memphis Mayor Henry Loeb III, 1920–1992: A Biographical Study." Ph.D. diss., University of Memphis, 2002.

Smith, Thomas F. X. *The Powerticians.* Secaucus, NJ: L. Stuart, 1982.

Squires, James D. *The Secrets of the Hopewell Box: Stolen Elections, Southern Politics, and a City's Coming of Age.* New York: Times Books, 1996.

Steed, Robert P., and Laurence W. Moreland, eds. *Writing Southern Politics: Contemporary Interpretations and Future Directions.* Lexington: University Press of Kentucky, 2006.

Stein, Judith. *The World of Marcus Garvey: Race and Class in Modern Society.* Baton Rouge: Louisiana State University Press, 1986.

Sterne, Emma Gelders. *His Was the Voice: The Life of W. E. B. Du Bois.* New York: Crowell-Collier, 1971.

Strub, Whitney. "Black and White and Banned All Over: Race, Censorship and Obscenity in Postwar Memphis." *Journal of Social History* 40, no. 3 (2007): 685–715.

Suggs, Henry L. *The Black Press in the South, 1865–1979.* Westport, CT: Greenwood, 1983.

Sullivan, Patricia. *Days of Hope: Race and Democracy in the New Deal Era.* Chapel Hill: University of North Carolina Press, 1996.

———. "Henry Wallace's Campaign Foreshadowed the Movement as Well as the Rainbow." *Southern Changes* 10, no. 5 (1988): 11, 16–17.

———. *Lift Every Voice: The NAACP and the Making of the Civil Rights Movement.* New York: New Press, 2009.

Takaki, Ronald. *Iron Cages: Race and Culture in Nineteenth-Century America.* Rev. ed. New York: Oxford University Press, 2000.

Taylor, Nikki. "The Democratic Machine as a Vehicle for African-American Civil Rights? The Politics of Peter H. Clark, 1882–1888." Paper presented at the Conference on Race, Labor and Citizenship in the Post-Emancipation South, Charleston, SC, 11–13 March 2010.

Terrell, Mary Church. *A Colored Woman in a White World*. 1940. Reprint, with an introduction by Nellie Y. McKay, New York: G. K. Hall, 1996.

Thomason, Sally P. "The Three Eds: Memphis 1948." *West Tennessee Historical Society Papers* 52 (1998): 150–58.

Thornton, J. Mills, III. "Challenge and Response to the Montgomery Bus Boycott of 1955–56." In *Gonna Sit at the Welcome Table*, ed. Julian Bond and Andrew Lewis, 278–311. New York: American Heritage Custom Publishing, 1995. First published in *Alabama Review* 33 (July 1983): 163–235.

———. *Dividing Lines: Municipal Politics and the Struggle for Civil Rights in Montgomery, Birmingham, and Selma*. Tuscaloosa: University of Alabama Press, 2002.

Tindall, George B. *The Emergence of the New South, 1913–1945*. Baton Rouge: Louisiana State University Press, 1967.

Tobey, Frank T., Claude A. Armour, Joseph P. Boyle, O. P. Williams, and John T. Dwyer. *The City of Memphis: Nucleus of the Mid-South, Municipal Report for 1955*. Memphis: Board of City Commissioners, 1955.

Topping, Simon. *Lincoln's Lost Legacy: The Republican Party and the African American Vote, 1928–1952*. Gainesville: University Press of Florida, 2008.

Trotter, James M. *Music and Some Highly Musical People*. Boston: Lee & Shepherd; New York: Charles T. Dillingham, 1881. http://www.gutenberg.org/files/28056/28056-h/28056-h.htm#.

Truman, Harry S. "Executive Order 9980—Regulations Governing Fair Employment Practices within the Federal Establishment." 26 July 1948. American Presidency Project. http://www.presidency.ucsb.edu/ws/?pid=78208#axzz2fve1Hv00.

Tucker, David M. *Black Pastors and Leaders: Memphis, 1819–1972*. Memphis: Memphis State University Press, 1975.

———. *Lieutenant Lee of Beale Street*. Nashville: Vanderbilt University Press, 1971.

———. *Memphis since Crump: Bossism, Blacks, and Civic Reformers, 1948–1968*. Knoxville: University of Tennessee Press, 1980.

Turner, Allegra W., and Jini M. Kilgore. *Except by Grace: The Life of Jesse H. Turner*. Jonesboro, AR: FOUR-G, 2004.

Tyler, Pamela. *Silk Stockings and Ballot Boxes: Women and Politics in New Orleans, 1920–1963*. Athens: University of Georgia Press, 1996.

Tyson, Timothy B. *Radio Free Dixie: Robert F. Williams and the Roots of Black Power*. Chapel Hill: University of North Carolina Press, 1999.

Umfleet, LeRae. "The Wilmington Race Riot—1898." *Ncpedia*, 2010. http://www.ncpedia.org/history/cw-1900/wilmington-race-riot.

US Commission on Civil Rights. *Hearings Held in Memphis, Tennessee, June 25–26, 1962.* Washington, DC: US Government Printing Office, 1963.

US House Committee on the Judiciary. *Mail Fraud Charges against Marcus Garvey.* 100th Cong., 1st sess., 28 July 1987.

Valien, Preston. "Expansion of Negro Suffrage in Tennessee." *Journal of Negro Education* 26, no. 3 (Summer 1957): 362–68.

Van West, Carroll, and Jen Stoecker. "Thomas Oscar Fuller." 1 January 2010. *Tennessee Encyclopedia of History and Culture.* http://www.tennesseeencyclopedia.net/entry.php?rec=528.

Wade-Gayles, Gloria. *Pushed Back to Strength.* Boston: Beacon, 1993.

Walk, Joe. *A History of African-Americans in Memphis Government.* Memphis: Joe Walk, 1996.

Walker, Randolph Meade. "The Role of the Black Clergy in Memphis during the Crump Era." *West Tennessee Historical Society Papers* 33 (1979): 29–47.

Walton, Hanes, Jr. *Black Politics: A Theoretical and Structural Analysis.* Philadelphia: J. B. Lippincott, 1972.

———. *Black Republicans: The Politics of the Black and Tans.* Metuchen, NJ: Scarecrow, 1975.

Ward, Brian, ed. *Media, Culture, and the Modern African American Freedom Struggle.* Gainesville: University Press of Florida, 2001.

———. *Radio and the Struggle for Civil Rights in the South.* Gainesville: University Press of Florida, 2004.

Wax, Jonathan I. "Program of Progress: The Recent Change in the Form of Government in Memphis, Pt. 1." *West Tennessee Historical Society Papers* 23 (1969): 81–109.

———. "Program of Progress: The Recent Change in the Form of Government in Memphis, Pt. 2." *West Tennessee Historical Society Papers* 24 (1970): 74–96.

Weiss, Nancy J. *Farewell to the Party of Lincoln: Black Politics in the Age of FDR.* Princeton, NJ: Princeton University Press, 1983.

West, Guida, and Rhoda Lois Blumberg. "Reconstructing Social Protest from a Feminist Perspective." In *Women and Social Protest,* 3–36. New York: Oxford University Press, 1990.

White, Deborah Gray. *Too Heavy a Load: Black Women in Defense of Themselves, 1894–1994.* New York: Norton, 1999.

Wilkerson-Freeman, Sarah. "The Second Battle for Woman Suffrage: Alabama White Women, the Poll Tax, and V. O. Key's Master Narrative of Southern Politics." *Journal of Southern History* 68, no. 2 (2002): 333–74.

Williams, Chad L. *Torchbearers of Democracy: African American Soldiers in the World War I Era.* Chapel Hill: University of North Carolina Press, 2010.

Williamson, Joel. *The Crucible of Race: Black/White Relations in the American South since Emancipation.* New York: Oxford University Press, 1984.

Woodward, C. Vann. *Origins of the New South, 1877–1913*. 3rd rev. ed. Baton Rouge: Louisiana State University Press, 1951.

———. *The Strange Career of Jim Crow*. New York: Oxford University Press, 1974.

Wrenn, Lynette B. *Crisis and Commission Government in Memphis: Elite Rule in a Gilded Age City*. Knoxville: University of Tennessee Press, 1998.

Wright, Gavin. *Old South, New South: Revolutions in the Southern Economy since the Civil War*. 2nd ed. Baton Rouge: Louisiana State University Press, 1996.

Wright, Sharon D. *Race, Power, and Political Emergence in Memphis*. New York: Garland, 2000.

Wright, William E. *Memphis Politics: A Study in Racial Bloc Voting*. Eagleton Institute Cases in Practical Politics, no. 27. New York: McGraw-Hill, 1962.

Yellin, Carol Lynn, and Janann Sherman. *The Perfect 36: Tennessee Delivers Woman Suffrage*. Memphis: Wilson Graphics, 1998.

Young, Richard P., ed. *Roots of Rebellion: The Evolution of Black Politics and Protest since World War II*. New York: Harper & Row, 1970.

Index

Civil Rights Crossroads: Nation, Community, and the Black Freedom Struggle
Steven F. Lawson

Selma to Saigon: The Civil Rights Movement and the Vietnam War
Daniel S. Lucks

In Remembrance of Emmett Till: Regional Stories and Media Responses to the Black Freedom Struggle
Darryl Mace

Freedom Rights: New Perspectives on the Civil Rights Movement
edited by Danielle L. McGuire and John Dittmer

This Little Light of Mine: The Life of Fannie Lou Hamer
Kay Mills

After the Dream: Black and White Southerners since 1965
Timothy J. Minchin and John A. Salmond

Fighting Jim Crow in the County of Kings: The Congress of Racial Equality in Brooklyn
Brian Purnell

Roy Wilkins: The Quiet Revolutionary and the NAACP
Yvonne Ryan

Thunder of Freedom: Black Leadership and the Transformation of 1960s Mississippi
Sue [Lorenzi] Sojourner with Cheryl Reitan

Art for Equality: The NAACP's Cultural Campaign for Civil Rights
Jenny Woodley

For Jobs and Freedom: Race and Labor in America since 1865
Robert H. Zieger